Great Debates in Commercial and Corporate Law

Great Debates in Law

Series Editor
Jonathan Herring, Professor of Law, University of Oxford

Commercial and Corporate Law
Andrew Johnston & Lorraine Talbot (eds)

Company Law
Lorraine Talbot

Contract Law
Jonathan Morgan

Criminal Law
Jonathan Herring

Employment Law
Simon Honeyball

Equity and Trusts
Alastair Hudson

European Convention on Human Rights
Fiona de Londras & Kanstantsin Dzehtsiarou

Family Law
Jonathan Herring, Rebecca Probert & Stephen Gilmore

Gender and Law
Rosemary Auchmuty (ed.)

Jurisprudence
Nicholas J McBride & Sandy Steel

Medical Law and Ethics
Imogen Goold & Jonathan Herring

Land Law
David Cowan, Lorna Fox O'Mahony & Neil Cobb

Great Debates in Law

Great Debates in Commercial and Corporate Law

Andrew Johnston
Professor of Company Law and Corporate Governance
School of Law, University of Sheffield
(University of Warwick School of Law from July 2020)
&
Lorraine Talbot
Professor of Company Law in Context
Birmingham Law School, University of Birmingham

 macmillan international HIGHER EDUCATION

 RED GLOBE PRESS

First published 2020 by
RED GLOBE PRESS

Red Globe Press in the UK is an imprint of Macmillan Education Limited, registered in England, company number 01755588, of 4 Crinan Street, London, N1 9XW.

Red Globe Press® is a registered trademark in the United States, the United Kingdom, Europe and other countries.

ISBN 978-1-352-00931-6

This book is printed on paper suitable for recycling and made from fully managed and sustained forest sources. Logging, pulping and manufacturing processes are expected to conform to the environmental regulations of the country of origin.

A catalogue record for this book is available from the British Library.

A catalog record for this book is available from the Library of Congress.

CONTENTS

An Introduction to Great Debates in Commercial and Corporate Law

Andrew Johnston and Lorraine Talbot

In a broad sense, commercial law is about the facilitation and regulation of trade, as well as the creation of assets, such as intellectual property (IP), which can be traded, and the provision of credit to finance transactions and businesses. Likewise, in a broad sense, company law is about the constitution and regulation of the dominant business form that exists to trade, employ people and produce, but also encompasses financial matters such as the creation and trading of securities that give their holders claims on companies or funds. On the face of it, one might expect a rich teaching and research dialogue to occur between these subject areas. Indeed, the interconnections between them are so evident that many non-commercial or non-corporate scholars treat these two subject areas as, more or less, interchangeable. However, the complexity of the various areas that together make up commercial and company law lead to their becoming siloed in different subdisciplines and discussed in specialised language, so that they appear to share little common ground. Despite the lack of a systemic, macrolevel approach to teaching and researching these subjects, commercial and company law are fundamentally connected, constituting the legal framework that underpins and steers the operation of our economy. For this reason, they are highly political, creating and conferring power within economic relations. They normalise unequal claims and unequal bargaining positions. As such, they are worthy of critical analysis both in their own right and as interconnected areas of law.

The purpose of this book is to look at a wide spread of commercial subjects and areas of company law (such as would be found in a typical law degree) and by critical analysis to expose the rationales for, and drivers of, the rules that have emerged in these areas. Many of the contributions to this book also show that, although the law presumes formal equality of the various parties to, or affected by, the transactions and institutions in question, the effect of the current configuration of laws is to entrench existing power structures and to polarise the distribution of wealth in society. Hence, this book aims to introduce students to critical approaches to a number of core law subdisciplines and to encourage them to begin the process of exploring the interconnections between them. For example, students might ask how they perpetuate inequality within our economic relationships or why lawmakers do not introduce reforms.

The book begins with two chapters on contract law, which is the essential foundation of a whole swathe of commercial and corporate law. Students will be familiar with the story of an early contract law that did not recognise inequality of bargaining power and the injustices to those dealing with large business, such as consumers, summed up in the phrase *caveat emptor*. It is the background against which to understand the development of vitiating factors in common law and, in particular, to understand legislation intended to protect consumers and to ensure that they have something approximating a fair deal. Catherine Mitchell (Chapter 2) shows how this progressive story is now radically outdated. Increasingly, private rules are developed between independent firms to determine contracts in respect of their economic activity rather than developed in the courts. She adds that the 'substantive rules of contract law apply only to the extent the parties have not expressly stipulated for an alternative', but generally, and following sophisticated legal advice, they have stipulated an alternative. Indeed, in a global economy characterised by complex contracting practices, specialist arbitrators are much more likely to pronounce on contractual disputes than the courts. The outcome, argues Mitchell, is that the courts have retreated into their old formalistic ways rather than rise to the challenges of a world in which people routinely enter 'contracts' through the click of a mouse. Thus, instead of considering the inequality of bargaining power between a multinational like Amazon and the average consumer, the courts – fed largely on a diet of business-to-business litigation and starved of cases involving consumers – have returned to 'more formal interpretation tests which uphold the plain meaning of terms' and are loathe to interfere in agreements, regardless of the parties involved.

Jonathan Morgan (Chapter 1) highlights the role of contract law as regulation and the difficult question of whether contract law should be made by the legislator, the courts or the parties themselves. He also emphasises the extent to which contract law is driven by market forces. Globalisation, he argues, has led to a 'market for laws' in which more permissive regimes attract more contract 'business' and leaving all jurisdictions cautious about imposing constraints on contracting practice. This obviously constrains those responsible for making contract law and creates pressure for default rules over mandatory rules. Of course, there are mandatory rules that insist on the validity of consent of the parties, so that duress and fraud continue to act as vitiating factors. But, beyond that, party autonomy tends to take over, so that terms that exclude liability for non-fraudulent misstatements or fraudulent misstatements by an agent, for example, may be allowed in some contexts. Similarly, a society's moral position on particular issues will affect contract law. It is not possible, for example, to enter into a contract for a commercial surrogacy. However, furthering other aspects of public policy through contract law will be balanced by the courts against the potential harm this does to the attractiveness of contract law for footloose commercial parties. For this reason, among others, redressing substantive inequality through contracts is far from the agenda of both the courts and governments.

No contract is more contentious in respect to creating and maintaining inequalities than the employment contract. As Charlotte Villiers and Roseanne Russell show in Chapter 3, contracts between employers and employees (capital personified as the company and labour) are grounded in serving the best interests of the employer and in transferring as much risk and uncertainty as possible onto the employee. At the extreme end of the current regime is 'precarious labour', a synonym for those on 'zero hours' contracts, which at best guarantees no working hours for the worker and at worst precludes workers from refusing offered assignments.

The chapters on IP illustrate, in different ways, how the 'free' global market is further shaped by the presence of property rights over 'intangible products of the intellect', which are strongly protected by law and serve to enhance global inequalities. Peter Harrison (Chapter 4) is particularly acute on this point. The problems, he argues, arise from the accepted justifications for the protection of IP through patents. Patents exist, it is supposed, to 'amplify market forces by rewarding those who get to an inventive idea first (and file a patent application for it) by giving them a limited monopoly over that idea'. However, the effect is to unjustly shape the market in the interest of patent holders and to hinder innovation because patents direct innovation in a particular way. Patent protection is intended to allow property owners to profit and so it ignores human needs and restricts access of other users to those ideas when those other users might otherwise take the 'base' innovation in other directions to the potential benefit of themselves and wider society. There are other problems with the patents regime. As Harrison notes, the system encourages the 'patenting of everything', known in IP as 'thicketting', to ensure that all possible future revenues are protected. The effect is to shut down innovation per se, and even in its own terms, to create an unworkable system. It is, of course, difficult to identify the end of an idea in the same way as one can identify the end of a country estate. However, as Harrison notes, these 'fuzzy edges' generally benefit the patent owner and increase the extent of their entitlement. It is a system, he states, that has a particularly bad impact on the Global South, which is subject to Western-derived IP law that restricts access to vital innovations. The pharmaceutical industry, shows Harrison, is particularly egregious in the barriers it sets up against developing countries gaining access to essential medicines cheaply.

In Chapter 5, Robert Burrell identifies a number of serious defects in the trade mark system. Although the system began as a means to guarantee the origin of products to consumers and has been justified on the basis that it allows producers to differentiate themselves on the grounds of quality, the range of marks and other identifiers that may be protected has expanded significantly. Indeed, there are now concerns that the short and memorable words that function best as trade marks may be running out. Although significant reform is required in relation to these matters, greater concern arises out of the (unjustified) expansion of protection against blurring and tarnishing that has been given to well-established brands through the doctrine of dilution. In addition to lacking any justification from a psychological perspective, this doctrine makes it very difficult for new traders to gain any legal certainty as to whether they can use a particular brand or sign. The harmful effects of this doctrine are exacerbated by aggressive brand management strategies on the part of companies and their lawyers. All this creates a danger of information overload for consumers arising out of the proliferation of brands whilst potentially crowding out social labelling and making it legally more risky for activists to use logos to criticise companies. Finally, an entire enforcement industry has emerged which means that trade mark litigation has taken on a life of its own, moving far away from its origins.

In Chapter 6, Emily Hudson explores a number of emerging normative and practical questions in the field of copyright. First, since copyright protection arises automatically, this poses difficulties for the legal system in the form of orphan works where no author can be identified. Second, she explores the role of copyright exceptions and the different ways in which they are administered so that, even where there are problems of ownership, copyright material may be used for the purposes of parody or education. Third, she explores the possibility of reintroducing formalities, such as registration, to prevent protection arising automatically. This leads into a discussion about the extent to which other concepts drawn from property law might be useful in developing a less exclusionary approach to copyright, underpinning a vibrant public realm that is able to draw more freely on cultural products. This is particularly salient in light of the emergence of what she describes as 'extensive, privately-written copyright codes' that govern consumers' ongoing rights of access to purchased digital content.

All three of the IP chapters draw attention, in different ways, to the distributive effects of IP regimes. The main beneficiaries of these powerful rights are not individual inventors working in laboratories or artists and authors working in attics but large global corporate groups. The largest corporate groups span the globe, extracting value from host states, their subsidiaries and suppliers through the use of monopsonistic buying power and control over IP rights. The cheap labour that is used by suppliers or subsidiaries in the Global South is readily exploitable, being easily replaceable and possessing few legal rights under domestic law. They are the precariat of the developing world. Patents, copyright and trade marks, on the other hand, are unique and irreplaceable, and they enable value extraction. IP rights can be vested in subsidiaries located in low-tax jurisdictions, and licensed to operating companies within the same group, enabling profits to be shifted from the jurisdictions in which production or consumption occurs to the jurisdiction in which the IP is located. Growing attention is being paid to the aggressive tax management strategies of the planet's largest companies, and in Chapter 10, Kerrie Sadiq and Bronwyn

McCredie explore the recent efforts of the Organisation for Economic Co-operation and Development (OECD) to combat this and ensure the continued viability of national tax systems. In contrast, less attention is paid to the huge profits made by corporations from the efforts of workers living in poverty. Legal challenges are very difficult, whilst political and moral complaints are addressed by business-friendly corporate social responsibility activities, which all too rarely focus on the specific impacts of companies on their stakeholders and the environment.

The acceptance (or even celebration) of corporations' ability to exploit their power and operate in such socially irresponsible ways is explained by Lorraine Talbot and Daniel Attenborough (Chapters 7 and 8, respectively). Talbot draws on the history of corporate capitalism to argue that we accept these patterns of corporate behaviour because we have grown to accept that shareholders are not responsible, either legally or morally, for what is done to produce their dividends and capital gains. It was not always this way, and she argues that, in Victorian factories or mines, the direct connection between the human misery of the workers and the owners' wealth was well understood. The one led to the other. However, once the company form became more widely used, the relationship between shareholder wealth and human misery became more opaque. This process of obfuscation, she argues, first emerged when the share ceased to be a property interest in the whole business and became instead a property interest in the profits generated by that business. It was completed when businesses opted in large numbers to operate as limited liability companies, rather than partnerships, at the end of the nineteenth century. These two key changes transformed shareholders from active and visible owners in an identifiable business to rentiers investing in financial property, and the business was run by professional managers. Other changes in relation to dividend law and corporate capacity, for example, strengthened the notion of the corporate entity but at the same time had the effect of distancing the shareholders in the eyes of the public from responsibility for what the company actually did. So, to take a modern example, the public's knowledge that the profits of say, Primark, are built on the misery of garment workers in Bangladesh's factories does not result in a societal demonisation of shareholders (although the directors may not be so lucky, and the company's reputation may also take a hit, at least in the short term).

In Chapter 8, Attenborough explores changing theories of corporate legal personality, highlighting the shifting justifications offered for the law's grant of separate legal personality to business people. He shows how an early theory of the company in the US reflected the legal reality that companies were created by the various states of the union and were therefore a 'concession' from the state. 'Fiction' or 'artificial entity' theory therefore conceived of the company's juristic personality as something that existed only as a 'metaphor, established in the eye of the law, to grant it the legal capacity to act… a legal fiction'. Attenborough then moves to Morton Horwitz's famous book in which he argued that, once the business operations of American companies expanded beyond the states that created them, they were clearly operating independently of their state of incorporations and this undermined the fictional idea of the company as a creature or concession of the state. Following case law, which made it clear that companies could incorporate in one state and yet locate their business in another, legal scholars began to conceptualise the company as an aggregate of individuals rather than a creation of the state. The legal entity reflected the already-existing real entity, which emerged from the collective activity of real individuals towards a common purpose.

Thus far, the project to define and explain the company was influenced by the shifting historical, economic and social context. However, the latest 'development' of corporate theory reflected a seismic shift in the political context and seeks to legitimate the shareholder rights and entitlements discussed by Talbot. The neoliberal agenda, which emerged following the Second World War in opposition to corporate managerialism and the emergence of the welfare state, gained political acceptance only from the late 1970s. It opposed regulation and the idea that business had social responsibilities; instead, it sought to promote the company as a profit-maximising business focused only on the interests of shareholders. The creation of shareholder value became the driving force of corporate governance after that. Not only did the relationship between human misery and shareholder wealth remain hidden; shareholder value became a moral imperative, justified on the basis that it reflected rising social wealth. Anything that reduced returns to shareholders was tantamount to 'expropriation' of their assets. Real entity theory collapsed into 'contractarianism', a theory that essentially did away with the 'entity' part of the earlier theory, leaving only the various individuals contributing their resources to corporate activity, connected to each other in a 'nexus of contracts'. Shareholder entitlement under this theory derives from the 'contract' between shareholders and directors, in which directors 'agree' to maximise shareholder returns in return for shareholders being the sole bearers of the 'residual risk' of the business. This contract was not an express agreement and, indeed, is not even a contract in the eyes of the law; rather, it is formed from economists' assumptions about what self-interested, abstract individuals would have agreed in an express contract had they gone through a bargaining process. This reduces company law to mere facilitation, to the reduction of the costs of setting up, running and governing a business, whilst the wider corporate governance system ensures that the directors do not pursue interests unrelated to those of the shareholders.

One symptom of this relentless pressure on companies to produce shareholder value is the emergence of a new precariat, discussed by Villiers and Russell in Chapter 3. Labour, they argue, is used to create shareholder value but is treated as exploitable and expendable, a cost that can be cut as and when shareholder value so demands. Under neoliberalism, companies no longer build up long-term relationships with their workers, developing their competences in order to improve productivity. Instead, labour is treated as a fungible input, supplied on the basis of short-term contracts. In pursuit of shareholder value, companies put in place the various short-term arrangements that make up the 'gig' economy, commodifying their workers in the process. The effect of this process, Villiers and Russell argue, is to transfer risk from the company and its shareholders (who in contractarian theory are supposed to be the 'residual risk bearers') to workers, who have fewer resources to absorb economic shocks and less opportunity to diversify. Their working life is unstable, unfulfilling and poorly remunerated but at the same time is also highly controlled, as the Amazon warehouse workers example shows.

Much of the pressure to pursue gig arrangements with workers derives from the shareholder value orientation of the UK's corporate governance system. A central component of this system, alongside executive pay practices and soft law corporate governance codes, is the UK's approach to takeover regulation. It facilitates hostile takeovers as a means of protecting the interests of shareholders. In Chapter 9, Andrew Johnston argues that the hostile takeover is the most striking feature of the UK's corporate governance system. Whether it is actually carried out, or just threatened, the hostile takeover is one of the main sources of pressure on corporate directors and managers to produce shareholder value. The hostile takeover may have emerged by chance, he argues, but its continued operation was ensured by financial interests, which used their political power to introduce self-regulation. Although the hostile takeover disrupted existing patterns of corporate management, it was given an efficiency makeover by the same group of neoliberal US scholars who reframed corporate theory from the 1970s. They claimed that a 'market for corporate control' was the best way to ensure that managers served the shareholder interest. Control of companies would move to the shareholder or group of shareholders who valued it most highly, and managers who wanted to keep their positions had to keep the shareholders happy with dividends and capital gains. Whilst a critical account of takeovers has emerged, emphasising that they drive short-termism, reduce investments in innovation and drive down the quality and quantity of employment, this has made little impact on policymakers, who have continued to follow the regulatory blueprint laid down by financial interests in the late 1960s. Although the lines of causation may be complex, the decline of stable employment accompanied the emergence of the hostile takeover and, later, the more general drive for shareholder value. Historically, employment in the post-war period was marked by stability, the idea of a job for life. Unions were legally protected and collective labour activity ensured that wages were relatively high. Inequality was the lowest in recorded history. The rise of takeovers destabilised corporate management, which had important knock-on effects on corporate strategy and working conditions. The evisceration of trade union power during the 1980s only made matters worse from the standpoint of labour. Hence, we can see the emergence of the hostile takeover as the first indication of a wholesale reorientation of corporate governance away from companies balancing the interests of the various groups with a stake in the enterprise towards an absolute prioritisation of the short-term interests of capital. In Johnston's words, 'takeover regulation is not merely a technical exercise;

it is a politically charged decision that reflects assumptions about the purpose of companies and scope of company law, as well as the interests of dominant actors'.

Faced with the social, environmental and economic dislocations that result from changes in corporate governance, technology, globalisation, and so on, the state has a number of tools in its armoury, including regulation and taxation. In Chapter 10, Kerrie Sadiq and Bronwyn McCredie offer a critical account of how the state ought to proceed in order to construct an effective tax system that can be used to fund public services, to compensate the losers of these far-reaching changes and even to steer economic activity towards internalising its social and environmental costs. They emphasise a number of the challenges confronting modern national tax systems, including globalisation and automation, and survey some of the international efforts to ensure their future integrity.

The state also has another, less appreciated tool at its disposal: its control over the money that is used to discharge commercial liabilities, to finance companies, to purchase IP and to pay workers. In Chapter 11, Andrew Johnston, Jay Cullen and Trevor Pugh argue that law scholars and students should pay more attention to the role played by the state and private banks in influencing the allocation of societal resources through the creation of money. Drawing on the topical (but heterodox and controversial) economic theory of money known as Modern Monetary Theory, they show that the state creates a certain amount of base money, which is spent into circulation and given value through its ability to discharge citizens' tax liabilities. However, the vast bulk of money is created out of nothing by private banks, credited to the accounts of borrowers in return for their promise to repay, and circulated between private bank accounts as it is spent. Bank money creation feeds into the real economy, increasing or reducing demand, which is expressed in the spending of money. It also tends to inflate asset prices, as more money chases a fixed supply of assets; residential property is perhaps the most obvious example. Not only does this skew the distribution of wealth towards those who own assets, it also leads to financial instability, as Chapter 12 by Jay Cullen shows.

Cullen shows the extent to which financial regulation has been informed by the flawed 'efficient markets hypothesis', which has no space for the asset bubbles that have been regularly observed in financial markets since the inception of financial capitalism. He then offers an overview of the more realistic 'financial instability hypothesis' (developed by Hyman Minsky), which operates on the basis that positions in assets are financed by debt. Given flaws in human psychology, which have been well documented by psychologists and behavioural economists, the way in which positions in assets are financed means that 'stability creates instability' without the need for any 'exogenous shock'. This more realistic explanation of financial crises gained some traction in the aftermath of the 2008 financial crisis, and there have certainly been some improvements to the way in which banks are regulated. However, there is still more to be done. When banking regulation fails, we are in uncharted territory. Should we allow asset markets to enter a vicious cycle of price falls, followed by insolvency of borrowers, followed by further price falls and contagious bank insolvencies? Or should we intervene to prop up asset prices, effectively bailing out reckless borrowers, reinforcing the distribution of wealth that resulted from those borrowing activities and sowing the seeds of the next crisis (as Minsky points out)?

Johnston, Cullen and Pugh show that after 2008 we chose the latter, and central banks pursued unconventional monetary policies that drove asset prices back up and further polarised wealth. This might not have mattered had it not been accompanied by the economically illiterate political argument that fiscal austerity was required alongside this extraordinary monetary largesse. Johnston, Cullen and Pugh show that the state's control over the monetary system could instead be used to transform society and to reallocate wealth. Indeed, at the time of writing, there was much political discussion around policies such as a Green New Deal, a jobs guarantee or guaranteed basic minimum income for all citizens.

Overall, then, the book begins the process of drawing out a number of social and economic themes that cut across the subfields that make up commercial and corporate law. The first relates to the role of business in society. Neoclassical economics has filled a large gap left by the law as to the purpose of the company, claiming that the success of companies should be measured by reference to their success in creating shareholder value (measured by the current share price, the dividends paid out and the shares repurchased). Other areas of law have come to support the achievement of this goal. For example, the creation, use and licensing of IP give companies distinct advantages in various markets as well as allowing them to reduce the amount of tax they pay. Thanks to the patent system, even the diseases that are targeted by the pharmaceutical industry are those whose victims are able to pay high prices for a cure or for relief. Likewise, neither labour law nor company law has done much to prevent the achievement of shareholder value through ever-greater levels of labour exploitation, whether this takes the extreme form of precarious labour or the even more extreme form of modern slavery. Any desire on the part of executives to take account of the social costs of their decisions, which is permissible as a matter of strict company law, is overcome by the carrot of performance-related pay and the stick of hostile takeovers. Under competitive pressure, contract law has retreated into formalism and is increasingly being privatised through standard-setting and arbitration.

The second relates to macroeconomic outcomes. The various subfields of commercial and corporate law could support the development and stability of the macroeconomy and drive more sustainable economic activity. Yet, as things stand, they arguably exacerbate growing inequality in society, as the interests of shareholders and the owners of assets prevail over those who rely on selling their labour to provide for their fundamental needs. One symptom of this problem is growing social discontent and the rise of populist politicians. The skewed distribution of wealth is not only unjust; it is also damaging from a macroeconomic perspective. It means lower consumption demand across the economy, as the wealthy consume proportionately less of their income whilst the poor in society are forced to rely on credit to fund consumption, creating stress, undermining future demand (as those debts must be repaid) and potentially resulting in financial (and further social and political) instability. At the same time, the wealthy are able to use their assets to finance further borrowing, driving up the prices of essential goods such as housing, further skewing the distribution of wealth, but also creating the danger of a serious economic downturn if the rate of borrowing falls. All of this is facilitated by private financial institutions whose executives and managers are powerfully incentivised to increase lending to borrowers, whether for consumption or the purchase of assets. The main effect of the 2008 financial crisis was to remind all concerned that, in the event of a serious downturn, states and their central banks will do everything necessary to underpin high asset prices so as to validate past lending and borrowing decisions. The main responses to a crisis driven by excessive borrowing were to encourage more borrowing and to cut benefits to those who were not borrowers. As some of the contributions to this book show, none of this is technically necessary or inevitable; rather, it is the product of policy choices.

The third relates to innovation. Corporate governance inculcates a short-term approach on the part of management; finance is focused on lending to enable the purchase of existing assets; and although IP is commonly justified on the basis that it encourages investment and incentivises creativity and invention, it is widely considered to be stifling the innovations needed to confront the global challenges we face. For example, if the computer technology developed by Alan Turing in the Second World War had been immediately patented, or if the underlying science had not been published as an open academic paper by John von Neumann, or if all this development had occurred under the umbrella of a corporate entity subject to the shareholder value imperative or had relied on a private bank providing finance, it seems very unlikely that computer technology would have developed in the way it did. Even so, subsequent patenting of computer technology, coupled with aggressive litigation practices, means that development in this critical field is determined by its alignment with large corporate interests. Similarly, takeovers create pressure for short-term returns to shareholders, syphoning capital away from research and development, unless that expenditure can be justified to shareholders. This steers the innovation process away from long-term investments, which carry no guarantee of success and often extend beyond the expected tenure of executives. The innovation that does occur takes place within smaller companies, which are gradually gobbled up by larger companies that have access to the bond markets and can obtain the finance required to acquire them but have no necessary interest in applying these innovations towards the common good. None of this is conducive to innovation.

There appears to be little political scope for change: states are discouraged from intervening in labour markets, changing the way companies are governed, pursuing social goals through contract law, or restricting the rights of IP own-ers by the threat of relocation of business to jurisdictions that adopt a more laissez-faire attitude. Although the financial crisis of 2008 offered the prospect of a reset or at least a fundamental rethinking of dominant assumptions, instead the owners of shares and various other forms of property benefitted from cen-tral bank monetary policy intended to prop up the value of their assets whilst another arm of the state retrenched on social provision in the name of fiscal austerity. As corporate structures become more complex and assets, including IP, are squirreled away in low-tax and secrecy jurisdictions, the future of the welfare state and even the ability of governments to preserve public goods are being called into question. We have moved a long way from the simple exchanges that make up the initial subject matter of contract law.

Whilst this appears to be a somewhat pessimistic conclusion, it serves to emphasise the importance of adopting a joined-up approach to commercial and corporate law and identifying the extent to which these subfields contrib-ute to pressing social and economic problems. Doing so creates the opportu-nity for discussion around reforms necessary to achieve social and economic justice, to encourage innovation whilst at the same time guaranteeing stability, and to address the pressing issues, such as climate change, that confront soci-ety. The question of reform is explicitly discussed in the chapter on tax but is implicit in all the chapters presented here. More balance is required, and law has the tools necessary to achieve it. We invite you, the reader, to take the debate further and reimagine our corporate and commercial law.

TABLE OF CASES

Author Biographies

Andrew Johnston is Professor of Company Law and Corporate Governance at the School of Law at the University of Sheffield until June 2020 and thereafter at the University of Warwick School of Law. He is also a member of the Sustainable Market Actors for Responsible Trade (SMART) Project (uio.no/smart) at the University of Oslo, a research associate at the University of Cambridge Centre for Business Research and a member of the GOODCORP Research Network. Recently he has been a visiting professor at Mines ParisTech and Queensland University of Technology. In the past, he has held positions at the Universities of Queensland, Cambridge and Warsaw. Before becoming an academic, he practised law with Herbert Smith and the Treasury Solicitor in London.

Lorraine Talbot is Professor of Company Law at Birmingham Law School, University of Birmingham. She previously held positions at University of York and University of Warwick. She has written widely on critical aspects of corporate law, corporate activity and the political economy of the corporation. Her books include *Progressive Corporate Governance for the 21st Century* (2013), *Critical Company Law* (2007, 2015) and *Great Debates in Company Law* (2014). She co-leads the corporate and financial stream for the International Panel for Social Progress.

Emily Hudson is Reader in Law at King's College London, and has previously held posts at the University of Oxford, University of Queensland and Melbourne Law School. She has a particular research interest in copyright law, including in relation to copyright exceptions and the ramifications of treating copyright as a form of property. Her chapter draws not only from her doctrinal work but from her extensive empirical research into the copyright experiences of cultural institutions in Australia, Canada, the United Kingdom and the United States. This work is described in detail in her monograph, *Drafting Copyright Exceptions: From the Law in Books to the Law in Action*.

Jonathan Morgan is Reader in English Law and a Fellow of Corpus Christi College, University of Cambridge. His teaching and research encompass contract, tort and public law. His books include *Contract Law Minimalism* (2013), *Great Debates in Contract Law* (3rd ed 2020, forthcoming) and *Great Debates in Tort Law* (2020, forthcoming).

Catherine Mitchell is Reader in Private Law at Birmingham Law School, at the University of Birmingham, where she teaches a variety of contract and commercial law courses. She has published widely on different aspects of contract law, including two monographs, *Interpretation of Contracts* (2nd ed 2018) and *Contract Law and Contract Practice* (2013). Her research has appeared in the *Journal of Contract Law, Legal Studies,* the *Oxford Journal of Legal Studies, Current Legal Problems* and the *Cambridge Law Journal.* Her work has been cited by the House of Lords, the Singapore Court of Appeal and the Law Commissions of England and Scotland.

Charlotte Villiers studied law at the University of Hull and the London School of Economics and Political Science and is a qualified solicitor. She has taught at the Universities of Sheffield and Glasgow and was a Visiting Lecturer at the University of Oviedo in Spain. She was appointed Professor of Company Law at the University of Bristol in 2005. Her publications include *European Company Law – Towards Democracy* (Ashgate, 1998) and, most recently, *Corporate Reporting and Company Law* (Cambridge University Press, 2006). She has written extensively on UK industrial relations. Her current research focuses on company law and sustainability, including reporting and on boardroom structures and cultures.

Roseanne Russell is Lecturer in Law at the University of Bristol and Co-director of its Centre for Law and Enterprise. Her research interests include corporate governance, employment law, and feminist legal theory. Before moving to academia, she held senior roles in private practice and in-house at the UK's former Equal Opportunities Commission. She has been a member of the Law Society of England and Wales Employment Law Committee, co-convenor of the Society of Legal Scholars Company Law Stream, and consultative committee member for the UK Office of Tax Simplification's review of employment status.

Peter S. Harrison is Lecturer in Law at the University of York. After a PhD and EU fellowship in neuropharmacology, he qualified as a solicitor with Linklaters, London. He has litigated high-profile patent and other IP actions in trial and appellate courts of England and Canada, the European Court of Justice, and the European Patent Office, becoming international IP practice head at Hill Dickinson LLP. His research focuses on the interface between biological innovation and IP protection, and he was awarded a PhD in Law for his work on indigenous peoples' rights to protect their traditional therapeutic knowledge, and genetic resources, from misappropriation.

Robert Burrell is Professor of Intellectual Property and Information Technology Law at the University of Oxford and Professor of Law at Melbourne Law School. He teaches and researches across all areas of intellectual property law. He is the author, with Allison Coleman, of *Copyright Exceptions: The Digital Impact* (Cambridge University Press, 2005) and, with Michael Handler, of *Australian Trade Mark Law* (Oxford University Press, 2010; 2nd ed, 2016). His most recent work includes an investigation of the role of rewards as an alternative to the patent system and an interdisciplinary project with a team of psychologists that tests trade mark law's assumptions about consumers.

Daniel Attenborough is Associate Professor in Corporate Law at Durham University and a Senior Fellow of the Higher Education Academy. He has held visiting posts at various institutions, most recently the University of California, Berkeley, and the Institute of Advanced Legal Studies, London. His principal and current research and teaching interests are in the fields of corporate and commercial law in the broadest sense. He has published widely on directors' duties, shareholder rights, comparative company law, and corporate governance theory. At Durham, he teaches Company Law on the LLB (Bachelor of Laws), and Corporate Governance and Mergers & Acquisitions on the LLM (Master of Laws) programme.

Kerrie Sadiq is Professor of Taxation in the School of Accountancy at the QUT Business School, Queensland University of Technology. She holds a B Com (UQ), LLB (Hons) (UQ), LLM (QUT), and PhD (Deakin). She is a Chartered Tax Adviser as designated by the Taxation Institute of Australia and a Graduate of the Australian Institute of Company Directors. She primarily researches in international tax, tax expenditures and capital gains tax. She is author of numerous publications in both Australian and international journals and has edited and co-authored textbooks on taxation. She is co-editor of *Australian Tax Review*, one of Australia's leading tax journals. Prior to joining Queensland University of Technology in 2012, she spent 20 years at the University of Queensland as a member of both their Law School and Business School.

Bronwyn McCredie is Senior Lecturer in the School of Accountancy at the QUT Business School, Queensland University of Technology. She holds a Bachelor of Commerce with first-class honours in Finance and the University medal (BCom Hons Class 1) from the University of Newcastle, a PhD in Finance from the University of Newcastle and a Postgraduate Certificate in Academic Practice from Queensland University of Technology. She is a fellow of the Higher Education Academy. She primarily focuses on financial law, taxation and regulation. Her current research focuses on the efficacy of the OECD Base erosion and profit shifting (BEPS) program and resultant tax transparency legislation and corporate social responsibility reporting.

Trevor Pugh is a financial markets professional with over 20 years of experience in trading. He worked at Barclays Capital for 18 years, becoming Managing Director and Head of Gilt Trading before joining HSBC in 2014 to run their Sterling Rates Trading desk. He is currently working with the Asset and Liability Management Association as well as delivering numerous guest lectures on banking, markets and finance generally.

Jay Cullen is Professor of Banking Regulation at the University of York and adjunct Research Professor at the University of Oslo. He was previously Reader in Law at the University of Sheffield and Director of the Sheffield Institute of Corporate and Commercial Law. He publishes on financial stability, bank regulation and corporate governance. He has held visiting positions at Columbia University and Oslo University, is an associated expert at INET, and a member of the SMART network. He co-founded the Law and Money Initiative, a research collaboration between Cornell, Sheffield and Manchester Universities.

CHAPTER 1

Contract Law as Regulation: Relational and Formalist Approaches

Jonathan Morgan

This chapter first considers how contract law best functions as a regulatory tool. The second debate asks which institutions should be responsible for devising contractual regulations. These lead into the third debate, which considers whether commercial contract law should aim to foster and support 'relational contracting' or a more 'minimalistic' approach. We move from abstract to concrete questions. Each is heavily contested. The chapter provides a *tour d'horizon* of the most important and divisive debates in commercial contract law.

Debate 1
Contract law as regulation: Choice of rules

The rules of contract law can be divided into those from which it is possible to contract out ('default' rules) and those from which it is not ('mandatory' or 'immutable' rules). The former seem likely to dominate given the theoretical foundations of the law of contract. It is founded on choice. Its role is to enforce parties' agreements. Parties should enjoy considerable freedom to decide on the content and substance of their agreements. All this is obvious. What role is left for the law? Why supply 'default rules' at all if the parties can decide for themselves? A number of answers are possible. First, some sort of background framework seems inevitable and essential. Second, 'immutable rules' arise from legal policy rather than party intention. Third, providing a more extensive set of 'default rules' could bring advantages, either instrumental (e.g., reducing the costs of contracting) or otherwise (e.g., guiding behaviour). However, at least in regard to the kinds of contracting parties who are sophisticated enough to choose not only the terms of their agreements but which legal system will enforce them, the more prescriptive a law of contract becomes, the higher the risk that parties will shun it in favour of more permissive alternative systems.

A 'BASIC FRAMEWORK'?

All systems of contract law have rules to decide a number of fundamental matters: when the parties have reached agreement; what their agreement means; whether the agreement is an enforceable legal 'contract'; whether there are any defences such as force, fraud, error or change of circumstances; and, finally, the consequence of breaking the agreement. The complex body of rules governing these questions is what we generally mean by contract law. Plainly, such questions need to be answered by any 'contract law' worthy of the name. At minimum, this basic framework must be legally supplied.

But should parties be permitted to give their own answers to these basic questions (e.g., their own definition of having reached binding agreement, or how the contract should be interpreted, or provision for when circumstances change, or their own remedies for non-performance)? Among sophisticated contractors (or those using standard forms drafted by experienced lawyers), such clauses are very common. An agreement-in-principle may be expressly designated 'subject to contract' – binding only when the parties formally sign it. Such written contracts frequently declare that they are the exhaustive source of obligations between the parties ('entire agreement clauses'), precluding reliance on collateral oral warranties or implied terms. 'Force majeure' clauses are also very common: they offer greater precision and breadth in the definition of relevant changes of circumstances and more flexible consequences (e.g., extension of time in which to perform) – compared with automatic absolute discharge of frustrated contracts at common law. Agreed remedy clauses are as popular and varied as they are important.

These clauses are usually enforceable. The 'framework' rules of contract law that they displace are nonetheless defaults – mere place-holders subject to contrary party agreement. Freedom of contract includes not just the 'content' of the contract in a narrow sense (i.e., the definition of the parties' primary obligations) but also 'process' questions: how is agreement established, how is its content ascertained, or what excuses and remedies are available for non-performance. This important point is at danger of being misunderstood. Much of what is taught as foundational contract law 'doctrine' can in fact be freely altered – and often it is.

'MANDATORY' OR 'IMMUTABLE RULES'

Although the 'basic framework' is subject to contrary agreement, contract law does impose some truly immutable rules. First are those protecting the integrity of agreement. A 'contract' induced by physical coercion (duress) or deception (fraud) cannot be viewed as freely agreed. These 'vitiating factors' are so extreme and clear-cut that attempts to exclude those doctrines must fail. The absence of force and fraud is integral to any plausible definition of true agreement. However, beyond such clear cases, there is little consensus. Parties often seek to exclude liability for *non-fraudulent* misstatements in negotiations or even for fraud on the part of their *agents* (rather than their own fraud). In each case, English law seems to recognise a qualified freedom to exclude such liabilities. But the exact circumstances in which this would succeed are not easy to state (owing to a statutory 'reasonableness test' in the first case and the limits of '*contra proferentem*' interpretation in the second).[1] The core case for mandatory rules to protect the integrity of free agreement is accepted but its extent is controversial.

More controversial still are limits on what parties are permitted to agree. Such rules are overtly paternalistic. Examples include the unenforceability of commercial surrogacy agreements or organ-donor agreements.[2] The rationale for these prohibitions includes moral distaste at the commodification of human body parts or child-bearing. There is also, clearly, a concern that if a market in such 'goods' and 'services' were enforced by law, disadvantaged persons would face economic pressure to degradingly 'sell their organs' or 'hire out their wombs'. (A sharp distinction is drawn between permissible *altruistic* blood/organ donation or surrogacy, such as within a family, and cash transactions.) Countervailing arguments point out that organ failure patients would benefit from an open market.[3] But society is entitled to make moral judgments about the proper limits of the market. For those limits to be effective, the law of contract must refuse to enforce prohibited transactions.

Third, mandatory rules prohibit contracts that would harm third parties. People should avoid activities that would impose costs on society as a whole ('externalities'). A clear example is the illegality/public policy defence. For obvious reasons, parties are not allowed to disapply it by agreement. Again, though, the precise limits of 'public policy' are debatable. Take 'restraint of trade': agreements not to compete may be legitimate when, for example, a business is sold and the seller undertakes not to lure former customers away. But there must be limits since competition benefits the public as a whole by lowering prices. The doctrine is bound to be controversial. In this very context, Sir George Jessel made his famous observation:

> if there is one thing which more than another public policy requires it is that men of full age and competent understanding shall have the utmost liberty of contracting, and that their contracts when entered into freely and voluntarily shall be held sacred and shall be enforced by Courts of Justice. Therefore, you have this paramount public policy to consider – that you are not lightly to interfere with this freedom of contract.[4]

---

[1] Misrepresentation Act 1967, s 3; *HIH Casualty Insurance v Chase Manhattan Bank* [2003] UKHL 6.

[2] Surrogacy Arrangements Act 1985; Human Tissue Act 2004, s 32.

[3] For example, AL Friedman, BMJ 2006; 333: 746.

[4] *Printing and Numerical Registering Co v Sampson* (1875) LR 19 Eq 462.

Jessel MR's suspicion of the 'public policy' doctrine underlines the point that when an immutable rule is not clearly justified, parties ought to be free to contract out of the law's rules ('defaults'). Indeed, attempting to impose too many mandatory rules may prove self-defeating given the optional nature of contracting. Let us postulate an imaginary contract law rich in mandatory rules designed to make contracting parties behave like good and moral people who would never seek to gain a commercial advantage and would always keep their promises, come what may. Some (probably most) commercial parties would be uneasy with compulsory co-operation and extravagant moralism. If prevented from excluding such rules by contrary agreement, two more radical courses would remain. First, parties could contract out of the law altogether by providing expressly that their agreement was not to create legal obligations. Second, they could include an express 'choice of law' clause to have their agreement governed by the contract law of another jurisdiction.

Such 'freedom of choice of law' is generally recognised. It imposes practical constraints on systems of contract law, which may lose 'customers' to more permissive and congenial rivals. There is now considerable literature on the 'market for laws' in which jurisdictions compete for the custom of mobile commercial parties.[5] There is scant empirical evidence of what drives choice between jurisdictions. But it seems plausible that the substantive rules of law must play a significant role (as, equally, must a system's procedural features).[6] A jurisdiction like England and Wales, which actively seeks to attract non-English contractors to use English law, will therefore aim to provide rules that meet such parties' expectations. Mandatory rules are inherently prone to repeal since they will inevitably prove uncongenial for some parties, save in the clearest cases discussed above.

'DEFAULT RULES': A WIDER PROJECT

It has been suggested above that any law of contract must supply a background 'framework' for contracting. Many parties do not seek to devise their own answers to all or any of these basic questions. Especially not small business and private individuals. Many agreements are still extremely brief – perhaps no more than a handshake. But unsophisticated parties are entitled to have their agreements legally enforced. The law must, by default, supply the minimum decencies to clothe such bare agreements.

In economic terms it can be put this way: A reason for the law to supply 'defaults' is to reduce the cost of making a contract ('transaction costs'). Doing so benefits the immediate parties and the wider economy since trade allocates resources to their highest-value use. If the law did not supply such terms, much contracting could become uneconomic: it would not be economically rational

---

[5] For example, EA O'Hara and LE Ribstein, *The Law Market* (OUP 2009).

[6] Compare with Catherine Mitchell (Chapter 2 in this book).

to expend resources negotiating an exhaustive set of terms for a low-value contract. So in the absence of legal defaults, very many contracts would be unenforceable because of being seriously incomplete. (Only high-value transactions enjoy bespoke contracts tailored by – expensive! – transactional lawyers.) In broad terms, the case for supplying default rules seems clear. It facilitates trade. But what should their actual content be?

An answer consistent with the 'transaction-cost lowering' rationale is that default rules should be what the contractors would have included had they considered the question (or had it been economically feasible to do so). In theory, this is an empirical question: what in fact do most contracting parties want? In reality, though, such data are unavailable. The 'majoritarian' approach[7] becomes a slightly different inquiry. The search is on for the best rule, all things considered, on the grounds that such an optimal rule is what most parties would (naturally) want to govern their transaction.[8]

This sounds fine. The difficulty, of course, is in discerning what the *optimal* rule is. Most debates about the substance of contract law concern the best rule for a given problem. Consensus is rare. The variables are quite intractable. Should the rule be designed with an eye to morality, or distributive concerns, maximising party autonomy, improving economic efficiency, or some combination of these – or some other goal entirely? Even if we follow Law and Economics and concentrate solely on efficiency (a highly controversial assumption), there is notoriously little agreement about the 'efficient' rule. Even the single most famous claim of (early) economic analysis – that expectation damages are the optimal remedy because they permit 'efficient breach' – has long been given up as too simplistic. There are just too many decisions demanding 'efficient' incentives (e.g., whether to contract, and on what terms; the extent to which to rely on the contract being performed; whether to perform or breach) that no single rule can simultaneously provide the right answer to all. Much depends on the incidence of transaction costs in particular situations (this could sometimes mean that specific performance is the optimal remedy). These costs are unmeasured and likely immeasurable. It emerges that all economic models are radically indeterminate – permanently resistant to consensus when applied to real-world situations. As will be seen, there is considerable concern about the institutional capacity of lawmakers (whether legislatures or courts) to resolve such knotty controversies in order to devise optimal, or even acceptable, default rules.

If these caveats are correct, the lesson seems to be that the law should supply default rules only where it is essential to do so (or if it, exceptionally, seems clear what the ideal rule is). But should we be so concerned about having the

---

[7] Compare for 'penalty' defaults: I Ayres and RH Gertner, 'Filling Gaps in Incomplete Contracts: An Economic Theory of Default Rules' (1989) 99 Yale LJ 87.

[8] SJ Burton, 'Collapsing Illusions: Standards for Setting Efficient Contract and Other Defaults' (2016) 91 Indiana LJ 1063.

'wrong' default? Given their *default* nature, parties can contract out of rules they dislike. And, certainly, this lessens the harm done by an inappropriate rule. But default rules' modifiability differs. Sometimes the law regulates contracting out, such as through statutory regulation or common law interpretive presumptions ('*contra proferentem*' or otherwise). There is not a simple dichotomy between mandatory and default rules – but a range of *more or less modifiable rules*. It is important to be clear just how modifiable a given 'default' rule is.[9] Of course, the harder it is to modify (and the more 'sticky' it becomes), the closer a 'default' rule comes to mandatory status, with the concerns noted above.

Note finally that even where there are no *legal* obstacles to modifying a given default, the mere fact of being the legal starting point endows the rule (whatever it is) with value – the 'status quo bias' noted by behavioural economists.[10] That is, parties' preferences can be shaped (in the fashionable terminology 'nudged') by legal doctrine, even where it applies only by default. Such soft regulation appears attractive. However, the concern that sophisticated parties may shun over-regulated systems of contract law applies equally to 'nudging' as to overtly mandatory regulation. We can reasonably conjecture that such parties prefer relatively few default rules that are readily modifiable, so that their own preferences will reliably govern.[11]

Debate 2

Which institutions should be responsible for regulating contract?

'Mandatory rules' must be imposed by statute or by common law. But with 'default rules' there is another option – which is not to have any rule at all. A more radical move towards autonomy simply leaves it to contracting parties to 'self-regulate'. There is no perfect solution. All institutions have different advantages and disadvantages as regulators. Realistically, we have to identify the least bad option from imperfect alternatives. Realism is important: idealised accounts of the legislative process, or common law evolution, or standard form contracts must all be avoided.

LEGISLATION

In theory, the legislature appears the superior regulatory organ. There are no legal constraints on its powers. It is not required to legislate within the confines of existing common law doctrine. Therefore, legislation can replace unsatisfactory judge-made rules. The classic example is exclusion clauses. In the mid-late

---

[9] I Ayres, 'Regulating opt out: An economic theory of altering rules' (2012) 121 Yale L.J. 2032.

[10] For example, C Sunstein, 'Switching the default rule' (2002) 77 NYULR 106.

[11] Of course, not all contractors are 'sophisticated' in this way: contrast with Catherine Mitchell (Chapter 2 in this book).

20th century, the English courts had struggled to regulate these. The doctrine of 'fundamental breach' rose and fell; restrictively narrow interpretations to the clauses were more durable.[12] These common law techniques were largely replaced by the Unfair Contract Terms Act 1977. Parliament enacted radical reforms – direct substantive regulation – which had been beyond the capacity of the courts. With relief the courts withdrew from 'linguistic gymnastics' (narrow construction of exclusion clauses),[13] a technique later described as a 'desperate' expedient.[14]

Legislation can resolve controversies about mandatory (and indeed default) rules. Parliament has the democratic legitimacy to resolve moral questions such as surrogacy arrangements. On technical commercial questions, legislation typically arises from a report of the Law Commission or some other expert group. Since the Law Commission invariably initiates public consultation, its reports embody a range of opinions in addition to the Commission's own research. Legal reforms from this quarter generally have widespread support.

But legislation suffers well-known drawbacks. Parliament must anticipate all questions that might arise in future – which is impossible given the limits of human foresight, notwithstanding the Law Commission's expertise and parliamentary counsel's ingenuity. Although in theory legislation could be kept under continuous review, 'post-legislative scrutiny' seems rare at Westminster. Notoriously indeed, pressures on the parliamentary timetable mean that most Law Commission reports are never implemented in the first place. 'Technical' law reform is a low political priority. We may, perhaps, feel optimistic that if a problem were pressing enough (if the common law proved inadequate in an important area and 'unreformable' by the courts), legislative impetus would be found. Commercial interest groups would lobby for intervention. As noted, the Government actively promotes the attractiveness of English law for transnational dispute settlement. But the reality is that a great deal of 'contractual regulation' still occurs through the common law. Some important legislation (e.g., the Sale of Goods Act) does little more than codify the common law rules.

Common Law

In England (and related systems), the basic outlines of contract law have arisen from the common law process. The previous section implies that this is an unfortunate second-best, *faute de mieux*. But some commentators praise the common law's regulatory potential.[15] Its rules are hammered out in the crucible of litigation – an incremental process of solving real problems in concrete

---

[12] For example, *Photo Production v Securicor Transport* [1980] A.C. 827.

[13] Ibid., 851 (Lord Diplock).

[14] *BCCI v Ali* [2001] UKHL 8; [2002] 1 A.C. 251, [60] (Lord Hoffmann).

[15] For example, H Collins, *Regulating Contracts* (OUP 1999) ch 4; A Schwartz and RE Scott, 'The Common Law of Contract and the Default Rule Project' (2016) 102 Virginia L.R. 1523.

cases. Common law is derived by induction from those individual cases (compare the abstract rules that characterise legislation). It is also sometimes suggested that a seriously defective rule will generate considerable litigation (perhaps through contracting parties' attempts to draft around it). Courts therefore become aware of perceived defects in the common law. Its development is an ongoing and dynamic process – compare the once-and-for-all nature of most legislative interventions (which in the absence of post-legislative scrutiny could be dubbed 'enact and forget'). Another point is that most senior judges were commercial practitioners before appointment to the bench. This gives them insight into parties' needs and the behaviour requiring regulation. All these features suggest that the common law process may have real advantages.

Again, however, we should not idealise it. The common law is 'reactive' in a less helpful sense. It can develop only if and when a suitable case arises. Sometimes this never happens. Disputes actually litigated are not, of course, a representative sample. Cases that reach judgment are probably highly unrepresentative – the cost is justified only with high-value transactions or when strategically contested as a test case. Also, as noted above (with regard to exclusion clauses), the historical mass of contract doctrine imposes real constraints on judicial development. Courts cannot simply wipe the slate clean.

These constraints may be for the best. Courts cannot issue public consultations on the issues before them. Just as they are prisoners of the cases which chance (or which are selected) to be litigated, so they are confined by how parties put their cases. As a great legal historian observed, that makes it implausible to view the common law as a species of social engineering, for courts are addressed by advocates who ultimately care only to win their client's case.[16] Counsel are not ultimately interested either in doctrinal purity or social regulation for their own sakes (although they may appeal to such concerns tactically). A court self-confident enough to embark on social regulation has to appreciate that it may well lack sufficient information about the implications. Finally, judges' experience at the Bar typically involved advising about the kind of disputes upon which they now adjudicate. This is at a considerable remove from being a transactional legal adviser, let alone in business themselves.[17]

SELF-REGULATION

Neither the common law or legislative process is a flawless promulgator of commercial law regulation. Some commentators take a pessimistic view of the regulatory capacity of the state (whichever of its institutions takes the lead). Alan Schwartz expresses doubts about the 'default rules' project. In particular, he suggests that such is the wide array of contracting parties that it is a mirage

---

[16] SFC Milsom, *Historical Foundations of the Common Law* (London 1981) 6–7.
[17] Cf. *Somerfield Stores v. Skanska* [2006] EWCA Civ 1732, [22] (Neuberger LJ).

to suppose that for any given problem there is *one* default rule that a majority of contractors want (or ought rationally to want) to govern their contracts. Heterogeneity makes such generalised law-giving impossible.[18] The indeterminacy of economic analysis of law and its incommensurable rival approaches (e.g., moral or distributive) was noted in the previous debate.

One possible response to this general regulatory scepticism is to leave as much as possible to the contracting parties. Apart from the exceptional categories of mandatory rules and the 'minimum decencies' that the law must supply as structural defaults (e.g., formation, interpretation and remedies), no further attempts at regulating contractual behaviour should be made. In other words, the category of default rules should be left as minimal as possible. The risk of error is high, and even though cast as 'defaults' the rules still apply to inadvertent parties. Plus, default rules' tenacity or 'stickiness' has been noted.

This scepticism seems compelling. But then is it realistic to leave so much to contracting parties? First, what of small businesses and consumers? These, surely, cannot be expected to devise their own exhaustive set of contract rules. Even for sophisticated contractors, individually negotiated contracts are rare. The cost is often prohibitive. However, many businesses will contract only on their standard terms (drafted with the benefit of legal advice – made affordable by the economy of scale). Whenever a detailed written contract is employed, one can be hopeful that it addresses the issues that may arise across the life of the deal; the need for legally supplied defaults fades accordingly.

But are standard form contracts really a satisfactory answer? At a theoretical level, many object that there is rarely 'true agreement' to the terms contained within them – and the rule that a signature irrebuttably proves agreement is a threadbare fiction.[19] But the signature rule is compatible with the objective approach to contractual agreement: perhaps the most important manifestation of it. Even if a party has failed to read (or understand) the terms, they can be taken to realise that when they sign a contract they are legally bound by its contents. Even consumers appreciate this. The rule is of great importance in practice.[20] It enables certainty about precisely when and on what terms a contract has been made. Perhaps then it should be justified not so much on the grounds of 'true agreement' but as a rule vital to the functioning of commerce in a mass-transaction economy.[21] Standard forms abound, and courtesy of the signature rule, they mostly serve their intended purpose. (Of course, failing to get a signature undermines this function – most notoriously when two

---

[18] A Schwartz, 'The default rule paradigm and the limits of contract law' (1993) 3 S. Cal. Interdisc. L.J. 389.

[19] *L'Estrange v F Graucob Ltd* [1934] 2 K.B. 394.

[20] For example, *Peekay Intermark v Australia & New Zealand Banking Group* [2006] EWCA Civ 386 [43] (Moore-Bick LJ).

[21] N Oman, *The Dignity of Commerce: Markets and the Moral Foundations of Contract Law* (Univ Chicago Press, 2016) ch 7. This rationale could, perhaps, include automated Smart and Blockchain contracts: see Catherine Mitchell, chapter two, this book.

businesses each have their own (different) standard terms, and the law must resolve the 'battle' between their inconsistent terms.)

Another criticism of regulation-by-standard-forms is that this reflects and entrenches power imbalances between contracting parties. There is long-standing and widespread concern about such unilateral regulation imposed on a take-it-or-leave-it basis ('contracts of adhesion'). In English law, such concern is reflected in the legislation which allows *businesses* to challenge clauses that exclude liability for breach of contract when contained in the breaching party's 'written standard terms of business'.[22] But the baby should not be thrown out with the bathwater. Not all standard forms are unreasonable or one-sided. Not infrequently, a given form is in widespread use across a given industry. The body responsible for its production is sometimes a conscious collaboration between different interest groups in that industry,[23] attempting to balance their competing interests to produce (as the Law Commission once put it) 'a document acceptable to all'.[24] Although, as the Law Commission recommended, the statutory 'reasonableness test' still applies to exclusion clauses in industry-wide terms, courts have proven reluctant to stigmatise these. For example, Gloster J upheld an exclusion's reasonableness relying on its presence in terms that were shown to be widely used as 'standard in the market'.[25]

Yet, again, caution is needed. Industry-standard terms could still reflect power imbalances. The role of standard-form contracts in the shipping industry has been praised: such standardisation enhances price transparency and thus a functioning market.[26] Yet laws like the Hague Convention limit shipowners' liability to cargo-owners. Shipping contracts have not been left entirely to the (sophisticated and well-resourced) participants. Or take construction, often cited as an industry where 'representative bodies' reconcile the competing interests of (say) architects, building firms and specialist subcontractors. But construction contract law has faced serious problems. A 1990s joint review by the Government and industry bodies aimed to reduce litigation and improve productivity.[27] Its reports made clear that contractual self-regulation by the construction industry had failed. Adversarial relationships were common and mutual trust low. The review recommended reform of payment and dispute-resolution provisions in the main industry standard forms – crucially with *legislative* underpinning to prevent contracting out. Parliament obliged in 1996.

---

[22] Unfair Contract Terms Act 1977, s. 3(1).

[23] See generally KE Davis, 'The Role of Nonprofits in the Production of Boilerplate' (2006) 104 Mich. L.R. 1075.

[24] Law Commission, 'Exemption Clauses' Report No. 69 (1975), para 152.

[25] *Springwell Navigation Corpn v JP Morgan Chase Bank* [2008] EWHC 1186 (Comm) [604]–[605].

[26] *The Maratha Envoy* [1978] AC 1, 8, (Lord Diplock).

[27] Sir M Latham, *Trust and Money* (interim report 1993) and *Constructing the Team* (final report, HMSO 1994).

This is a fascinating episode.[28] Construction industry groups concluded that self-regulation was failing and demanded legislation to restrict their own freedom of contract. Therefore, 'mandatory' rules cannot be dismissed as inherently repugnant to all commercial contracting. Legislation and self-regulation may work in harness. The only general conclusion is that solutions are situation-specific. Contract regulation requires a balance between the various institutions, and the optimal blend differs across sectors of the economy.

Debate 3

Should the law embrace relational contract or the 'new formalism'?

The 'formalist' (and individualistic) contract law tradition has proven remarkably durable in England. Many of its assumptions have been attacked by critical work from the 1960s onwards which could be grouped under the heading of 'relational contract'. There are signs that such ideas are filtering through into English doctrine. Yet a reaction to 'relational contract' has emerged among US commentators, termed 'neo-formalism' (although there is nothing new about it in England). The most important debate for commercial contract law is which approach to take. Again, the correct answer may ultimately depend on the precise commercial context – some requiring a highly formal approach, others greater 'relationism'.

TRADITIONAL CONTRACT LAW: FORMAL AND INDIVIDUALISTIC

This section contains a brief sketch of the approach and assumptions of traditional contract law. It prefers clear and formal rules to judicial discretion. Certainty and predictability enable parties to confidently assess their rights and obligations. One important example concerns the content and meaning of a contract. As seen, a signed contract is binding irrespective of whether it has in fact been read, or understood, by the signing party. Furthermore, according to the parol evidence rule, a written contract is the exclusive source of contractual obligation. On this approach, no terms can be derived from the broader context of the deal or any unwritten expectations. Written contracts are also traditionally interpreted 'textually'. One justification for these restrictive rules is (as noted) certainty. It is easier to ascertain what is written down in the contract than to decide precisely what 'context' should be taken into account and with what effect on the parties' legal obligations. Such formalism also accords greater control to the parties (or whoever drafted the contract). As Lord Neuberger notes, when defending a highly formal approach to a contract which

---

[28] See for discussion C Ellis, 'What can we learn from Part II of the Housing Grants, Construction and Regeneration Act 1996?' in TT Arvind and J Steele (eds), *Contract Law and the Legislature* (Hart 2020, forthcoming).

turned out desperately imprudent, parties determine the text of the contract but not the wider context that a court might use to interpret it.[29]

English contract law is also notoriously tolerant of self-interested behaviour. This is distinct from the formal approach but is consistent and overlapping with it. Self-interested behaviour is (within limits) permitted during both the negotiation and the performance of contracts. Of course, duress and fraud are prohibited (indeed, there is a wide doctrine of innocent misrepresentation).[30] But duress was traditionally limited to physical coercion and its recent expansion to 'economic' duress has mostly been cautious (although there has been recent judicial enthusiasm in some quarters for stigmatising 'commercially unacceptable' conduct).[31] Although positive misstatements are widely actionable, there is usually no redress for failure to disclose information. There is no general duty of good faith from which to derive a duty of disclosure. Quite the reverse. The leading case, *Smith v Hughes*, remains the pillar and exemplar of English law's approach.[32] Cockburn CJ and Blackburn J each emphasised that whatever *morality* might require from the better-informed party (on realising the 'self-delusion' of the other), he or she is not *legally* obliged to correct the false impression.

Nor is there any general duty to perform contracts 'in good faith' or even to co-operate. Each party is entitled to consider its own interest exclusively (absenting express obligations to the contrary). A sharp distinction is drawn between a typical contract and a 'fiduciary' relationship (which requires placing the other party's interest first). A contractor is entitled to terminate a contract for any reason or none (faced with breach of a relevant condition). When discretion is conferred by a contract, orthodoxy clearly allows it to be used in en entirely self-interested fashion without fear of judicial review.

A longer account would note all of the exceptions and qualifications to the points outlined above. They are not absolutely true in all circumstances: the trend, no doubt, is away from traditionally strict formality and stern individualism. Yet it remains broadly accurate – a portrait of the essence of English contract law. The tradition has been both questioned and defended in recent work.

'RELATIONAL CONTRACT': THE CHALLENGE TO ORTHODOXY

The traditional picture of contract law has been criticised as outdated and unrealistic. At the heart of the critique are reflections on how business deals actually work. In the real world of contracting, it is argued, parties place much more emphasis on their ongoing business relationship and very considerably less on

---

[29] *Arnold v Britton* [2015] UKSC 36, [17].

[30] See for criticism: M Bridge, 'Innocent Misrepresentation in Contract' [2004] CLP 277.

[31] For example, *Times Travel (UK) Ltd v Pakistan International Airlines* [2017] EWHC 1367 (Ch) (reversed on appeal [2019] EWCA Civ 828).

[32] (1871) L.R. 6 Q.B. 597.

the formal written contract. The 'relational' challenge stems from two great scholars: Ian Macneil and Stuart Macaulay.

Macneil's theoretical writing championed the importance of business relationships.[33] Nearly every contract is embedded in a relationship that develops over time. That perspective is quite at odds, of course, with the traditional emphasis on the formal contract agreed at the outset. To view it as settling, once and for all, the parties' relationship for the entire currency of the deal seems unrealistic when that relationship is dynamic and evolving. Even the most skilled contract drafter would find it impossible to anticipate all possible problems in advance. Such 'presentiation' is not how business relations work or ever could work.

A flourishing business relationship (one that maximises the parties' profits) instead requires flexibility and co-operation. Parties might (for example) share information and attempt to adjust the contract should difficulties arise – rather than acting with unbending priority for their (short-term) self-interest by strict adherence to the initial contract terms. Given this insight, traditional legal doctrine seems seriously defective. It does nothing to encourage such co-operation and is tolerant of selfish behaviour that may bring relationships to a premature end (ones that remained mutually beneficial – i.e., profitable – to the parties in the longer term). Macneil's research suggests that traditional contract law needs fundamental reform to absorb the lessons of relational contract theory.

Support is derived from Macaulay's ground-breaking 1963 paper, which is that rarest of things, empirical research into the reality of how business professionals make contracts and view the law of contract.[34] (That it is one of the most cited articles of all in contract research indicates both its importance and its rarity.) Having interviewed managers of small manufacturing firms, Macaulay found a widespread disuse and mistrust of contract law. Businesses worked problems out co-operatively when they arose, making adjustments to quantities or prices. The great concern was to preserve good commercial relationships. All agreed that even to cite a contractual provision at another party would be looked upon unfavourably. To threaten litigation would effectively end the relationship between the firms in question.

We might suppose that a number of sociological factors unconnected to the particular rules of contract law underlie Macaulay's celebrated findings of 'non-use'. Any evidence of a disputatious or litigious disposition is likely to cause alarm in all human relations. Legal advice is extremely expensive, and litigation especially so. Would the threats be any better received were contract law thoroughly 'relational'? But Macaulay has been emphatic that contract law mistakenly prioritises the 'paper deal' (the formal legal contract) over the 'real deal'

[33] IR Macneil (ed by D Campbell), *The relational theory of contract: Selected works of Ian Macneil* (London: Sweet & Maxwell, 2001).

[34] S Macaulay, 'Non-Contractual Relations in Business: A Preliminary Study' (1963) 28 American Sociological Rev 1.

actually governing the parties' relationship.[35] The implication is that contract law should transform itself to enforce the implicit dimensions of the parties' relationship, giving these priority over the mere formal contract (which bears little resemblance to the parties' true expectations, even at the outset, let alone as the relationship develops). An influential thesis explicitly calling for such a reorientation of the law is Hugh Collins' *Regulating Contracts*.

Such arguments have begun to influence the development of doctrine in England. In *Yam Seng Pte Ltd v International Trade Corp Ltd*, the High Court implied a term that the contract would be performed in good faith.[36] This entailed two specific duties on the supplier under a distribution agreement: that it would not provide misleading information and would not sell the same goods at a lower price in any market covered by the agreement. Leggatt J's reasoning was revolutionary. He rejected English law's traditional hostility to good faith with its 'ethos of individualism' and accompanying fears of uncertainty.[37] He thought 'too simplistic' the 'sharp distinction' drawn between fiduciary relationships 'in which the parties owe onerous obligations of disclosure to each other, and other contractual relationships in which no duty of disclosure is supposed to operate'.[38] Some contracts require information-sharing by their nature, even when fiduciary duties are absent. Leggatt J labelled these 'relational contracts' and gave examples: 'joint venture agreements, franchise agreements and long-term distributorship agreements'. Such contracts

> may require a high degree of communication, cooperation and predictable performance based on mutual trust and confidence and involve expectations of loyalty which are not legislated for in the express terms of the contract but are implicit in the parties' understanding.

Various criticisms have been made. Does good faith really meet the high threshold of necessary implication of a term 'in fact' (i.e., that the parties intended that the term should be part of the contract, although they failed to include it among the express terms)?[39] Alternatively, and perhaps more honestly, the term could be viewed as one imposed by default onto a category of contracts by legal policy (not the parties' intentions). But do 'relational contracts' form a sufficiently clear category to limit such 'implication by law'?

---

[35] S Macaulay, 'The Real and the Paper Deal: Empirical Pictures of Relationships, Complexity and the Urge for Transparent Simple Rules' (2003) 66 MLR 44.

[36] [2013] EWHC 111 (QB); [2013] 1 All E.R. (Comm) 1321.

[37] Ibid., [124].

[38] Ibid., [143].

[39] Leggatt LJ has recently asserted that the good faith term meets the extremely demanding test for implication reaffirmed in *Marks & Spencer Plc v BNP Paribas Securities Services Trust Co (Jersey) Ltd* [2015] UKSC 72, [2016] AC 742: see *Al Neheyan v Kent* [2018] EWHC 333 (Comm), [174].

Otherwise, the relational good faith term would seem to arise by default in all commercial contracts, which Leggatt J expressly declined to advocate. Perhaps such generalisation is the inevitable destination of the *Yam Seng* development if it takes root. Not all courts and commentators have welcomed it.[40] *Should* relational contracting be incorporated into contact law?

The 'Neoformalist' Response

Scepticism about 'relational contract law' questions both its desirability and contract law's capacity to implement it. The counter-argument on the first point is that formal rules of law do not preclude, or necessarily harm, extra-legal relational norms within a commercial deal. On the second, the argument is that many parties do not desire 'relational' rules imposed by law when they are perfectly able to write such contracts if they wished.

The first argument has been explained by using a distinction between 'relationship-preserving norms' and 'end-game norms'. Broadly, the suggestion is that very different norms govern relationships during their currency and at their end. A possible parallel – although it seems remote from commercial law – is marriage.[41] The norms that govern spouses' partnerships are almost entirely non-legal (i.e., other than the kinds of marital misconduct, such as adultery, which serve as legal grounds for divorce). It seems unlikely that marriages would be enhanced by legally attempting to enforce vital intra-marriage norms such as sharing, co-operation and respect. First, it would be hard to frame the obligations in sufficiently precise terms and difficult to 'observe' (prove to the court) whether breach of them was inexcusable or was justified retaliation for an earlier breach. Such matters are better worked out between the parties. Divorce laws do not attempt to enforce these norms either. Although (as noted) certain categories of marital misconduct have historically survived, the increasing trend is towards 'no-fault divorce' in which the only ground is the decision by one or both parties that the marriage should end. Courts no longer attempt to adjudicate on fault when apportioning the spouses' assets. Neither during a marriage nor at its end are the relational norms crucial to any successful marriage legally enforced.

Could commercial relationships work in a similar way? Trying to enforce co-operation during a relationship's currency faces the same problems of definition and proof as the matrimonial example. In addition to these practical difficulties, would enforcement anyway be desirable? Robert Scott has cautioned against the danger of displacing true commercial co-operation by a less

---

[40] Cf. *Al Neheyan v Kent* at [168–70] (round-up of decisions in which *Yam Seng* has received a warmer welcome).

[41] See Robert and Elizabeth Scott 'Marriage as Relational Contract' (1998) 84 Virginia LR 1225.

satisfactory legally enforced version.[42] Let us postulate a comprehensive legal duty to co-operate and compliance with it. Would it support relational contracting? There is a marked difference between grudging co-operation offered tactically in order to avoid a legal sanction and true, willing co-operation. Scott argues that it is much more difficult for contracting parties to ascertain whether the other is truly co-operative or trustworthy when 'relational norms' are legally enforced. Law may even 'crowd out' truly relational behaviour in addition to making it harder to distinguish from tactical, sanction avoidance. Traditional contract law's limited obligations may better facilitate truly relational behaviour 'in the gaps'. It is easier to signal co-operative commitment to the relationship. Co-operative behaviour (e.g., sharing commercially sensitive information) here goes beyond what is legally required and cannot be mistaken for mere compliance. Paradoxically then, the argument runs, a formal contract *law* could better accommodate relational *contracting*.

A different objection is more familiar. To come up with an adequate relational law of contract would exceed the capacity of the legal process.[43] Since the relevant norms are relationship-specific, general legislation is unlikely to be able to supply suitable rules (unless it delegates implementation to the courts). As for the judicial process, trying to discern and enforce contracts' 'implicit dimensions' poses obvious practical problems. Unspoken, relationship-specific understandings are difficult for outsiders to penetrate. By contrast, close adherence by courts to contractual texts is much more feasible – and its outcome more predictable. Even if the wholehearted enforcement of relational norms in precedence to the formal contract were desirable, there would be a high cost in attempting to do this through the legal process (including the 'error costs' of courts defining and enforcing the norms incorrectly).

EVIDENCE FROM PRACTICE: WHAT DO SOPHISTICATED PARTIES CHOOSE?

Some evidence suggests that commercial parties do not invariably choose 'relational' contract law in real-world situations. It comes from two sources: first, examining the dispute-resolution mechanisms in 'domestic' tribunals governing disputes between fellow members of a trade association; second, considering the popularity of different jurisdictions' contract laws as expressed through choice of law clauses.

Lisa Bernstein is the leading scholar on trade associations. Bernstein finds that the dispute resolution mechanisms of certain associations are clear and

---

[42] RE Scott, 'The Death of Contract Law' (2004) 54 Univ Toronto LJ 369.

[43] A Schwartz and RE Scott, 'Contract Theory and the Limits of Contract Law' (2003) 113 Yale LJ 541; J Gava and J Green, 'Do we need a hybrid law of contract?' [2004] CLJ 605.

formal, contrary to what relational contract theory would predict.[44] The trade bodies that Bernstein studied avoided 'relational' rules. Their domestic tribunals (resolving disputes between members) applied the rules strictly. Bernstein's hypothesis is that as US contract law has become less formalist, trade associations have 'contracted out' of public contract law in favour of more effective – i.e., *more formal* – private dispute-resolution. Bernstein argues that these empirical studies support the claim that optimal 'end-game norms' (appropriate for resolving disputes) are clear and formal.

The evidence is not wholly one-sided. British construction projects increasingly use the New Engineering Contract forms, which are replete with express obligations of good faith and co-operation, being designed to promote a collaborative ethos. Presumably, this meets the perceived needs of industry participants. The lesson is that sweeping assumptions should be avoided. Bernstein's research shows that lawyers should be cautious before assuming that relational contracts should be legally enforced wherever they are found to exist (as a sociological matter). Evidently, this is not always the optimal dispute-resolution mechanism according to the revealed preferences of trade association members. But sometimes it is, suggests the rise of 'relational' construction industry clauses. In the next section, we suggest that context is all.

Further real-world evidence suggests that sophisticated contractors may prefer more formalist laws of contract. A study of choice of law by American companies (in publicly filed contracts) revealed a marked preference for New York law.[45] Compare the much lower number of parties opting to be governed by (say) Californian law. The economic size and importance of the State of California rival those of New York. The study's author suggests that the contrasting contract laws in those states could explain the disparity. Californian contract law places greater emphasis on the background, context and implicit dimensions of the deal (compared with the wording of the contract), granting greater powers for courts to intervene to adjust contracts perceived to be unfair. Californian contract law seems more 'relational', whereas that in New York is rather closer to the English model and more 'formalist'. Therefore, the disproportionate popularity of New York contract law could suggest a preference for such formalist law.

Many English lawyers would enthusiastically concur. English law, too, is one of the most popular globally for international disputes. This could well be seen as a vote of confidence for its traditional formalist approach. But caution is needed. Studies generally just count the number of choices of law for England, New York, and so forth, but lack evidence of the reasons for the choice. Such evidence can be only indirect – perhaps even speculative. As Stefan

---

[44] L Bernstein, 'Merchant Law in a Merchant Court: Rethinking the Code's Search for Immanent Business Norms' (1996) 144 Univ Pennsylvania LR 1765 and 'Private Commercial Law in the Cotton Industry: Creating Cooperation Through Rules, Norms, and Institutions' (2001) 99 Michigan LR 1724.

[45] GP Miller, 'Bargains bicoastal: New light on contract theory' (2010) 31 Cardozo LR 1475.

Vogenauer argues, factors apart from substantive doctrine could also determine choice of law.[46] The fact that England enjoys a high-quality, independent and incorruptible judiciary is of great importance, as is the dominance in global trade of the City of London and the supposed political stability of the UK, as indeed is the use of the English language. It could be that the detailed rules of substantive law have little effect on the choice. Perhaps not – although can they have no effect whatever? English contract law is rule-based, non-interventionist and respectful of party autonomy. Such characteristics are presumably attractive to international 'customers'. Yet developments like *Yam Seng* could further enhance English law's commercial reputation if Leggatt J has correctly identified what parties to relational contracts want. The danger of complacent conservatism among English lawyers should be guarded against.

Synthesis: Pluralist Contract Law(s)

Perhaps deft compromise can resolve these debates. It seems overwhelmingly likely that different contracting parties have differing appetites for relational or formal laws of contract. (Again, these categories represent ends of a gradual spectrum rather than a binary choice.) If so, it would be no better to have an unvaryingly 'relational' contract law than the traditional 'formalist' variety. A variety of approaches seems preferable to one single rigid paradigm. But a rich and varied approach would also be complex – and potentially unpredictable. Could it be made to work with sufficient clarity? How is the choice to be made between different registers of relationism or formality – and who is to make it, the parties or the courts?

Arguably, the best compromise is to leave the choice to the parties. The court must fully accept that choice and enforce the contract accordingly. For example, parties that insert clauses requiring renegotiation in good faith in the event of problems emerging in a long-term contract expect this to be legally binding.[47] Despite suggestions to the contrary in the English case-law, there is no good reason to disappoint such expectations.[48] Full acceptance of party choice of relational rules runs with the grain of freedom of contract, not against it. Such a choice is surely understandable. As McKendrick puts it, 'long-term contracts must often be phrased in broad, flexible terms to enable the parties to adjust their bargain to meet changing circumstances' – and the role of the court is nothing other than the traditional one of giving effect to those expressed intentions.[49]

---

[46] S Vogenauer, 'Regulatory Competition Through Choice of Contract Law and Choice of Forum in Europe: Theory and Evidence' (2013) 21 Eur Rev Private Law 13.

[47] For example, *Associated British Ports v Tata Steel* [2017] EWHC 694 (Ch); [2018] 1 All E.R. (Comm) 170.

[48] Sir G Leggatt, 'Negotiation in Good Faith—Jill Poole Memorial Lecture' [2019] J.B.L. 104 .

[49] 'The regulation of long-term contracts in English law' in J Beatson and D Friedman (eds), *Good Faith and Fault in Contract Law* (OUP 1995) 305 (cited with approval *Total Gas Marketing Ltd v Arco British Ltd* [1998] CLC 1275, 1286 (Lord Steyn)).

But the need for sensitivity could equally point the other way. As seen, not all contracts are expected by the parties to be governed by relational norms. A proper appreciation of context may therefore lead (somewhat paradoxically) to a formalist approach (i.e., for the court to focus *acontextually* on the words alone). Thus, Lord Hodge has explained that some contracts require interpretation 'principally by textual analysis' – particularly sophisticated and complex agreements drafted by 'skilled professionals'.[50]

There is much to be said for leaving the choice to the parties. They know their own business better than the courts do. But two difficult and related points remain. What should the background approach or starting point be (the one that will apply by default unless parties signal otherwise)? And what about less sophisticated parties who are unable to 'signal' anything to the court because they lack 'skilled professionals' to draft their agreements?

A number of reasons support formalism as the default approach.[51] First, it is considerably easier for the courts to apply – as noted already, it places much lower demands on the tribunal's capacity to apply the words of the contract than to identify its 'implicit dimensions'. The more ambitious task should be assumed by the court only when the parties clearly mandate it. Second, formalism has long been the familiar approach in England. Contract drafters do not currently signal their preference for it: silence must be taken as tacitly approving the traditional approach (at least on the part of sophisticated parties). It would create considerable uncertainty (for a significant transitional period) were the law to switch to a relational default position.

Third, it may be harder to contract out of relational approaches than to stipulate for them. Perhaps it is sheer unfamiliarity that makes it seem strange, but there would be something odd about clauses saying that 'all good faith duties are to be excluded'. Would this be effective given the *contra proferentem* rule? Courts generally seem more accepting of parties that assume additional obligations (i.e., duties of good faith under the current law) than attempts to exclude the law's background obligations (i.e., good faith duties under a reformed 'relational' contract law). Another way to put it: if the law imposes relatively few, relatively clear-cut obligations, it is relatively easy for advertent parties to assume whatever additional obligations they wish. Party autonomy is maximised, whereas a rich array of 'relational' duties might prove harder to exclude. (At minimum, this would place greater demands on drafters, putting a premium on skilled legal advice.)

A wide measure of party autonomy arguably benefits all contractors, sophisticated or not. But the choice of paradigm remains.[52] Should the archetypal

---

[50] *Wood v Capita Insurance Services* [2017] UKSC 24; [2017] A.C. 1173, [13].

[51] J Morgan, *Contract Law Minimalism: A Formalist Restatement of Commercial Contract Law* (CUP 2013).

[52] See D Kimel, 'The Choice of Paradigm for Theory of Contract: Reflections on the Relational Model' (2007) 27 OJLS 233.

contractor be sophisticated and mobile (able to choose between rival laws of contract)? If so, leaving it to the parties to signal their preferred degree of formal or relational contracting is attractive. Or should law cater primarily for the small businesses and consumers ill equipped to make such choices? The nascent development of implied duties in 'relational contract' could be seen as the courts attempting to evolve a more complex set of background rules. This places considerable demands on the courts' regulatory capacity. To the extent that it improves the position of contractual 'small fry', it might drive away 'big fish' who prefer the chillier waters of formalism. Empirical questions lurk here. (Who litigates contract claims in English law? Why do they choose this jurisdiction?) That is inevitable whenever law attempts to satisfy preferences. We need to know what the preferences are. But in deciding *whose* preferences to satisfy (and whether it is feasible to offer different contract *laws* suitable for varied parties), normative choices are required. This chapter suggests how they could be made. But there are no easy answers.

FURTHER READING

L. Bernstein, 'Private Commercial Law in the Cotton Industry: Creating Cooperation Through Rules, Norms, and Institutions' (2001) 99 *Michigan Law Review* 1724.

H. Collins, *Regulating Contracts* (OUP, 1999).

S. Macaulay, 'The Real and the Paper Deal: Empirical Pictures of Relationships, Complexity and the Urge for Transparent Simple Rules' (2003) 66 *Modern Law Review* 44.

C. Mitchell, *Contract Law And Contract Practice: Bridging The Gap Between Legal Reasoning And Commercial Expectation* (Hart, 2013).

J. Morgan, *Contract Law Minimalism: A Formalist Restatement of Commercial Contract Law* (CUP, 2013).

A. Schwartz and R. E. Scott, 'Contract Theory and the Limits of Contract Law' (2003) 113 *Yale Law Journal* 541.

S. Vogenauer, 'Regulatory Competition Through Choice of Contract Law and Choice of Forum in Europe: Theory and Evidence' (2013) 21 *European Review of Private Law* 13.

CHAPTER 2

The Common Law of Contract: Essential or Expendable?

Catherine Mitchell

INTRODUCTION

The functions and significance of contract law, on the classical model at least, appear clear and undeniable. Along with the recognition and protection of property rights, a state-endorsed system of contract enforcement is one of the key constituents of a market economy. The law tells us how legally enforceable agreements are created, and it polices the contract contents, the excuses for non-performance and the remedies for breach. The principle of freedom of contract lies at its heart: individuals, rather than the state, are the best judge of their own preferences and are best equipped to identify opportunities for the pursuit and satisfaction of these preferences via a system of voluntary exchange. As well as providing the rules governing this process, contract law has generated a rich theoretical literature, using a variety of methodological perspectives to scrutinise the nature of contractual liability. There seems little room for doubt that a robust system of contract law lays legitimate claim to be a pillar of the liberal social and economic order and one of the hallmarks of a developed nation-state. Small wonder then that contract law occupies a distinct space in the curriculum of the UK undergraduate law degree. It is one of the foundations of legal knowledge and a core subject for the aspiring legal professional. It provides a grounding in common law method and forms the bedrock upon which the more specialised regulation of specific contracts (between employer–employee, consumer–business and landlord–tenant, for example) is built.

Though truncated, the above account is the familiar and enduring tale that contract law has been telling about itself for the past couple of centuries. This chapter explores some of the disruptive elements that undermine this story, in particular those that point to the common law's declining sphere of applicability and influence over the contracting process. Doubts about the importance and relevance in society of contract law, at least in its common law form, are nothing new. It has long been lamented that what is taught in most mainstream contract law courses in UK universities is largely an exercise in legal history or – worse – mythology, perpetuating and reinforcing a false narrative of the centrality of contract law to a functioning market economy.[1] In the 1970s, Grant Gilmore criticised contract law as little more than an elaborate patchwork of judicial opinions forced into existence as a distinctive field of law through the efforts of academics. He went on to predict the contract's death through the disintegration of its elegantly constructed doctrines because of encroachment by the law of tort and unjust enrichment.[2] Fragmentation and the development of specific rules to govern areas such as consumer contracts and employment rights also raised doubts about the future of the general principles of contract law. Further assault came from relational contract scholars and empiricists who exposed the relatively minor place of contracts and contract law in functioning business relationships.[3] Even the theoretical scholarship on contract, stressing its connection to promising, autonomy and the capacity for self-determination, though enlightening on why the state is ever justified in enforcing voluntarily assumed obligations, tended to be overshadowed by the less-than-ideal reality of economic exploitation, inequality of bargaining power and lack of meaningful choice for more vulnerable participants in the market, such as consumers and employees. Far from regulating contractual injustice, classical contract law appeared actively to contribute to it through a commitment to objectivity and a willingness to accept simulacra of consent established through acquiescence and inertia rather than informed and active engagement.[4] A lack of appropriate common law rules hampered judicial efforts to curb substantive unfairness in terms, although procedural measures, such as incorporation and interpretation of terms, allowed some measure of control.

This chapter does not intend to rehearse these familiar areas of contract controversy but rather explores the irony that the terminal blow to the common law of contract may come not from the established critiques outlined above but ultimately from contract itself. While generating doubts about the role of contract law in a modern economy, the foregoing debates yielded little in the way of radical common law reform. If anything, the merits of a more traditional, classical law of contract have been reasserted. Therein lies the irony. Having been relieved of the main responsibility for policing

---

[1] John Wightman, *Contract: A Critical Commentary* (London, Pluto Press 1996).

[2] Grant Gilmore, *The Death of Contract* (Columbus, Ohio UP 1974).

[3] Stewart Macaulay, 'Non-Contractual Relations in Business: A Preliminary Study' (1963) 28 *American Sociological Review* 55; Ian Macneil, *The Relational Theory of Contract: Selected Works of Ian Macneil*, D Campbell (ed) (London, Sweet & Maxwell 2001). See Chapter 1 by Jonathan Morgan in this collection.

[4] Margaret Jane Radin, *Boilerplate: The Fine Print, Vanishing Rights and the Rule of Law* (Princeton, Princeton UP 2013) 7–11.

business-to-consumer contracts by legislative intervention, the common law of contract should have found itself confined to the comfortable territory of regulating the 'arm's length' commercial agreement. However, in complex forms of economic activity involving exchange between independent firms, the substantive rules of contract law apply only to the extent the parties have not expressly stipulated for an alternative.[5] Along with the additional pressures of globalisation and technological advance, contract law's status as a default may finally tip it into oblivion, replaced with private rules created by the parties through contracts or developed by specialist industry bodies operating in discrete sectors of the economy. The common law still acts as arbiter of the legal validity of these systems, but its response has been to retreat to a formal, insular model, largely content to enforce the parties' self-governance under the principle of freedom of contract. This is manifest in the law's return to more formal interpretation methods which uphold the plain meaning of terms and a marked judicial reluctance to interfere in agreements, even in cases involving inequality of bargaining power.[6] The legal turn towards formalism appears to be motivated in part by a belief that a more formal law is the preference of commercial contractors, as well as a judicial perception that contract law is a product that must remain competitive in the international market for commercial law and legal services. As McBride has observed, there is a risk that contract law will '"eat itself" through the courts' too slavishly giving effect to the formalist ideal of "party autonomy"'.[7] Instead of providing the moral foundation for economic exchange, contract law in the hands of the courts is in danger of becoming wholly optional, a minor force in a world of private dispute resolution.

In drawing out this new source of debate about the relevance of contract law to a modern economy, we note first some general reasons for scepticism about contract law's role in the process of economic exchange. The chapter then explores the paradox that the law's turn towards formalism has coincided with the increased 'contractualisation' of society. Following that, we trace the implications of the diminishing practical importance of contract law and the growth of private regulation by third-party institutions (such as industry organisations) and through express contract terms. These include the risk of a stagnating common law and a lack of legal engagement with issues of substantive contractual justice. Finally, the chapter considers the future threat to domestic contract law posed by advances in information and communication technology (such as the phenomenon of 'smart contracts'). It concludes that though ostensibly contributing to the redundancy of the common law, these innovations may hold the key to its future development.

---

[5] Alan Thomson, 'The Law of Contract' in Ian Grigg-Spall and Paddy Ireland (eds) *The Critical Lawyers' Handbook* (London, Pluto Press 1992) 69, 71.

[6] *Office of Fair Trading v Abbey National plc and Others* [2009] UKSC 6, [2010] 1 AC 696; *Arnold v Britton* [2015] UKSC 36, [2015] AC 1619; *ParkingEye Ltd v Beavis* [2015] UKSC 67, [2016] AC 1172.

[7] Nicholas J McBride, *Key Ideas in Contract Law* (Oxford, Hart 2017) 18.

INDICATIONS OF CONTRACT LAW DECLINE

(a) Contract Law or Social Norms?

On a superficial level, it is easy to establish the centrality of law to the process of contracting. A contract is, by definition, a *legally* enforceable agreement. Creating a contract, as opposed to implementing a transaction by some other method (e.g., through a forced exchange), appears crucially dependent on the existence of a background set of legal rules governing the process. However, placing contract law centre-stage tends to marginalise the variety of social norms and institutions that support economic activity. Even the most cursory consideration of everyday contracts reveals this. First, many simple agreements are self-enforcing, as when items for sale in a shop are purchased by cash payment in a more or less instantaneous trade of goods for money. Making the contract (if it is even right to think of this process as one of 'contracting'[8]) is simultaneous with performance of it. The idea that contract law facilitates this kind of simple transaction appears absurd, although it has sometimes been necessary to determine the exact moment of contract formation in circumstances such as these in order to pursue a broader policy objective.[9] The transaction may give rise to rights concerning the quality of the goods received in exchange for payment, but most of those rights are derived from statute, not the common law.[10] Indeed, the common law of contract resolutely refuses to engage with one of the most basic issues concerning the transaction – whether the goods are worth the price paid – on the grounds that freedom of contract entails that this is fundamentally a matter for the parties.

Second, mutual trust may allow the parties to trade without the background machinery of legal enforcement, even when the exchange is not simultaneous. Complex systems of non-legal norms governing agreement-making and performance, developed organically through patterns of repeated interaction, have been observed to replace contract law in small insular communities.[11] Of course, trust may break down, in which case the most appropriate remedy may be a reputation sanction and not a costly attempt to secure legal remedies. Fulfilling a similar function in a more impersonal setting are the internet platforms and online review sites that encourage us to publicly share our experience of 'contracting' with others. Though imperfect in many respects (reviews may be fabricated and customers may exaggerate or may be more likely to recount a negative experience than a positive one), such platforms reduce the risk of dealing with complete strangers by giving some indication of broad

---

[8] Doubts have been expressed by Macneil, above n 3 at 129 and P S Atiyah, 'Contracts, Promises and the Law of Obligations' in *Essays on Contract* (Oxford, OUP 1986) 10, 19–22.

[9] Such as controlling unfair terms: *Thornton v Shoe Lane Parking* [1971] QB 163.

[10] Notably the Consumer Rights Act 2015.

[11] Lisa Bernstein, 'Opting Out of the Legal System: Extralegal Contractual Relations in the Diamond Industry' (1992) 21 *Journal of Legal Studies* 115.

trustworthiness or lack of it. These reputation-based systems are found even in complex industries. Dietz, for example, shows how reputational networks facilitated by information and communication technologies are more important than state-enforced contract law in cross-border trading in the software industry.[12] Empirical studies consistently demonstrate that maintaining reputation is a more important motivator than the law in ensuring contract performance, certainly amongst traders who want to continue to do business with one another.[13] The trust-building process can be replicated at the international level by specialist industry organisations, which seek to mimic the spontaneous order that emerges from repeated personal dealings by crystallising (or imposing) uniform standards and expectations on participants in the industry through model contract terms. Examples of such organisations are the Grain and Feed Trade Association and the International Swaps and Derivatives Association (ISDA) or the UK Joint Contracts Tribunal and the International Federation of Consulting Engineers (FIDIC) in the construction industry. These bodies seek to reduce the costs of contracting through standardisation, providing a set of ground rules that facilitate trading by aligning the parties' expectations, minimising risks and the possibility of disputes.[14] In effect, the trust necessary to contract is not generated between the parties at the personal level but at the level of the trade association and its bespoke contract documentation.

The existence of these alternatives does not eradicate the need for a law of contract. After all, these systems operate within the law's shadow and most commercial relationships will rely on the presence of contract law to some degree, even if they seek to avoid the operation of its default rules. Nonetheless, the availability of alternatives does suggest that high dependence on legal norms is likely to be displayed amongst only a minor subset of commercial contractors: those who lack trust and the opportunity to develop it, where support mechanisms provided by interested industry organisations are absent, or where contract performance does not depend on cultivating a long-term cooperative relationship with a counterparty.[15] Trading in fungible commodities in spot markets provides an example of where the parties' expectations may be derived principally from contract law norms. Macneil referred to these trades as 'discrete' exchanges, where the strict legal obligations assumed by the parties under a contract were neither connected to nor dependent on the other elements of their commercial relationship.[16] On this understanding, *contracting* is simply one method of effecting an economic exchange, suitable for the impersonal transaction requiring heavy reliance on the insurance of legal

---

[12] Thomas Dietz, *Global Order Beyond Law* (Oxford, Hart 2014) 167–72.

[13] Lisa Bernstein, 'Private Commercial Law in the Cotton Industry: Creating Co-operation Through Rules, Norms and Institutions' (2001) 99 *Michigan Law Review* 1724.

[14] Mitu Gulati and Robert E Scott, *The 3½ Minute Transaction* (University of Chicago Press 2013) 33ff.

[15] Oliver Williamson, *The Economic Institutions of Capitalism* (New York, Free Press 1985) 72.

[16] Macneil, above n 3, 154.

enforceability. Here, the existence of the law of contract saves a party from undertaking their own costly pre-contract enquiries into whether the other can be relied upon to perform their side of the bargain. It also means a party does not have to expend resources on security, monitoring and enforcement measures to guarantee performance. The background threat of an action for breach may be sufficient to ensure compliance. This version of what contract law is for also informs the paradigm of whom it is for. Contractors that rely on legal norms are assumed to act wholly in their own self-interest, informed by hard economic rationality and a reduced capacity to demonstrate the finer qualities necessary to maintain a continuing and long-term commitment.[17] The extent to which contractors actually fit this model, and whether contract law should be predicated on it, is a source of ongoing debate in contract law scholarship. Indeed, one of the reasons for common law decline may be the gulf between the classical law's one-dimensional image of the contractor and the more complicated reality found in most business relationships.

(b) Private Ordering as a Replacement for Public Regulation

Even in contracting contexts where we might expect the law to play a more central role, contract law's status as default rules, together with its commitment to upholding party autonomy, encourages private ordering. Forms of private ordering are diverse, ranging from the relatively minor (a set of comprehensive standard terms and conditions that attempt to oust the majority of local contract law) to major rule-systems that effectively govern specific kinds of contract (e.g., the UN Convention on the International Sale of Goods 1980) or elements within it (as with the International Chamber of Commerce Uniform Customs and Practice for Documentary Credits or 'UCP 600'). Though dependent on law for background legitimacy (through either a process of ratification and incorporation into domestic law or the contract law of a nation-state that governs the agreement to use these systems), contract parties are generally free to opt into these schemes. Express contract terms stipulating choice of law, jurisdiction and forum for disputes can also be used to prescribe the contract rules applicable to an agreement. The shift to privatisation of contract regulation is exacerbated by the prevalent use of arbitration to resolve disputes in commercial contracts. The potentially deleterious effect of arbitration on domestic contract law has long been a matter for concern.[18] We return to this point later in the chapter.

---

[17] See Lord Ackner's dictum in the House of Lords decision in *Walford v Miles* [1992] AC 128, 138, for the classic judicial statement of these supposed characteristics of commercial contractors.

[18] For a recent example, see Lord Thomas, 'Developing Commercial Law Through the Courts: Rebalancing the Relationship Between the Courts and Arbitration', The Bailii Lecture, 9 March 2016 (available at <https://www.judiciary.uk/wp-content/uploads/2016/03/lcj-speech-bailli-lecture-20160309.pdf> accessed 11 December 2018).

Perhaps more significant for the privatisation of civil justice in the commercial sphere is the development of industry-specific standard contract terms that may be used without material variation throughout the trade. In 'thick markets' with many participants, trade associations will often do the necessary work in developing standard forms to facilitate contracting.[19] The trade association terms are likely to be efficient in the sense of reflecting what parties would have chosen (or a reasonable compromise) and in responding to specific market conditions. This accords the terms a degree of acceptance amongst participants, such that they constitute the rule book for anyone wanting to engage in that particular trade. The standard terms enhance certainty and reduce the risks of contracting. Dispute resolution services may also be mandated by trade association governance processes within particular industries, especially those operating on a global scale.[20] The procedures are assumed to reflect the parties' preference for speedy and relatively inexpensive dispute resolution conducted by industry experts, which inflicts minimal damage on any broader and enduring trading relationship.

The effective ousting of legal norms in favour of trade association rules and procedures has been observed in markets as diverse as New York diamond merchants, cotton merchants and the international timber industry.[21] Though reckoned to be superior forms of contract governance, these attempts to conduct the entirety of productive activity outside the confines of a national legal system raise issues about legitimacy, accountability and the rule of law. First, the fact that a rule has evolved from trade usage, or appears within a standard form developed by industry insiders, may be a reliable indicator that the rule is familiar but not that it is fair. An industry-prescribed dispute resolution procedure may become essentially compulsory, putting trade rules and practices beyond the scope of legal oversight. Second, a powerful international trade association is likely to lobby hard with law-makers to protect its contract norms from legal interference, irrespective of the effect on third parties, the public interest or social welfare. Consequently, if an industry standard form is reviewed during litigation, courts may be reluctant to disturb customary understandings about the form's meaning and effect. The legal response to the ISDA Master Agreement, which governs almost all trading in over-the-counter financial derivatives, is a case in point. It has been asserted that the ISDA contract standardisation project has been 'highly successful in assuring public actors that the OTC derivatives industry was in fact

---

[19] Ronald J Gilson, Charles F Sabel and Robert E Scott, 'Contract and Innovation: The Limited Role of Generalist Courts in the Evolution of Novel Contract Forms' (2013) 88 *New York University Law Review* 170, 176–7.

[20] Bernstein, above n 13.

[21] See, respectively, Bernstein, above n 11 and n 13, and Wioletta Konradi, 'The Role of *Lex Mercatoria* in Supporting Globalized Transactions: An Empirical Insight into the Governance Structure of the Timber Industry' in Volkmar Gessner (ed) *Contractual Certainty in International Trade* (Oxford, Hart Publishing, 2009) 49.

capable of largely self-regulating'.[22] This certainly appears to accord with the attitude of the courts. In *Lomas v JFB Firth Rixson Inc*, the Court of Appeal considered the operation of certain provisions of the ISDA Master Agreement.[23] After some inconsistent approaches in the lower courts, the case has, according to one commentator, 'restored, more or less intact, to its status quo ante the common understanding of market practitioners as to how the ISDA Master Agreement works following an Event of Default'.[24] Even if courts were minded to intervene, there is some evidence to suggest that a negative assessment of legality by courts does not necessarily lead to amendment of the standard form (a quality often referred to as the 'stickiness' of the form[25]). Standard terms are more likely to respond to the pressures emanating from organisational, economic or market-driven imperatives operating in that business, rather than legal considerations. The danger here is that the 'law' is whatever is accepted and promulgated by the relevant trade association or body, rather than the general rules of the national legal system. Agreements are not enforced by the power of the law but by the conventions of the relevant contracting and interpretative community that develops (or dictates) the rules.

(c) The Ascendancy of Contractualisation and the Retreat of Common Law

It is paradoxical that the common law of contract has declined in importance at a time when private ordering in the provision of goods and services has flourished following the privatisation and marketisation of previously publicly owned or administered sectors of the economy. Private ordering relies on contracts. It has become much more apparent that many aspects of our lives – and our significant relationships – are predicated on highly formal contractual structures that often fail to embody the liberal contract ideal. Technology has also played an important role in facilitating the 'contractualisation' of society. Two simple examples will illustrate this general point. Thirty years ago, a student entering higher education in England would find a system of financial support through gifts (i.e., means-tested but non-repayable maintenance grants) and tuition fees paid from public funds. This has been replaced by a system of repayable loans facilitated through the 'student loan agreement'.

---

[22] John Biggins and Colin Scott, 'Public-Private Relations in a Transnational Private Regulatory Regime: ISDA, the State and OTC Derivatives Market Reform' (2012) 13 *European Business Organization Law Review* 309, 323.

[23] *Lomas & Ors v JFB Firth Rixson Inc* [2012] EWCA Civ 419.

[24] Edward Murray, 'Lomas v Firth Rixson: 'As you were!'' (2013) 8 *Capital Markets Law Journal* 395, 395.

[25] Gulati and Scott, above n 14; Omri Ben-Shahar and John A E Pottow, 'On the Stickiness of Default Rules' (2006) 33 *Florida State University Law Review* 651.

The accompanying marketisation of higher education has transformed the relationship between student and university into one of consumer and service provider with a contract at its core, albeit one unlikely to be scrutinised or enforced by general contract law.[26] Oversight of the sector is undertaken by the recently established Office for Students, whose regulatory goals include ensuring that students receive value for money from their higher education experience. Another example of contractualisation is provided by the simple purchase of goods for cash at a high-street outlet. This straightforward transaction generates multiple layers of contract complexity when transferred away from physical premises and into an online environment. Standard terms and conditions are ubiquitous in the online purchase. Of course, the small print has been an enduring feature of contracting for decades but rarely evident (and certainly not necessary) in a face-to-face sale of tangible products in a bricks-and-mortar shop.[27] However, conducted over the internet, the same sale will be subject to a dense array of retailer standard terms and conditions that purport to govern most aspects of the transaction. The increased use of these terms is a reflection of the complicated and opaque nature of the online process, not least that successful performance depends on essential contributions from intermediaries responsible for various aspects of the transaction: facilitating payments, warehousing, shipping and delivery of the goods, and so on (contract law will treat these intermediaries as 'third parties', suggesting a degree of remoteness from the central object of the exchange). The existence of these vast networks behind a simple purchase creates many more points of potential failure over which the retailer may exercise little direct control, presenting a need for more detailed risk and expectation management. However, an additional reason for the proliferation of standard terms is the ease with which automation makes it possible to 'contractualise' many common types of agreement. A consumer is effectively prevented from making an online purchase if they do not agree to the terms. Similarly, the supply of software or other products provided via digital download is subject to the customer's acceptance of an impenetrable 'end user licence agreement'. Consent to these contracts is often procured through processes that are less than transparent, augmenting the control that the superior economic actor has over the transaction.[28]

The classical law of contract, with its focus on objectivity and freedom of contract, enables and informs this heavily bureaucratic model of what it means to contract. Although there are external efficiency grounds (connected to the higher costs of negotiating individual agreements) to explain the increasing standardisation of transactions, the rise of standard terms and conditions is

---

[26] See the Competition and Markets Authority, *Higher Education: Guide to Consumer Rights for Students* available at <https://www.gov.uk/government/publications/higher-education-guide-to-consumer-rights-for-students> accessed 11 December 2018. See also Wightman on this process of 'contractualisation' of modern society, above n 1, 3–4.

[27] Mark A Lemley, 'Terms of Use' (2006) 91 *Minnesota Law Review* 459, 466.

[28] Lemley, ibid.

difficult to disentangle from the legal willingness to enforce them. This is not necessarily a problem in contracts between big businesses where negotiated risk management is essential, but the model has potential to work considerable mischief in agreements that are a poor fit with its underlying assumptions (such as that contractors will read, understand and give their genuine consent to the terms). This is particularly the case where autonomy is supposedly established through proxies for genuine agreement, such as clicking a box indicating that one has agreed to a non-negotiated set of standard terms. The legality of many of these terms is largely untested but taken on trust.

Counterintuitively, the ascendancy of contracting in society has not led to the emergence of a reinvigorated contract law. The common law response to this perfect storm of contractualisation, complexity and private ordering has been to revert to an abbreviated party-autonomy model that perceives its primary function as enforcing the terms provided that the process of reaching agreement was free of vitiating factors such as fraud or duress.[29] The protection of weaker parties, such as consumers, is left to other forms of regulation. The re-emphasis on broadly formalist virtues in contract law can be observed in a number of legal developments over the past few years: a return to plain-meaning contract interpretation; an emphasis on upholding express contract terms at the expense of established contract doctrine; and a generally negative response in superior courts to attempts in lower courts to develop a more contextual or expectations-led approach to contract law.[30] There is also burgeoning acceptance that contract terms can be used to nullify the operation of legal claims and rights that a party might otherwise enjoy under general contract law.[31] Written contracts are marked by increasing introspection. Express terms seek to control the immediate contracting environment and inhibit the creation of any obligations beyond those written into the contract text. The 'acknowledgement of non-reliance' clause in a contract can prevent a claimant from bringing an action for misrepresentation.[32] The 'entire agreement' clause can preclude collateral warranties and obligations arising outside the main statement of express terms and conditions.[33] The 'no oral modification' clause can prevent attempts to undermine the original contract text by reference to agreed but informal variations.[34] Similarly, there has been some liberalisation of the operation of the penalty rule. A contract clause setting a level of liquidated damages, or fine, that exceeds the claimant's likely losses from breach may be enforceable

---

[29] For a comprehensive defence of formalism in contract law, see Jonathan Morgan, *Contract Law Minimalism* (Cambridge, Cambridge UP 2013).

[30] For a fuller examination of these factors, see Catherine Mitchell, *Interpretation of Contracts*, 2nd ed (Abingdon, Routledge 2018).

[31] Radin, above n 4, explores this phenomenon in great depth in the consumer context.

[32] *Springwell Navigation Corp v JP Morgan Chase Bank* [2010] EWCA Civ 1221.

[33] *Inntrepreneur Pub Co Ltd v East Crown* [2000] All ER (D) 1100.

[34] *Rock Advertising Ltd v MWB Business Exchange Centres Ltd* [2018] UKSC 24.

if the claimant can demonstrate a legitimate interest in securing performance of the primary contractual obligation.[35] Although such terms may be subject to legislative control in a consumer contract, regulation in commercial contracts is largely a common law matter. It appears to have gone unnoticed that by mounting such a strong defence of the contract text, contract law is creating the perfect conditions for its own demise.

Does Formalism Risk Contract Law Redundancy?

The resurgence of formalism in contract law is explained partly by the judicial concern to limit unjustified interference in contracts in the wake of increasing commercial contract complexity and self-regulation by the parties. The re-emphasis on party autonomy and freedom of contract is also a reflection of general shifts in the political climate of the UK since the latter part of the 20th century. It is perhaps unfortunate that the rhetoric surrounding the virtues of privatisation and free markets appears to have penetrated English contract law itself. Judges are increasingly concerned with whether English commercial law is competitive against rival jurisdictions in capturing commercial legal business. Below, we explore these themes and their implications for the law.

(a) Freedom of Contract and Judicial Abdication of Responsibility

Though long regarded as a strong champion of party autonomy, English contract law wavered between more or less robust interpretations of freedom of contract over the course of the last century. A more welfarist and paternalistic turn in contract law was detected in the decades from the 1940s to the 1970s, prompted by the need to address the problems generated by mass consumer contracting on standard terms.[36] The welfarist strand within contract law during this period also chimed with the social and economic policy of post-war governments that recognised the state's important role in providing for its citizens public goods and services that were not procured effectively through markets. The reassertion of freedom of contract and the return to a more formalist style of legal reasoning can be interpreted as the natural, perhaps even inevitable, counter-trend that emerged after the common law was liberated by legislation from responsibility for regulating business-to-consumer transactions. Key enactments here were the Consumer Credit Act 1974 and the Unfair Contract Terms Act 1977. More broadly, it reflects the ideological shift in government policy since the late 1970s back towards the philosophy of free markets. Contract law is showing demonstrable caution in how it responds to commercial contract texts with renewed emphasis on party autonomy and a reluctance to interfere in contracts on abstract grounds of fairness. Contract judgments

---

[35] See *ParkingEye Ltd v Beavis*, above n 6.
[36] Wightman, above n 1, 114–15.

are replete with statements concerning the role of the judge in a contract dispute: to uphold the terms of the contract, assuming that it is otherwise valid, and not to improve or alter the bargain. The reassertion of a more formal legal approach to the contract terms is also illustrated in the recent tendency of the Supreme Court to uphold strict obligations (such as termination rights) over softer-edged standards in the contract documents (such as duties to co-operate) and a plain-meaning interpretative default.[37]

The formalist turn in legal reasoning responds to criticism that a broader contextualist approach to establishing obligations, which allows reference to contract background in interpreting contracts and implying terms, allows judges too much scope to interfere in contracts using vague and open-ended criteria such as reasonableness and commercial sense. There are both principled and pragmatic justifications for judicial restraint. The principled justification is that contracts are voluntarily assumed obligations based on consent. This rationale for contracts as a means to protect and advance private interests resists judicial interference with the agreement except on very narrow grounds. That a deal has turned out unexpectedly badly for one of the parties is no justification for intervention. Private ordering is also regarded as superior from an efficiency point of view. Interference may alter the contract balance of liability in unexpected ways, giving rise to a risk allocation different from the one the parties believed they were undertaking (and hence priced for). The anti-activist approach also upholds the constitutional and institutional limits of the common law: judges are there to interpret and apply the law as derived from the recognised sources. They are not empowered to undertake a broad policing role or impose unbargained-for responsibilities on the parties on the grounds of some ill-defined policy or moral criteria.

Overlapping with these constitutional, separation-of-powers concerns are the more pragmatic reasons for curbing judicial activism, notably that judges lack knowledge and expertise to make assessments of what is in a party's best interest, still less to make judgments about what might be good or bad for commerce. Ultimately, judges are not there to regulate the operation of the market but to decide on the legal rights of the parties. In relation to contract law, this is usually done by asking two simple questions. First, have the parties reached a legally enforceable agreement? Second, what have they agreed? The latter question is answered primarily by reference to the express terms of the agreement. The judge's role is simply to interpret the terms and uphold whatever result follows.

These kinds of arguments for judicial restraint appear convincing at first sight but fail to withstand serious scrutiny. It is difficult to draw a neat line clearly distinguishing an acceptable extension of the rules according to common law reasoning from an unjustified exercise of judicial discretion. Attempting to create such a distinction, and holding judges to account if they fail to uphold

---

[37] See case law at n 6 above.

it, seems likely only to stifle legitimate common law development. Progress in the common law depends to a large extent on a judicial ability to reinterpret rules and to take some risks. In the current climate of formalism, it is hard to imagine that innovations such as the doctrine of economic duress, a 'practical benefits' approach to consideration, or restitutionary damages – all of which required some willingness to exercise creative and imaginative judicial thinking – could take root. Certainly, these developments have not escaped sometimes trenchant criticism for making the law unpredictable or uncertain. However, they are evidence of serious judicial engagement with the limits of freedom of contract, and the problems of applying a general law, fashioned with a particular class of contractor in mind, across a wide variety of contracting contexts. It would be unfortunate if the judiciary's ability to use a common law reasoning method to address issues of substantive and procedural injustice disappeared from the judicial skill-set. Of course, courts do recognise that contracts might have unwelcome or negative social effects. Yet, currently, it appears that it is not reckoned to be any part of the common law to act as a corrective to this. The judicial role is presented as a relatively neutral one of simply enforcing the agreed terms. In *Arnold v Britton*, Lord Neuberger expressly rejected any active regulatory role for the judiciary in contracts. He appeared to take some solace from the fact that a contract which worked wholly unexpectedly and manifestly unfairly for one party could be renegotiated and the dispute settled. In his view, a problem arising from the operation of contract law and the contract terms was ultimately resolvable by contract.[38] Specific legislation, or the parties' ability to negotiate their way around the law, is expected to pick up the slack in ameliorating the worst effects of the legal disengagement from the issue of contractual justice, leaving the common law free to uphold the traditional liberal virtue of freedom of contract.

(b) Contract Law as a Product in the Market for Law

The re-emergence of a more classical style of law may also be linked to the conviction that a formal contract law is more attractive to commercial contractors in the competitive market for law and legal services. Improving the appeal of a particular legal system to the business user might be thought more a matter of minimising delay and costs in civil procedure and judicial case management rather than tinkering with the substantive contract law rules. However, there is a line of scholarship suggesting that contract law principles should be adapted to meet the preferences of the commercial contracting community.[39] There is little empirical evidence one way or the other to support the assertion either that commercial contractors prefer a formal contract law or that they will contract out of a more contextual law. Nevertheless, concerns over

---

[38] *Arnold v Britton*, above n 6, at [64–5].
[39] For the academic support for this position, see Morgan, above n 29, at 87–9.

competitiveness and customer satisfaction appear to have resonated with elements of the judiciary. Writing extra-judicially, Lord Justice Thomas has argued that English law needs to stay competitive against France and Germany, noting that France has made changes to its Civil Code in order to ensure that it does not 'fall behind'. He also asserts that 'Singapore has been developing its contract law so that it provides the certainty that some argue English contract has to a degree lost. Again, we can see the intention is to establish a robust competitor to English law'.[40]

This perception of contract law as a commodity serving a particular market is worrying.[41] As parties seek to control more of the elements of their agreement through the contract terms, which contract law is content to enforce, there may be some profound effects on the capacity of the common law to exercise any form of regulatory control over innovations in contracting practice. The danger is that contract law and adjudication by courts become a private service where justice is equated to matters of speed and cost in legal proceedings. The rhetoric surrounding the importance of London in a competitive market for dispute resolution services contributes further to the 'privatisation of justice' which renders invisible the important public functions that litigation serves, notably the production of general legal rules rendered authoritative through the doctrine of precedent.[42] As Davies points out, '… the purpose of adjudication by courts is not, or not just, the resolution of private disputes; it is to deliver justice according to law, which has a public purpose of declaring and enforcing the law, thereby giving effect to the underlying values of the community'.[43] This sort of claim is met with profound scepticism from formalists that commercial litigants are interested in contributing to the ruleset for future litigants,[44] still less a public debate about societal values expressed by the rules of contract law. Rather, the rules are a product to be shaped and dictated by the needs of their primary consumers – commercial contractors – with minimal regard to any wider public interest in contract law development.

It is axiomatic that principled development of the common law relies on precedent, which in turn depends on disputes being heard in a public forum and a sufficient number of these reaching appeal where senior judges can deliver authoritative statements of the law. It would be unfortunate if commercial considerations were allowed to excessively shape the general character of contract law since the law has widespread, and sometimes unpredictable,

---

[40] Lord Thomas, 'Keeping Commercial Law Up to Date' Jill Poole Memorial Lecture, Aston University, 8 March 2017 (available at <https://www.judiciary.uk/announcements/the-jill-poole-memorial-lecture-by-the-lord-chief-justice-keeping-commercial-law-up-to-date> accessed 11 December 2018) at [8–9].

[41] See Attenborough on Easterbrook and Fischel (Chapter 8).

[42] Linda Mulcahy, 'The Collective Interest in Private Dispute Resolution' (2013) 33 *OJLS* 59.

[43] G L Davies, 'Civil Justice Reform: Why We Need to Question Some Basic Assumptions' (2006) 25 *Civil Justice Quarterly* 32, 35.

[44] Morgan, above n 29, 87.

application. An unduly rigid approach to contract law enforced by a risk-averse judiciary threatens to render the common law stagnant and redundant. Possibilities for revision to common law contract doctrines are already limited, so it is disconcerting to see opportunities not taken when they arise. A recent illustration is provided by *Rock Advertising Ltd v MWB Business Exchange Centres Ltd*.[45] The Supreme Court was content to dispose of a dispute concerning an alleged contract variation on the basis of an express 'no oral modification' clause in the contract. The clause was interpreted to mean exactly what it said. The court chose not to provide any detailed assessment of the contract law doctrines of consideration and the part-payment rule that also impinged on the case, arguments over which have occupied a generation of academics. For the court, the more important issue to resolve concerned the interpretation and enforcement of the express terms, not the issue surrounding the default contract law rule. In a contract law world where the main judicial role is to rule on the interpretation of bespoke terms, it may be difficult to find a dispute which generates a question of wide-reaching public importance or upon which authoritative resolution is necessary and beneficial for the wider community. Issues surrounding the interpretation of contract texts raise few issues of substantive law beyond determining what interpretation test to apply. Even outcomes in large, complex commercial cases may have little precedential value (except for those to whom the decision is of immediate interest) since the arguments may revolve around terms of art, specific issues relating to an industry, whether to plug gaps in the paperwork, or other very context- and fact-specific problems that render a case easily distinguishable. If contract law is reduced to ruling on the interpretation of terms, parties may prefer to rely on expert arbitrators to undertake this task with reference to the shared contextual understandings of the parties rather than a remote and acontextual approach of a judge. Market practice may not come in for sustained judicial scrutiny except on the occurrence of some unanticipated crisis or global shock – conditions hardly conducive to principled common law development. That private law may particularly suffer the effects of a stultified common law is somewhat paradoxical since it is private law where the rights of the parties to choose have greatest resonance. To the extent that lack of authoritative case-law may hamper the private efforts of commercial actors to write efficient agreements in the light of contract law default rules, the commercial contracting community would seem to have much to lose from a diminished common law.

(c) Contract Law Futures: Blockchains and Smart Contracting

A further threat to contract law comes from the increasingly sophisticated ways in which contracting processes can be automated. Domestic contract law has lagged behind international and European initiatives dealing with issues such

---

[45] [2018] UKSC 24.

as exactly when a contract is created through a process of email exchanges, the status of e-signatures, or whether parties can be bound to terms through processes such as shrink-wrap, browse-wrap and click-wrap. Common law supporters may draw comfort here from previous case-law demonstrating the ability of judges to mould the law in response to novel developments in how people interact and make agreements. For example, it is assumed that the rules of offer and acceptance, though developed in relation to traditional methods of communication over long distances, can be adapted to fit new situations. Common law gives the impression of easily assimilating innovation without too much disruption to its underlying principles, although it has long been conceded that this involves 'forcing the facts' to fit the existing legal categories.[46] Nevertheless, it is questionable how far the classical contract model can stretch before it becomes so distorted that it is transformed into something else or rendered obsolete. One might also argue that the relative lack of judicial engagement with the effects of technology on contracts reflects the arbitrary nature of common law development rather than the malleable quality of the law itself. Lack of specific laws dealing with new technologies may be indicative of the general ability of commercial contractors to adjust working practices in the light of innovation without too much difficulty and certainly without the need for a ruling on the legal implications of their actions. Nothing here necessarily disturbs the law's confidence that it still fulfils the function of background enforcer keeping everyone broadly in line, even if the rules have not developed markedly since the 19th century. It may be a different story, however, if the technology effectively aims to displace the operation of law in ensuring enforceability.

Emerging information and communication technologies, such as distributed ledgers, blockchains and smart contracts, may force the domestic law of contract to confront this issue head-on. These technologies have the potential to remove the requirement for state institutions to enforce certain varieties of agreement, replacing them with private and autonomous forms of control facilitated electronically through computer software and cryptography.[47] Automated processes are attractive because of their relatively low cost, greater efficiency and responsiveness to the individual features of the particular contracting environment in which they are found. Theorising about the implications of these innovations for contract law is still relatively new. The issue has largely escaped the notice of all but a few contract law scholars, but it brings into view one possible endgame for the contribution of classical contract law to private ordering. Space precludes a thorough examination of all the ramifications of

---

[46] Lord Wilberforce in *New Zealand Shipping Co Ltd v A M Satterthwaite & Co Ltd (The Eurymedon)* [1975] AC 154, 167; Mark Giancaspro, 'Is a 'Smart Contract' Really a Smart Idea? Insights from a Legal Perspective' (2017) 33 *Computer Law & Security Review* 825, 829.

[47] Kevin Werbach and Nicolas Cornell, 'Contracts *Ex Machina*' (2017) 67 *Duke LJ* 313; Kevin Werbach, 'Trust, But Verify: Why the Blockchain Needs the Law' (2018) 33 *Berkeley Tech LJ* 487.

blockchain for contact law. The discussion is intended to give a flavour of the technology's capacity to supersede contract law as an enforcement mechanism for the market transaction and is necessarily speculative.

Blockchain and smart contracts are related technologies but not exactly the same thing. A blockchain is a 'distributed digital ledger that uses cryptographic algorithms to verify the creation or transfer of digital records in a distributed network'.[48] We don't have to grasp the finer points of how the processes work to comprehend that blockchains facilitate peer-to-peer interactions that can be executed, recorded, stored and validated by way of a shared digital ledger. Depending on whether the ledger is public or private, it is accessible to anyone who has the necessary permission and digital key. It is supposedly tamper-proof. The ledger is not held or administered by any individual or central organisation and hence it dispenses with the need for third-party intermediaries, or 'authorities', that might perform functions of recording, enforcing and otherwise enabling the transactions undertaken via the ledger. Distributed ledger technology enables cryptocurrencies such as Bitcoin and Ethereum and the phenomenon of smart contracts. Giancaspro describes a smart contract as 'a computer program which verifies and executes its terms upon the occurrence of predetermined events. Once coded and entered into the blockchain, the contract cannot be changed and operates in accordance with its programmed instructions'.[49] The legal status of the smart contract is a matter of debate (in what sense is it a 'contract' if it does not rely on some background conception of legality in its definition?), but becoming mired in the semantics may lead us to overlook the broader significance of the technology.

As we saw in the opening sections of the chapter, one of the functions of contract law is to provide a state-endorsed system of contract enforcement that facilitates exchange between strangers, overcoming some of the risks associated with trust. Smart transacting performs the same task but relies on the underlying computer code and software to execute an agreement automatically. Performance of the smart contract is therefore autonomously guaranteed by the code, generating a further 'trust-less trust' alternative to the law. It is tempting to regard smart contracting as just another method of performing an underlying agreement, much in the same way that email may be a novel way of creating what is in every other respect a traditional contract. However, this would underestimate the potential implications of smart technology. The development of smart contracts reimagines a contract not as a legally enforceable agreement at all but as a code-enforceable agreement. Despite its name, the smart contract does not rely on the law (or any central enforcing institution) to ensure performance.[50] Though at present a somewhat remote

---

[48] Michèle Finck, 'Blockchains: Regulating the Unknown' (2018) 19 *German Law Journal* 665, 667.

[49] Giancaspro, above n 46, 826.

[50] Finck, above n 48, 670–1.

possibility, a smart contract could be envisaged that terminates an agreement on the occurrence of some event, such as a stipulated payment not being received by a certain date, which is simultaneously enforced by cutting off access to the subject matter of the contract. For example, non-payment of rent could be enforced by automatic denial of entry to the affected premises.

Are there circumstances in which smart contracts in such a form can replace legal contracts and obviate the need for contract law? It seems unlikely that innovations such as distributed ledger technology, blockchain and smart contracts will render national law redundant but this ultimately depends on the functions of law in relation to the contract and also the limits on the technology. Blockchains and distributed ledgers do not regulate transactions in accordance with an external set of rules. A blockchain-enabled smart contract simply executes automatically in accordance with the underlying computer code. Performance is supposedly inevitable and irrevocable, rendering breach impossible and removing the need for specific enforcement measures provided by law or performance-encouraging contract terms provided by the parties (such as liquidated damages provisions). The smart contract may operate simply as a method of performing the obligations contained in an underlying written or oral agreement that satisfies the existing legal tests for determining that a contract exists. This idea of 'smart execution', as an instrument to ensure enforcement of a 'traditional' contract, appears distinguishable from the 'smart contract' properly (i.e., a self-contained, autonomous system or platform capable of generating and executing a transaction between two, possibly anonymous, parties without any substantive input or oversight from an intermediary). Such systems may be set up deliberately to bypass national legal and other institutions (such as fiat currency and state-based banking organisations). Nevertheless, regulation must be required here to deal with unforeseen contingencies affecting the smart contract. There is a question, however, over what form this regulation might take. On one hand, it must be doubted whether the common law of contract would have any enhanced role – smart contracting stretches the 'offer and acceptance' analysis of formation to breaking point. On the other hand, although contract performance may be a certainty, this will not preclude disputes. However, many practical difficulties may present themselves in the pursuit of legal remedies when things go wrong with the smart contract, particularly in the case of systemic failure, software defects or malicious interference in the ledger. These difficulties include identifying who, if anyone, should be held legally responsible and for what.

In relation to the limitations on the technology, smart contracting at present appears suitable only for certain kinds of agreement, notably those involving obligations that are relatively fixed and certain. This might be a transaction to buy goods on the occurrence of a specified event (e.g., a sale/purchase which is triggered automatically when the price index for a commodity reaches a certain level), where it is necessary to track the movement of goods and facilitate payment mechanisms,[51] or where complex financial products and digital assets (such as virtual currencies) are traded. One potential use for the technology is to facilitate peer-to-peer platforms for payments, dispensing with the reliance on banks and other intermediaries (in which case the technology has the potential to transform merchant-created payment mechanisms, such as the system of letters of credit in international commercial sales). Smart contracting in this wholly autonomous sense seems a way off, although it is interesting to observe that in many ways it replicates the simplicity of the self-enforcing, cash-based, simultaneous exchange with the added attraction of the ability to project the exchange into the future (to use Ian Macneil's terminology) without compromising certainty or the ability to rely on performance.

It is difficult to predict how English contract law might react to these developments. Given the law's current autonomy-driven stance, if the parties have consented to execute their arrangement via smart methods (assuming that the parties intend the law to have any role at all in the agreement), then presumably this will be enforceable, subject to consumer protection legislation or other bespoke regulation that might be developed. Once contract law gives the green light to the possibility that contracts could be performed automatically (and potentially irreversibly) in this way, then it appears to have little further role to play, except in cases where the transaction may be affected by fraud, mistake, misrepresentation, illegality, and so on. An action for breach of contract would seem to be precluded by the impossibility of breach. Similarly, we might conjecture that there is limited scope for the possibility of judicially implied terms (how would the existence of a contract gap be determined?) or contract interpretation. Some varieties of boilerplate, such as the entire agreement clause or the no-oral modification clause, would become obsolete. At this point, we might speculate that a contract law that is content to enforce terms in a formal manner may find a competitive edge in relation to enabling and facilitating smart contract technology. A formalistic and plain-meaning approach by courts to contract interpretation and enforcement seems conducive to the endeavour to reduce obligations to machine-readable code and automatic execution. Presumably, it is much easier to facilitate routine transactions on standardised terms by smart contracts. The law may not have a role in enforcing such agreements since that is automatic, but there may be some reassurance to be had for the 'smart contractor' in the low likelihood of the transaction being subject to a serious legal challenge if the software simply mimics the formality of the legal system in executing the contract as written, irrespective of the outcome. Code may become the ultimate formalist contract enforcer. This possibility is borne out by a recent decision from the Singapore International Commercial Court. The judge ruled that it was a breach of contract for a human programmer to reverse a cryptocurrency trade undertaken automatically by two computer systems. Owing to a software defect, the trade

---

[51] Finck ibid., 672.

was made at around 250 times the market exchange rate for the currencies. The terms of the underlying agreement between the claimant and defendant noted that trades were irreversible. The argument that the computers were legal agents of human principals was rejected. Nor was the trade held void for mistake.[52]

Smart contract technology appears less suited to facilitating complex, more uncertain and longer-term contracts involving ongoing collaboration, co-ordination or repeat commitments (such as infrastructure projects, strategic alliances, or in areas of innovation). Parties here may avoid legalistic express terms in favour of more reassuring, informal norms. Soft obligations to co-operate or act in a spirit of trustworthiness, or 'partnership', can be written into a traditional contract text straightforwardly, but their open-ended and value-laden nature makes them difficult to interpret and, one assumes, more difficult to capture in computer code that can judge reliably whether these standards have been reached or breached.[53] This development, however, may be only a matter of time and computing power. It is an interesting irony that to the extent that future contract law has to develop a jurisprudence that engages with vague terms, it may no longer be able to ignore those relational qualities of contracting parties (the capacity to act in good faith, reasonably, co-operatively, with common sense, and so on) to which it has so long resisted ascribing meaning and effect in its legal analysis. Formalistic legal reasoning encounters difficulties with these commitments since they stipulate behaviours and qualities to be displayed rather than precise objectives to be achieved. If current contract law is unable to adapt to this new role in interpreting and enforcing flexible obligations, it might simply fall into disuse.

CONCLUSION

In this chapter, we have explored some doubts over whether contract law plays an essential role in supporting market activity. Although in theory the general rules of contract law play an important role in facilitating exchange, the evidence is sparse that the specific rules of English law perform this function for the vast majority of commercial contractors. The implications of contract law's reduced role in society are potentially significant, for both the teaching and practice of law but also the legal enterprise more generally. In terms of contract law teaching, it is no longer justified (if it ever was) to present the classical law rules as an important facilitator and regulator of economic activity. There is still room for analysis of the traditional rules but in the context of real-life contracting behaviour and an appreciation of the multiple normative frameworks within which economic exchange occurs. A larger proportion of the syllabus should be given over to matters of contract interpretation and the meaning and effect

---

[52] *B2C2 Ltd v Quoine Pte Ltd* [2019] SGHC(I) 03.
[53] See Werbach, above n 47, 36; Giancaspro, above n 46, 831, 833.

of commonly used express terms of the contract. Alternative systems of contract governance should be explored and compared. Common forms of business relationship established through contract (franchising, for example, or supply chains) could be examined and critiqued, and the limitations of the classical model exposed.

The substantive erosion of the common law of contract might appear as a matter for little regret. But a weakened common law raises real concerns in a society that has seen a massive expansion in private ordering through contracts in the provision of goods and services over the last 40 years. The methods by which contracts come into existence, and notionally create binding obligations, have become more insidious. Increasingly, we enter into contracts via automated processes on terms over which we have little control. Separate legislation is available to offer some protection to consumers; nevertheless, the legal validity of many standard terms is unquestioned and untested. Owing to the vagaries of litigation and the inadequacy of common law rules now fashioned to appeal predominantly to commercial contractors, there may be no realistic prospect of a determinative ruling on these issues. The dwindling significance of contract law is also evident in the commercial sphere. Whereas the process of commercial exchange is managed through complex, multi-faceted contractual mechanisms, the enforcement of these contracts relies on social systems and norms (trust and reputation networks) rather than domestic contract law. Similarly, international trade is governed largely by model rules, standard form contracts, bespoke regulation and dispute resolution promulgated by specialist industry organisations, not legal institutions. Developments in information and communication technology, such as the advent of 'smart contracts', appear destined to further reduce the need for a general law of contract and usher in private forms of contract enforcement subject to minimal legal scrutiny.

Instead of engaging with the increased complexity and pervasiveness of contracting in society and attempting to curb its worst effects, the English common law response has been to shrink to a minimalistic model, content simply to enforce terms on the basis of freedom of contract. The resurgence of formalism is motivated in part by a judiciary concerned with improving the commercial competitiveness of English contract law against alternatives in the international market for laws. The remoulding of domestic contract law as a 'product' further reduces the generality, scope and regulatory effectiveness of contract law in society and erodes the other non-autonomy normative values of consent, promise-keeping and the protection of reasonable expectations, upon which it should be based. In the wake of all this, contract law appears rather like an ageing, loyal, but ultimately redundant servant allowed to continue rattling around an ancestral home because now and again they can be called upon by the (commercial) masters to do something useful. Somewhat counterintuitively, technological developments may herald contract law's potential revival in the hands of the judges but this entails abandoning the classical model once and for all and embracing a more contextual and relational account of contract.

FURTHER READING

L. Bernstein, 'Opting Out of the Legal System: Extralegal Contractual Relations in the Diamond Industry' (1992) 21 *Journal of Legal Studies* 115.

R. Brownsword, *Contract Law: Themes for the 21st Century*, 2nd ed (2006).

H. Collins, *Regulating Contracts* (1999).

T. Dietz, *Global Order Beyond Law* (2014).

J. Gava, 'How Should Judges Decide Commercial Contract Cases?' (2013) 30 *Journal of Contract Law* 133.

M. Gulati and R. E. Scott, *The 3½ Minute Transaction* (2013).

I. Macneil, *The Relational Theory of Contract: Selected Works of Ian Macneil*, D Campbell (ed) (2001).

N. J. McBride, *Key Ideas in Contract Law* (2017).

C. Mitchell, *Interpretation of Contracts*, 2nd ed (2018).

J. Morgan, *Contract Law Minimalism* (2013).

M. J. Radin, *Boilerplate: The Fine Print, Vanishing Rights and the Rule of Law* (2013).

K. Werbach and N. Cornell, 'Contracts *Ex Machina*' (2017) 67 *Duke Law Journal* 313.

J. Wightman, *Contract: A Critical Commentary* (1996).

O. Williamson, *The Economic Institutions of Capitalism* (1985).

CHAPTER 3

Labour Law and Practices: Workers Paying the Price for Capitalist Failure?

Charlotte Villiers and Roseanne Russell

INTRODUCTION

In this chapter, we investigate the interaction between company law, corporate governance and labour law. As we examine some of the key debates that feature within this interaction, we advance the argument that company law allows, and the corporate governance system encourages, corporations to hire workers under highly exploitative terms. Exploring the issue from a corporate governance perspective, we argue that the regulation of companies and broader corporate governance framework have features that encourage and depend on precarious labour. Our consideration of the debates leads us to suggest that the corporate governance imperative is to cut costs and transfer risks and that precarious labour appears as a logical response to this challenge.[1] The traditional contractarian view would support a suggestion that any precariousness is met by robust protection provided by labour law. However, we argue that this does not reflect either the structure of the employment contract or the current deficiencies of statutory law, neither of which is capable of accommodating current labour practices in an entirely convincing manner. Moreover, we argue, this assumption brings with it new risks for corporate governance. What is needed is systemic change so that workers are valued and respected.

---

[1] S. McKay, 'Disturbing equilibrium and transferring risk: confronting precarious work', in N. Countouris and M. Freedland, *Resocialising Europe In a Time of Crisis* (Cambridge University Press, 2013) 191, especially her Table 9.1, at 193.

ARE COMPANY LAW AND CORPORATE GOVERNANCE SEPARATE AND UNRELATED TO LABOUR LAW?

One side of this debate would argue that these are distinct and unrelated areas of law: company law is concerned with the relationship between company directors, companies and their shareholders, whereas labour law is concerned with the relationship between management and labour. Those on the other side of the debate would argue that labour is a key participant in the economic activities of a corporation and that corporate managers should be concerned not only for the interests of their shareholders but also for the interests of all the company's stakeholders. This debate forms a part of the broader shareholder versus stakeholder discussion in corporate governance in which the position of workers is particularly relevant. Team production theorists highlight the firm-specific investments made by labour, giving them a claim to be taken into account by managers in their corporate decision-making.

Corporate governance theory has undergone significant developments since the latter part of the 20th century. Stakeholder theory has received significant attention with associated calls for greater worker voice or representation in the boardroom. In continental Europe, this is supported by corporate governance structures that include codetermination and supervisory boardrooms. Overall, however, recent decades have largely witnessed a narrowing of the vision of the corporation so that a shareholder primacy, contractarian model of the corporation has come to prevail, particularly in the UK and the US.

In market-based models of company law, the idea of 'contract' is central. Unlike the legal concept of contract which is typically based on the assumption that parties have freely negotiated its terms, the economic view that companies can be reduced to a 'nexus of contracts' assumes that company law reflects the contract that the parties would have reached had they bargained for it.[2] Shareholders are privileged under this model because they are presumed to be at greater risk than other contributors to the nexus. Whereas (some) creditors may bargain for additional security and employees may look to employment law for protection, shareholders are thought to be at the mercy of how the company performs. Critics of the contractarian model, however, have argued that this view of the company is highly problematic. Far from being residual risk-bearers, Ireland has argued, for example, that investors 'enjoy the best of all possible legal worlds'.[3] His argument is based on the fact that shareholders are treated as distinct from the companies in

---

[2] F. Easterbrook and D. Fischel, *The Economic Structure of Corporate Law* (Harvard University Press; Cambridge, MA, 1996).

[3] P. Ireland, 'Limited liability, shareholder rights and the problem of corporate irresponsibility' (2010) 34 *Cambridge Journal of Economics* 837 at 848.

which they invest and enjoy limited liability but that companies are operated so as to generate maximum profit that can be returned to those same investors in the form of dividends. Ireland has termed this a 'shareholder's paradise: a body of law able to combine the ruthless pursuit of "shareholder value" without any corresponding responsibility on the part of the shareholders for the losses arising out of corporate failure or the damage caused by corporate activities or malfeasance'.[4]

Arguments for shareholder primacy, based on reduction of the company to a nexus of contracts (see Daniel Attenborough, Chapter 8, herein), have inspired a corporate governance system that highlights the relationship between the company's directors – both executive and non-executive – its shareholders and the auditors. This triangular relationship between the directors, shareholders and auditors was reflected in earlier versions of the UK's Corporate Governance Code that did not mention workers. In such a setting, the connection between corporate governance and labour law was barely visible. Labour law has thus been treated as distinct and separate from corporate governance. Indeed, Moore has observed that 'one of the most distinctive characteristics of Anglo-American corporate governance is its traditional neglect of the interests of labour'.[5]

Company law's indifference to labour can be seen when considering how the law describes a director's duty to the company historically. Section 309(1) of the Companies Act 1985 stated that 'matters to which the directors … are to have regard in the performance of their functions include the interests of the company's employees in general, as well as the interests of its members'. The rather weak wording coupled with the fact that only directors and shareholders (via a derivative claim) have standing to enforce a breach of duty by a director meant that the provision was relatively meaningless. Section 172 of the Companies Act 2006 arguably subordinates employee interests further as they are merely one matter to which directors may have regard when considering how to act in order to promote the success of the company for the benefit of its shareholders as a whole. For the late Lord Wedderburn, the duty in section 172 was not simply the result of Parliamentary draftsmen maintaining a disciplinary distinction between company and labour law (with the needs of labour being regulated by the latter) but reflected a political choice to defer to the 'requirements of transnational capital and the hegemony of the "promotion of shareholder value"'.[6] Moore is equally critical of the subordination of labour to the

---

[4] Ibid.

[5] MT Moore, 'Reconstituting Labour Market Freedom: Corporate Governance and Collective Worker Counterbalance' (2014) 43 (4) *Industrial Law Journal* 398 at 399.

[6] Lord Wedderburn of Charlton, 'Employees, Partnership and Company Law' (2002) 31 (2) *Industrial Law Journal* 103.

needs of investors and argues that 'it is lamentable that recent decades have, if anything, witnessed an even greater divergence between these two fields of thought, as company law scholarship in the UK has become increasingly subsumed within a US-led law and economics paradigm, which – generally speaking – has served to further emphasise the relative primacy of financial capital within the notional "firm" over the countervailing demands of labour'.[7] For those who observe company law from a law and economics perspective, the indifference of the sub-discipline towards workers can be logically explained. In Jensen and Meckling's account of the company as being a market in which a fictional firm operates as a nexus for contracting parties, shareholders are thought to have incomplete contracts with the company and bear the residual risk if a company fails.[8] Workers, on the other hand, have complete contracts with guaranteed returns in the form of fixed payments for labour rendered. In the event that the employment contract is incomplete, statutory labour law and trade unions are presumed to fill any gaps and ensure that workers are protected.

However, as we shall demonstrate later in this chapter, it is arguably not enough to rely on labour law as a separate area of protection for employees. Companies such as Amazon and Sports Direct came under fire in recent years because of their poor treatment of their workers. This was picked up by the Business, Innovation and Skills Committee and was treated as a corporate governance problem, leading to a White Paper on Corporate Governance and changes to the Corporate Governance Code. Principles D and E of the 2018 Code require boards of large companies to ensure effective engagement with, and encourage participation from, both shareholders and stakeholders and boards should also 'ensure that workforce policies and practices are consistent with the company's values and support its long-term sustainable success. The workforce should be able to raise any matters of concern'. Whilst these are small steps and arguably need to go considerably further, they do demonstrate that it is possible for policymakers to recognise that employees have interests at stake in corporate governance and therefore that there is a connection between labour law and corporate governance. It remains to be seen how far these changes to the soft law Corporate Governance Code change practice. However, it is possible that as corporate governance evolves, this will in turn impact on labour law and the protections available to workers.

This leads us to consider a second debate, which asks, if workers are required to accept risks arising from corporate governance, does this give rise to a need for protections and for dialogue between management and labour?

---

[7] Moore (2014) at 426.

[8] M. Jensen and W. Meckling, 'Theory of the Firm: Managerial Behavior, Agency Costs and Ownership Structure' (1976) 3 *Journal of Financial Economics* 305.

Does Our Corporate Governance Framework Encourage Risks to Be Passed to Labour?

Some will argue that all stakeholder constituents – and not only labour – endure risks inherent in business activity, whereas others will argue that the emphasis on financialisation in corporate governance has the effect of encouraging corporations to view their workers instrumentally, and this particular problem should be addressed.

Risk management is a central concern of corporate governance. Whilst risk management is important, the scope of the governance standards is somewhat limited, focusing primarily on internal control and audit functions and financial risk, and this has led company boards to review their incentive structures.

This emphasis on financialisation has encouraged corporations to view their workers instrumentally. Rather than build long-term relationships with their workers, companies have shifted towards treating them as 'human capital'. This commodification dehumanises workers and treats them as costs that must be kept at a minimum, either by paying them as little as possible or by keeping the size of the workforce as small as possible. Increasingly, workers are viewed as expendable, and very often, when companies hit financial trouble, the company, in order to uphold the share price, is restructured and the workforce is reduced to save on costs. As Joly suggests, '"Human resource" expenditures get slashed, firings multiply. Share price capital trumps human capital'.[9] Evidence shows that investors pursuing financial interests motivate firms to engage in tactics that increase shareholder value in the short term and to engage less in long-term strategic decision-making.[10] With shareholder primacy being so firmly embedded in the corporate governance system, companies are managed in ways designed to satisfy the shareholders' financial goals. The new Code provides a bridge towards more long-term thinking and consideration of other stakeholders' interests in Provision 5, which requires, on a comply-or-explain basis, engagement with the workforce and that one or a combination of the following methods should be used: a director appointed from the workforce, a formal workforce advisory panel, and a designated non-executive director. Provision 6 requires that there should be a means for the workforce to raise concerns. Whilst this marks a distinct shift in the approach to corporate governance, and welcome recognition that employee interests are at stake, it falls far short of the mandatory employee representation on boards promised by the Prime Minister at the Conservative Party conference in October 2016 following the Brexit referendum in June of that year. These limited recent provisions aside, however, the workers' role, from the corporate

---

[9] C. Joly, 'Why we should stop talking about 'Human Capital'' *Social Europe*, 13 January 2016, at https://www.socialeurope.eu/inhuman-capital-and-human-value.

[10] J. Adam Cobb, 'How firms shape income inequality: Stakeholder power, executive decision making, and the structuring of employment relationships' (2016) 41 (2) *Academy of Management Review*, 324 at 336.

governance system's financialised perspective, is primarily to help the company generate levels of profit that will attract and retain investors. The workers are then managed in ways to support the organisation's goals and to maintain its efficiency, resulting in threats to their welfare and job security.[11] The indifference of company law to labour's interests is reflected in increasing reliance on precarious labour.[12]

Does the Narrow Scope of Corporate Governance Encourage Greater Reliance on Precarious Labour? Is Precarious Labour a New Phenomenon and Is It a Problem?

A variety of terms have been used to describe precarious labour including contingent or atypical work. These terms are not entirely satisfactory. Atypical work is often used as a 'catch all' to include part-time and fixed-term work, neither of which is particularly atypical in 2018. 'Zero-hours' contracts, often used as a synonym for precarious labour, can take a variety of forms, with some contracts obliging workers to accept an assignment when offered, while others impose no obligation to be offered or to accept work. Kalleberg has defined precarious work as 'employment that is uncertain, unpredictable, and risky from the point of view of the worker'.[13] The International Labour Organization (ILO) identifies a precarious job 'by uncertainty as to the duration of employment, multiple possible employers or a disguised or ambiguous employment relationship, a lack of access to social protection and benefits usually associated with employment, low pay, and substantial legal and practical obstacles to joining a trade union and bargaining collectively'.[14] Hence, we can say that the position of labour is precarious when some or all of the following are present: low-quality work, lack of control over the work for the individual, low wages, lack of certainty or job security, limited social protection and obstacles to trade union membership or collective bargaining.

Kalleberg and Vallas suggest that precarious work 'has historically been the norm'.[15] Indeed, talk of an emerging 'precariat' risks obscuring the fact that, for many, work has always been scarce and unstable. As Monk argues:

> It is a bold hypothesis to suggest that a new social subject has emerged: a 'precariat', which now constitutes a 'dangerous class' as did the urban poor in

---

[11] MA O'Connor 'Human Capital ERA: Reconceptualizing Corporate Law To Facilitate Labor-Management Cooperation' (1992) 78 *Cornell Law Review* 899.

[12] E. Ndzi, 'UK Company Law and Precarious Employment Contracts' (2017) 59 (4) *International Journal of Law and Management* 571 at 576.

[13] AL Kalleberg, 'Precarious work, insecure workers: Employment relations in transition' (2009) 74 (1) *American Sociological Review*, 1 at 2.

[14] ILO, 2012 at 27.

[15] AL Kalleberg and SP Vallas, 'Probing Precarious Work: Theory, Research and Politics' (2018) 31 *Precarious Work: Research in the Sociology of Work* 1 at 6.

Victorian Britain. It is a term that perhaps captures some of the feelings among Northern academics, themselves subject to casualisation and the end of job security. But is the term novel or even relevant, for the millions of workers and urban poor in the global South for whom precariousness has always been a seemingly natural condition?[16]

Indeed, precarious labour has always been a feature of capitalism. From a Marxist perspective of capitalist production, precarious labour underpins the labour market, and the surplus that is generated during the production process is generated by labour. Marx's critique of capitalism maintained that keeping labour costs low meant that maximum value could be extracted during production for the benefit of capitalists who, as a result, could enjoy as large a surplus as possible.[17]

Minimising labour costs can be as simple as paying low wages, but value can be extracted in more nuanced and complex ways. Maximising productivity through minimal rest breaks and long hours, two practices which have become culturally embedded; structuring the workforce so that workers are engaged only on an 'as required' basis; and ensuring that the supply of labour remains high compared with the amount of work available, all contribute to the suppression of the value of labour. For companies, the resulting surplus could be distributed in a variety of ways: reinvesting in corporate development, rewarding workers and directors, and returning profit to shareholders in the form of dividends and share buybacks. In fact, distributions to shareholders tend to prevail at the expense of the workers and the long-term sustainability of the company, although executive directors and senior executives are very well rewarded for serving the shareholder interest in this way. (See Talbot, Chapter 7.) This type of remuneration is not available to rank-and-file employees or casualised workers.

In recent decades, there has been a move from the post–Second World War phenomenon of job security and wage growth to a labour market characterised by flexibility and choice. 'Flexibility' became a defining characteristic of New Labour's employment policy and has been extended by subsequent Governments. Labour has been transformed into 'human resources', a liquid factor of production capable of being deployed and redeployed to suit organisational demands. Precariousness appears to be simultaneously deepening and encroaching into other areas where work has traditionally been more stable. Even Monk concedes that since the last financial crisis in 2008, 'globalisation' has 'increased the precarious and insecure nature of most work'.[18] By 2014, almost half of the population of large British employers had made use of workers on insecure contracts.[19] Precarious forms of contracts and working practices

---

[16] R. Monk, 'The Precariat: a view from the South' (2013) 34 (5) *Third World Quarterly* 747.

[17] K. Marx, *Capital: Critique of Political Economy Vol 1* (Penguin Books Limited, 1990)

[18] Monk (2013) *supra*.

[19] D. Milliken, Almost Half of Big UK Employers Use Insecure Contracts – ONS, 30 April 2014, available at: http://uk.reuters.com/article/uk-britain-employment-idUKKBN0DG0TB20140430.

are also a growing trend in the European labour market. In the EU in 2016, 2.3 per cent of employees were in precarious employment.[20]

In 2016, in the EU, open-ended full-time contracts represented 59 per cent of the labour market share, indicating a decreasing trend, whilst the 2 per cent of fixed-term contracts remained stable and part-time work increased in its percentage of the labour market share to 7 per cent (25 per cent of which were involuntary part-time contracts). The UK had the highest number of zero-hour contracts at 5 per cent of its labour market share and of temporary agency work at 1.7 per cent (1.5 per cent across the EU). More vulnerable still, freelancers represented 10 per cent of the EU's labour market share, carrying a high risk of bogus self-employment status, and informal or undeclared work took up 4 per cent of the labour market. Almost half of young workers between 18 and 35 years (46 per cent) across the EU had completed an internship by 2016.[21]

According to Bivand and Melville, the number of insecure workers in the UK rose from 2.4 million in 2011 to 3.1 million in 2016, so that by 2016 one in ten of those employed were in insecure employment. Insecure employees (precarious labour) are half as likely to be supported by trade unions as secure employees – over the 2011–2016 period, only 14 per cent of insecure employees were in workplaces covered by trade union representation compared with 30 per cent of secure employees.[22]

The drivers of this change are complex and multi-faceted. The current precariousness of labour can be explained by a number of factors related to the workplace, such as shifts in modes of production; post-recession austerity; differential tax treatment of self-employed contractors and employees; smart technology devices; hefty tribunal fees to complain to an employment tribunal until these were repealed in 2017; and low levels of trade union membership. The rise of precarious labour can also be attributed to the wider economic context of globalisation, financialisation, and competition, reinforced by policies of regulation and deregulation driven by neoliberal ideology. Multi-national companies operating through global value chains are able to benefit from paying low wages to labour in less developed economies, by imposing their own demands on local employers and by creating competition among those offering to provide labour to their production processes, leaving labour, globally, more vulnerable to pay cuts and even more exploitative conditions. A global labour arbitrage is effectively created.[23] Similarly, they can take advantage of low tax

---

[20] Eurostat, 9 February 2018, at http://ec.europa.eu/eurostat/web/products-eurostat-news/-/DDN-20180209-1.

[21] Precarious Employment in Europe, Part 1: Patterns, Trends and Policy Strategy (European Union, 2016).

[22] P. Bivand and D. Melville, 'What is Driving Insecure Work? A Sector Perspective: Report to the TUC' (Learning and Work Institute, July 2017) at 2, available at https://outlook.office.com/owa/?realm=bristol.ac.uk&path=/attachmentlightbox.

[23] Wise, R. D., & Martin, D. (2015). The political economy of global labour arbitrage. *Handbook of the International Political Economy of Production*, 59–75.

and secrecy jurisdictions, locating intangible assets there to reduce their tax liabilities, reducing the ability of the state to spend to counteract the consequences of downward pressure on the quality of jobs.[24] (See Sadiq and McCredie, Chapter 10.)

However, the privileging of shareholder interests in company law and corporate governance is particularly problematic for labour, especially in a market with high investor turnover which requires corporate management to continuously stimulate a market for their shares by making them desirable to both existing and potential investors.[25] Yet, although shareholders are often considered to drive short-term, financialised strategies, the main corporate governance policy response since the global financial crisis has been to empower shareholders further through 'say on pay' and the Stewardship Code.[26] The interests of labour thus become subordinated to the profit-maximising demands of those investors. Indeed, as Cushen and Thompson observe, 'value extraction via cost cutting is associated with labour and the labour process through headcount reduction interventions such as redundancies, outsourcing, centralization and supply chain harmonization, as well as increasing reward insecurity. Headcount reduction is central to financialized "downsize and redistribute" strategies and share buybacks'.[27]

Employers justify precarious employment contracts as contributing to the efficiency of the company's business. Only those with the required skills are hired on a permanent basis, whilst a pool of workers on precarious contracts are available to engage as need and market demand dictate. Precarious labour is likely to 'work very hard to impress the employers so that they can be called again whenever there is work. By working so hard to impress the employers, their hard work goes a long way to promote the success of the company'.[28] Thus, the directors may see themselves as fulfilling their duties to the company by increasing its profitability through this flexibilised workforce. For example, the costs of employment can be cut by keeping contractual payments below the relevant threshold for paying National Insurance and pension contributions as well as other employment-related benefits.

---

[24] Zummo, H., McCredie, B., & Sadiq, K. (2017). Addressing aggressive tax planning through mandatory corporate tax disclosures: An exploratory case study. *eJTR, 15,* 359.
[25] J. Cushen and P. Thompson, 'Financialization and value: why labour and the labour process still matter' (2016) 30 (2) *Work, employment and Society* 352 at 356.
[26] Talbot 'Why shareholders shouldn't vote: A Marxist-progressive critique of shareholder empowerment' (2013) 76 *Modern Law Review* 791.
[27] Ibid., at 358. See also Lazonick W and O'Sullivan M (2000) Maximizing shareholder value: a new ideology for corporate governance. *Economy and Society* 29(1): 13–35; and Lazonick W (2013) The financialization of the US corporation: what has been lost, and how it can be regained. *Seattle University Law Review* 36(2): 857.
[28] Ndzi, *supra* n 12 at 576.

Amazon Case Study[29]

Amazon is a global phenomenon and e-commerce success story. Its online retail model allows consumers to purchase a staggering range of products from multiple retailers from a single site and for these goods to be delivered directly. Its founder is reportedly worth $138.8 billion and the world's only 'centi-billionaire', but the online retail giant has been criticised in the media for its treatment of workers. Orders are picked from a vast range of products stored in its 'fulfilment centres' (warehouses) by robots and humans. The pressure to meet productivity targets is intense, and some staff have reportedly urinated in waste-bins rather than take a toilet beak. The work is also physically demanding and staff have complained that they are treated like robots. In September 2018, after 115 ambulances had been called out for staff over the previous three years, GMB union protested about these conditions outside the company's Rugeley warehouse. In one case, a pregnant woman was allegedly forced to stand, bend, and push a heavy cart around the warehouse for 10 hours a day. Amazon's business model is designed around dominating the market and profiting in the long term rather than pursuing short-term returns. Worker exploitation in this model leads to minimised costs and helps create a future monopoly.

Precarious labour might be seen as both a cost and risk reduction strategy through an 'externalization process' that could lead to what Frade and Darmon identify as 'the organization of an "insecurity-and-risks transfer chain"'.[30] Rather than reduce risk, precarious work as a strategy *shifts* risks onto the workers. Indeed, as is noted by the ILO, precarious work is a means for employers to maximise flexibility and to shift risks and responsibilities onto workers.[31]

These precarious arrangements could be viewed as beneficial for some workers. Young workers, for example, might regard the flexibility of this sort of labour as liberating, enabling them to pursue other activities and education and to avoid the oppressiveness of the old 'job for life' represented by the standard employment contract. However, workers who are hired under precarious arrangements have to accept risks of falling into poverty and social exclusion (with the associated reliance on social welfare) as well as increased risks to their health and safety as the Amazon case study suggests. Risk is not reduced by precarious employment; rather, as Kalleberg and Vallas argue, it is transferred by the corporation away from the shareholders towards workers and society.

---

[29] The employment practices of Amazon have been widely reported in the media. See, for example, F. Onasanya, Amazon must be forced to change, for the sake of its workers, *The Guardian* (20 July 2018).

[30] C. Frade and I. Darmon 'New modes of business organization and precarious employment: towards the recommodification of labour?' (2005) 15 (2) *Journal of European Social Policy* 107 at 116.

[31] ILO, 2012, above note 14, at 5 and ILO 2011, Policies and regulations to Combat Precarious Employment, at 5 and 6.

The workplace and societal consequences of this cultural shift towards precarious contracts, even if they are not universal, can be devastating. In the workplace, those hired on precarious contracts obviously experience generally poor and exploitative working conditions. One extreme example is Sports Direct.

Sports Direct Case Study

According to the Business, Innovation and Skills Committee, 'corporate governance is there to ensure that in running companies, boards balance the interests of the many different stakeholders, including the employees and workers. In a well-run company, widespread evidence of poor working practices would be detected at an early stage, reported to the board and properly addressed'. In 2016, this Committee found that this corporate governance ideal was not being fulfilled at Sports Direct, a company that was, instead, being run on a business model that involved 'treating workers as commodities rather than as human beings with rights, responsibilities and aspirations'. The low-cost products for customers, and the profits generated for the shareholders, came 'at the cost of maintaining contractual terms and working conditions which f[e]ll way below acceptable standards in a modern, civilised economy'.[32] Witnesses described the company as operating more like a gulag or Victorian workhouse than a distribution centre. Corporate management had unreasonable and excessive powers to discipline or dismiss at will, reinforced by their power to control the hours offered to each worker. Workers would be unlikely to challenge decisions, because they knew if they did, they probably would not be offered any more hours in the future. The Inquiry also found no convincing reason why Sports Direct engaged the workers through agencies on short-term, temporary contracts, other than to reduce costs and deflect responsibility. The Inquiry found that workers were not being paid the national minimum wage. It also found that staff were penalised for taking a short break to drink water and for taking time off when ill. Despite having recognition rights to directly represent employed warehouse workers at the Shirebrook distribution warehouse since September 2008, the union stated that only limited negotiations had taken place, and there were no meaningful negotiations despite requests for meetings since 2012.

Even workers who are not on precarious contracts are working longer hours, accepting poorer wages and accepting changes that are disadvantageous to them. The talk of precarious work makes all workers feel less secure, less certain and less willing to cause trouble for fear of losing their jobs. Kalleberg and Vallas have argued that precarious labour becomes a threatening new form of control as well as a political instrument. They have suggested that these exploitative labour conditions lead to problems of poor physical and mental health that place burdens and costs on the National Health Service and on taxpayers; they contribute to decreased quality of family and social life; and

---

[32] Business, Innovation and Skills Committee, *Employment Practices at Sports Direct*, Third Report of Session 2016–17, HC 219, 22 July 2016, at 27.

they lead to deeper wealth and income inequalities that make for poorer societies generally. This is seen in the works of Dorling,[33] who argues that the richest 1 per cent in our society enjoy their luxuries and benefits at the expense of the poorer 99 per cent, and of Wilkinson and Pickett,[34] who have demonstrated that inequality creates a much less healthy society with serious individual physical and psychological costs.

Whilst the corporation is relieved of the burden of labour costs, it is possible to envisage that this strategy also creates new risks for the corporation. As Cushen and Thompson observe, as labour is instrumentalised, this affects workers' behaviours and perceptions. The effect is reduced 'trust and employee engagement levels, rising cynicism and a more general crisis of attachment and disaffection for companies ...'. In turn, this prompts 'cynical and calculative behaviours in circumstances where employees understand themselves as a quantifiable, disposable commodity, and as a distinct stakeholder with interests that conflict with, and lose out to those of capital'.[35] Thus, despite short-term gains for shareholders, exploitation of workers may have negative long-term repercussions for the corporation and its shareholders as well as for corporate governance and the economy. KPMG notes the following:

> Higher turnover and increased churn: The use of temporary workers increases risk of higher turnover, as these employees are more likely to leave organizations. This can lead to churn and increase the resources organizations must invest in activities such as orientation and training. Reduced engagement and alignment: Workers in precarious employment relationships were observed to be less engaged than their permanent counterparts, and are less inclined to invest more time and effort into their responsibilities. Additionally, these workers are less aligned with organizational goals, which was thought to reduce return on an organization's labour investment. Reduced Performance: Workers in a secure employment relationship were generally thought to have more skills and knowledge when compared to their precarious counterparts. Those in precarious employment relationships were, in general, thought to be less productive, thus reducing overall organizational performance. Health and safety risks: Workers in precarious employment relationships were thought to pose additional health and safety risks to an organization as they do not have the same knowledge and experience as their permanent counterparts. Reduced customer satisfaction: Full-time employees were thought to improve customer satisfaction, particularly in customer facing businesses, such as those in the hospitality sector. One poor customer interaction can permanently fracture a relationship, and some employers felt that having non-permanent workers in these positions posed an unacceptable risk. [36]

---

[33] D. Dorling *Inequality and the 1%* (Verso Books, 2014).

[34] R. Wilkinson and K. Pickett *The spirit level: Why equality is better for everyone* (Penguin UK, 2010), and *The Inner Level* (Allen Lane, 2018).

[35] Cushen and Thompson, at 360.

[36] KPMG, 'Precarious Employment: The Employer's Perspective' (2014) at https://pepso.ca/documents/kpmg-uw-report-precarious-employment-may-2014.pdf at 11. See also KPMG and United Way (2017). Better Business Outcomes Through Workforce Security.

Does Labour Law Adequately Protect Labour from the Consequences of Corporate Governance?

It is clear that the push towards more precarious labour is problematic. If company law and corporate governance are identified as causal factors for precarious labour, the question arises to what extent they might be protected by labour law. If their interests are not sufficiently protected within the corporate governance arrangements because of the dominance of the shareholder-centric model, then workers will call upon labour law to operate as a protective system. Unfortunately, there are limits to what labour law can do, partly because of its structural features and partly because of inadequate statutory provisions.

We noted the contractarian approach to company law above. In labour law, the idea of contract also plays a dominant role. The employment relationship is typically considered to be based on the contract of employment and the employee *choosing* to work for her employer. Yet, while there may be elements of the contract that can be negotiated (depending on the seniority and experience of the worker), most terms are prescribed by the employer. The demise of collective bargaining through trade unions has further eroded the ability of workers to negotiate terms. Viewing the employment relationship as one that has its theoretical foundation in contract is therefore problematic, particularly when the inequality of power between the two parties to the agreement is taken into account. The hierarchical nature of the employment relationship and 'the nature of the social relations involved', argues Collins, mean that it is not appropriate to characterise the employment relationship as one of contract.[37] This insistence effectively masks an inequality that leaves the employee exposed to the risk of exploitation by a far more powerful employer who is capable of dominating the employee. Thus, the contractual analysis of labour law perpetuates the potential for employer companies, and therefore executive directors and shareholders, to profit at the expense of the workers. Such an analysis obfuscates the exploitative relationship and thereby reduces the potential political pushback. Capitalism, in this way, is the extraction of value from labour.

A second problem with conceding that labour law 'fills the gaps' left by company law lies in the statutory protections given, which depend entirely on the nature of the work undertaken. These might be viewed as a cushion that protects against the exploitative possibility left open by contractual inequalities. However, these are also insufficient. Two of the most important employment law protections – the right not to be unfairly dismissed from your job and the right to receive a redundancy payment if your role is redundant – apply only if you are an employee who has two years of continuous service. Other rights apply to employees and another category – workers – but not to those who are

---

[37] H. Collins, 'Market Power, Bureaucratic Power and the Contract of Employment' (1986) 15 *Industrial Law Journal* 1.

self-employed. It follows therefore that legal status in relation to the 'employer' is of vital importance in determining the rights of the worker. The Employment Rights Act 1996 is limited in its definition of 'employee', stating at section 230(1) that it means an individual who has entered into, or works under, 'a contract of employment'. A 'contract of employment' is then defined in section 230(2) as a 'contract of service or apprenticeship, whether express or implied, and (if it is express) whether oral or in writing'.

In order to interrogate whether a contract is one of employment or something else entirely (such as a contract between an organisation and an independent contractor to provide consultancy services), the courts have developed a range of tests. These include the need for the employer to have control over the employee, for there to be mutuality of obligation (the employee agrees to work and the employer agrees to pay for the work done), and for the employee to provide her service personally.[38] One difficulty with these tests is that they have developed over time and do not always map neatly on to the nature of the modern working world. For example, the working pattern of a sales executive who spends her time working either from home or on the road may not fit with our traditional idea of what it means to be subject to an employer's control. Likewise, someone who is engaged on a 'zero hours contract' where there may be no obligation to accept work if it is offered may be an employee for the short duration of the shift she is working, but gaps between assignments may mean that insufficient continuous service can be accrued to benefit from important statutory protections.

The somewhat opaque treatment of employment status, coupled with the reverence given to the contract of employment, has led to some employers drafting terms in which the true relationship between the parties is purported to be something that it is not. An example of this is the case of *Autoclenz Limited v Belcher and others*.[39] In this case, valets who worked at a car cleaning company claimed that they were workers, entitled to be paid the national minimum wage and to enjoy the protections of the Working Time Regulations 1998. The written contract that the valets signed, however, stated that the valets were self-employed sub-contractors. A later document given to the valets made clear that they were entitled to substitute someone else to provide work and that there was no obligation on Autoclenz to provide work or on the sub-contractors to accept the work offered. These later two clauses can clearly be read as attempts to make it clear that no mutuality of obligation was owed and that the sub-contractors were not required to give personal service. The problem for Autoclenz was that these contractual terms bore little resemblance to how the parties conducted themselves in practice. In this case, the Supreme

---

[38] *Ready Mixed Concrete (South East Limited) v Minister for Pensions and National Insurance* [1968] 2 QB 497; *Carmichael v National Power plc* [2000] IRLR 43; *Pimlico Plumbers Limited and another v Smith* [2018] UKSC 29.

[39] [2011] UKSC 41.

Court departed from orthodox principles of contractual interpretation[40] to look beyond what the parties had signed to consider the reality of the relationship. Lord Clarke commented on the unique nature of the employment bargain when he said:

> So the relative bargaining power of the parties must be taken into account in deciding whether the terms of any written agreement in truth represent what was agreed and the true agreement will often have to be gleaned from all the circumstances of the case, of which the written agreement is only a part. This may be described as a purposive approach to the problem. If so, I am content with that description.[41]

Even if employers do not deliberately set out to mislead, the law affords considerable latitude to employers in structuring work, and this allows companies to organise labour so as to avoid the triggering of important legal protections. The growth of the 'gig economy' and the push towards precarious work means that large parts of the workforce will not qualify for fundamental labour law protections such as the right not to be unfairly dismissed.[42] Thus, contrary to the standard company law view, labour law does not 'fill the gap' left by company law's indifference to workers.

Uber Case Study

Over 2 million people are registered to use Uber's services in London, where there are around 30,000 Uber drivers. Using a smartphone app, Uber connects drivers and passengers as an alternative to a traditional taxi service. In December 2018, the Court of Appeal set down its judgment on the question of whether Uber drivers are 'workers' for the purposes of certain labour law protections (the right to holiday and the right to the national minimum wage).[43] The drivers claimed that they were workers engaged by Uber and that they were 'working' when the app was on and they were available for hire. Uber argued, in line with the written contract between it and the drivers, that it merely acted as an intermediary

---

[40] See Chapter 2 (Mitchell) for a discussion on the return to formalism in contractual interpretation

[41] Ibid. per Lord Clarke at [35]; A. Bogg, 'Sham Self-Employment in the Supreme Court' (2012) 41(3) *Industrial Law Journal* 328.

[42] M. Taylor, 'Good Work; The Taylor Review of Modern Working Practices' (UK Government, 2017). Available at https://www.gov.uk/government/uploads/system/uploads/attachment_data/file/627671/good-work-taylor-review-modern-working-practices-rg.pdf; V. De Stefano, *The Rise of the 'Just-in-Time Workforce': On-demand work, crowd work and labour protection in the 'Gig-Economy'* ILO Working Paper http://www.ilo.org/travail/whatwedo/publications/WCMS_443267/lang%2D%2Den/index.htm.

[43] [2018] EWCA Civ 2748.

between passenger and driver for the purposes of providing booking and payment services.

The Court of Appeal held, in a majority judgment, that the drivers were workers. One thing that was particularly influential in the Court's view was the element of control. Drivers could be disconnected from the app if they declined too many offers for rides. In this way, Uber exerted a degree of control over the drivers that was inconsistent with their claim that the drivers were genuine freelancers. The Court also held that the drivers were working when the app was on and they were available for hire and not merely when, as Underhill LJ maintained in his dissenting judgment, they had actually accepted a fare. Uber has been granted permission to appeal to the Supreme Court.

WHAT REFORMS SHOULD BE INTRODUCED TO PROTECT LABOUR? SHOULD THEY BE LABOUR LAW REFORMS OR CORPORATE GOVERNANCE REFORMS OR BOTH? IS A POLITICAL SHIFT NECESSARY?

One option is to strengthen labour law's protection especially in relation to those who currently fall outside its scope. It had been hoped that the Taylor Review of Modern Working Practices, which reported in July 2017, would take steps to address this. One factor that prompted the Review was the confusing and unclear three-tier structure of work relationships (employee, worker and self-employed), which, as we noted above, has been exacerbated in the gig economy. The Review proposed a clearer distinction between those who are genuinely self-employed and those who are 'workers', who will be known as 'dependent contractors'. In addition, the Review considered replacing the current framework, in which there is only a limited statutory definition of employment, with a statutory framework embodying the current common law tests. The difficulty with legislating in this area is that any statutory test risks being insufficiently subtle to capture the actual realities of the working relationship. This might prevent courts in the future from looking beyond the contract to actual working practices as the Supreme Court was able to do in *Autoclenz*. They might prefer to adopt a more formalistic, rather than purposive, approach when interpreting the contractual provisions in order to avoid the controversies that have long beset this area of law.

The Review also proposed making clearer the distinction between employees and workers. One suggested way of doing this is to give greater weight to the test of control. The consequence of emphasising control as a defining characteristic of the employment relationship is that it may have unintended repercussions for certain groups. A carer, for example, is likely to visit clients' homes without supervision. On one view, such a worker has a high degree of autonomy when delivering care. On another view, she is likely to be subject to regular monitoring of her work by the client, client's family and care provider. How we interpret 'control' and the place we give it in defining what it means to be an employee or worker can result in a person being given or denied important labour law protections.

Following consultation on the Review's proposals, in December 2018, the Government published its 'Good Work Plan'. The Plan contains a variety of proposals, including the following: legislation to improve the clarity of the employment status tests; a right of zero hours contract workers to request 'a more stable and predictable' contract after six months' service; a right to a written statement of employment rights from day 1 for both employees and workers; a new duty on employers' businesses to provide a Key Facts page, which would benefit agency workers; holiday pay reference period extended from 12 weeks to 52 weeks; aggravated breach penalties on employers and the maximum penalty raised from £5,000 to £20,000.[44] Whilst these proposals will go some way towards providing greater clarity for many workers, they arguably do not go as far as is required to ensure that workers are free from exploitative conditions. Indeed, the response of the General Secretary of the union Unison was that the Good Work Plan 'looks set to fall at the first hurdle. It's no good, it won't work and it isn't a plan. Britain's worst employers need to be dragged kicking and screaming into the 21st century, but sadly this response won't do that'.[45]

A second reform option in addition to expanding labour law's protection is to consider whether company law holds any potential for redressing its current indifference to labour. One point that is often made in respect of section 172 of the Companies Act 2006 is that it holds considerable emancipatory potential. The argument is that by asking directors to have regard to matters falling outside traditional shareholder concerns – such as the interests of the company's employees, the impact of the company's operations on the community and environment, and the likely consequences of any decisions in the long term – directors are compelled to be more holistic in their decision-making. There are, however, considerable flaws with this argument. One is the weak formulation of the duty which requires directors to act in the way most likely to promote the success for the benefit of members (i.e., shareholders) but only to 'have regard' to other concerns. There is no absolute requirement to take any of these into account, nor is there any guidance as to how to conduct a balancing exercise when the interests may compete. However, there are new reporting requirements in relation to section 172 of the Companies Act 2006 which require companies to report in their strategic report on how they have had regard to the goals and persons listed in section 172(1)(a) to (f).[46] Another

---

[44] HM Government, *The Good Work Plan* (HM Government; London, December 2018) at 7–8.

[45] Unison, The government's good work plan is no good, it won't work and it isn't a plan, says UNISON, 7 February 2018 (sic) available at https://www.unison.org.uk/news/article/2018/02/governments-good-work-plan-no-good-wont-work-isnt-plan-says-unison/.

[46] The Companies (Miscellaneous Reporting) Regulations 2018, No 860, Regulation 4, inserting new Section 414CZA into Companies Act 2006.

flaw relates to how such a duty may be enforced. Employees have no standing to enforce directors' duties directly. Duties are owed to the company and so it is the company acting through the directors or exceptionally through a derivative claim by a shareholder who can seek to enforce any breach. Even then, such claims are always in respect to losses to shareholders rather than to employees; in any case, the long-standing deference of courts to matters of 'business judgment' suggests that any action challenging the considerations given to, or balancing of, other concerns would be doomed to failure. Company law, then, appears to offer little scope for reform as it is currently drafted.

One factor to which directors should have regard in the context of section 172 is the desirability of the company maintaining a reputation for high standards of business conduct. Despite this, matters of 'reputational risk' appear to have had little influence over how companies have decided to structure their labour force. During a visit by journalists in 2016 to a Sports Direct warehouse, amidst widely reported concerns about worker treatment, its CEO Mike Ashley withdrew a large number of £50 notes from his pocket while going through a security scanner, joking that he had just been to the casino. If appeals to the risk of reputational damage – or even to basic decency – are likely to fall on deaf ears, how can we get companies to take seriously the risks that are being passed to labour?

The great challenge for reform in this area is that while existing legal formulations might do little to protect labour, and precarious labour in particular, the problem is a systemic one. As we have shown, corporate governance is implicated in creating an environment in which risk is transferred from investors to labour (and other stakeholder groups). The imperative behind that risk transfer is a legal obligation (directors have wide discretion under s172 CA 2006). Rather, it is a system of corporate governance, embedded within a capitalist system, which incentivises those with decision-making power to minimise the cost of labour in order to maximise value extraction. Whilst policy makers have tinkered with the corporate governance system since 2008, reliance on voluntary measures of corporate social responsibility, weak soft law rules about employee participation and pro-social shareholder activism is unlikely to reap results. A more positive step instead might be to revive trade union power and strengthen collective bargaining rights so that these can be used as a counterveiling force in the contractual imbalance we have identified above.

Companies have developed as the key vehicle to facilitate the production process but the companies' focus on shareholder value is driven by the self-interest of capitalists. Thus, for many thinkers, reform can never be sufficient. For Harvey, there is an 'absolute necessity for a coherent anti-capitalist revolutionary movement', the aim of which 'has to be to assume social command over both the production and distribution of surpluses'.[47] He is equally clear

---

[47] D. Harvey, *The Enigma of Capital and the Crises of Capitalism* (Profile Books; London, 2011) at 228.

that reform cannot come from *within* capitalism itself despite what some advocates of so-called responsible capitalism might suggest. As he argues, 'an ethical, non-exploitative and socially just capitalism that redounds to the benefit of all is impossible. It contradicts the very nature of what capitalism is about'.[48]

Imagining a future outside capitalism is difficult but not impossible. Indeed, across the world, there are important counter-movements formed by those who seek a genuine alternative to an economic system that is divisive, exploitative and ultimately unsustainable. Their environmental and social activism stands in stark contrast to shareholder activism, which is advanced as the mainstream way of making companies more robust, more economically and environmentally sustainable, and less risky.

Further Reading

H. Arthurs and C. Mumme, 'From Governance to Political Economy: Insights from a Study of Relations Between Corporations and Workers' (2007) 45 (3) *Osgoode Hall Law Journal* 439–470.

Business, Innovation and Skills Committee, *Employment Practices at Sports Direct*, Third Report of Session 2016–17, HC 219, 22 July 2016.

A. Bogg and T. Novitz, 'Investigating 'Voice' at Work' (2012) 33 *Comparative Labor Law & Policy Journal* 323–354.

K. Ewing et al. (eds), *A Manifesto for Labour Law: Towards a Comprehensive Revision of Workers' Rights* (IER, 2016).

T. M. Hanna, 'The Next Economic Settlement: The Return of Public Ownership' (2018) 26 (2) *Renewal: A Journal of Social Democracy* 17.

D. Harvey, *A Companion to Marx's Capital* (Verso; London, 2010).

M. Jensen and W. Meckling, 'Theory of the Firm: Managerial Behavior, Agency Costs and Ownership Structure' (1976) 3 *Journal of Financial Economics* 305.

A. L. Kalleberg and S. P. Vallas, 'Probing Precarious Work: Theory, Research and Politics' (2018) 31 *Precarious Work: Research in the Sociology of Work* 1–30.

OECD, *Risk Management and Corporate Governance* (Corporate Governance, OECD Publishing, 2014) At http://www.oecd.org/daf/ca/risk-management-corporate-governance.pdf.

G. Standing, *The Precariat: The Dangerous New Class* (Bloomsbury Academic, 2011).

G. Standing, 'Understanding the Precariat Through Labour and Work' (2014) 45 (5) *Development and Change* 963–980.

P. Zumbansen, 'The Parallel Worlds of Corporate Governance and Labor Law' (2006) 13 *Indiana Journal of Global Legal Studies* 261.

---

[48] Ibid. at 239.

A Good Idea Gone Bad.
Can We Still Justify Patent Monopolies?

Peter S. Harrison

INTRODUCTION

Intellectual property (IP) is a surprisingly strange beast. Whilst society as a whole seems to have become somewhat accustomed (or, as some critics might argue, inured) to the concept that the products of intellectual effort are protected by property rights, the true (and problematic) character of IP itself, the normative questions which surround its existence, and its deep societal impact sometimes appear unappreciated.

Students who first encounter the subject understandably focus on not confusing a patent with a copyright, a copyright with a trade mark, or a trade mark with a design right. They then grapple with subject matter of protection, validity requirements, duration periods, and infringement exemptions for a seemingly endless spectrum of disparate rights. However, although getting to grips with the basics of the individual rights is clearly important, this effort can lead to a misapprehension that the world of IP is (save for some minutiae) relatively settled and without substantial normative problems. That is very far from the truth. The aim of this chapter is to highlight some of the key societal challenges created by the control of inventions by way of patents and why critical lawyers may wish to take issue with the current position. The societal problems of patents fall under two main heads.

Imprecise Effect

The first set of problems arises from the imprecise effect of patents on technology innovation. The propertisation of ideas through the existence of patents is a cornerstone of the economic model in which the market is the key driver in determining the direction of innovation. At the heart of the patent system is a paradox – that the grant of monopolies to inventors will enhance overall development within a market by incentivising innovation. Patents serve to amplify market forces by rewarding those who get to an inventive idea first (and file a patent application for it) by giving them a limited monopoly over that idea. However, as we see in this chapter, the 'market + patents' model, in which innovation activities are directed towards maximising profit, is a very blunt (or at least imprecise) instrument that can result in technological development priorities and market behaviours, which arguably do not always seem to be to the benefit of broader society.

We will also see that there is a risk that those granted a monopoly will look to overstep the limits of their grant to the extent that the aims of the granting of that monopoly become undermined. Often, that behaviour is a function of the inherent 'fuzzy edges' of IP protection and the direct (and indirect) response of actors to that fuzziness within a market economic environment.

This chapter will look in particular detail at the patenting behaviour of the pharmaceutical industry, for it is often here that the greatest criticism of the patent system is levied. It will then look at two other key targets of criticism of the patent system: the development of patent thickets (particularly within the fields of consumer electronics) and the impact of the so-called patent 'troll'.

Effects Upon the Global South

The second set of problems relate to the impact that the imposition of a Western-style strong patent system has had upon societies in the Global South. For some, this is little more than a way of ensuring that the states and peoples of the Global South remain controlled by global multi-national corporations (and their Western state sponsors) and that the technologically strong maintain their dominance over those who are creative but who are, in relative terms, technologically weak.

We will look at the argument that the problems of the patent system seen in the Global North are often magnified when we look at its impact on the South – particularly in relation to pharmaceutical patents. We will also look at the accusations of hypocrisy levelled at the Global North in relation to the worldwide imposition of a strong patent system.

DEBATE: INVENTIONS DEFY DELINEATION

Those rights which are bundled up as 'intellectual property' are, at heart, property rights in *intangible* products of the intellect, and this immediately creates problems (see also Hudson, Chapter 6). The idea of property rights in those things which you can touch, whether physical goods or land, seems intuitive – I can understand *how* I might lock away my Fabergé egg, or fence off my Scottish deer estate, as they are tangible things. Although there are, of course, very live normative questions as to whether I *should* have the right to keep my Fabergé egg out of the public gaze or stop others from productively using my otherwise little-used tracts of Scottish wilderness, in both cases the thing which is subject to legal protection can be relatively easily defined. Indeed, real property lawyers are sometimes parodied as delighting in using their trusty set of coloured pencils to delineate land holdings on maps. However, when we turn to the idea of property in intangible *concepts*, we find that this relative certainty slips away.

Since an intangible concept cannot be physically held, locked away, or fenced off, I can protect that concept only through the application of positive law. However, in such an application, there will often be a deep-seated problem of definition – I cannot simply draw around an idea with a red coloured pencil – I need to somehow describe it in enough detail for others to know what I am referring to. I have to be able to state in what way my concept is different from all the concepts that went before it. It would seem unfair if I were able to claim control over something that had already been conceived or was merely trivially different to something that had gone before. Considerations of such 'backward facing' boundaries are the key to answering questions concerning the subsistence of a right over a concept.

In addition, I need to make it clear where my right ends in relation to the set of 'yet to be had' concepts. It would, again, seem unfair if I were permitted control over *anything* new that was distantly inspired by 'my' concept. On the other hand, it might also be unfair if someone were able to profit by exploiting a relatively trivial change to my 'hard-won' invention. Obviously, considerations of such 'forward facing' boundaries are the key to answering questions concerning third-party infringement of a right over a concept. The establishment of what is 'fair' in this battleground between the subsistence of a right and the freedom of third parties to act free of the right has exercised legislators and courts around the world for centuries.

Intuitively, one might feel that this balancing of rights is in some way all about 'reward' and go on to frame the question of proper scope of protection along the lines of: 'How much new do I have to do to "deserve" my right in a concept?' or 'How much new does a third party have to do to deserve to "avoid" my right?'. One might further intuitively think that if I have made some significant contribution to humanity I should deserve stronger protection than that given in reward for a minor 'tweak' to a piece of technology; perhaps protection that would entitle me to exert control over a wider range of third-party activity (and activities that were more different from my original concept) than the protection I would get for a mere tweak.

This idea that rights granted are in some way a reward for (and should be in some way coterminous with) 'contribution' is a constant thread within the discourse on the justifications for IP.[1] However, reliance on reward encounters an immediate problem in its detailed application: How do you *actually* go about objectively determining something as subjective as 'contribution'? Is it

---

[1] Justin Hughes, "The Philosophy of Intellectual Property" (1988) 77 Geo LJ 287; Edwin C. Hettinger, "Justifying Intellectual Property" (1989) 18 Philosophy and Public Affairs 30.

about volume of work? Degree of effort? Potential future impact? Impressiveness of inspiration? Elegance of solution? A mixture of all of the above? In addition, we have the particular problem that what might be thought to be a significant development in one field of endeavour may be deemed relatively trite in another.

Given the obvious subjectivity of these tests, there can be no absolute standard of 'contribution'. We find, therefore, that patent laws across the globe, whilst they seem broadly to reflect the idea of a right based on reward, cannot in operation be based upon any inherent natural law 'lode-stone'. However, if the patent validity and infringement tests created by statute (and operated by patent offices and judges) are not to be merely arbitrary, they need to be informed by some other normative justification. What might this be?

Before we come to that, we need to look at the argument that, whatever the justification for patents rights is, it had better be a good one. Whether a particular *physical* entity can be propertised will likely impact on a relatively small pool of potential users of that entity. In contrast, the inherently non-rivalrous nature of an intellectual concept means that a limitless number of persons can use the concept at any one time without any one individual's use limiting the enjoyment of that concept by another. Therefore, propertising that concept through the granting of a patent (and thereby taking it out of use for others) can affect a very wide number of potential users. However, the impact of allowing patent protection over a concept goes beyond the mere numbers of persons affected (important as that may be). There is also a strong argument that the ability to use intellectual concepts without hindrance is an important part of individual freedom. It is surely not an overstatement to say that the movement and adaptation of abstract concepts have been at the centre of the development of human civilisation. Indeed one might ask: What *is* human civilisation without such knowledge? For Bronowski:

> Man is distinguished from other animals by his imaginative gifts. He makes plans, inventions, new discoveries, by putting different talents together; and his discoveries become more subtle and more penetrating, as he learns to combine his talents in more complex and intimate ways.[2]

In the light of this, it might be argued that the freedom to use information is not one to be interfered with lightly. Accordingly, a restriction on the right of others to use concepts might, at the very least, be seen to be one where

(a) a particularly high justificatory threshold is required and

(b) there is a need to be particularly cognisant of not improperly restricting the action of third parties.

---

[2] Jacob Bronowski, *The Ascent of Man* (Book Club Associates, London 1977), 20.

With both those points in mind, that brings us to the question of what patents are *for*.

DEBATE: INDIVIDUAL INCENTIVES PROMOTE THE INNOVATION SOCIETY NEEDS

The pro-IP argument most commonly employed by businesses, and the advocates for business growth within governments and inter-governmental bodies, is essentially consequentialist/utilitarian. It goes like this: innovation (and through it the development of new means of production, new products and enhanced prosperity) enhances the greater utility of society and such innovation will be adequately incentivised only through giving protection to innovators such that their efforts are not copied by others (what economists would term 'free riders').

For some commentators, IP rights (and patents in particular) are the very basis of a modern technical society and are the potential saviour of those nations who are seeking to rely upon the so-called 'knowledge economy' as a way of maintaining a competitive advantage over lower cost-base economies in the less-developed world. For Rand:

> ...patents are the heart and core of property rights, and once they are destroyed the destruction of all other property rights will follow automatically, as a brief postscript.[3]

Perhaps, more poetically, for Burke:

> Because the rule of law exists, and above all because it encourages and protects acts of innovation ... we in the modern world expect that tomorrow will be better than today. Our view of the universe is essentially optimistic because of the marriage between law and innovation. Law gives the individual the confidence to explore, to risk, to adventure into the unknown, in the knowledge that he as an inventor will be protected by society.[4]

These are very significant claims to make and would seem to imbue patent law with a heavy burden of supporting technological industrial society and human development. However, others are fearful that this focus on commercial development, and the use of patents in an attempt to support it, detracts from the fundamental advancement of science. For example, Robert B. Laughlin (winner of the 1998 Nobel Prize in Physics) expresses grave concerns:

> ... biology has now evolved from science to highly profitable engineering. This distinction strikes most people as a label change, but it is actually a tectonic shift,

---

[3] Ayn Rand, *Capitalism: The Unknown Ideal* (New American Library, New York 1966), 128.

[4] James Burke, *The Day the Universe Changed* (Guild Publishing, London 1985), 19.

for science and engineering differ in one central respect: in science, you gain power by telling people what you know; in engineering you gain power by preventing people from knowing what you know. Chronic confusion and ignorance are the rule, rather than the exception, in engineering for the simple reason that everyone is withholding information from everyone else on intellectual property grounds.[5]

The consequentialist argument for patents certainly has the benefit of initial simplicity. However, the problems in its logical steps are equally apparent. The key questions come down to these:

(a) Do new means of production and products *really* enhance the utility of society?

(b) To what extent is the advent of such new means of production really incentivised though the creation of patent rights?

With regard to question (a), there are a number of key sub-questions. First, there is the fundamental question (which goes back to the very beginning of utilitarianism as a philosophy[6]) of what actually constitutes societal utility and how you might measure it. How does one go about balancing the felicific calculus of a society? For example, is some measure of gross domestic product (GDP) sufficient[7] or do we need to look to a broader sense of well-being?[8] Such questions are, of course, one of the bedrocks of political debate and are not easily answered.

Second, there is the question of whether societal utility (whatever that may be) is actually enhanced through the development of new means of production and products. Crucially, the answers to all such questions are predicated upon which particular 'society' (or part of society) we choose to consider. Is the relevant society all humans on Earth, just those within a certain territory, or those within a socioeconomic class or a particular class of consumers? It would be nice to believe that in all cases equal consideration would be given to *all* possible societies in *all* possible situations. However, history teaches us that (likely since the advent of human hierarchies) interested groups, states or empires will more often focus their 'utilitarian' analysis upon the 'society' that most closely aligns with their own constituency, whilst ignoring, underestimating or explaining away the impact on other (perhaps less advantaged) societies.

---

[5] Robert B Laughlin in *A Different Universe – Reinventing Physics from the Bottom Down* (Basic Books, New York 2006), 162.

[6] See, for example, Maurice Mandelbaum, "Two Moot Issues in Mill's Utilitarianism" in JB Schneewind (ed) *Mill: A collection of Critical Essays* (Macmillan, London 1968) 206; JJC Smart and Bernard Williams, *Utilitarianism For and Against* (Cambridge University Press, Cambridge 1973).

[7] Estelle Derclaye and Tim Taylor, "Happy IP: aligning intellectual property rights with well-being" [2015] 1 IPQ 1.

[8] Estelle Derclaye and Tim Taylor, "Happy IP: replacing the law and economics justification for intellectual property rights with a well-being approach" [2015] EIPR 197.

A temporary inequality in the availability of the fruits of innovation is arguably inherent within the 'market + patents' model. Although, on a product-by-product basis, there will likely be some immediate winners and losers within broader society, the existence of a patent system is intended to create a predictable environment that rewards and protects innovative effort and investment and leads to an overall growth in number and quality of products and a general enhancement of technology which, in time, will come to benefit all members of society. There is something of a 'trickle-down' element to this argument: today's high-technology 'toys' for the rich will eventually become the essential tools for everyone – it is just that the poorer members will just have to wait a little longer until they can access such goods. This might be summed up as 'short term pain (for some) in return for long term gain (for all)' – a classic 'rule utilitarian' trade-off. Many may consider this as being a justifiable *quid pro quo* when we are looking at (say) access to a new high-definition, wide-screen TV. However, the balance of utilities becomes more challenging when an element of society is being denied access to a new, very high-cost, anti-cancer drug.

The second key question ('b' above) is whether the existence of patent monopolies actually *does* encourage product innovation in the first place. Intuitively, one would imagine this to be the case – surely, if I know my invention will not be 'stolen' the moment I make it available to the public, I will be prepared to invest more during its development. In fact, the degree to which innovation is stimulated by the existence of patents is likely to vary from industry to industry.

At one end of the spectrum are the so-called 'non-sequential' industries (such as pharmaceuticals and biotechnology), in which development tends to occur in relatively large step-changes from what went before and where each of those step-changes will likely require major investment. It is broadly argued that the existence of patents is crucial in incentivising this sort of development. At the other end of the spectrum of development are the so-called 'sequential' industries (such as consumer electronics), where advances in technology are more often made through a number of smaller incremental steps, each of which of itself requires less investment. Here, the role of patents in genuinely incentivising development is less clear.

In a good number of sequential industries (notably consumer electronics) there is a vast proliferation of patent applications and a significant degree of patent litigation activity. One might intuitively suppose that this is a reflection of the importance of patents in supporting innovation in this field. It might equally point to a system that incentivises actors in the field to engage in unjustified, anti-competitive behaviour.

Before we look at such behaviour, we will examine the main areas of complexity encountered in applying the incentivisation of innovation justification for patents to the field of pharmaceuticals, an area where the utilitarian conflict between incentivising innovation for the benefit of broader society and the alleviation of individual suffering is arguably at its most acute.

PHARMACEUTICAL PATENTS

The pharmaceutical and biotechnology industries are most usually held out to be the classic examples of those using 'non-sequential' development and are often seen as something of a 'poster child' for the 'market + patents' model of incentivising innovation. However, they are also the area in which the inherent conflicts of that model are clearest. First, we will look at why patents are perceived as being crucial to supporting innovation in this sector. We will then look at some of consequences that arise out of the operation of a 'market + patents' model.

Incentivising Pharmaceutical Development

What if you were a pharmaceutical company looking to develop a groundbreaking drug? Such development is very expensive, and a company may experience many development failures before one of their candidate products can be demonstrated to be safe and efficacious in humans (and in some regulatory systems good value for public money) and becomes a commercially successful product. In contrast, the actual production costs of making the active constituent of a tablet are often small in comparison with the huge upfront development costs of the product. As such, a successful pharmaceutical product is a perfect target for economic 'free riders' who, in the absence of IP rights keeping them out of the market, would be able, at minimal investment cost to themselves, to take advantage of a pharmaceutical company's development efforts. Indeed, this is what almost always happens when the monopoly period of a patent for pharmaceutical product expires. During that monopoly period, the pharmaceutical company seeks to recoup its development cost for the product (and, indeed, the costs of failure of other candidate products which did not make it to market) as well as make profits to distribute to shareholders. On patent expiry, a range of so-called 'generic' drug companies will immediately step into the market, selling the identical product at a small fraction of the price of the original product.

Here, the incentivisation justification for patents seems, at first sight, to stand up well. Without patent protection, you really would not invest the hundreds of millions required to develop (and obtain regulatory approval for a new drug) and the existence of new drugs leads to the enhancement of social utility (directly in the form of improved welfare and by improving GDP). However, pharmaceutical companies, wanting to ameliorate risk and maximise returns, will rationally direct their efforts towards those areas that are more likely to be technologically and commercially successful. This can have a number of outcomes.

'Me-Toos'

The first of these is the drive to develop so-called 'me-too' (or less pejoratively, 'follow-on') drugs. Although these are new chemical entities that will attract patent protection, they will be members of the same class of drug as the existing market leader – acting through an identical biological mechanism. Whilst they may offer some technical enhancement, that enhancement may be relatively marginal over what went before. The result is a proliferation of products that act in the same way against the same disease states.[9]

One might argue that that seems fine – surely, an industry is allowed to develop to a level of optimum provision through an evolutionary 'fine-tuning' of products. Perhaps less justifiable is that the fine-tuning effort tends to be concentrated within those disease areas that will guarantee a commercial return at the expense of those that will not. Even if development goes beyond mere fine-tuning and a drug with a new mechanism of action is found, development efforts will often continue to focus on therapeutic areas that guarantee a significant return on investment.

Tropical Diseases

For many years, the best-selling pharmaceuticals were for treatment of heartburn and peptic-ulcers, a classic disease of the stressed Western professional and middle-manager. The slot of global best-selling drug would be held by an anti-ulcer drug and would be replaced in that slot by an enhanced anti-ulcer drug that in turn would be replaced by another, enhanced, anti-ulcer drug. Following that, there was a period over which the top spots were dominated by cholesterol-reducing statins. Today, competition for the top slot is primarily amongst a raft of anti-arthritis treatments – crucial for those suffering from an extremely debilitating disease – but with an arguable bias towards the large profitable markets in the Global North.

This is not to say that there is no development being undertaken in respect of drugs to treat the tropical diseases endemic in the Global South, but there is a clear degree of bias towards developing those drugs that pay well. Indeed, much of the development effort directed at tropical diseases is funded by philanthropic giving, such as that directed and funded by the Bill & Melinda Gates Foundation.

'Orphan' Drugs

However, it is not only the Global South that is the victim of this bias towards profitability. There are diseases that affect the many and there are diseases that affect the few. Some diseases are relatively easy to find a treatment for, whereas others are refractory to attempts to find treatment. Given that the potential profitability of a drug is a function of the size of its potential market, the cost of its development, and the price that the market will bear, there will be disease

---

[9] S. Regnier, "What is the value of 'me-too' drugs?" (2013) 16(4) Health Care Manag Sci. 300.

states (even in the affluent Global North) that will not be a profitable target for drug development efforts. Although definitions differ, these commercially 'unloved' conditions where there are very few sufferers (or where there are relatively few sufferers and where treatment is exceptionally difficult to arrive at) are often referred to as 'orphan' diseases, and the drugs for their treatment as 'orphan' drugs. Governments do look to encourage development of drugs for these disease states through financial incentives and allowances within the pharmaceutical regulatory system.[10] However, alone, the 'market + patents' model rarely provides sufficient incentive for pharmaceutical companies to investigate such conditions. The recent example of Glybera (described in Box 4.1) demonstrates some of the problems inherent in this incentive model.

Box 4.1 Glybera® – The Lost Orphan

Lipoprotein lipase deficiency (LPLD) is an autosomal recessive inherited disorder in which there is a defective gene for the enzyme lipoprotein lipase. This is an enzyme that is an important part of normal fat metabolism and the defect in the gene for this enzyme can lead to fat deposits under the skin, pancreatic and liver problems, and diabetes. Though a serious disorder that can result in early death, LPLD is relatively rare; the prevalence is only 1 in 500,000. In October 2013, the European Medicines Agency approved a gene therapy treatment for LPLD, the first-ever gene therapy treatment approved in Europe or the US. The therapy, alipogene tiparvovec (sold under the trade name Glybera), uses a virus vector to inject a functioning version of the faulty gene into the cells of the muscles of the patient. The patient starts to produce functioning lipoprotein lipase and corrects (in part) their faulty fat metabolism.[11] Although this sounds (relatively) simple, the technology was cutting-edge in human therapy. As a result of high development costs combined with a small target market, the cost per dose of Glybera was over €1.1 million – making the drug the 'most expensive in the world'. At this price, the manufacturers found difficulty in persuading any healthcare providers to justify this level of expenditure. With disappointing sales – it is possible that only one patient ever paid for treatment – in October 2017 the manufacturers chose not to renew their marketing authorisation for Glybera[12]. The story hardly serves as an encouragement for other potential entrants into the gene therapy for orphan diseases market. Indeed, the surprising element of this story is that the manufacturers pursued this commercial course, and were able to convince investors to support this course, in the first place.

---

[10] See, for example, Regulation (EC) 141/2000 (the Orphan Regulation).

[11] ES Stroes et al. (2008). "Intramuscular Administration of AAV1-Lipoprotein LipaseS447X Lowers Triglycerides in Lipoprotein Lipase-Deficient Patients" 28(12) Arteriosclerosis, Thrombosis, and Vascular Biology 2303.

[12] http://www.ema.europa.eu/ema/index.jsp?curl=pages/medicines/human/medicines/002145/human_med_001480.jsp&mid=WC0b01ac058001d124 (Accessed March 2019).

Antibiotic Resistance

A further complexity in the relationship between patents and pharmaceutical innovation is seen in the area of development (or lack of development) of novel antibiotic agents. Antibiotics have undoubtedly revolutionised the world. Before their development, deaths and significant morbidity from micro-organism infections were widespread. For example, it was relatively common for people to die of septicaemia caused by a graze or even a shaving cut.[13] The evolution and spread of antibiotic-resistant micro-organisms, caused by over- and mis-use of antibiotic drugs, are threatening to bring to a close the 'golden age' of freedom from micro-organism infection. With time, fewer and fewer classes of antibiotic drugs are retaining their capability to treat extreme cases of infection. The use of drugs that are still effective in extreme cases of infection are being carefully conserved by governments to ensure that resistance against them does not develop and that medics have something left in their antibiotic arsenal. The finding of new effective antibiotic drugs is a global health-care priority. However, within the commercial sector, development activity in this area seems to be slow.[14] Why is this? Finding such drugs is not easy – much of the 'low hanging fruit' of the easily found antibiotics has been harvested, and accordingly we need to look harder to find new active substances. That is not cheap. Neither is it cheap to demonstrate to modern standards that these drugs are safe and efficacious. Notwithstanding this, however, one might imagine that, given the potential market, the 'market + patent system' model would incentivise such investment.

Maybe it would, but there are two problems. First, in comparison with chronic conditions, the course of treatment of an effective antibiotic is very short – and with that the opportunity of making profit is reduced. Second, as soon as a truly effective drug is developed, governmental medical systems (keen to avoid the mistakes of the past) will, through prescribing guidance and regulatory means, be keen to restrain use of that drug such that it is preserved for *in extremis* cases. Potential commercial drug developers would likely fail to see a sufficient return on their investment during (and indeed beyond) the

---

[13] Ernst Bäumler *In Search of the Magic Bullet: Great Adventures in Modern Drug Research* (Thames and Hudson. London 1965), 48.

[14] C Lee Ventola, "The Antibiotic Resistance Crisis Part 1: Causes and Threats" (2015) 40(4) Pharmacy & Therapeutics 277; S Ragnar Norrby et al., "Lack of development of new antimicrobial drugs: a potential serious threat to public health" (2005) 5(2) The Lancet Infectious Disease 115.

monopoly period of any patent. In the absence of other bespoke compensatory mechanisms, the patent/market system alone seems to be insufficient to stimulate development in the area. It is also worth noting that there is a potential irony here: un-checked reliance on a market solution, without governmental interference, might well lead to the same mis/over-use of drugs which led us to the development of antibiotic resistance in the first place.

The 'Evergreening' of Patents

That patents are an imprecise instrument in their effect can also be seen when we look to the phenomenon of so-called pharmaceutical patent 'evergreening'.

The crown jewels of pharmaceutical patents are those that cover a new chemical entity (NCE) for a therapeutic purpose. Ideally, such a patent will also cover classes of chemical derivatives of that NCE, thereby preventing competitors from manufacturing and marketing that particular chemical entity (and the derivatives claimed) for a period of 20 years. Twenty years may seem like a long time, but it is often considered to be a relatively short time in which to recoup the investment costs of drug development.

This is mainly because a pharmaceutical company is often unable to sell a product covered by that patent for the entire duration of the patent monopoly. For a good part of that period, the company will be looking to obtain a marketing authorisation for the drug from the relevant regulatory agency. Without such an authorisation, the drug will be unable to be sold. In a good number of sequential industries (notably consumer electronics) there is a vast proliferation of patent applications and a significant degree of patent litigation activity. One might intuitively suppose that this is a reflection of the importance of patents in supporting innovation in this field. On the other hand, the drug company will often wish to file its patent for the NCE as early as possible to avoid its work being rendered irrelevant by the research activity (and patent filing) of others. The patent systems of most countries recognise this problem and will permit a drug company to obtain a (limited) extension of the monopoly period for the authorised drug for up to five years to take account of the time taken to obtain marketing authorisation.[15] The protection provided by this extension, however, will be limited to the NCE for which the authorisation was received rather than covering all the chemical entities claimed within the patent.

However, once a pharmaceutical product has established a market presence, every week that it can remain on the market without effective competition will ensure a greater return for the manufacturer. That is a great deal to give up and, accordingly, there is a significant drive for the manufacturer to restrict effective competition for as long as possible.

---

[15] See, for example, the European Union Supplementary Protection Certificate provided under Regulation (EC) 469/2009.

How would you go about this? You might reckon that there are more elements to a pharmaceutical product than the NCE alone and start to think which of these elements might be independently protectable. You might think about the formulation of the drug (whether a liquid, a tablet, a topical cream, pessary, or suppository) and how through changes to the formulation you might enhance the product's stability or biological deliverability or both. You might look at the dosage regime and, through that, at ways to maximise efficacy and minimise side effects. You might think of the process of manufacture and of ways in which that might be made more efficient or more reliable. You might look at the NCE itself and, if it is a mixture of chemical optical isomers, look to determine whether the selection of one particular optical isomer can enhance efficacy and safety of the product. Of course, all these (and more) tactics are employed by pharmaceutical companies that look to build a series of rings of 'secondary' patent protection around the original product.[16] Commonly, patents in relation to such secondary technology are filed towards the end of the period of monopoly protection of the NCE.

Views in relation to this so-called patent 'evergreening' are understandably mixed. If one believes that the grant of a monopoly under a patent to the use of an NCE (and any relevant patent term extension) is sufficient reward for the development the NCE, then one might also believe that any further attempt to extend a *de facto* (if not a *de jure*) monopoly which denies patients cheaper access to the NCE could be considered unjustified. On the other hand, new delivery systems, formulations, dosage regimens and the like require considerable time, effort and money to develop and you may perhaps consider that that effort should be rewarded.

The position is often complex, and, for this author, needs to be examined on a case-by-case basis. In particular, it should be noted that such secondary patents do not act as a *de jure* restriction to the access to the NCE *per se* but act to keep the originator 'ahead of the game' and make life difficult, but not impossible, for generic competitors.

Perhaps then, the key consideration should be to what extent the 'rings' of secondary patents act as an effective *de facto* restriction to keep the NCE away from competitors and patients. For example, a patent covering a process of manufacture of the NCE would not necessarily keep it away from use in patients, provided that there were alternative methods to make the compound. Here, again, we see a delicate (and difficult-to-resolve) balance of utilities between encouragement of innovation and the direct impact on patients.

---

[16] For problems with this, see Graham Dutfield "Healthcare Innovation, Personalisation and the Patent System: Where is the public interest?" in Harikesh Singh, Alok Jha and Chetan Keswani (eds) *Intellectual Property Issues in Biotechnology* (CABI Wallingford Oxfordshire, 2016) 165, 173.

DEBATE: PATENTEES SHOULD BE FREE TO FULLY EXERCISE THEIR MONOPOLY RIGHTS

It is the role of a patent attorney to convert an inventor's concept into a valid, enforceable patent, a process that requires a process of iterative negotiation with examiners in patent offices. Some applications will fail, others succeed. In a process reliant on human judgment, errors will be made, but one's overall chance of success as a patent applicant might be thought to be enhanced with the number of applications made: I might take the view that the more applications I launch at a patent office the more applications will have a chance of being granted as a valid patent (even if some of my applications are of questionable quality).

This probabilistic (and entirely rational) 'numbers game' strategy has metamorphosed over time as applicants found that the greater number of pending applications and granted patents they had, the greater overall exclusive (and deterrent) affect there was on competitors. The possession of large portfolios of patents was also found to be useful when engaging in patent litigation settlement and cross-licensing deals – the more patents one can present for the negotiation 'pot', the better. The rational applicant now found that they had to file an even greater number of applications (often of marginal individual value) to keep pace with their competitors, creating, in some industry sectors, something of a patent 'arms race'. Indeed, the aggregation of a patent 'armoury' can often be the motivation for merger-and-acquisition activity. It has been suggested that the motivation behind Google's $12.5 billion acquisition of Motorola Mobility in 2012 was (in part) driven by Google's desire to enhance its patent portfolio by the addition of Motorola's 17,000 existing patents and pending patent applications.[17]

A stage is eventually reached where, even if a party wanted to step off the strategic patenting treadmill, they fear it would be disadvantageous to be the first of their peers to do so. Accordingly, as a new technical area develops, a 'thicket' of patents is rapidly built up such that it becomes difficult to determine whether there is any clear intellectual space in which to operate and where (owing to overlapping and contiguous patent claims) no single party may, in fact, be able to act freely.[18] Such a thicket may operate to cement the dominance of larger entities that have the resources to conduct efficacious patent searching, the market power to conduct fruitful cross-licensing negotiations, and the skill-set to engage in further strategic patenting to back up future negotiations.[19]

---

[17] Tom Nicholas "Are Patents Creative or Destructive?" Harvard Business School Working Paper (2013), 19. https://www.hbs.edu/faculty/Publication%20Files/14-036_88022f59-a293-4a6f-b643-b205304bce91.pdf (Accessed March 2019).

[18] Carl Shapiro, "Navigating the Patent Thicket: Cross Licenses, Patent Pools, and Standard Setting" (2000) 1 Innovation Policy and the Economy 119.

[19] Ian Ayres and Gideon Parchomovsky, "Tradable Patent Rights" (2007) 60 Stan. L. Rev. 863 (December 2007).

The inevitability of this process has been recognised by Jacob:

'... every patentee of a major invention is likely to come up with improvements and alleged improvements to his invention...'; and

'... it is in the nature of the patent system itself that [patent thickets] should happen and it has always happened'.[20]

There is little reason to believe that there is any industry area that is inherently immune to thicket development, but classic examples include the US 'sewing machine war' of the 1850s (see Box 4.2), the US patent thicket surrounding the invention of powered flight in the early 1900s[21], and the global smartphone patent thicket that has grown from the early 2000s to today.[22]

Box 4.2 The Sewing Machine Wars – The 'First Patent Thicket'[23]

The phenomenon of the patent 'thicket' is not new, and their creation under current patent systems seems inevitable where there is a major technology advance in a commercially important sector that has a number of powerful market actors. Those circumstances are well illustrated in the case of what has been called the first patent thicket.

In 1846, Elias Howe received US Patent 4750 for a machine to increase the speed and efficiency of clothes manufacture. His 'sewing machine' could sew seven times faster than an experienced seamstress. However, it was originally seen as an expensive curiosity, of limited utility, and Howe had difficulty finding people who would invest in manufacturing his machine. After an unsuccessful marketing trip to the UK, Howe returned to the US to find that versions of his machine were being made and used by unauthorised parties. Howe was not himself a manufacturer but embarked on a patent enforcement campaign of threatening unauthorised users with litigation. This tactic gained a large number of licensees under his patent – earning himself retrospective infamy as America's first patent 'troll'. Howe's policy eventually met opposition in 1854 in the form of Isaac Merritt Singer, who sought to invalidate Howe's patent on the basis of lack of novelty and inventive step. In particular, Singer sought to demonstrate that the invention of Howe's particular combination of known mechanical techniques had been anticipated by 10 years by an earlier machine. This claim involved Singer's attempting

---

[20] Sir Robin Jacob "Presentation of the Directorate-General of Competition's Preliminary Report of the Pharma-sector inquiry" (2008).

[21] Herbert A. Johnson "The Wright Patent Wars and Early American Aviation" 69 J. Air L. & Com. 21 (2004).

[22] For a discussion, see Ronald A. Cass "Lessons from the Smartphone Wars: Patent Litigations, Patent Quality, and Software" (2015) 6 Minn. J.L. Sci. & Tech. 1.

[23] Adam Mossoff, "The Rise and Fall of the First American Patent Thicket: The Sewing Machine War of the 1850s (2011) 53 Arizona Law Review 165.

(unsuccessfully) to rebuild the alleged prior art from rusty parts found in an attic.[24] Singer's action eventually failed. However, such was the market impact of Howe's machine that other manufacturers were keen to develop improvements of it and gain patents for those improvements. A thicket of competing patents soon built up, and with it a gathering storm of reciprocal patent infringement suits.

By 1856, a group of three major manufacturers realised the futility of their actions and came together (with Howe) to form the 'Sewing-Machine Combination'. This operated as a patent 'pool' allowing the members reciprocal licences to the key patents within the pool (including Howe's original patent and Singer's improvements) and a cartel threatening non-members with infringement proceedings if they refused to pay licences under the pool patents controlled by the Combination. The number of external licensees was limited to 24 to enhance the commercial desirability of being a licensee. The cartel behaviour of the Combination provoked criticism at the time for stifling innovation and preventing new entrants to the market. The Combination arrangement lasted until 1877 (due to expiry of the key patents) but its demise does not appear to have resulted in a burst of new innovation from non-parties. The reason for this is unclear, but it may be that by then the Combination members had gained a difficult-to-challenge market position. Patent pools are found today – usually in relation to agreed standards that provide for interoperability of devices. Crucially, however, competition laws and authorities (undeveloped in mid-19th-century America) ensure that access to the pool patents is not numerically limited and that licences are provided on fair, reasonable and non-discriminatory (FRAND) terms.[25]

What, however, of new market entrants? Without significant resources, they cannot safely determine whether they have freedom to operate, do not have a patent portfolio to act as leverage in cross-licensing deals and are deterred from entering the market. In this way, the creation of thickets through the strategic mass filing of patent applications of marginal merit could be argued to subvert the incentivisation of innovation argument for the existence of patent rights and indeed represents obvious rent-seeking behaviour by the holders of patent portfolios. However, some might argue that this position is somewhat simplistic in that we do not know what type of innovation is in fact valued by society. Perhaps it does not matter that new entities are excluded from entering a market provided that society, in the end, still gets its progressively cheaper and more awesome electronic 'toys'. This again brings us back to the question of what societal utility we are looking to promote.

However, an important point to note is that (as we will see below) it is likely that strategic patenting and the existence of thickets will deter innovation in those economies in the Global South which are most in need of such stimulus

---

[24] Ruth Brandon, *A Capitalist Romance: Singer and the Sewing Machine* (Lippicott Philadelphia, 1977), 92.

[25] Mathias Dewatripont and Patrick Legros 'Essential' Patents, FRAND Royalties and Technological Standards (2013) 61(4) Journal of Industrial Economics 913.

whilst cementing the advantage of established entities in the Global North behaviour that would appear to represent a still clearer example of rent-seeking on the part of those creating strategic patent armouries.

THE PHENOMENON OF THE TROLL – A NATURAL CONSEQUENCE OF THE MARKET?

The existence of patent thickets shows (if any demonstration was necessary) that policy can result in unintended consequences arising from rational actors acting in their perceived self-interest. The same effect can be seen in the phenomenon of the patent 'troll'. The definition of a troll (less pejoratively known as non-practising or patent enforcement entities or, amongst their apologists, as patent 'traders') is greatly contentious. However, at its core, a troll is an entity that acquires patents and uses them (through actual or threatened litigation) as a mechanism to obtain an income stream from alleged infringers of the acquired patents.[26]

Most commentators recognise that trolls are an inevitable consequence of the market – if one creates a freely tradable right to take action against third parties, then it will naturally follow that entities will acquire the rights to do with them what is inherent within such a right (i.e., to sue, or threaten to sue, people to obtain money). However, apologists for the trolls have gone further. They argue that, by providing a ready market for patents, trolls enhance (through enhanced market liquidity and price-setting) the efficiency of a market in a tradable commodity[27] – being analogous to shareholders in a secondary equity market. Whilst it is not inconceivable that trolls can provide such a market setting function in certain patent markets, it should be noted that their presence in a market may actually serve to distort that market by excluding (through price) potential patent purchasers who may have far less piratical aims.

It would be fair to say that the troll apologists are in the minority – most see the troll phenomenon as having greatly negative effects upon entrepreneurism. Entities are fearful of entering a new field for fear of litigation, so the growth of actors in a market is inhibited, with harmful consequences for competition. The spectre of trolls operating within existing patent thickets becomes particularly concerning to new market entrants. In return, trolls themselves rarely have anything to fear from counter actions as they have no business reliant on patents (other than that of extorting others).

To many, the action of trolls feels inherently wrong. Perhaps it is because they seem not to 'deserve' the patents they employ – more often than not, the troll is not the inventor but has bought the patent it will seek to enforce from

---

[26] Raymond P Niro "Who Is Really Undermining the Patent System – Patent Trolls or Congress?" (2006) 6(2) J. Marshall Rev. Intell. Prop. L. 197.

[27] James F McDonough III, "The Myth of the Patent Troll: An Alternative View of the Function of Patent Dealers in an Idea Economy" (2007) 56 Emory Law Journal 189.

a third party. In contrast, their victims are often perceived to be entities seeking to make money through 'legitimate' entrepreneurialism. This understandable gut reaction is, however, rather simplistic. Whilst it is true that the activities of trolls certainly can have a 'localised' anti-innovation effect and litigation costs accrued fighting trolls can result in the diversion of funds away from innovative activity, it is less clear whether the existence of trolls has a broader and fundamental impact on the incentive to innovate justification for patents *as a whole*. Trolls have to buy their patents from someone, so arguably inventor patentees are, in fact, compensated within the system. Trolls are also remarkably policy-sensitive – notably to changes in litigation cost regimes[28] – so are arguably less of an *inherent* problem than, say, strategic patenting activity and the growth of thickets within a particular technology area.

DEBATE: THE IMPOSITION OF A PATENT SYSTEM UPON THE GLOBAL SOUTH IS NEW COLONIALISM

The second head of the societal problems of patents identified in this chapter is the adoption of strong patent rights within the Global South.

Ha-Joon Chang[29] has argued that the story that the wealth of the Western industrial powers was built upon free trade is a myth. For Chang, many states (Britain and the US in particular) built their economies in the nineteenth and twentieth centuries on the back of protectionism that allowed their infant industrial sector to flourish in the absence of outside competition and though free trade enforced on weaker entities. On occasion, this protectionism extended to preventing colonies from developing industry in competition with their colonial Motherland. Such protectionism was allied to weak or one-sided IP regimes (or both) which allowed the copying of overseas ideas whilst protecting 'home-grown' innovation. Only once domestic industry was established were stronger IP regimes put in place.

May[30] has argued that, notwithstanding what Western developed countries did during their own development, those countries have, through various economic and political pressures, sought through the Trade-Related Aspects of Intellectual Property Rights (TRIPS) agreement to ensure that the Global South follows a neoliberal IP model in which all nations sign up to a minimum standard of IP (including strong patent rights). See Box 4.3.

---

[28] Aria Sodouri "Defeating Trolls: The impact of Octane and Highmark on Patent Trolls" (2015) 35 Loy. L.A. Ent. L. Rev. 319.

[29] Ha-Joon Chang, *Kicking Away the Ladder: Development Strategy in Historical Perspective*. London: (Anthem Press, London 2002); Ha-Joon Chang, "Intellectual Property Rights and Economic Development: Historical Lessons and Emerging Issues" (2001) 2(2) Journal of Human Development 287.

[30] Christopher May, "The hypocrisy of forgetfulness: The contemporary significance of early innovations in intellectual property" (2007) 14 Review of International Political Economy 1.

Box 4.3 TRIPS

The Agreement on Trade-Related Aspects of Intellectual Property Rights (TRIPS) was agreed in 1994 as part of the Uruguay Round of the General Agreement on Tariffs and Trade negotiations. TRIPS seeks to ensure that all signatories to the World Trade Organization (WTO) put in place minimum IP standards. Amongst the provisions of TRIPS are requirements that:

> patents shall be available for any inventions, whether products or processes, in all fields of technology, provided that they are new, involve an inventive step and are capable of industrial application;

and that

> patents shall be available and patent rights enjoyable without discrimination as to the place of invention, the field of technology and whether products are imported or locally produced.[31]

Despite the many concerns of parties in the Global South, they were persuaded that they needed to accept the 'TRIPS package' as an indivisible element of the whole of the WTO system.[32] Bargaining inequalities have often meant that subsequent regional and bilateral trade arrangements have resulted in the imposition of stronger IP rights than even those seen under TRIPS – an effect referred to by Drahos as 'the global ratchet' for IP rights.[33]

The requirement that patents need to be respected without discrimination 'as to the place of invention, the field of technology and whether products are imported or locally produced' is crucial in its impact – arguably, developing nations cannot on the whole 'protect' themselves from Western-originating patents. Why is this a problem? Surely, patents are there to encourage innovation and developing nations need home-grown innovation to grow their economies? The problem is that patents tend to give the greatest support to those that have an effective innovation infrastructure already in place.

As we have seen with the effect of strategic patenting and thicketing, patents can act effectively against new market entrants – cementing the existing *status quo*. In this respect, countries in the Global South (many with very early-stage innovation infrastructure) can be seen as new entrants into the global 'market'.

---

[31] TRIPS Article 27.

[32] Duncan Matthews *Globalising intellectual property rights: the TRIPS Agreement.* (Routledge London 2002).

[33] Peter Drahos *The global ratchet for intellectual property rights: why it fails as policy and what should be done about it.* (2003) New York: Open Society Institute. https://www.anu.edu.au/fellows/pdrahos/reports/pdfs/2003globalipratchet.pdf (Accessed January 2020).

'Biopiracy'

The imbalance of market and IP-based power can also be seen in the cases where more sophisticated foreign entities appropriate local and indigenous knowledge by 'translating' that knowledge into scientific understanding and obtaining a patent for it.[34] A large number of currently prescribed drugs have had their origin in chemical compounds found in the plants used by indigenous peoples in their traditional medicine systems.[35] Indigenous knowledge can play a vital role in determining which plants can have beneficial medicinal effects. However, such knowledge is usually held within indigenous knowledge systems (often mixed in with other societal, cultural and religious elements) which are alien to Western scientific discourse. Historically, Western science has treated indigenous therapeutic knowledge as a 'public good', and the originators of such knowledge as being undeserving of reward for its subsequent use. In addition, the trans-generational nature of such knowledge (in which the originators are lost to history) renders the knowledge as being inherently incapable of patent protection for lack of novelty.[36] In marked contrast, products 'inspired' by traditional knowledge – for example, the development of a drug from the chemical identified by scientists as being responsible for the beneficial effect understood from the traditional knowledge – are often capable of being patented. Attempts to prevent the misappropriation of indigenous knowledge are the subject of a significant international effort.[37]

The Impact on Public Health

Initial fears following the introduction of TRIPS particularly concerned the access by patients in the Global South to medicines (restricted by the price created by newly introduced patent monopolies) – most crucially access to anti-HIV drugs in sub-Saharan Africa. These developing nation concerns were addressed through the November 2001 Doha 'Declaration on the TRIPS Agreement and Public Health', which served to provide certain 'flexibilities' to address public health problems.[38] These flexibilities are allowable under Articles

---

[34] Graham Dutfield, "A critical analysis of the debate on traditional knowledge, drug discovery and patent-based biopiracy" (2011) 33(4) EIPR 238.

[35] Londa Schiebinger, *Plants and Empire, Colonial Bioprospecting in the Atlantic World* (Harvard University Press 2004); Michael J Balick and Paul A Cox, *Plants, People, and Culture: The Science of Ethnobotany* (Scientific American Library 1997).

[36] Graham Dutfield, *Intellectual Property Rights, Biogenetic Resources and Traditional Knowledge* (Earthscan Publications, London and Sterling, VA 2004), 101.

[37] See Frantzeska Papadopoulou, *The Protection of Traditional Knowledge on Genetic Resources* (Edward Elgar, Cheltenham 2018); Peter S. Harrison "Grasping Frankenstein's Monster: Uncertainty in the Downstream Scope of the Nagoya Protocol" [2019] 1 IPQ 61.

[38] Dianne Nicol and Olasupo Owoeye, "Using TRIPS flexibilities to facilitate access to medicines" (2013) 91 Bulletin of the World Health Organization 533.

30 and 31 of TRIPS which establish that WTO member states may, in the event of a 'national emergency or other circumstances of extreme urgency', unilaterally provide limited exceptions to the exclusive rights conferred by a patent – essentially allowing member states to determine the terms of a compulsory licence under a patent. Article 5 of the Doha Declaration confirms that such compulsory licences to access pharmaceutical patents can be granted in the event of public health crises and that such crises can include epidemics related to human HIV infection, tuberculosis, malaria and other diseases. Of course, what one person describes as a 'crisis' can look to others like a long-term, chronic, situation. There are strong incentives on governments in the Global South to declare almost constant and broad 'states of emergency' in the face of long-standing problems, with the potential for development of concomitant stresses within the WTO system.

It is worth noting that in their funding of research into tropical diseases, the Bill & Melinda Gates Foundation have been cognisant of the problems inherent in the existence of pharmaceutical patents in the Global South. Whilst being broadly supportive of the existence of patents generally, they are, through their 'Global Access' policy, insistent that grantees of their funding:

> commit to making the products and information generated by foundation funding widely available at an affordable price, in sufficient volume, at a level of quality, and in a time frame that benefits the people we're trying to help.[39]

This policy extends to collaborations with for-profit entities that are permitted to market products developed with Foundation funding at a profit in the developed world, provided that Global Access conditions apply in relation to those territories in which the relevant disease is endemic.

The public health concerns identified here are important, but owing to their high profile, they have tended to overshadow the broader systemic concern that innovation and the growth of commerce in developing nations have been stifled by the introduction of a patent system that gives advantage to existing innovators in the North.

Conclusions: Do Patents Have Social Value?

We have seen that patents are imprecise in their effect. The existence of a patent system is intended to create an environment in which innovation is encouraged and, through such innovation, the common weal is enhanced. However, as we have seen, there is an inherent rule-utilitarian trade-off here: society overall will benefit, even though some elements of society – namely those who cannot afford new products – will be temporarily disadvantaged. One might argue that all that is potentially being denied is something that would not have existed but for the patented invention. However, that trade-off becomes more difficult to

---

[39] http://globalaccess.gatesfoundation.org/ (Accessed March 2019).

accept when what is being 'temporarily' denied is a life-saving medicine. The 'trade-off' also becomes more difficult to accept when monopolists behave in ways – such as strategic patenting and the creation of patent thickets – that arguably undermine the reason for the existence of the rights in the first place. We have also seen that a reliance on a 'market + patents' model (in which development decisions are directed by the likelihood of making a profit) can result in investment decisions that are not always ideal for broader society. A very acute example is the relative failure of the pharmaceutical industry to develop new antibiotic drugs and drugs for the treatment of tropical and orphan diseases.

Patents have, from their very beginnings in mediæval Europe, often been used to secure narrow national technological and economic advantage.[40] Arguably little has changed. Certainly, in the imposition of a 'strong' patent system on the Global South through TRIPS, the negotiators from the Global North could be said to be following in the footsteps of their mediæval ancestors. We have seen that, dressed up as the creation of a beneficial global environment for innovation, this system likely acts to the advantage of the Global North at the expense of the Global South – a system that the infant economies of the industrial revolution did not impose upon themselves.

One can clearly engage in significant debate over whether patents are inherently good or evil. We have seen, however, that they are undoubtedly powerful. They are powerful in the hands of individual right holders and as a policy tools for government and super-governmental bodies. They cannot be ignored, nor can they be seen in isolation from other normative debates. Patent policy should be a crucial aspect of any effort to create fairer societies on a domestic and (in particular) a global scale. However, the effect of changes in patent law can be hard to predict and, as might be expected of such a powerful right, there are many opportunities for unintended consequences. Such effects, however, may be better understood the better one appreciates the inherent conflict of rights and the paradoxes at the heart of using patents to incentivise innovation.

Further Reading

H. J. Chang, 'Intellectual Property Rights and Economic Development: Historical Lessons and Emerging Issues' (2001) 2(2) *Journal of Human Development* 287.

M. Fisher, 'Classical Economics and Philosophy of the Patent System' (2005) 1 *Intellectual Property Quarterly* 5.

D. Matthews, *Globalising Intellectual Property Rights: The TRIPS Agreement* (Routledge; London, 2002).

---

[40] See, for example, the Statute of Venice of 1474. Mikulas Teich and Roy Porter *The Industrial Revolution in National Context: Europe and the USA* (Cambridge University Press, Cambridge 1996), 160.

C. May, 'The Hypocrisy of Forgetfulness: The Contemporary Significance of Early Innovations in Intellectual Property' (2007) 14 *Review of International Political Economy* 1.

J. F. McDonough III, 'The Myth of the Patent Troll: An Alternative View of the Function of Patent Dealers in an Idea Economy' (2007) 56 *Emory Law Journal* 189.

R. P. Merges, *Justifying Intellectual Property* (Harvard University Press; Cambridge, MA, 2011).

T. Nicholas, 'Are Patents Creative or Destructive?' Harvard Business School Working Paper (2013), 19 (https://www.hbs.edu/faculty/Publication%20Files/14-036_880 22f59-a293-4a6f-b643-b205304bce91.pdf).

D. Nicol and O. Owoeye, 'Using TRIPS Flexibilities to Facilitate Access to Medicines' (2013) 91 *Bulletin of the World Health Organization* 533.

C. Shapiro, 'Navigating the Patent Thicket: Cross Licenses, Patent Pools, and Standard Setting' (2000) 1 *Innovation Policy and the Economy* 119.

C. L. Ventola, 'The Antibiotic Resistance Crisis Part 1: Causes and Threats' (2015) 40(4) *Pharmacy & Therapeutics* 277.

CHAPTER 5

Is Trade Mark Law Fit for Purpose?

Robert Burrell

INTRODUCTION

For many intellectual property (IP) scholars, trade mark law can be divided into two parts: the part that needs to be reformed and the part that needs to be abolished. The part that needs to be reformed is the traditional, consumer-focused element of trade mark law. Although there is general acceptance that signs and symbols that denote the trade origin of goods and services deserve some degree of legal protection, there is also now widespread concern that trade mark law has become misshapen. The problems are manifold but include the fact that bars to registrability have been set too low; tribunals routinely apply the likelihood of confusion test too broadly; the notion of 'confusion' has been expanded in ways that are problematic; the circumstances in which we are prepared to tolerate some risk of confusion have not been properly articulated; defensive doctrines within trade mark law remain underdeveloped; mechanisms for detecting marks that should be removed from the register are ineffective; and remedies for trade mark infringement have become draconian. This long list of problems now needs to be viewed alongside recent scholarship that is challenging two of the largely unspoken assumptions on which the consumer-focused branch of trade mark law rests: first, that the supply of traditional trade marks such as words and devices is effectively infinite and, second, that the law's only concern is to increase the supply of reliable information in the marketplace.

The part of trade mark law that many argue should be abolished is the brand-focused element. Over recent decades, trade mark law has expanded to allow owners to protect their marks against so-called 'dilution'. These harms are often described as not requiring any confusion as to origin, instead going to such things as impairing the communicative power of the mark ('blurring') and damaging its reputation ('tarnishment'). This aspect of trade mark law has attracted a significant degree of scholarly attention, but the more dilution is examined the less sense it seems to make. Critics have pointed out that dilution has had a protean quality that means it ought to be approached with care; that elements of the current law are incoherent; that psychological studies fail to support the need for this branch of trade mark law; that the economic case for anti-dilution protection is weak; that the moral case is no stronger; that such protection may have a chilling effect on free speech; and that such protection fits very uncomfortably with the mechanics of trade mark registration.

The two sets of problems identified above continue to be refined and developed, but the sense that modern trade mark laws suffer from serious defects is now widely accepted in the academic trade mark community. There is also the sense that these defects are compounded by aggressive brand management strategies that see teams of lawyers generating clouds of cease and desist letters in cases of doubtful merit. Threats actions and other procedural mechanisms designed to prevent spurious claims are proving inadequate to counter these abuses. There also appears to be a reluctance to pull other levers (such as using professional codes of conduct) to discourage misuse of the trade mark system.

The above reads like a long and gloomy list of problems. There are, however, signs that judges and policymakers are beginning to listen to concerns, and in some areas of trade mark law and practice there are signs of progress. This is obviously welcome. But towards the end of this chapter, I want to suggest that there may be another previously undiagnosed problem with the trade mark system. This problem does not flow from a defect in the legal rules, nor even from how these rules can be deliberately misused. Rather it flows from the way decisions about trade marks become embedded in the processes and work practices of brand owners, law firms and trade mark offices. The suggestion is that these elements of the trade mark system, which are only just beginning to attract attention from trade mark scholars, also contribute to the problem of overreach. If this diagnosis is correct, we may need to develop additional strategies if we are to tackle the full range of problems that beset the trade mark system.

WHY DO WE PROTECT TRADE MARKS?

For the uninitiated, it may be far from obvious that trade mark law warrants a place in a volume that provides critical perspectives on commercial law. On the contrary, when trade mark law is first encountered, much of what it is seeking to achieve makes intuitive sense. As consumers, we understand that every time we buy, say, a pair of 'Nike' running shoes, these shoes come from a particular trade source – that is, from a particular company that uses the word 'Nike' and associated symbols such as the 'Swoosh' so that consumers can distinguish its products from those of its competitors. Under modern market conditions, this does not so much mean that the products come from a particular factory or workshop – the manufacturing process may well be entirely outsourced – but rather that there is a company that exercises ultimate control over the goods that bear the mark.

Over time, trade marks may come to be associated with particular ideas and attributes. For example, we may come to associate Nike with sporting prowess and associated values such as discipline, hard work and self-motivation. These attributes are often the thing that prompts consumers to return to buy the company's products in the future. Consumers want to 'access brands'; they want to associate themselves with what the brand 'means'. Consequently, it is often brand meaning that produces consumer loyalty and hence brand value. In commercial terms, brand loyalty is essential for success. It is widely accepted that for many companies their brands are their most important asset. It is therefore hardly surprising that brand owners are keen that trade mark law be reshaped to protect brand value (of which more below). However, there can be no question that trade marks remain, at their core, 'badges of origin'. Consider, for example, the words TIFFANY & CO and '24-carat'. Both function as indications of quality in relation to jewellery, but they do so in very different ways. We understand that in the former case the 'guarantee' of quality results from the fact that the goods originate from a particular trade source that has a reputation for producing high-end goods. Similarly, if we are given cause to wonder about whether goods are real or fake, we are directing our attention to whether goods have a particular commercial provenance. We understand that goods can be fake but of the same quality. Thus, although trade marks may convey a range of messages and meanings, it is their function as an indication of trade source that remains central. This continues to be how the essential function of trade marks is conceptualised.

Moreover, it is not difficult to find convincing justifications for preventing third parties from interfering with the functioning of trade marks as guarantees of commercial origin. By providing a reliable indication of source, trade marks allow consumers to identify goods that they tried previously, such that they can steer their purchases towards goods that they like and away from goods that they want to avoid. Consequently, it is often said that trade marks promote market efficiency by reducing consumer 'search costs': consumers can find what they want quickly and easily. It seems that most of us have had the experience of shopping on 'autopilot', of being in a supermarket while we are preoccupied with something else (talking on the phone, keeping children away from the confectionery aisle, or writing an essay or lecture in our heads) and yet find that we have managed to procure most of the items we wanted. The ability of trade marks to convey the 'I am what you are looking for' message so efficiently is central to our being able to rely on unconscious information processing when shopping for everyday items. For more expensive goods, of course, we do not rely (and do not want others to rely) on unconscious decision-making, but trade marks can still allow us to direct our choices towards a subset of the full range of products on offer.

The ability of trade marks to connect consumers with the 'same' goods over time is connected to the other important economic function that trade marks are said to perform, namely that they provide traders with incentives to compete on grounds other than price. To understand this argument, imagine a world without trade mark protection. In such a world, it would be impossible for companies to develop a reputation for producing high-end goods. As soon as a trader developed such a reputation, competitors could step in and trade off this reputation by branding their goods in the same way while undercutting the first trader on quality and price. It is therefore said that trade marks provide an incentive for traders to develop products with particularly desirable characteristics and to ensure that these characteristics remain stable over time. Indeed, it is probably true to say that in order for a market economy to function in anything like the fashion with which we are familiar, there is an irreducible core of trade mark protection that has to be secured by the State.

THE EXPANSION OF TRADE MARK SUBJECT MATTER

The question is therefore not whether trade mark protection can be justified, but rather how is it that a branch of the law that is so easy to justify has become so controversial? The answer lies in the manner in which trade mark law has been recast by a combination of legislative reform, judicial decisions and changes in administrative practice. Take, for example, issues of registrability. Many countries amended their trade mark law in the decade following the conclusion of the 1994 TRIPS (Trade-Related Aspects of Intellectual Property Rights) Agreement. One common reform was to expand the range of signs that could be registered as trade marks. Most importantly, there was a move towards allowing the registration of three-dimensional shapes. This expansion of trade mark subject matter was justified on the basis that there are some shapes that serve to indicate trade source, the Coca-Cola contour bottle being the most famous example. However, this reform also creates new and significant competition concerns in that it risks giving traders a potentially perpetual monopoly over product design and features of packaging. Most countries tried to offset this risk by introducing accompanying provisions that exclude from registrability shapes that perform a technical function or that offer significant market advantage in other ways. But ultimately the law has still been extended to include a potentially problematic form of subject matter. The question of whether this reform was really necessary, given that there are probably only a handful of shapes that can be said convincingly to serve a trade mark function, has never been reopened by policymakers.

The expansion of trade mark subject matter is an obviously significant and controversial change. In terms of the day-to-day operation of the trade mark system, however, a more important development has been the lowering of the general bars to registrability. Take the requirement that a trade mark be 'distinctive'. This requirement ensures that trade mark owners cannot secure a monopoly over, amongst other things, common descriptive and laudatory words, these being words that other traders have a legitimate need to use when describing their goods and services. But the distinctiveness requirement has been lowered in various ways. In Europe, for example, we find cases that suggest that a trade mark can be distinctive if it contains a 'syntactically unusual juxtaposition' of words. Consequently, the words BABY-DRY were held to be inherently distinctive for disposable nappies. The potential impact on traders who might want to use a phrase such as 'these nappies will keep your baby dry' was disregarded.[1] In Australia, there has been significant relaxation of the rules governing the registration of foreign words, with the result that CINQUE STELLE, Italian for 'five stars', was held to be inherently distinctive for coffee.[2] This was despite the presence of a sizeable Italian community in Australia that has traditionally been heavily involved in the coffee industry. To be clear, these examples are not intended to suggest that the cases have run in a single direction or that other decisions have not taken a robust position in relation to distinctiveness. The overall pattern is nevertheless clear, namely that there has been an overall lowering of the distinctiveness bar in the post-TRIPS period.

A further example of the relaxation of registrability requirements is the treatment of marks that previously would have been rejected on the grounds that they are contrary to public policy as being scandalous or immoral. In Commonwealth countries, these types of exclusion have a long history, having appeared in the first British statute dealing with trade mark registration.[3] These provisions have been used to prevent the commercial appropriation of terms with significance for particular religious communities, such as HALLELUJAH and MECCA[4], as well as the registration of marks that might offend a significant section of the general public, such as TINY PENIS for clothing.[5] The US has gone furthest in rolling back immorality exclusions; the US Supreme Court held in the *Tam* and *Brunetti* cases that the relevant provisions of the US trade mark statute (generally referred to as the 'Lanham Act') are incompatible with the First Amendment and hence unconstitutional.[6] For some trade mark scholars, this has been a welcome development. In particular, it has opened up the possibility that other elements of modern trade mark law, including protection against dilution, may be open to constitutional challenge. However, the outcome in these cases is a product of the exceptional nature of First Amendment jurisprudence and is therefore unlikely to have traction elsewhere.[7]

Other jurisdictions have nevertheless travelled in the same direction, largely as a consequence of resistance within trade mark offices to applying scandalous marks provisions in anything other than the most clear-cut cases. Unlike in the

---

[1] Cf. D. , 'About Kinetic® Watches, Easy Banking and Nappies that Keep a Baby Dry: a review of recent European case law on absolute grounds for refusing to register trade marks' [2002] IPQ 131.

[2] *Cantarella Bros Pty Ltd v Modena Trading Pty Ltd* [2014] HCA 48.

[3] *Trade Marks Registration Act* 1875, s. 6.

[4] *Hallelujah Trade Mark* [1976] RPC 605; *Mecca Trade Mark* (1955) 25 AOJP 938, respectively.

[5] *Ghazilian's Trade Mark Appn* [2002] RPC 33.

[6] *Matal v Tam* (2017) 137 S Ct 1744; *Iancu v Brunetti* (2019) 588 U. S. __.

[7] See J. Griffiths, 'Is there a Right to an Immoral Trade Mark?' in P. Torremans (ed.), *Intellectual Property and Human Rights* (Kluwer Law International, 2008).

US, therefore, these developments do not offer a platform for positive reform in other elements of trade mark doctrine. Some commentators would no doubt still welcome this trend, and it must be admitted that at first sight there is something strange about provisions that prevent the registration of certain words and images as trade marks on the ground that they are 'scandalous' but leave those signs free for use in trade. Scandalous marks provisions do, however, provide a way of the state refusing to sanction the use of terms that are likely to cause significant offence, without taking the more draconian step of imposing an outright ban. Moreover, these provisions signal that the trade mark system respects values other than market efficiency, and this author at least struggles to see how the world is a better place for allowing FUCT and KÜNT to be registered as trade marks.[8]

THE EXPANSION OF RIGHTS AND REMEDIES

Moving away from registration to questions of enforcement, the overall pattern has been one of the gradual strengthening of trade mark rights. It must be remembered that we are not at this point talking about the introduction of protection against dilution. Rather, the focus is on the additional protections that have been afforded to owners within the traditional, consumer-focused, limb of trade mark law. These changes have taken place over a very long time frame, and providing a summary of developments is further complicated by the fact that the pattern of change has varied considerably between jurisdictions.[9] However, one more or less universal change has been the expansion of 'confusion' to include not just cases where consumers might wrongly conflate the trade mark owner and the defendant but also cases where consumers might erroneously assume that the trade mark owner has some sort of licensing relationship with the defendant. In this way, the concept of confusion as to 'trade source' has been extended considerably beyond its original meaning. In Commonwealth countries, this change can be seen as much in passing off cases as in cases involving registered trade marks. One consequence is that celebrities have been given greatly expanded rights to control the use of their name and image. Consequently, whereas in 1977 the band ABBA were unsuccessful in preventing the unauthorised use of their image on T-shirts, by 2013 Rihanna was able to prevent Top Shop from selling unauthorised T-shirts bearing her image.[10]

---

[8] See, respectively, *In re Brunetti* (2017) 125 USPQ2d 1072; *Kuntstreetwear Pty Ltd's Appn* (2007) 73 IPR 438, [39] (but finding that the word KUNT alone was unregistrable as a 'colourable imitation of an obscene English word').

[9] For example, there is considerable variation between jurisdictions in the extent to which so-called 'pre-sale' and 'post-sale' confusion are actionable. These types of harm are not considered further in this chapter, but the move to expand the notion of confusion beyond traditional point-of-sale confusion has also been a significant development, particularly in the US.

[10] *Lyngstad v Anabas Products Ltd* [1977] FSR 62; *Fenty v Arcadia Group Brands Ltd (t/as Topshop)* [2015] EWCA Civ 3, respectively.

The academic community has tended to be supportive of expanding rights to control unauthorised character and personality merchandising and indeed of the expansion of the notion of trade origin (and hence confusion more generally).[11] It is hard to justify allowing defendants to misrepresent that a celebrity has lent his or her endorsement to a product, be that product a chocolate bar, an album of ballroom music or a new radio station.[12] It is also difficult to summon too much sympathy for Top Shop, not least because the company had previously paid Rihanna to act as a brand ambassador. There is, however, real danger in the self-fulfilling and self-reinforcing chain of reasoning that runs as follows: (1) consumers expect merchandise to be licensed and are confused when they encounter unauthorised merchandise; (2) therefore, the law should intervene to restrict the supply of unauthorised merchandise; (3) consumers see only authorised merchandise; (4) consumers expect merchandise to be licensed and are confused when they encounter unauthorised merchandise. Expansion of merchandising rights looks rather different when we think about the impact on established traders who have built businesses selling unofficial merchandise clearly marked as such in the vicinity of music venues. The same is true of traders who have built similar businesses outside football grounds, who find themselves pursued by premier league football clubs with an aggressive approach to policing their registered trade mark rights.[13]

The way in which trade mark rights have been strengthened can also be illustrated by changes in the application of central elements of the test for trade mark infringement. In broad terms, trade mark owners are afforded rights to prevent the use of similar marks on similar goods or services.[14] In recent decades, notions of 'similarity' have been stretched and expanded. This is most obviously true in the case of word marks, such that we now find cases where MYSTERY and MIXERY, and WACKOS and DOGS GO WACKO FOR SCHMACKOS, have been held to be similar.[15] In cases involving devices or compound word and device marks there has been the same tendency to apply the similarity test broadly with the result, for example, that a frontal view of a buffalo skull above the word 'Carabao' was held to be similar to an image in

---

[11] But see M. Lemley and M. Mckenna, 'Irrelevant Confusion' (2010) 62 *Stanford Law Review* 413.

[12] Cf. *Tolley v JS Fry and Sons Ltd* [1931] AC 333; *Radio Corp Pty Ltd v Henderson* [1960] NSWR 279; *Irvine v Talksport Ltd* [2003] EWCA Civ 423, respectively.

[13] Cf. *Arsenal Football Club Plc v Reed* [2003] RPC 710.

[14] In most jurisdictions, there is a requirement that these similarities result in confusion. Confusion is not, however, a free-floating inquiry. Rather, it colours how the assessments of similarity of marks and similarity of goods are undertaken: R. Burrell and K. Weatherall, 'Towards a New Relationship between Trade Mark Law and Psychology' (2018) 71 *Current Legal Problems* (forthcoming).

[15] *Mystery Drinks* [2003] ECR II-43; *Effem Foods Pty Ltd v Wandella Pet Foods Pty Ltd* [2006] FCA 767, respectively.

profile of two bulls locking horns beneath the words 'Red Bull'.[16] If cases involving devices and compound marks less obviously represent a departure from long-standing practice, this is only because some jurisdictions have long taken a remarkably expansive view of the scope of protection that should be given to such marks.[17]

As regards similarity of goods and services, it has been held in the EU that the assessment is to be made in light of the fame of the senior mark, as part of the 'global appreciation inquiry'.[18] In other words, the more famous the earlier mark, the easier it will be to demonstrate infringement, and a consequence is that a determination that the goods or services are 'similar' no longer functions as a threshold inquiry. Australia, in contrast, has not gone down this route – a finding that the goods are similar remains a threshold matter – but nevertheless we find the similarity of goods and services inquiry being applied more broadly, with the consequence, for example, that it has been indicated that motor insurance services and repair inspection services are probably now to be regarded as similar.[19]

The strengthening of trade mark rights has put considerable additional pressure on defensive doctrines within trade mark law. A defensive doctrine in this context means either an express defence or some other element of trade mark law that serves to excuse liability despite there being a *prima facie* case of infringement. The difficulty is that in some jurisdictions defensive doctrines remain woefully underdeveloped. This is particularly true in Europe, where a limited range of express defences cover narrowly defined forms of third-party use. For example, European trade mark law contains a defence to allow for use of a mark in comparative advertising. This defence, however, has been read narrowly and is available only to the extent that the defendant has complied with the restrictive requirements of the comparative advertising directive.[20] Consequently, the defence applies only where the advertisement 'objectively compares one or more material, relevant, verifiable and representative features' of goods or services, such that more allusive or playful forms of comparative advertising are outside the scope of what is permissible. For example, it would not be possible in Europe to show the pizza box of a rival being filled with

---

[16] *Carabao Tawandang Co Ltd v Red Bull GMBH*, HC Wellington CIV-2005-485-1975, 31 August 2006 and see *Red Bull GmbH v Carabao Tawandang Co. Ltd* [2006] ATMO 60 (successful opposition brought by Red Bull in Australia against the trade mark 'Red Carabao' with the same device).

[17] See, e.g., *Jafferjee v Scarlett* (1937) 57 CLR 115 (picture of two runners crossing a finishing line held to be similar to an image of an athlete throwing a javelin).

[18] *Canon Kabushiki Kaisha v Metro-Goldwyn-Mayer Inc* [1998] ECR I-5507, [24].

[19] *Australian Associated Motor Insurers Ltd v Australian Automotive Motor Inspection Centre Pty Ltd* [2003] FCA 1088.

[20] Directive 2006/114/EC concerning misleading and comparative advertising [2006] OJ L376/21, Art 4.

money and loaded onto a plane bound for the US as a way of making a mildly humorous point about the destination of corporate profits.[21]

The limited scope of defences to trade mark infringement under European law has also meant that defendants have had to look elsewhere to justify use of trade marks in keyword advertising. The practice of keyword advertising has arisen as a result of some search engines, particularly Google, selling 'keywords' consisting of trade marked words to third parties, including competitors of the trade mark owner. The consequence of this practice is that searches using keywords will bring up advertisements in the form of sponsored links to websites operated by those third parties. Often, these will consist of a hyperlinked title, a URL, and a brief description of the advertiser's website. Keyword advertising can play an important role in drawing attention to competing goods and services but also to alternative suppliers of the original product (that may be offered at a lower price or on better terms). Keyword advertisements thus have the capacity to enhance consumer decision-making. The Court of Justice of the European Union (CJEU) has recognised that many forms of keyword advertising ought to be permissible and has operationalised this view by building on suggestions in its earlier case law that unauthorised uses of a sign that are not 'liable to affect one of the functions of the mark' cannot constitute an infringement. Consequently, in *Google France*,[22] the CJEU indicated that an advertiser who paid to use another's mark to ensure that its own advertisements were prioritised on search result pages would not, by this action alone, harm any of the functions of a mark.

However, even taking the CJEU's development of functions analysis into account, there remain significant gaps in the protections afforded to defendants. Indeed, there is a danger that particular uses become fetishised. There is a danger that we privilege uses like keyword advertising and trade mark parodies that attract a good deal of attention from academics and other critical commentators, but that these are mere illustrations of types of use that are unlikely to cause consumer confusion. To illustrate, consider the position in the EU, where after *Google France* it is clear that many uses by a trader of a competitor's trade mark in a keyword advertisement are unobjectionable. However, the CJEU has also told us that use of trade marks in product comparison lists (that provide valuable information but do not fall within the definition of comparative advertising) may be infringing.[23] The highly publicised keyword advertising problem gets addressed, but much of the rest of the system remains unsatisfactory.

Given that rights have been extended in ways that are problematic and defensive doctrines remain underdeveloped, there is good reason to be concerned about another expansion to trade mark law: the strengthening of

---

[21] Cf. *Thompson v Eagle Boys Dial-A-Pizza Australia Pty Ltd* [2001] FCA 741.

[22] *Google France SARL v Louis Vuitton Malletier* [2010] ECR I-2417.

[23] *L'Oréal v Bellure* [2009] ECR I-5185.

remedies for infringement. One such example is the greater use of criminal law to protect trade mark rights. The TRIPS Agreement requires signatories to provide for criminal penalties in cases of 'wilful trademark counterfeiting on a commercial scale', but many countries have extended the scope of criminal liability considerably further. The penalties are also draconian. In the UK, for example, the maximum sentence for convictions on indictment is a 10-year term of imprisonment.[24] A punitive element has also crept into civil proceedings. For example, some Commonwealth countries have introduced statutory 'additional damages' for trade mark infringement. Such damages result in a payment to the owner that is unconnected to that person's loss. It is said that such damages are designed to deter trade mark infringement, but the efficacy of this deterrent has not been empirically established.

Courts have also taken steps to strengthen the remedies available to trade mark owners. In Australia, for example, it has been held that courts can award damages for loss of reputation in trade mark cases. The logic is that trade mark infringement can make consumers accustomed to being able to acquire goods at a discount and this can make it more difficult for owners to maintain a price premium. Such damages have an obvious connection to the idea that trade mark law should seek to preserve brand value. For present purposes, however, the key thing to note is that damages for loss of reputation are awarded 'at large'. In other words, they are awarded on the basis that the claimant has been able to convince the court that it has suffered a loss but that loss cannot be quantified.[25] A more cynical description might be that such damages are awarded on the basis on a convincing sob-story.

Two More Fundamental Problems

The previous two sections provided an overview of a well-worn list of problems. Many of these problems require significant additional attention from courts and policymakers, but as has already been noted, steps have now been taken to address at least some of them. At the same time, however, academic work has begun to emerge that challenges two assumptions on which the trade mark system has been built. The first such assumption is that there is an infinite supply of potential trade marks. At one level, this is clearly true: there is an unlimited supply of combinations of letters, pictures and other signs and symbols (including letters in other scripts) that might be used as trade marks. Trade mark law has therefore been founded on the assumption that the law needs only to prevent traders from monopolising signs that have a natural connection with the goods, such as descriptive and laudatory terms or shapes that confer an ongoing competitive advantage. However, trade marks are not freely interchangeable. The trade marks that work best are short, memorable words

---

[24] Trade Marks Act 1994, s 92(6)(b).
[25] See R. Burrell and M. Handler, *Australian Trade Mark Law*, 2nd ed. (Oxford University Press, 2016), pp. 631–2 and the cases cited therein.

(including readily pronounceable neologisms) and common surnames. Writing in the context of the US, Barton Beebe and Jeanne Fromer have conducted an ambitious and multifaceted empirical study that demonstrates that the supply of words that can function as effective trade marks is already severely depleted, and the problem is particularly acute in areas such as electronic goods, clothing and computer-related services.[26] This trend is forcing later applicants to rely on less effective trade marks and is making the entire trade mark system complex and difficult to navigate. Beebe and Fromer argue convincingly that their work points toward a number of possible reforms, including raising renewal fees and tightening proof-of-use requirements to ensure that unused marks are removed from the Register; becoming more cautious about accepting evidence of 'acquired distinctiveness' (which will allow owners to overcome a finding that a mark lacks inherent distinctiveness)[27]; and narrowing tests for infringement and expanding defensive doctrines. They are, in other words, calling for an overhaul of much of the current trade mark system. In this, their conclusion chimes with that of many other trade mark scholars. But their reasons for reaching this conclusion are fundamentally different, and in this respect, Beebe and Fromer's work makes a powerful addition to the case for root-and-branch reform of the current system.

The second assumption that has begun to be challenged is in many ways still more fundamental. Trade mark law has been built around the related ideas that the law's only concern is to increase the supply of reliable information in the marketplace and that increased choice for consumers is always a good thing. However, there has long been a strand of literature that has taken a more cautious view of these propositions. One long-standing concern is that consumers are being presented with choices that are meaningless. In its strongest form, this claim blurs into radical critiques of consumerism generally: that consumerism serves as a distraction from our spiritually empty lives, the act of purchase giving us an all too brief dopamine hit before the pointlessness of modern existence sweeps back over us; current patterns of consumption are environmentally disastrous and threaten our survival as a species, and so on.

Radical critiques of consumerism need to be taken seriously, but they are so far-reaching in their implications that it is not easy for trade mark scholars to engage with them.[28] Trade mark scholars, however, are beginning to deal with a related, but less sweeping criticism, namely that increased choice for consumers can produce undesirable outcomes when judged within the current economic and social paradigm. In particular, there is now concern that a proliferation of choice can cause a form of 'information congestion'. This occurs in cases where the cost to consumers of sorting through their options outweighs the

---

[26] B. Beebe and J. Fromer, 'Are We Running Out of Trademarks? An Empirical Study of Trademark Depletion and Congestion' (2018) 131 Harv. L. Rev. 945.

[27] See also L. Anemaet, 'The Public Domain is Under Pressure – why we should not rely on empirical data when assessing trade mark distinctiveness' (2016) 47 IIC 303.

[28] But see A. Griffiths, 'Trade Marks and the Consumer Society' (2018) 15 scripted 209.

benefits that flow from the presence on the market of a variant[29] that produces a marginal increase in the preference satisfaction of a small number of consumers. This concern has found its way into the trade mark literature[30] and is clearly deserving of more attention, since it disrupts the way in which trade mark scholars have traditionally thought about consumer search costs.

Further disruption of our understanding of search costs comes from work that takes a critical view of the marketing strategies of some large and established market actors. The most detailed account, from a trade mark perspective, has been developed by David Adelman and Graeme Austin.[31] Adelman and Austin demonstrate that the proliferation of 'green trade marks' is having serious adverse consequences. 'Green trade marks' in this context are signs that indicate that goods have been produced in accordance with certain ethical or environmental standards. Persuading consumers to choose products that are environmentally sustainable and ensure fair returns for workers is crucial to tackling pressing ecological and social problems. This is particularly true in a world where direct Government action remains either politically unpopular (as in the US) or practically difficult (because it requires international coordination). Adelman and Austin argue that the potential of this form of private environmental governance has not been realised, largely because consumers are overwhelmed by competing green trade marks based on different standards or criteria.

Part of the problem is that there are simply too many green trade marks jostling for our attention: marks promising fair returns to producers compete with organic certification schemes, with marks promising sustainable agriculture, with marks promising carbon offsets and so forth. There is the danger that, faced with these competing claims, consumers either disengage entirely or are content with having made a 'green choice' without engaging with the nature of that choice. The latter point is intertwined with concerns about the problem of a regulatory race to the bottom. Over and above the fact that there are lots of different types of green trade marks competing for our attention, there is the problem that within any given category of green trade mark there are now likely to be competing certifying bodies.[32] From the perspective of

---

[29] For example, yet another variety of breakfast cereal or yet another flavour of ice cream.

[30] L. Larrimore Ouellette, 'Does Running out of (Some) Trademarks Matter?' (2018) 131 Harv. L. Rev. F. 116, drawing in particular on the work of psychologist Barry Schwartz:

B. Schwartz, 'More Isn't Always Better' (2006) 84 Harv. Bus. Rev. 22. See further,

B. Schwartz, *Paradox of Choice – Why More is Less* (Harper Perennial, 2005).

[31] D. Adelman and G. Austin, 'Trademarks and Private Environmental Governance' (2017) 93 Notre Dame L. Rev. 709. 'Green trade marks' are more commonly described as 'ecolabels', but the former language serves to draw attention to the fact that the use of these signs is controlled in large part by trade mark law.

[32] It should be noted that here we are not concerned only with trade marks that have been formally registered as certification marks. There is a trend towards relying on standard forms of registered trade mark to underpin green labelling. The reference to certifying body must be read accordingly.

corporate actors, selling environmentally friendly products is not about securing social goals but about securing market advantage. We must expect corporate actors to seek to secure the relevant market advantage at the lowest
possible cost – this is what the shareholder value paradigm of corporate governance demands.[33] If consumers do not look behind what green trade marks
denote, companies are likely to gravitate to regimes that have the least onerous
standards.

Other concerns about information congestion have also begun to be aired,
in particular about the ability of established market actors to use misleading
marketing strategies to maintain market share in the face of increased competition or changing consumer preferences. For instance, there has been media
coverage of the phenomenon of large and established breweries seeking to
'pass off' their products as craft beer by choosing brand names and product
packaging that consumers would more naturally associate with the craft beer
industry.[34] A more extreme example is provided by the litigation in Australia
involving various sub-brands of NUROFEN, the so-called NUROFEN 'specific pain range'. Products in this range were sold under sub-brands that
included 'NUROFEN – Back Pain' and NUROFEN – Period Pain', and the
accompanying packaging promised 'Fast Targeted Relief from Pain'. In fact,
however, these products all contained the same active ingredient and hence
worked in the same way. It was not, therefore, the case that consumers were
buying a product that was ineffective; rather, it was that they were not buying
a product that had any special advantage over generic ibuprofen. The Australian
Competition and Consumer Commission argued and the defendant eventually
conceded that the specific pain range was misleading, leading to the imposition
of a $6 million fine.[35] It is, however, important to remember that consumers
only had to look at the active ingredients to make an informed decision. But
the defendant was eventually forced to acknowledge that this rested on an
unrealistic model of consumer decision-making: the arrival onto the market of
a rash of apparently new pain relief options was enough to persuade consumers
to change their purchasing habits; they could not be expected to look behind
the branding. This must add to the argument that more thought needs to be
given to how the law should respond to mass-produced products that are
being packaged and sold as if they had been made using more traditional arti-
sanal modes of production. Much the same applies to attractively priced products that bear a green trade mark that (as far as the consumer is concerned)

---

[33] See Johnston, Chapter 9.
[34] See, for example, *The Guardian*, 11 July 2017, 'Indie Brewers Fight Back in Bitter Row over
Beer Brands' Craft Credentials'.
[35] *Australian Competition and Consumer Commission v Reckitt Benckiser (Australia) Pty Ltd*
[2016] FCAFC 181. But cf. the outcome in *Boris v. Wal-Mart Stores, Inc.*, No. CV 13–7090
2014 WL 1477404 (C.D. Cal. Apr. 9, 2014) holding that it was not misleading to market
painkillers with the same active ingredients under different names, colours, and price points.
My thanks go to Rebecca Tushnet for bringing this case to my attention.

promises the same environmental or social benefits as a different green trade mark appearing on more expensive goods.

Running through the examples considered in this section is the concern that trade mark law's model of consumer search costs is simplistic. Moreover, it is important to emphasise that the problem is not simply that other areas of law are not picking up the slack. The Nurofen example, in particular, could be thought to indicate that the solution is a more robust consumer law to deal with types of consumer confusion that have never been within trade mark law's ambit. We may well need a more robust consumer law, but the point being made here is that trade mark law is not a neutral vehicle in some of the conduct that causes consumer confusion or, to say much the same thing another way, conduct that causes an increase in consumer search costs. It enables large breweries to secure legal protection for the names of their faux craft beers, and it allows organisations with doubtful environmental credentials to secure rights over green trade marks. At a higher level of abstraction, it helps create a regulatory environment in which the multiplicity of trade signs is almost invariably perceived as a good thing. It helps create a hollowed-out understanding of what we mean by consumer choice.

PROBLEMS WITH THE BRAND PROTECTION LIMB

One of the most important changes in the trade mark landscape has been the acceptance by policymakers that trade mark law should go beyond the prevention of consumer confusion. Trade mark law has therefore been extended to protect the investment that trade mark owners make in developing their brands. The principal mechanism through which brand investment is protected is the doctrine of 'dilution'. Protection against trade mark dilution is said to preserve the brand owner's investment by preserving the attractive force of the mark. This is generally said to mean that brand owners need to be protected against both 'blurring' and 'tarnishment'. Blurring is said to occur where a well-known mark is used in relation to unrelated goods or services. The idea is that use on unrelated goods or services may not cause confusion but nevertheless may impair the ability of the mark to reach out to consumers. Most famously, it was claimed that, left unchecked, the use of ROLLS-ROYCE for restaurants, cafeterias and clothing would lead to the eventual destruction of the ROLLS-ROYCE mark as an effective commercial identifier.[36] Protection against tarnishment attempts to prevent a mark from being linked with goods or services that are antithetical to the brand's core values. The idea is that things such as NIKE burger bars, TIFFANY refuse services or DUREX sieves can undermine the original brand by causing consumers to associate the mark with 'incompatible' goods or services.

---

[36] F. Schechter, statement at *Trade Marks: Hearings Before the House Committee on Patents*, 72d Cong, 1st Sess, 15 (1932).

More recently, it has been held in Europe that dilution might also extend to protect against a third form of harm, styled 'free-riding'. Free-riding goes beyond blurring and tarnishment. Under this limb, it is enough to demonstrate that the defendant is taking advantage of the trade mark owner's investment in the brand. It therefore can apply in cases where the defendant's use is unlikely to harm the mark's distinctive character or reputation. The key case is *L'Oréal v Bellure*, a 2009 decision of the CJEU.[37] The defendant in that case produced perfumes that smelled similar to L'Oréal fragrances (which it was entitled to do since the smell of a perfume does not generally attract IP protection). The defendants also distributed product comparison lists to retailers. These lists set out L'Oréal brands and gave details of the matching Bellure product. L'Oréal claimed for the use of its trade marks in these lists, in part on the basis of dilution. The problem for L'Oréal was that that it could not demonstrate either blurring or tarnishment. There was no blurring because the comparison lists actually reinforced the idea that the marks denoted perfumes manufactured by L'Oréal. There was no tarnishment because there was no real brand dissonance between the two sets of goods, merely a price differential. The CJEU nevertheless agreed that the defendant's use might be actionable, holding that anti-dilution protection in Europe also extends to 'free-riding' (i.e., to taking advantage of the brand owner's investment), even in cases where the distinctive character and reputation of the mark are not damaged.

Protection against dilution was first proposed in the 1920s.[38] It is, however, important to note that dilution has not had a fixed meaning over time. As the consumer protection limb has been expanded, anti-dilution advocates have sought to push protection for brand owners ever further. The result is a degree of protection, particularly in the EU, that goes far beyond anything that early proponents of anti-dilution protection could have imagined. This unstable or protean quality of anti-dilution protection is one of the things that has enlivened critics of this branch of trade mark law. However, this is only one concern among many, and over time a significant body of scholarship that is highly critical of dilution has emerged.

One challenge to dilution is that this branch of the law suffers from internal incoherence. To understand this criticism, one needs to bear in mind that not all trade marks are eligible for protection against dilution. It is only trade marks that have acquired a certain level of public recognition that gain the benefit of anti-dilution protection. In the EU, it is only marks 'with a reputation' that enjoy this protection. In a similar vein, in the US, trade marks have to be 'famous', whereas in New Zealand and Singapore marks have to be 'well known'. However, it is not at all clear that this reputation threshold serves as a sensible precondition for the establishment of liability, particularly in cases of 'blurring'. It was seen that the harm in blurring cases is said to be that the use

---

[37] *L'Oréal SA v Bellure NV* [2009] ECR I-5185.
[38] F. Schechter, 'The Rational Basis of Trademark Protection' (1927) 40 Harv. L. Rev. 813.

of a similar mark on dissimilar goods or services can inhibit the ability of the trade mark to 'reach out' to consumers. It seems strange to suggest that this type of harm can occur only in cases where the mark enjoys a reputation. Such marks are, by definition, already firmly fixed in the public mind and the risk that third-party uses will diminish consumers' ability to recall the mark and its associations must be relatively limited. In contrast, in cases where the mark has not yet established a reputation, unauthorised use of the mark on unrelated goods might have a much more significant impact on consumer recognition.[39]

A rather different sort of internal critique is that anti-dilution protection does not sit comfortably with the mechanics of trade mark registration. The trade mark register is intended to act as a valuable source of public information. In particular, it helps traders determine a whether a mark remains available for use. Thus, the trade mark register is said to help reduce 'business clearance costs'. The problem with anti-dilution protection is that it reduces the value of the register as a source of information. Traders can no longer rely on the fact that no one has registered a similar mark for similar goods or services since anti-dilution protection can apply even in cases where the goods or services are entirely unrelated. This makes searching the register much harder. Moreover, if the trader does discover that a similar trade mark has been registered for very different goods or services it will not be apparent from the register whether that mark enjoys sufficient public recognition to qualify for anti-dilution protection. This is a particular problem in jurisdictions like the EU, where the reputation bar is set relatively low since the question of whether the mark enjoys a reputation will not be a matter of common knowledge.[40]

The above internal critiques of anti-dilution protection are important in that they show up problems with this form of protection that bite even if one accepts the premises on which anti-dilution protection is founded. The most telling criticisms of dilution, however, suggest that these premises are in any event not well founded. Consider, for example, what we know about tarnishment. In an important study, Christo Boshoff attempted to measure tarnishment effects. He did so by exposing participants in a laboratory experiment to advertisements for well-known brands and to advertisements for tarnished versions of these brands. When the participants were exposed to the tarnished versions first their subsequent reactions to the original brands were actually *more positive* than in cases where they were exposed to the original brands first.[41] It has been pointed out that this finding, though counterintuitive, is not

[39] R. Burrell and M. Handler, 'Reputation in European Trade Mark Law: A re-examination' (2016) 17 *ERA Forum* 85.

[40] See further R. Burrell and M. Handler, 'Dilution and Trademark Registration' (2008) 17 Transnat'l L & Contemp Probs 713.

[41] C. Boshoff, 'The Lady Doth Protest Too Much: A Neurophysiological Perspective on Brand Tarnishment' (2016) 25 *Journal of Product and Brand Management* 196. Reactions were determined by using electroencephalography (or 'EEG') to measure brain activity and electromyography (or 'EMG') to measures changes in facial muscles.

out of step with what we know about unpopular brand extensions – the available evidence suggests that even when consumers are disappointed by a new product produced by the brand owner, their negative evaluation of the extension will not feedback to impact on their view of the original.[42]

Blurring fares little better when viewed through a consumer psychology lens. Although there are studies that purport to demonstrate that blurring does occur, it has been argued convincingly that evidence of a delay in consumer recognition time that has to be measured in milliseconds does not begin to make the case for legal intervention.[43] Moreover, even within the most famous study of this type, we find examples where use of a mark on dissimilar products actually served to increase recognition of the original brand.[44] Historical evidence also fails to provide any obvious evidence of the attractive force of a mark being harmed by unauthorised use on unrelated goods or services. It has been pointed out, for example, that two unrelated entities have been using the mark 'Rolls-Royce' for more than 40 years without the Rolls-Royce name suffering any obvious loss of prestige or distinctive character.[45] More comprehensive historical surveys suggest that, even in the absence of anti-dilution protection, uses of famous marks on dissimilar goods are in any event likely to be rare.[46]

If blurring and tarnishing harms cannot be demonstrated to occur, then a case might still be made for free-riding. However, when the case for allowing protection against pure free-riding is examined closely, it is no more convincing. This is true irrespective of whether free-riding is understood in economic or moral terms. In economic terms, free-riding is a problem insofar as it causes underinvestment in an activity. Free-riding occurs where a party enjoys a benefit from the investment or actions of another economic actor outside of a voluntary transaction. Free-riding is a concern because it means the market signal will fail to reflect the full value of the activity that generated the benefit. For example, keeping bees may create benefits for neighbouring farmers. The beekeeper is, however, unlikely to see a benefit from the increased crop yields that his or her neighbours enjoy. The beekeeper may therefore decide to get rid of the bees and, say, build a golf course instead, even though the total value to the economy of the golf course is lower than the value of the bees. Conferring IP rights is one way in which the state can correct for free-rider problems: the owner of the IP can then charge anyone who uses its creation. However, it

---

[42] M. Handler, 'What Can Harm the Reputation of a Trademark? A Critical Re-Evaluation of Dilution by Tarnishment' (2016) 106 Trademark Reporter 639, 680.

[43] R. Tushnet, 'Gone in 60 Milliseconds: Trademark law and cognitive science' (2008) 86 Texas L. Rev. 507. See also B. Beebe, R. Germano, C. Sprigman and J. Steckel, 'Testing for Trademark Dilution in Court and in the Lab (2019) 86 U Chi L. Rev. (forthcoming).

[44] M. Morrin and J. Jacoby, 'Trademark Dilution: Empirical Measures for an Elusive Concept' (2000) 19 *Journal of Public Policy and Marketing* 265.

[45] S. Malynicz, 'Applying the Law on Trade Mark Dilution' (2015) *ERA Forum* 49, 54.

[46] P. Heald and B. Brauneis, 'The Myth of Buick Aspirin: An Empirical Study of Trademark Dilution by Product and Trade Names' (2011) Cardozo L. Rev. 2533.

must be remembered that legal intervention is the exception not the rule. In the real world, our actions often generate benefits and costs for others. Generally speaking, as the beekeeping example also helps demonstrate, we allow those benefits and costs to fall where they will. Furthermore, even in situations where we determine that some form of legal intervention is required, there is a strong case that such intervention should go no further than is required to provide the incentive to invest. One of the reasons why patent and copyright law have become so controversial is that these regimes now provide a level of protection that would seem to go well beyond that which is required to preserve incentives. It is difficult to see that there is a danger of an 'undersupply' of trade marks that the law needs to guard against given the advantages that accrue to the owner of an established brand.

The language of free-riding, however, can also suggest a moral case for intervention: that we should prevent people from seizing the benefits of the labour and investment of others. Brands are valuable commercial assets and firms invest huge sums in the development and maintenance of 'brand image'. But brands exist in the minds of consumers and it is not just brand owners but also public figures, the media and consumers themselves who construct brand meaning. As a consequence, it is far from obvious that trade mark owners are entitled to capture all of a brand's value or to try to freeze its meaning in time. More generally, it must be remembered that capitalism turns on the right to copy. Take the example of trader who has invested considerable time and money in creating consumer demand for a product newly imported from overseas. Later traders are perfectly entitled to compete in the market for that product even though in so doing they will be benefitting from the efforts of the first mover. IP protection is the exception not the rule, and any case for extending such protection, irrespective of whether it is framed in ethical or economic terms, has to explain why we should deviate from the default position, namely, that copying is allowed.[47]

A third body of critical commentary on the brand protection limb focuses on the negative social and political impacts of this branch of trade mark law. In particular, the concern has been expressed that anti-dilution protection has a chilling effect on free speech.[48] It is anti-dilution protection, in particular, that owners have relied upon when seeking to use trade mark law to prevent activists from reproducing company logos in a critical context. Thus, to take some of the better-known examples, anti-dilution protection was relied upon (i) by a South African brewery when suing a small activist company for producing T-shirts that commented on the brewery's labour practices; (ii) by a

---

[47] See further, D. Gangjee and R. Burrell, 'Because You're Worth It: L'Oréal and the Prohibition on Free Riding' (2010) 73 MLR 282.

[48] See, for example, M. LaFrance, 'No Reason to Live: Dilution Laws as Unconstitutional Restrictions on Commercial Speech' (2007) 58 SC L. Rev. 709; A. Kur, L. Bently and A. Ohly, 'Sweet Smells and a Sour Taste – The ECJ's L'Oréal Decision' [2009] *Max Planck Institute for Intellectual Property, Competition & Tax Law Research Paper*, No 09–12, available at: <http://ssrn.com/abstract=1492032>.

well-known American retailer seeking to prevent an activist from selling merchandise that mocked the retailer's commitment to family values; and (iii) by a multinational oil company seeking to stop an environmental group, *inter alia*, from using its marks as metatags to increase traffic to its website.[49] Admittedly, in each of these cases, the trade mark owner was ultimately unsuccessful, but only after protracted litigation.

TRADE MARK LAW IN ACTION

The final point made above about defendants being successful, but only after time-consuming and expensive litigation, goes to a broader point about the nature of problems with the trade mark system. However serious the problems outlined above might be, it is arguable that they are less significant than the impact of aggressive brand enforcement strategies. The phenomenon of the 'brand bully' – the large corporation that goes after a small and medium-sized enterprise or not-for-profit organisation for using a trade marked word or image in circumstances that are never going to cause confusion – has become a media staple. Anyone who has practised in the trade mark field can almost certainly add their own horror stories. There have also been attempts, particularly in the US, to document how trade mark rights are being enforced. This research has added weight to the claim that the phenomenon of overclaiming is widespread.[50] There are, admittedly, procedural mechanisms that ought to help address the problem. For example, many Commonwealth jurisdictions have a 'threats action' that allows defendants to bring proceedings in relation to an unjustified threat to sue for infringement of a registered trade mark. The existence of these provisions has not, however, been sufficient to head off the problem, and there seems to be little prospect that recent reforms to threats actions will alter the position substantially.[51] In a similar vein, so-called 'anti-SLAPP' laws[52] in some US states, which are intended to restrict the ability of plaintiffs to use frivolous threats of civil proceedings to silence critics, appear to have had a limited impact on trade mark overclaiming. This is despite the willingness of some courts to apply such laws in cases where there is a genuine underlying commercial dispute between the parties.[53]

---

[49] *Laugh It Off Promotions CC v South African Breweries International (Finance) BV t/a Sabmark International* [2005] ZACC 7 (Constitutional Court of South Africa); *Smith v. Wal-Mart Stores Inc.* (2008) 537 F. Supp. 2d 1302 (N.D. Ga. 2008); *Esso SA v Greenpeace France* [2009] IIC 241 (Cour de Cassation), respectively.

[50] See, for example, W. Gallagher, 'Trademark and Copyright Enforcement in the Shadow of IP Law' (2012) 28 Santa Clara Computer & High Tech. L.J. 453; W. McGeveran, 'The Imaginary Trademark Parody Crisis (and the Real One)' (2015) 90 Wash. L. Rev. 713.

[51] See, in the UK, The Intellectual Property (Unjustified Threats) Act 2017.

[52] The acronym stands for Strategic Lawsuit Against Public Participation.

[53] See, for example, *Shire City Herbals, Inc v Blue* (2016) WL 2757366 (D. Mass. 12 May 2016).

The analysis thus far suggests that trade mark law has become plagued by serious problems. While there is some difference in the nature and scale of these problems between jurisdictions, the overall pattern is clear. The picture is not, however, entirely bleak. There are signs that policymakers are beginning to take seriously at least some of the concerns canvassed above. For example, trade mark offices have become genuinely alarmed about the possibility that in some fields the stock of available trade marks is becoming depleted. More generally, while advocates of reform may be disappointed that more has not yet been achieved, critical voices are now at least being heard in official circles. There are also signs that members of the judiciary who deal with trade mark cases regularly are aware that something is amiss. There is, therefore, reason to be optimistic about the future direction of executive, legislative and judicial rule-making.

Optimism about the future direction of the trade mark system must, however, be tempered if the problems with the system flow as much from aggressive brand enforcement strategies as they do from defects in the rules. It is for this reason that there is frustration in some quarters at the reluctance of policymakers to consider whether changes to professional codes of conduct might be used to produce changes in the cultures of brand management and trade mark enforcement. No one believes that tinkering with the ethical standards governing trade mark attorneys and other professionals would produce a radical change in behaviour. But a signal that there are public interest considerations to which lawyers need to pay attention might help generate some change in the culture of a branch of the profession whose members are quick to shelter behind their duty to the client when pressed on their behaviour in unmeritorious cases.[54] Moreover, some of the reforms that might be introduced – such as imposing restrictions on lawyers applying to register or renew a trade mark in cases where they have actual knowledge that the client has no intention of using the mark – ought to be relatively uncontroversial.[55] Courts also need to be convinced of the need to adopt an approach to case management that recognises the potential for abuse. This will require scholars to collect additional evidence of the scale of the problem. Thought is also being given in some quarters to whether there is scope to help level the playing field by providing a degree of legal protection to attempts to use social media to expose trade mark bullying, for example, by providing a defence to any claim for copyright infringement that might be brought against a threatened party that publishes the letter containing the threat online.[56]

---

[54] Gallagher, *supra* n. 48, p. 38.

[55] It might be noted that such an ethical obligation would be difficult to enforce, but this is to misunderstand the ways in which lawyers' ethical obligations can influence behaviour – the signalling effect and the ability to point to a regulatory requirement as a justification for resisting client demands can be more important than the fear of sanction.

[56] L. Grinvald, *Shaming Trademark Bullies*, [2011] WIS. L. REV. 625.

These are all potentially important measures, but if we are to respond effectively to the problem of trade mark owners asserting overly broad and unmeritorious claims, we need to ensure that we understand the drivers for this behaviour. In the literature, the phenomenon of overclaiming is invariably presented as being underpinned by a series of conscious decisions: we need to find ways of addressing the problems created by aggressive brand enforcement *strategies*. This idea undoubtedly captures an important part of the problem, but we might want to be wary of concluding that this provides the entire story. Part of the problem may also be that decisions around trade marks become embedded in bureaucratic processes that identify 'conflicts' between marks when in reality there is no prospect of the later market entrant causing the trade mark owner harm. The suggestion, in other words, is that actors within the trade mark system have adopted ways of working that contribute to the over-enforcement of trade mark rights.

Consider, for example, the industry that has grown up around trade mark 'watching'.[57] Many large brand owners employ the services of trade mark watching agents who monitor trade mark applications. Watching agents promise to identify competitors who are looking to register similar marks. However, the marks that watching agents identify as providing cause for concern will be thrown up on the basis of algorithms that are designed to be over- rather than under-inclusive. This is only rational. Clients will soon turn elsewhere if potentially problematic marks are missed by the agent. It is far better to send the client details of all marks that might possibly interfere with its market presence. The client can then exercise its judgment as to whether to take action. There must, however, be the concern that the actions of agents help construct a paradigm in which trade mark rights are construed broadly.

Law firms also contribute to an expansionist construction of trade mark rights. In some cases, brand owners will use law firms to filter the results generated by watching agents. In other cases, the law firm itself will identify the potential conflict, either as a consequence of its own monitoring processes or because they have identified a potentially problematic mark serendipitously. Much like watching agents, law firms have a strong incentive to report more rather than fewer conflicts. Like watching agents, they will want to 'err on the side of caution'; that is, they will want to ensure that they do not fail to identify marks that subsequently cause their clients cause for concern. In addition, however, law firms will be hoping to secure work from challenging the later market entrant. This is not to suggest that lawyers routinely advise their clients to bring opposition proceedings or to send out letters of demand solely in order to increase their billable hours. But it does help construct a paradigm in which trade mark rights are understood broadly and in which the need to maintain 'space' for the brand is given a high priority.

---

[57] J. Bellido, 'Towards a History of Trade Mark Watching' [2015] IPQ 130.

The paradigm in which trade mark rights are understood broadly and preserving brand space is given a high priority is also reflected within corporate structures. In the author's experience, for example, it is not uncommon to find that a decision to launch a trade mark opposition will be made by someone within a corporate structure who occupies a relatively junior position (whether as a manager or as an in-house lawyer). However, that person may well not be authorised to settle a case insofar as reaching a settlement involves entering into a coexistence or division-of-use agreement. Again, this makes sense within the existing paradigm – threats to brand space must be taken seriously and acted upon rapidly. It therefore makes sense to devolve responsibility down the corporate structure to someone who can be expected to err on the side of caution. In contrast, a decision to allow a third party to occupy a similar brand space (as constructed through a set of processes that throw up uses that in market terms are not very similar at all) is one that needs to be taken by someone more senior, who can be trusted to weigh up the threat to the business. This contributes to an environment in which trade mark overclaiming is the default position. It also helps normalise overclaiming for other actors within the trade mark system, including IP offices handling opposition disputes. Indeed, it is perfectly possible that all of us who interact regularly with the trade mark system are in danger of losing sight of how far the trade mark system has moved from its foundations: when we think of trade mark overclaiming, we may be thinking of only the most egregious examples of a much bigger problem. Changing how repeat players think about trade marks and brands may therefore be both more important and more difficult than at first appears.

CONCLUSION

IP law is not like other areas of commercial law. Critical perspectives are now mainstream across copyright, patent and trade mark law. As a consequence, debates within trade mark circles tend to focus on understanding the nature and depth of problems with the current system. This chapter has sought to demonstrate that the problems with the current system are manifold. Indeed, recent research suggests that the 'trouble with trade mark'[58] goes even further than we had thought. For all that judges and policymakers are becoming aware of the need for reform, we remain a long way from an intellectually justifiable trade mark system.

FURTHER READING

L. Bently, 'From Communication to Thing: Historical Aspects of the Conceptualisation of Trade Marks as Property' in G. Dinwoodie and M. Janis (eds), *Trademark Law and Theory: A Handbook of Contemporary Research* (Edward Elgar, 2008).

R. Bone, 'Enforcement Costs and Trademark Puzzles' (2004) 90 *Virginia Law Review* 2099.

---

[58] Cf. S. Carter, 'The Trouble with Trademark' (1990) 99 Yale L.J. 759.

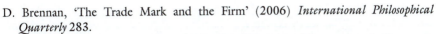

D. Brennan, 'The Trade Mark and the Firm' (2006) *International Philosophical Quarterly* 283.

M. Chon, 'Trademark Goodwill as a Public Good: Brands and Innovations in Corporate Social Responsibility' (2017) 21 *Lewis & Clark Law Review* 277.

R. Cooper Dreyfuss, 'Expressive Genericity: Trademarks as Language in the Pepsi Generation' (1990) 65 *Notre Dame Law Review* 397.

G. Dinwoodie, 'Trademarks and Territory: Detaching Trademark Law from the Nation-State' (2004) 41 *Houston Law Review* 885.

S. Dogan and M. Lemley, 'The Merchandising Right: Fragile Theory or *fait accompli*? (2005) 54 *Emory Law Journal* 461.

J. Litman, 'Breakfast with Batman: The Public Interest in the Advertising Age' (1999) *Yale Law Journal* 1717.

M. McKenna, 'Testing Modern Trademark Law's Theory of Harm' (2009) 95 *Iowa Law Review* 63.

K. Weatherall, 'The Consumer as the Empirical Measure of Trade Mark Law' (2017) 80 *MLR* 57.

CHAPTER 6

Copyright and Invisible Authors: A Property Perspective

Emily Hudson

I. Introduction

The inspiration for this chapter is the debate as to whether copyright, and indeed other forms of intellectual property (IP), are proprietary in nature. Some contributions to this debate have been formalistic in nature, focusing on the attributes of property and whether copyright works share sufficient characteristics with other types of thing that the law accepts can be the object of property rights. Other contributions have had a more explicit normative or philosophical focus. For instance, one line of argument doubts whether some explanations for property in tangible things apply to intangible 'things' such as copyright. Consider justifications based on the tragedy of the commons. The essence of this argument is that when resources are held in the commons, free to be used by all, people will typically maximise their individual, short-term interest even if this degrades the resource and is inimical to its long-term sustainability.[1] Private property rights have been identified as one way to counteract this tendency, on the basis that they give owners a direct stake in the ongoing existence and quality of the resource. But it has been said that this justification is inapt for copyright because copyright works, being intangible, can be used simultaneously and repeatedly by many people (i.e., are non-rivalrous) with no depletion or degradation (i.e., are non-exhaustible).[2] In fact, it has been said that the problem for copyright is the 'tragedy of the anticommons': that works end up being *underused* because of difficulties in clearing

---

[1] Garrett Hardin, 'The Tragedy of the Commons' (1968) 162 *Science* 1243. Examples include over-fishing the ocean, over-grazing land, and belching pollution into the atmosphere.

[2] But note William M. Landes and Richard A. Posner, 'Indefinitely Renewable Copyright' (2003) 70 *University of Chicago Law Review* 471 (arguing some forms of IP can suffer these harms).

rights.[3] With this and other concerns about a proprietary conception of copyright, numerous scholars explain copyright not as property but as a limited monopoly granted by the state to encourage and reward certain forms of intellectual and artistic endeavour.[4]

This chapter does not seek to address the formalist's question of whether copyright is property as there is already a preponderance of contributions to this topic. Instead, it starts from the proposition that irrespective of whether copyright is *truly* proprietary, the system developed in jurisdictions such as Australia, Canada, the UK and the US is based on ownership and property-style rights. Looking to the UK, for example, the Copyright, Designs and Patents Act 1988 (CDPA) states in section 1 that copyright is 'a property right'; identifies the first 'owner' of copyright in section 11; and in section 90 states that copyright 'is transmissible by assignment, by testamentary disposition or by operation of law, as personal or moveable property'.

The aim of this chapter is therefore to explore a number of normative and practical questions in relation to ownership in copyright law, thus drawing from debates in relation to orphaned works, copyright formalities, works generated by artificial intelligence (AI), and so forth. In section II, it explores the underlying doctrinal framework of copyright ownership, including one feature that differentiates copyright from patents and registered trade marks: that copyright protection is automatic, meaning that rights arise irrespective of the knowledge and intention of the author. Automatic protection combined with the long term of copyright can lead to a number of problems, the most extreme of which is orphaned works: those for which permissions are impossible because the copyright owner cannot be identified or located. But section II also notes the challenges presented by other types of 'invisible' author, such as works produced without any direct human participation and works of unknown authorship.

In section III, this chapter analyses possible recalibrations to a system which is built around ownership but for which authorial intent is irrelevant, possession is inapposite, and formalities such as registration are prohibited. In assessing the suite of options, it is important to bear in mind that international copyright instruments such as the Berne Convention limit the hands of domestic legislatures, meaning that certain responses could not be rolled out without a fundamental change to the international legal order. The (re)introduction of formalities is one such example, meaning that countries could not, at this stage, link copyright subsistence to (say) the deposit of a copy of the work at a national library or its entry on a central register.

The analysis concludes in section IV with a brief provocation. Although the chapter discusses philosophical and practical challenges with copyright's conception of ownership, it may be that some of these problems have been

---

[3] Michael Heller, 'The Tragedy of the Anticommons: A Concise Introduction and Lexicon' (2013) 76 *Modern Law Review* 6.

[4] As discussed in Mark Lemley, 'Property, Intellectual Property, and Free Riding' (2005) 83 *Texas Law Review* 1031.

overtaken by the growth in copyright works (especially digital and online works) being distributed subject to detailed licences. These licences have been criticised on numerous grounds, including that they function as privately written copyright codes that often extend beyond, and contract around, the inbuilt limits of the statutory regime. This development in licensing presents a major challenge for copyright law, and this chapter concludes by asking whether property concepts might be relevant to some of the problems with this new type of 'ownership' issue.

II. Doctrinal Indications

A. The Problem of Allocating Ownership: Existential and Evidentiary Issues

One of the central ideas of copyright law is that rightsholders enjoy certain rights in relation to copying, public performance, online communication, and so forth. In the UK, this is framed within the language of ownership: that the 'owner of copyright in a work has ... the exclusive right'[5] to do certain acts. The CDPA contains provisions to allocate initial ownership, stating that 'the author of a work is the first owner of any copyright in it'.[6] This rule is subject to two exceptions: for works created by employees in the course of employment (where, subject to any agreement to the contrary, copyright is owned by the employer)[7] and for Crown copyright.[8] Compared with other copyright principles, ownership and authorship are less well developed in international and supranational copyright instruments, and different countries take different approaches.[9] One example relates to the transmissibility of copyright. Common law countries such as Australia, Canada, the UK and the US tend to emphasise freedom of contract and, for the most part, allow copyright to be dealt with freely. In contrast, civil law jurisdictions are more likely to impose restrictions on the exploitation of rights. In Germany and Austria, for example, there is a prohibition on the 'sale' (assignment) of copyright.

One challenge is how to deal with works that have existential or evidentiary issues in relation to authorship from the very moment of their creation. Existential issues arise for works whose creation did not involve any direct human participation, such as monkey selfies[10] and works generated by AI. Do

---

[5] CDPA s. 16(1).

[6] Ibid., s. 11(1).

[7] Ibid., s. 11(2).

[8] Ibid., s. 11(3).

[9] See Paul Goldstein and Bernt Hugenholtz, *International Copyright: Principles, Law, and Practice* (Oxford: Oxford University Press, 3rd ed, 2013) Ch. 7.

[10] *Naruto v Slater*, No. 16-15469 (9th Circuit, 2018) (monkey does not have statutory standing to sue under the US Copyright Act).

such works fall within accepted justifications for copyright protection, and is there a person or entity with legal standing to exploit or enforce rights? In some cases, the copyright system defines the author not by reference to creatorship but to the person or entity that 'made the work possible'[11] (e.g., as seen in UK provisions in which producers, broadcasters and publishers are 'authors' of sound recordings, films, broadcasts and published editions[12]). The UK adopts a similar approach for literary, dramatic, musical and artistic works that are computer-generated; for these works, the author is 'the person by whom the arrangements necessary for the creation of the work are undertaken'.[13] This can be contrasted with the position in Australia, where case law has said that human authorship is essential, with the result that copyright did not subsist in a telephone directory that was produced by a computer program that assembled the underlying information and put the directory into material form.[14] With the power of AI growing, it has been asked whether existing understandings of authorship and ownership need to be revised – although alternatively, one might ask why we should recognise property rights in the outputs of AI merely because they *look* like copyright works. These debates encompass a number of themes, including philosophical matters (such as whether copyright protection might incentivise the development of AI) and pragmatic questions about how to determine which contributors to AI should be rewarded with copyright ownership.

Evidentiary issues, on the other hand, relate to works which clearly had a human author but for which that author cannot be identified. The CDPA, for example, has provisions for works of 'unknown authorship', being works where 'it is not possible for a person to ascertain [the author's] identity by reasonable inquiry; but if his identity is once known it shall not subsequently be regarded as unknown'.[15] For these works, certain rules have been adjusted because of the lack of an identifiable author. One example is duration, which is calculated by reference to the year the work was made or first publicly disseminated, rather than the life of the author.[16]

Interestingly, despite appearing to accept what is, in practice, ownerless copyright, the CDPA does not exclude such works from its provisions regarding infringement. This is significant. If we think about the classification system for legal relationships developed by Guido Calabresi and Douglas Melamed,[17]

---

[11] Lionel Bently, Brad Sherman, Dev Gangjee and Phillip Johnson, *Intellectual Property Law* (Oxford: Oxford University Press, 5th ed, 2018) 126.

[12] CDPA s. 9(2).

[13] Ibid., s. 9(3).

[14] *Telstra v Phone Directories* [2010] FCAFC 149.

[15] CDPA s. 11(5).

[16] Ibid., s. 12.

[17] Guido Calabresi and A. Douglas Melamed, 'Property Rules, Liability Rules, and Inalienability: One View of the Cathedral' (1972) 85 *Harvard Law Review* 1089.

the economic rights of copyright fall most obviously into property rules, being entitlements that may be bought by a third party in a voluntary transaction at a price agreed by the seller. But if there is no known author and hence no known copyright owner, it is no longer possible for third parties to secure assignments or licences for acts of consumption and re-use. At a purely practical level, an answer might be found in risk assessment: that if an author cannot be identified, users might also be confident that no owner will ever come forward to assert rights. But the fact that the copyright system even contemplates ownerless copyright is significant, because (1) it sits uneasily with rationales for copyright (which would seem to require an author who is incentivised or rewarded or whose authorial personality is being respected) and (2) it can cause us to tolerate a degree of artificiality in copyright transactions. This second point will be seen later in the discussion on centralised and extended collective licensing.

B. The Problem of Unaware Authors

So far, this section has focused on works of unknown authorship. But a further issue relates to works of unaware authors: individuals who do not appreciate that the work they have created is protected by copyright. The possibility that copyright owners can be oblivious to their legal status arises because of the automaticity of copyright protection. There is no requirement that authors intend or desire copyright protection, and the linking of subsistence to formalities such as registration, deposit or the assertion of rights (e.g., by writing © Your Name 2020 on the work) is, in practice, prohibited by Article 5(2) of the Berne Convention.[18] Instead, rules regarding subsistence focus on the qualities of the work, such as whether it falls within the types of subject matter that copyright protects or is original in terms of being its 'author's own intellectual creation'[19] or 'possess[ing] some creative spark'.[20] If these requirements are met, copyright will subsist upon making or publication.

The position for copyright can be contrasted with tangible property, where owing to the role of such preconditions as registration and possession, it is far more difficult for ownership to be thrust upon the unaware. For instance, case law makes it clear that possession requires physical control and an intention to possess (an *animus possidendi*). Although this does not necessarily require knowledge of the specific chattel in one's custody, an intention to control must still be present.

A number of justifications have been offered for automatic copyright protection. Many of these revolve around concerns that formalities requirements

---

[18] A qualification is warranted: Berne's principle of national treatment is such that Member States could, if they wished, impose formalities requirements for their own nationals. But the approach across Convention countries has been to abolish such requirements.

[19] The European test: *Infopaq International A/S v Danske Dagblades Forening* (C-5/08) [2009] ECDR 16 at paras. 35–7.

[20] The US test: *Feist Publications, Inc v Rural Telephone Service Co*, 499 US 340, 345 (1991). Other countries use different formulations.

can be difficult to comply with, assume wrongly that authors have a good working knowledge of the law, and create devastating consequences – i.e., no protection – if not fulfilled. More recently, it has also been questioned whether formalities map onto a digital world characterised by user-generated content, memes, and large, distributed authorship networks (such as that which sits behind Wikipedia). The prohibition on formalities in Berne must also be understood alongside that Convention's central idea of national treatment: that Member States must treat the works of authors from other Convention countries the same way they treat the works of their own nationals. A system in which authors must comply with formalities in different countries, or in which judges must determine whether the formalities of other countries had been complied with, would be problematic and undermine this goal. The solution eventually arrived at was therefore the removal of formalities requirements.[21]

But the absence of formalities has become a growing concern on the basis that it is one of a number of factors that have led to difficulties in clearing rights. Consider a library that wishes to create a website about, say, the 1975 constitutional crisis in Australia, in which Prime Minister Gough Whitlam was dismissed by the Governor-General. It may wish to digitise collection items such as newspaper articles, photographs, cartoons, radio broadcasts and television footage. With no requirement for copyright owners to register or assert rights, obtaining information about the ownership of each individual item may be time-consuming and generate costs out of all proportion to the value of each individual use. It is likely that important material will be orphaned, such that no copyright owner will be identifiable. Finally, these challenges will likely be exacerbated by the copyright term, which can extend well beyond the life of the author or any meaningful commercial interest in the work.

As discussed above in relation to works of unknown authorship, it may be that, in practice, some of these issues can be dealt with through risk management. However, it is again noteworthy that we have a system which is built around property rules and which relies on voluntary licensing and assignment as the main way to facilitate the efficient use of works, but for which owners seem to have minimal, if any, obligation to maintain *any* ongoing connection with their works.

To illustrate, consider the outcome in *Fisher v Brooker*.[22] This case pertained to copyright in the song 'A Whiter Shade of Pale', recorded by the band Procol Harum in 1967. Matthew Fisher was at that time a member of the band – he left a few years later – and came up with the song's famous organ solo. He was not, however, credited as one of the writers of the music, and over the subsequent decades, royalties were distributed on the basis that the music for the

---

[21] Stef van Gompel, 'Formalities in the digital era: an obstacle or opportunity?' in Lionel Bently, Uma Suthersanen and Paul Torremans (eds), *Global Copyright: Three Hundred Years Since the Statute of Anne, from 1709 to Cyberspace* (Cheltenham: Edward Elgar, 2010).

[22] [2009] UKHL 41, [2009] 1 WLR 1764.

song was written by Gary Brooker and the lyrics by Keith Reid. In May 2005, some 38 years after the song was released, Mr Fisher commenced proceedings seeking, amongst other things, declarations in relation to authorship and copyright ownership. One of the key ideas to come from the case was that Mr Fisher's delay did not bar his request to be declared a joint owner of copyright, there being no limitation period for such claims in English law,[23] no copyright equivalent to adverse possession, and no evidence that might ground a proprietary estoppel (especially given that the defendants had, for many years, benefited from not having to share royalties with Mr Fisher). Lord Hope observed:

> There is no concept in our law that is more absolute than a right of property. Where it exists, it is for the owner to exercise it as he pleases. He does not need the permission of the court, nor is it subject to the exercise of the court's discretion. The benefits that flow from intellectual property are the product of this concept. They provide an incentive to innovation and creativity. A person who has a good idea, as Mr Fisher did when he composed the well-known organ solo that did so much to make the song in its final form such a success, is entitled to protect the advantage that he has gained from this and to earn his reward. These are rights which the court must respect and which it will enforce if it is asked to do so.[24]

The House of Lords stated that its recognition of Mr Fisher's joint ownership of the musical copyright in 'A Whiter Shade of Pale' did not render his delay irrelevant to his legal position, as defences such as laches and estoppel might limit his ability to obtain injunctive relief in the future. But the decision was consistent with the proposition that copyright owners can be inactive for many years without losing their claim *to* copyright. Indeed, without a substantive limitation period or doctrine similar to adverse possession, it could appear that copyright is a kind of uberproperty that is not even subject to the same vulnerabilities as tangible property. This is particularly significant for orphaned works, where concerns arise that copyright owners can resurface at any time to assert rights. But very similar issues also exist for 'apathetic' copyright owners who, for whatever reason, do not wish to exploit or enjoy their rights.

The issues generated by various types of 'invisible' authors raise the question of whether the copyright system needs to be changed to facilitate the use of orphaned and other works, on the basis that socially desirable uses are not taking place because of fears amongst users that proceeding without a licence may lead to legal and reputational harm. This is discussed further in section III, which analyses some of the solutions that have been deployed (or proposed) to deal with ownership-related problems.

---

[23] In contrast, there is a limitation period from the accrual of the cause of action for claims arising out of copyright, and the claimant limited its claim for royalties for a period of six years: ibid., at para. 15.

[24] Ibid., at para 8.

III. Solutions

A. Conceptualising Ownership Problems

In thinking about how to deal with copyright works that have ownership-related problems, it is worth pausing to clarify what exactly are the problems that we might wish to address. This chapter focuses primarily on instances where there is a fundamental failure of copyright as a system built on property rules, for instance because of the absence of an identifiable owner or because the owner is unaware of their rights or because the owner is apathetic, in terms of being completely uninterested in exploiting the rights granted automatically by law.

Another failure arises where there are willing buyers and sellers, but transaction costs are an impediment to consensual negotiations. This is a particular problem for high-volume, low-value uses, where the costs of clearing so many rights can be disproportionate to the value of those uses. One way to respond to this sort of problem is via collective administration, in which a copyright collective manages the rights of many copyright owners and can offer individual or blanket licences across its repertoire. There are therefore well-established collectives that manage rights in relation to the playing and broadcast of music and the use of copyright works in education.[25]

Separately to this, it has been said that certain uses ought not to be left to voluntary negotiation since we cannot rely on the market to deliver normatively desirable outcomes. Parody is often used to illustrate this point.[26] Parodies can be subversive and critical – consider, for example, video responses to 'Blurred Lines' by Robin Thicke and Pharrell Williams, which criticised the misogyny said to characterise the original song and music video. However, these sorts of critical elements or twists can lead to problems with holdout: that the copyright owner may be disinclined to grant *any* licence. In addition, parody is often said to be desirable as a creative output – i.e., have important benefits for society – but 'society' does not have a seat at the negotiating table. Instead, the societal interest in parody is represented by the parodist. Whether this interest is supported will depend on whether the parodist can pay the (possibly exorbitant) licensing fee.

For the preceding reasons, it has been said that parody should not be within the copyright owner's control. For parody, this outcome is typically effected through a free exception: a statutory provision that provides a defence for conduct that is prima facie infringing.[27] Importantly, the issue here is not the failure of property rules because there is no active owner but that property rules ought not to apply in the first place. Whilst parody exceptions are typically

---

[25] See Goldstein and Hugenholtz, n. 9 above, 275–81.

[26] See Robert P. Merges, 'Are You Making Fun of Me?: Notes on Market Failure and the Parody Defense in Copyright' (1993) 21 *AIPLA Quarterly Journal* 305.

[27] For example, via fair dealing in CDPA s. 30A and Copyright Act 1968 (Cth) ss. 41A, 103AA.

unremunerated, reliance on other exceptions and limitations is tied to the payment of money to the copyright owner. These provisions can have the effect of converting property rules to liability rules insofar as the copyright owner cannot withhold consent to a use but retains the right to be paid. For instance, in Australia, there have for many years been remunerated statutory schemes ('compulsory licences') to facilitate educational copying.[28]

Free exceptions have an indirect impact on works with problematic ownership because they remove the need for permission and the payment of remuneration. If a user proposes to rely on an exception for a use rather than securing permissions, such a strategy can be deployed for works with active owners as well as those whose ownership presents difficulties. In some cases, the factors that lead to the absence of an active owner – e.g., that commercial interest in the work receded long ago or that the creator never had a relationship of 'auteurship' with the work – may make it more likely that an exception will be applicable. As such, we should not overlook exceptions and limitations in any discussion about problematic ownership. However, there is only so much we can rely on these provisions (at least in their current form) as they do not cover the full gamut of cases where there is a failure in a system built on property rules.

B. Legal and Non-legal Solutions to the Orphaned Works Problem

To return to the central issue of problematic ownership, let us consider possible solutions to the orphaned works problem. As hinted at above, there is no statutory provision that exempts orphaned materials from infringement or that provides a general defence where a defendant undertook a reasonable search for the copyright owner but was unable to identify or locate that individual. In Australia, there has for many years been a narrow exception facilitating the publication of certain very old, unpublished works held by libraries and archives.[29] To rely on this exception, the identity of the copyright owner must be unknown and the user must, using the prescribed form, give public notice of their intention to publish. In the EU, the Orphan Works Directive aims to facilitate the digitisation programmes of European cultural institutions by providing that a 'relevant body' does not infringe copyright in an orphaned 'relevant work' by various acts of digitisation, making available, etc.[30] Bodies wishing to use this exception must satisfy a number of requirements, including that (1) they have undertaken, and maintain records of, a diligent search for the rightsholder and (2) that information about the work and the body's use has been reported to the European Union Intellectual Property Office

---

[28] Now found in Copyright Act 1968 (Cth), Part IV, Division 4. These were formerly known as Part VA and Part VB licences.

[29] Copyright Act 1968 (Cth), s. 52.

[30] Directive 2012/28/EU of the European Parliament and of the Council of 25 October 2012 on certain permitted uses of orphan works; implemented in the UK in CDPA, Schedule ZA1.

(EUIPO). If a rightsholder comes forward, fair compensation is payable. In the UK, the CDPA provides that this amount shall be determined by the parties or, if they are unable to agree, set by the Copyright Tribunal.

Although orphaned works have long been a by-product of the copyright system, they have occupied a prominent spot in copyright debates over the last two decades. These debates have identified a number of legal and non-legal solutions to the orphaned works problem. Proposed legal responses often fall into one of three categories.

In the first category are solutions that uphold the appearance of property rules through measures in which permission is supplied for the use of an orphaned work – just not from the copyright owner. This can be achieved via a centrally administered licence granted by a state tribunal or body, as illustrated by the Canadian scheme for unlocatable owners and, more recently, the UK scheme run by the Intellectual Property Office (IPO),[31] which operates along-side the EU-mandated exception. Alternatively, a similar result can be achieved by extended collective licensing, in which the repertoire of a collective extends to all works of a particular class and thus includes works of non-members.

The second category limits the remedies that a judge may award in relation to the defendant's conduct, should the copyright owner resurface.[32] Such limi-tations can take a number of forms, such as withdrawing any form of monetary relief, restricting damages to a reasonable licence fee, and/or limiting the cir-cumstances in which an injunction may be granted (e.g., by withdrawing that remedy where orphaned material has been incorporated into a new work and it would not be appropriate to prevent continued exploitation of that work by the defendant). Though not cast as a remedies limitation, the exception in the EU Directive – at least as implemented in the UK – shares many of the same intellectual foundations as a remedies limitation because of the requirement for fair remuneration should a copyright owner come forward. It differs from other proposals for remedies limitations, however, through its reporting requirements.

The third category will be explored in detail in Part C, and involves a more fundamental reappraisal of the copyright system and its ownership concepts in order to reduce or eliminate the existence of orphaned works. Leaving that to one side for now, the two solutions above deal with orphaned works in differ-ent ways: the first through identifying a body or representative that is given the power to grant permissions and the second by anticipating that negotiation may take place, but retrospectively, and only upon the resurfacing of the rightsholder.

---

[31] Copyright Act, RSC 1985, c. C-42, s. 77 (scheme for unlocatable copyright owners; licences granted by the Copyright Board of Canada); Copyright and Rights in Performances (Licensing of Orphan Works) Regulations 2014 (SI 2014/2863) (scheme in which the UK Intellectual Property Office may grant licences for the use of orphaned works).

[32] For example, the approach of the US Shawn Bentley Orphan Works Act of 2008 (never passed).

An obvious question in relation to the first solution pertains to licencing fees. In the UK scheme run by the IPO, for example, applicants are charged a 'reasonable licence fee',[33] which must be retained by the IPO in a separate ring-fenced bank account for at least eight years.[34] If no rightsholder comes forward during that time, the fee may be put towards the reasonable costs of running the licensing scheme or, if there is a surplus, for 'social, cultural and educational activities'.[35] This raises numerous practical and philosophical questions. What success rate do these schemes have in locating copyright owners? How much do they cost to administer, and do they generate benefits that render them preferable to other less bureaucratic interventions? Are we comfortable with the artificiality of these arrangements, which could be said to revolve around the idea that everything is okay so long as *someone* is paid, even if that person is not the copyright owner? Thinking about all the costs of a centralised licensing scheme, both for applicants and for the administering body, could those resources be used in more productive and socially desirable ways?

But there is a bigger question: in devising these legal solutions for orphaned works, with all the delays and conflicts inherent in legislative reform, are we crafting solutions that do not work for a problem that no longer exists? One must be very careful not to oversimplify since different users will have different experiences and perspectives. However, empirical evidence suggests two things. The first is that orphaned works licensing schemes tend to have low take-up rates. Analysis of decisions from the Copyright Board of Canada shows that from 1990 (when the first licence was issued) to December 2018, the Board issued approximately 298 licences[36] and denied 22 applications.[37] In the UK, from the launch of the licensing scheme in 2014 to January 2019, the IPO received a total of 160 applications in relation to 892 works, and granted licences in relation to 801 works.[38] When one considers the volume of creative activity in both countries, these numbers are extremely low. Reasons for the lack of utilisation include the administrative costs of making applications,

---

[33] Copyright and Rights in Performances (Licensing of Orphan Works) Regulations (SI 2014/2863), para. 10(1)(a).

[34] Ibid., para. 10(2).

[35] Ibid., paras. 13(1), (2).

[36] Copyright Board of Canada, *Unlocatable Copyright Owners: Decisions/Licences Issued* <http://www.cb-cda.gc.ca/unlocatable-introuvables/licences-e.html> (last visited 13 January 2019). That website lists 303 sets of reasons, but at least five are in relation to the same licence or application.

[37] Copyright Board of Canada, *Unlocatable Copyright Owners: Applications Denied (Reasons)* <http://www.cb-cda.gc.ca/unlocatable-introuvables/denied-refusees-e.html> (last visited 13 January 2019).

[38] IPO, *Orphan Works Register*, <https://www.orphanworkslicensing.service.gov.uk/view-register> (last visited 13 January 2019). Applications were withdrawn for 80 works, and there were 11 pending applications.

the need to document a reasonable search, and limits in the licences themselves.[39] For instance, licences granted by the IPO have a term of seven years (with renewal for a further seven years possible) and apply only in the UK.

The second thing suggested by empirical research is that users and the nature of their legal concerns have changed over time. For instance, interviews with staff at leading UK and Australian cultural institutions conducted by the author as part of a long-term project suggest that, over the last decade, staff have become progressively more knowledgeable about copyright and their institutions more tolerant of risk.[40] This is not to suggest a copyright free-for-all – far from it – but that for many members of the sector, orphaned works are less of a problem because of the deployment of more robust risk management practices. The interviews also suggested a positive feedback loop, in which the appropriateness of risk-informed uses of orphaned works was reinforced by the lived experience that copyright owners did not resurface very often and, when they did, were often delighted by the institution's use. In such an environment, many interviewees did not see any benefit in applying for an IPO licence, especially given that they did not tend to use orphaned works on merchandise or other commercial endeavours. The EU exception was more palatable but seemed to replicate risk management norms – albeit with greater administrative burden – although the potential for smaller and less experienced institutions to appreciate the added certainty was noted.

With institutions becoming more confident in their handling of orphaned works, an emerging question for the cultural institution sector is how to deal with the works of non-responsive copyright owners. Crafting a strategy for such works is, in certain respects, trickier than for orphaned works because the problem is not the lack of an identifiable copyright owner but that this individual fails to answer institution correspondence. Many institutions take the approach that such works should be treated as though permission has been withheld. But should inaction be taken as a positive desire to reject licensing, or that the copyright owner does not care about exploiting or enforcing rights, or that the copyright owner is not even aware of his or her status? It may be that, as with orphaned works, much of the answer will be found in risk management. But do these ownership issues around orphaned materials, ignorant owners and apathetic owners suggest that more radical reform is required or that a system built around 'ownership' is not fit for purpose, at least in its current form? These ideas are explored next in Parts C and D.

---

[39] See Emily Hudson, *Drafting Copyright Exceptions: From the Law in Books to the Law in Action* (forthcoming, Cambridge: Cambridge University Press) Ch. 3.

[40] Ibid, Chs. 3 and 8.

C. Is It Time to Re-introduce Copyright Formalities?

A number of scholars considering such things as orphaned works and mass digitisation have debated whether we need to consider more radical reform to the copyright system, including the re-introduction of formalities requirements such as notice, deposit and registration.[41] As noted above, a number of objections have been made in relation to such requirements. However, a century after the Berne Convention was amended to state, in Article 5(2), that the 'enjoyment and the exercise of these rights shall not be subject to any formality', the case for formalities is being prosecuted with greater fervour. In some but not all cases, these suggestions would require the revision of Berne.

A central plank of the pro-formalities case is that such measures help to create legal and evidentiary certainty in relation to, amongst other things, the nature and boundaries of the work in which rights are claimed and the identity of the author and copyright owner. This has been predicted to have various flow-on benefits, for instance by making licensing easier, aiding in dispute resolution, and reducing the likelihood that works will become orphaned. In addition, because formalities require an active step by the author to claim rights, they have been identified as a mechanism to reduce the number of works protected by copyright, increase the flow of protected works into the public domain, or both. These benefits might be thought to help deal with many issues associated with problematic ownership.

Some proposals in relation to formalities involve a rollback of automatic copyright protection. But it is important to appreciate the variety of forms that formalities can take. As discussed by Stef van Gompel, these might include (1) constitutive formalities (required for copyright to *subsist*), (2) renewal formalities (required for existing rights to *continue*), and (3) declarative formalities (required for *court enforcement* to be permitted or for *certain remedies* to be awarded).[42] Consider, for example, the proposal of William Landes and Richard Posner for 'indefinitely renewable copyright'.[43] The core of their idea was that authors would receive an initial automatic grant followed by 'a right to renew copyright as many times as the owner (including the original owner's heirs and successors) wants', for a fee.[44] Landes and Posner suggested that this would cause the average copyright term to decrease since many works would never be renewed. One attraction of the Landes and Posner model is that it does less violence to the current legal framework, given that all authors would receive an initial grant.

---

[41] For example, van Gompel, n. 21 above.
[42] Ibid.
[43] Landes and Posner, n. 2 above.
[44] Ibid., 473.

D. Should We Treat the Proprietary Nature of Copyright More Seriously?

One matter that is striking about many suggestions for reform is that they involve the (re)introduction into copyright law of ownership principles that exist for tangible property. Consider registration. There are ways in which owners can physically signal their rights to land, such as erecting fences and putting up signs. However, in land law, we make extensive use of registers to define the plot and record those who claim an interest in it. Although registration may not necessarily be required for an interest to arise, failure to register will often result in that interest being more easily lost, thus providing a strong incentive to register and leading to a comprehensive record of interests.[45] Another use of registration is to record security interests over personal property, and in some systems this is the main way to perfect the creditor's interest (i.e., ensure that person obtains the strongest rights possible).

This leads to the question of whether ownership problems in copyright relate not to copyright being understood as a species of property (such that we should reject that characterisation in favour of something else) but that the proprietary underpinnings of copyright have not been taken seriously enough. For example, the arguments in favour of formalities in IP law might be even stronger than for tangible property, given the lack of a physical thing to which rights relate. Tangible things have an existence in time and space. Possession is important not just for its legal significance but because it provides useful rules of thumb (e.g., that people tend to own the things that they possess). For intangible creations, how do we identify the parameters of the work? What heuristics do we tend to apply in relation to the identity and preferences of the copyright owner? To the extent that our starting point is often 'all rights reserved', does that accurately reflect the mind-set of most people? One argument in favour of formalities is that they help with some of these matters – for instance, by requiring authors to identify the work claimed and by signalling that (at least at some point) there was an owner who wished to assert rights.

One further thing to bear in mind is that analysis of property law might reveal other ways to respond to ownership problems, being strategies that unlike (some) formalities can be implemented without change to international copyright law. For instance, might answers be found in general law principles in relation to abandonment, admixture, limitation periods and estoppel – doctrines that might be relevant to the loss of rights or the ability to sue? Some of these arguments were considered in *Fisher v Brooker*, where it was concluded that they did not oust claims *to* copyright. But should that be the inevitable outcome? Even if copyright protection is automatic, should we require that copyright owners take some steps to maintain a connection with their works?

---

[45] Molly Shaffer Van Houweling, 'Land Recording and Copyright Reform' (2013) 28 *Berkeley Technology Law Journal* 1497.

In Europe, there has been an implicit push-back against one possible response – greater use of implied licence – in CJEU cases such as *Soulier v Premier Ministre*.[46] Implied licence is relevant for infringement. It recognises that there will be no infringement where a user acts within the scope of a licence from the copyright owner, but that sometimes this licence can be implied from the circumstances rather than manifesting as an express grant. The *Soulier* case related to legislation in France to permit the mass digitisation of out-of-print books in a scheme intended as the French equivalent to the Google Books project. Relevantly for the case, books identified as candidates for digitisation would be entered on a publicly-available register. If, in the six months following a book's entry on the register, no author or publisher came forward to assert rights, then it was possible for digitisation to be authorised by a collective – although the author or publisher could subsequently withdraw this consent. The Third Chamber held that the legislation was incompatible with European copyright law. It stated that the Information Society Directive gives a high level of protection to authors, and that the 'circumstances in which implicit consent can be admitted must be strictly defined in order not to deprive of effect the very principle of the author's prior consent.'[47] Although there was a mechanism to advertise the books that had been identified for mass digitisation and a six month period before digitisation could commence, it could not be assumed that the *absence* of any communication by the author was an implied consent. Every author had to 'actually be informed' about the proposed use and had the ability to object.[48] The French legislation was therefore held to be incompatible with the Information Society Directive.

Since *Soulier*, there has been some attempt to facilitate mass digitisation by European cultural institutions via Article 8 of the new Directive on Copyright in the Digital Single Market (DSM Directive). Article 8 applies to 'out-of-commerce works' and has some similarities with the French scheme. It has two limbs: (1) extended collective licensing (ECL) for works where there is a representative collective; and (2) an exception or limitation for works for which no such collective exists, and which allows institutions to digitise those works and make them available on non-commercial websites. There is much to critique in relation to Article 8, including the extremely broad definition of 'out-of-commerce' works, which apparently includes works never intended for commerce. Relevantly for this discussion, it is possible for authors to opt out not only from any licence but from the exception. Having an opt out for the ECL limb makes sense if we take seriously the idea that authorial consent is paramount in a system built on property rules. In contrast, the extension of the opt-out to the exception is far less principled.

---

[46] (C-301/15) [2017] ECDR 23 (CJEU, Third Chamber).
[47] Ibid., at para 37.
[48] Ibid., at para 38.

There are two inter-related issues. The first is the reasoning behind the exception: is it that we would *prefer* licensing to take place but appreciate that for many works in cultural collections there are market failures due to transactions costs, invisible authors, and so forth; or are we of the view that the use covered by the exception is *outside* the copyright owner's market? The opt-out suggests the former. But here the second issue arises: if the activity covered by the exception is within the rights of the author, then is Article 8 in substance a requirement for formalities that contravenes Article 5(2) of Berne? This raises matters in relation to international copyright law that are complicated and beyond the scope of this chapter, including whether 'exceptions' and 'limitations' are functionally distinct. For now, the key question is whether authors start with, in effect, a derogation from their rights, and must comply with a formality – some mechanism in which they opt out – in order to enjoy those rights. If so, this could be argued to be contrary to Berne – although there may be people who are not dissatisfied with such an outcome.

IV. Concluding Remarks

This chapter has analysed problematic ownership in copyright law. It has identified options for reform that can be rolled out within the current system, options that would require a more fundamental revision of the international copyright order, and has noted that we could also consider responses that derive from general property law principles. But it is worth ending with a brief provocation since a very different type of 'ownership' problem has emerged in the last few decades: the mediation of relationships between owners and users via technological measures and extensive, privately written copyright codes.

The emergence of this problem can be connected in large part to digital and online technologies. These technologies have changed how we acquire copyright content. Instead of buying physical infrastructure onto which the work is recorded (books, magazines, CDs, DVDs, and so forth), purchasers often receive electronic copies or no (permanent) copy at all (e.g., where content is streamed or accessed from a remote server). This gives the content provider much greater power to control the terms of access and to withdraw content or have it subject to digital locks and other controls. The contracts that accompany such electronic content can be problematic for a number of reasons. In some instances, they place extensive restrictions on how the works the subject of the licence may be used, including by purporting to contract out of exceptions.[49] In addition, contract has been used to assert copyright-style controls in relation to works that are not protected by copyright (e.g., because they are not original).

---

[49] In some copyright statutes, this has led to prohibitions on contracting out: e.g., CDPA, ss. 29(4B), 29A(5), 30(4), 30A(2), 32(3).

To the extent that these contracts can overreach, there are a number of legal regimes that might help supply answers, including consumer protection law. However, it is also worth considering the contributions that property law might make. One question that warrants further attention is whether IP needs a more robust *numerus clausus* principle: a doctrine that fixes and limits the number of forms that property may take.[50] In addition, it may be that property does a better job than contract at reflecting the various interests that the law needs to accommodate in relation to intellectual and artistic works. Although we can debate whether the right balance has been struck, copyright law can be seen as responding to a variety of imperatives – for instance, to reward authors but also encourage new authorship, and to provide a legal infrastructure that allows authors to monetise their labour but with carve-outs for uses that are outside the author's reasonable market. Even when a natural law justification for copyright is applied, rights are not absolute but must be seen in the light of the rights and freedoms of others.[51]

In sum, copyright's current idea of ownership can create problems, including in relation to various types of invisible author. But in a world where the statutory regime is being overtaken by technological locks and aggressive licensing practices, there may be good reasons for arguing that the solution is to be found in an even more serious engagement with the proprietary underpinnings of copyright.

FURTHER READING

M. Carrier, 'Cabining Intellectual Property Through a Property Paradigm' (2004) 54 *Duke Law Journal* 1.

P. Chapdelaine, 'The Property Attributes of Copyright' (2014) 10 *Buffalo Intellectual Property Law Journal* 34.

D. S. Gangjee, 'Copyright formalities: A return to registration?' in Rebecca Giblin and Kimberlee Weatherall (eds), *What if we could reimagine copyright?* (ANU Press; Canberra, 2017).

J. Ginsburg, 'Berne-Forbidden Formalities and Mass Digitization' (2016) 96 *Boston University Law Review* 745.

E. Hudson and R. Burrell, 'Copyright, Abandonment and Orphaned Works: What Does it Mean to Take the Proprietary Nature of Intellectual Property Rights Seriously?' (2011) 35 *Melbourne University Law Review* 971.

W. M. Landes and R. A. Posner, 'Indefinitely Renewable Copyright' (2003) 70 *University of Chicago Law Review* 471.

M. Lemley, 'Property, Intellectual Property, and Free Riding' (2005) 83 *Texas Law Review* 1031.

L. P. Loren, 'Abandoning the Orphans: An Open Access Approach to Hostage Works' (2012) 27 *Berkeley Technology Law Journal* 1431.

---

[50] See generally Thomas W. Merrill and Henry E. Smith, 'Optimal Standardization in the Law of Property: The *Numerus Clausus* Principle' (2000) 110 *Yale Law Journal* 1.

[51] See generally Hugh Breaker, *Intellectual Liberty: Natural Rights and Intellectual Property* (Farnham: Ashgate, 2012).

J. McCutcheon, 'Curing the Authorless Void: Protecting Computer-Generated Works Following ICETV and Phone Directories' (2013) 37 *Melbourne University Law Review* 46.

C. Mulligan, 'A Numerus Clausus Principle for Intellectual Property' (2013) 80 *Tennessee Law Review* 235.

CHAPTER 7

Shareholders and Directors: Entitlements, Duties and the Expansion of Shareholder Wealth

Lorraine Talbot

Introduction

Company law and governance exist for one purpose: to expand and protect shareholder income and power. This chapter explores some of the implications of this and some of the resulting paradoxes. A core paradox is that by promoting shareholder value, company law and modern corporate governance simultaneously and necessarily promote the interests of company executives whose own fortunes are bound to that value. However, while achieving shareholder value is considered a success, and a rising Financial Times Stock Exchange (FTSE) a marker of economic good health, high executive pay is considered a modern-day scandal, a societal blight. Other curiosities include the considerable scholarship that links shareholder value-driven corporate activity to societal problems such as inequality, or lack of investment in innovation and productivity, but that simultaneously clears shareholders of culpability. Executives, not shareholders, are to blame. Indeed, shareholders and other claimants on corporate profit are thought to be part of the solution to shareholder value-driven corporate activity. They are entrusted with increasing monitoring responsibilities and with control of key corporate governance mechanisms, manifest in such developments as shareholder say on pay, the Stewardship Codes and the Shareholder Rights Directives.[1] That these contradictions can co-exist evidences the considerable debate, not to mention confusion, in company law and governance around shareholders, directors and their varying duties and entitlements.

---

[1] DIRECTIVE (EU) 2017/828 of the European Parliament and of the Council 17 May 2017, amending Directive 2007/36/EC as regards the encouragement of long-term shareholder engagement.

In assessing the issues of entitlements, duties and the expansion of share-holder wealth, this chapter first presents arguments that may explain why the enrichment of shareholders is (largely) accepted whereas the enrichment of directors is not. It begins with the proposition that shareholder enrichment is accepted because of changes in company law, which made shareholder claims less controversial at a time when they could be perceived as both political and exploitative. We see this through consideration 19th century company law on the changing property of the share, reflected in dividend law. The next section considers the impact of the law on shares upon directors' duties, which require that directors pursue the interest of shareholders and eschew alternative inter-ests. The chapter then explores how the environment that shapes shareholder entitlement is not fixed or natural. It shows how post-war company practice and policies were more in keeping with social expectations that companies should be managed to balance the interests of a variety of stakeholders, which included shareholders but did not make them paramount. This period was fol-lowed by a forceful reassertion of the centrality of the shareholder and was accompanied by an ideological reshaping of social expectations to align them with shareholder primacy. The chapter then considers how this reassertion led to a rapid rise in executive directors' remuneration, which in turn led to regula-tory measures to rely on shareholders to control remuneration. The chapter argues that the ineffectiveness of these regulations in curtailing excessive remu-neration largely results from the binding of policymakers to an unwavering and uncritical commitment to shareholder entitlement.

Debate 1
History shows us that the legal structuring of companies freed shareholders from the charge of exploitation previously levelled at industrial owners

As a cursory glance at history and literature show us, the typical Victorian fac-tory was a dangerous and exploitative environment in which men, women and even children worked long hours for pitiful wages. In contrast, factory owners enjoyed safe and lavish lifestyles on the wealth created from an immiserated workforce. In this stereotypical – though not necessarily inaccurate – account of social conditions under early industrialisation, it was the factory proprietors who were the bad guys and the beneficiaries of its profits. Under modern con-ditions, the shareholders are the beneficiaries. However, we do not demonise shareholders. On the contrary, if there are perceived injustices in the behaviour of companies, we encourage them to get more involved in the running of the company. So what has changed? First, the relationship between profit and human misery became obfuscated. This obfuscation began when the share stopped being a property interest in the whole business and became instead a property interest in the profits generated by that business. The obfuscation became complete when businesses later opted to operate as companies rather than partnerships. These two key changes (and several more between these two) transformed shareholders from active visible owners in an identifiable business to rentiers investing in financial property.

So when did these changes occur? The wholesale shift of business to the corporate form at the end of the 19th century followed some decades after legal changes to the share and the rights of shareholders. A profound change occurred in the nature of the property of the share in the 1830s. For centuries, the property of the share was understood to be a beneficial interest in the whole business, but, as Williston revealed, this property was reconceptualised and the share was thereon understood as an interest in surplus value only. Williston proved this by analysing a number of early cases involving the fraudulent transfer of shares, theft of shares and transfer of shares upon intestacy. He found that the courts decided these cases on the basis of whether they considered the share to be realty or personalty. In all cases, the courts based their decision on the type of property owned by the company. Was it primarily realty or personalty? He surmised, therefore, that a share represented a beneficial interest in the company as a whole, which included its productive assets. In contrast to this long-standing legal understanding of shares and shareholders, the 1837 decision in *Bligh v Brent* held that shareholders were beneficial *and legal owners* of the *surplus* created by company assets but not the assets themselves.[2] Over the following decades, this ruling on the nature of the share became the general understanding of the proprietary rights attaching to all shares, in all companies.

Subsequent company legislation, which aimed to encourage businesses to adopt the company form, further enhanced the separateness of the shareholder from the company and increased the transferability of shares. The Joint Stock Companies Act 1844 aimed to increase incorporations by offering the privileges of incorporation to all who complied with the Act. It further required existing partnerships with over 25 members and all existing joint stock companies (understood under the Act as 'every partnership whereof the Capital is divided or agreed to be divided into Shares, and so to be transferable without the express Consent of all Copartners') to register as companies under the Act.[3] Joint stock companies were also known as deed of settlement companies because they operated in accordance with bespoke deeds of settlement, which set out the arrangement between investors and directors. The 1844 Act, in large part, aimed to displace these business practices because of their pervasiveness and association with financial scandal. However, the Act continued some of their practices by providing that registration would be complete only when a deed of settlement, covering specified issues, was signed and sealed by the shareholders and registered with the relevant authority. The Act also required a minimum of three directors and one auditor. Directors were empowered to 'conduct and manage the affairs of the company' whereas shareholders were

---

[2] S. Williston, 'History of the law of business corporations before 1800: part II' (1888) 2(4) *Harvard Law Review* 149–C66, citing the case of *Bligh v Brent* (1837) 2 Y&C 268.

[3] An Act for the Registration, Incorporation and Regulation of Joint Stock Companies (Victoria 7&8) 1844. Section III.

not. Shareholders merely collected dividends provided that they had made sufficient upfront payments. Another key piece of legislation was the Limited Liability Act 1855, which limited the liability of shareholders and thereby severed them from the debts of the company. This further underlined the distinction between shareholder and company property, as the company retained unlimited liability for its own debts.

Subsequent company legislation continued to enhance the benefits (for shareholders at least) of the company form. The 1855 provisions on limited liability were quickly superseded by the Companies Act 1856, which removed many of the previous Act's onerous solvency requirements. The 1856 Act introduced further reforms to mimic the deed of settlement company because this organisational form had proven success in facilitating outside investment. The clauses of the newly introduced articles of association closely mirrored clauses typical in the deeds of settlement used by business prior to the 1844 Act. The 1856 Act constituted in effect 'a statutory adoption of the deed of settlement form'.[4] From 1856 on, the clause empowering directors to manage the affairs of the company would be included in the articles by default, rather than arise by statute, as it had under the 1844 Act noted above and as is the norm in common law countries. In so doing, English company law adopted a contractual form more suited to private ordering and is part of the explanation for the reliance on contractual and quasi-contractual mechanisms in company law as discussed by Attenborough (Chapter 8). The 1856 Act and the following Companies Act 1862 both simplified and streamlined registration to further encourage incorporation. Finally, the Companies Act 1867 allowed companies to cancel uncalled capital and to break up existing shares into small denomination shares. In this way, shares became more practical to transfer and were able to become a fungible property form.

However, although the legal shape of the company share was established by the courts and by legislation, these changes did not immediately influence attitudes to the abuses carried out by factory owners because the most visibly exploitative businesses were not companies but partnerships. Most industrial businesses did not want to use the corporate form. After the 1844 Act was passed, on average only 377 business each year were incorporated under the Act, and a large percentage of these either never began trading or were wound up after a short period of trading.[5]

The 1844 Act did not give company shareholders limited liability since parliament believed it subverted ethical business and was 'contrary to the whole genius and spirit of the common law'; so it is arguable that the low take-up for incorporation was due to the strict rules on unlimited liability set out in the

[4] S. Watson, 'Derivation of Powers of Boards of Directors in UK Companies' in P.M. Vasudev and S. Watson, *Corporate Governance after the Financial Crisis* (Elgar, 2012), 56.
[5] B.R. Cheffins, *Corporate Ownership and Control. British Business Transformed* (Oxford 2008) pp. 166–7.

Act.[6] Moreover, the growing political agitation for limited liability companies indicated that access to limited liability might enhance the desirability of incorporation. Working men's collectives sought limited liability as a protection against debt, while rich investors sought limited liability to give them safe access to company profits. However, a Royal Commission set up to enquire into the merits of limited liability, consulting with key manufacturers, merchants, bakers, lawyers, academics and MPs, was less conclusive. Nonetheless, the government opted to facilitate limited liability, a move that commentators have concluded was intended to give wealthy (and emerging middle-class) investors access to the profits of manufacturing and thereby to bridge the gap between industrial capital and investment capital, 'the "gentry" and the "trading class"'.[7] But, whatever the intention was, established manufacturing businesses remained uninterested in incorporation, even with limited liability (largely because they already had more-than-adequate capital).

The new company form, however, was adopted by start-ups and more risky businesses, particularly speculative finance. This could have led the legislature to back away from limited liability but it did not. Undeterred, it continued to develop the company form as a vehicle for investment. So, when the Overend Gurney bank fell and financial crisis ensued in 1866, instead of abandoning limited liability, they doubled down on it by passing new legislation allowing companies to cancel unpaid capital and to create small denomination shares (Companies Act 1867). The government believed that by making it easy to break down large denomination shares and to cancel unpaid capital on large denomination shares, the de facto unlimited liability this affected would gradually cease.

Nonetheless, these attempts to shape business through company law had little effect on business. Why was this? The answer is largely agreed to be economic. Industrial capitalists were making too much profit to want what the company form offered – limited liability, corporate identity and outside investment in exchange for regulation. The labour-intensive productive sector, which included child labour, profited from the low wages offered to the workforce and long arduous hours they worked. In terms of profitability, manufacturing was the jewel of the British economy and the source of spectacular returns. The average real rate of return on fixed capital in manufacturing is calculated as 39.8 per cent from 1855 to 1874, and the high point was 1860.[8] In contrast, other parts of the economy, such as finance and infrastructure, which had already embraced the corporate form, either were volatile or produced low returns. For example, the return on railway shares was around 5 per cent from

---

[6] Bishop Carleton Hunt, 'The Joint Stock Company In England 1830–1944' (1935) 43 *The Journal of Political Economy* 331, 358.

[7] R.A. Bryer, 'The Mercantile Laws Commission of 1854 and the Political Economy of Limited Liability' (1997) 1 *Economic History Review* 37, 55.

[8] E.E. Maito, 'And yet it moves (down)', *Weekly Worker*, 14th August 2014. http://weekly-worker.co.uk/worker/1023/profit-debate-and-yet-it-moves-down [Accessed 27 February 2016].

1870 to 1910.[9] The high profits enjoyed by manufacturing meant that owners had no need for incorporation, limited liability, or outside investors. Manufacturers largely preferred the freedom of a private partnership arrangement in which they owned, controlled and claimed the profits of the business. Thus, the company legislation passed throughout the 19th century to encourage a corporate, investor-based capitalism was largely unused by Victorian manufacturers.

The continued aversion of manufacturing firms to the company form had another interesting effect on company law development: company law in the courts was being shaped by finance and infrastructure companies, which tended to be very large with many outside, non-controlling shareholders. That is, judgments were made on the understanding that shareholders were outside rentiers and that directors rather than shareholders made decisions on the company's behalf. This was because that was the reality within railway companies, banks and so on. For example, the common law doctrine of *ultra vires* – that the company did not have the power to enter into contracts that fell outside its business purpose as stated in its constitution – was established in a case involving a railway company.[10] This doctrine enabled those without management control, including creditors as well as shareholders, to challenge directors' decisions in these extreme circumstances.[11] Likewise, a railway company case established that company funds could not be used for non-commercial or charitable purposes. Companies were commercial businesses without a public purpose, or to put it more famously, 'there are to be no cakes and ale except such as are required for the benefit of the company'.[12] This decision is all the more striking in its focus on shareholders' interests (the challenged payment would have reduced the amount payable to shareholder) because railway companies were incorporated by statute and had an express public purpose.

The early rules on *ultra vires* underlined the outside nature of shareholders – they were non-managing owners of profit with a limited right to challenge

---

[9] R.J. Irving, 'The profitability and performance of Britain's railways, 1870–1914', *Economic History Review* 2nd ser., XXXI (1978).

[10] *Ashbury Railway Carriage & Iron Co v Riche* (1875)LR HL 653.

[11] This strict application of the doctrine was radically modified in the courts to include contracts that were 'reasonably incidental' to the objects. Later, the courts allowed objects that allowed directors to enter into any contracts they deemed to be in the interest of the company. Johnston emphasises the strong managerialist orientation of these decisions (A. Johnston, 'The Shrinking Scope of CSR in UK Corporate Law' 74 *Wash. & Lee L. Rev.* 1001 2017); however, Talbot emphasises the marginalisation of creditors and minority shareholders to the benefit of both directors and larger shareholders. See L. Talbot, 'Critical Corporate Governance and the Demise of the *Ultra Vires* Doctrine' (2009) 38 *Common Law World Review* 170.

[12] *Hutton v West Cork Ry Co* (1883) 23 Ch D 654. This ruling is much curtailed since *Horsley v Weight*. However, Marc Moore argues that the importance of *Re Hutton* is its assertion of a director's right to determine what is in the interests of the company provided they are acting in good faith Marc T. Moore, *Shareholder Primacy, Labour and the Historic Ambivalence of UK Company Law* 19 (Univ. of Cambridge Legal Studies Research Paper Series, Working Paper No. 40/2016, 2016).

contracts if they concerned something that was substantially different from the business purpose in which they had invested and set out in the company's objects. Second, they underlined shareholder entitlement to profit from an entity that was required to be profit-making and commercial.

The ownership and control relationships in the sorts of companies whose cases were coming before the courts were clearly different from the ownership and control relationships in industry. But, of course, these legal norms would apply to those businesses when they finally adopted the company form. By the end of the century, they had done so. Business had substantially shifted to the company form.

However, this did not occur because of the new privileges attached to companies or, as often claimed, because the corporate form enables the most effective economy. It occurred because capitalism failed. In the face of an entrenched economic slump, the company form facilitated protectionism. In the last quarter of the century, prices and then profits fell and remained depressed until the end of the century: an extended economic depression known as the 'Long' or 'Great Depression' (1873–1896). Industrial capitalists responded to this challenge by merging with competitors in order to reduce competition and so arrest the slump in prices. The company form provided a convenient way of doing this. In so doing, industrial capitalists were transformed from owner/managers into non-managing shareholders, owners of a property form that was transferable and disconnected from the business's activities and liabilities. The shift of manufacturing from partnerships to companies can be evidenced by stock market statistics. By 1913, railway companies represented 15 per cent of the total equity market, down from 76 per cent in 1870.[13] Industrial company shares now dominated the stock market.

Other areas of company law also illustrate that the owners of industrial companies were, by the end of the century, merely rentiers. For example, the changing rules on dividends recognised that a shareholder had a proprietary interest in profit but not company assets. Before those changes, the courts took account of reductions in the value of company assets in its calculation of profits available for distribution, connecting, in this context, shareholder interest to the company's assets. However, from 1889, the court calculated profit and therefore distributions independently from any loss to assets. The court considered only the profit made from those assets. This severed the link between what shareholders owned (a claim to profit) and the value of the assets that created those profits.

The early approach was set out in the case of *Burnes v Pennell*.[14] This case concerned an action against a shareholder who refused unpaid calls on his shares, claiming that the price he had paid for the shares was artificially inflated because it was based upon dividends that the directors had declared when there

---

[13] R.S. Grossman, 'New indices of British equity prices 1870–1913', (2002) 62 *Journal of Economic History* 121–146.

[14] *Burnes v Pennell* (1849) 9 English Reports 1181 (House of Lords).

was insufficient profit to do so (an unlawful act that involved paying dividends from company capital). The court held that this misrepresented the company's finances and was a fraud by the directors.[15] This approach was taken further in 1877, when Jessel M.R. stated that dividends could not be paid when there has been a loss of capital in trading unless the court had approved a statutory reduction.[16]

Then, in *Lee v. Neuchatel Asphalt Co.* (1889), a shareholder claimed that, as the value of the company's assets had fallen, the company should make good that loss before declaring a dividend. Although the loss itself was disputed, the court, in a sharp departure from previous authorities, held that a company could declare dividends notwithstanding that its assets were depleted; a wasting asset could still produce a profit. Lindley LJ[17] therefore introduced an interpretation of what constituted distributable profit that reflected the shareholder as *rentier*. The *Lee* position was followed in subsequent cases that confirmed the disembeddedness of the shareholder from the company.

By the end of the 19th century, the claimants of industrial profits were shareholders, to whom applied all the legal doctrines on shares and shareholders developed throughout the century in the context of non-industrial companies and corporations (*Foss v Harbottle, Bligh v Brent, Ashbury Railway co*), as well as later rulings, such as on dividends, which concerned industrial companies. These doctrines, together with company legislation, conceptually severed shareholders from actual production and reconceptualised the shareholder as a rentier. Shareholders were therefore not responsible for exploitative work practices; they were merely owners of financial property that entitled them to company profit (legally conditional on the directors declaring a dividend).

Of course, it might be supposed that in the shift from factory owner to shareholder, the moral culpability of the capitalist could be amplified, in the eyes of the public, because the shareholder enjoys the value extracted from exploited labour without taking responsibility for managing the work environment or even being responsible for the debts of the business. This, as we know, is not the case. As Marx makes clear, the manifest exploitation of labour by capital under late- 19th-century capitalism was not revealed, but obfuscated and politically neutralised, when the share ceased to confer ownership of the business entity and instead simply commodified the corporate surplus.[18] Furthermore, from a liberal, property rights perspective, shareholders are entitled to corporate profit because that is in the nature of the property of the share. Accordingly, the shareholders' extraction of value from the company is not controversial; it is in the character of their property. Thus, once shares were concretised as a *legal* entitlement to surplus, shareholders' right to profit

[15] Op cite *Bligh v Brent*.
[16] *Re Ebbw Vale Steel, Iron &Coal Co.* (1877) 4 Ch.D 827.
[17] *Lee v. Neuchatel Asphalt Co.* (1889) 41 Ch.D 1.
[18] K. Marx *Capital: A Critique of Political Economy Vol III* (Foreign Languages Publishing House 1962) p. 380.

became an incontestable and natural attribute of share ownership. This first applied to the discrete elements of the economy that used the company form and, later, to the economy as a whole as manufacturing businesses of any size incorporated. As shareholders have gradually abandoned their earlier passive stance, this conceptualisation has become an effective licence to pressure for more profit, not as a form of social or class power but as a quality of the property of the share. These developments in company law ensured the shareholders' right to expect that directors would manage the company with a view to prioritising their interests, a view that has become the cornerstone of judicial and legislative thinking (Box 7.1).

Box 7.1 The Modern Consequences of the Dis-embedded Share

That a share was conceived in law as an entitlement to profit detached from the company assets has had a number of consequences. First, and together with limited liability, it has enabled shareholders to be free from legal and moral responsibilities for any harms the company commits. This has shifted the impact of companies' externalities onto creditors (including involuntary creditors) and the environment. Second, in the context of a modern globalised society, it has enabled business to form itself into corporate groups, headed by a lead company that may own all or sufficient of the shares in the group (as one example of the forms that groups of companies may take). This allows the lead or parent company to be protected from the other companies' liabilities while holding full entitlement to the profits.

Debate 2

Directors' duties arise from shareholder entitlement

The historical development of shareholder claims led to the imposition of corresponding duties on directors to meet those claims. Company law has developed many principles, which ensure that directors create wealth for shareholders (*Re Hutton* above) and prohibit them from extracting wealth for themselves. Directors' duties, first established in the courts and more recently embedded in statute, aim to ensure that directors focus on creating value for shareholders and impose strict rules against directors' self-dealing.

The overarching common law duty of a director was to act in good faith in the interests of the company. But, this was generally interpreted as the promotion of shareholder interests rather than wider concerns such as the development of the enterprise's productive capacity or employee welfare. Attempts to construe the benefit of the company as that which benefits non-shareholder interests have invariably been dismissed by the courts. In *Parke v Daily News*[19], Plowman J. rejected the notion that the benefit of the company could be that

---

[19] *Parke v Daily News* [1962] Ch. 927.

which benefits employees and that a directors' duty might also be to the employees, stating 'in my judgment such is not the law'.[20] As the case concerned a company that had ceased trading, there could be no benefit to shareholders in making payment to redundant employees. Leaving little room for ambiguity on the matter, Lord Evershed M.R. had earlier stated that 'the benefit of the company meant the benefit of the shareholders as a general body'.[21] This general duty is now found in the Companies Act 2006 under section 172 and has been reformulated as promoting the success of the company for the benefit of its members (Box 7.2).

Box 7.2 Section 172: Duty to Promote the Success of the Company

(1) A director of a company must act in the way he considers, in good faith, would be most likely to promote the success of the company for the benefit of its members as a whole, and in doing so have regard (amongst other matters) to

    (a) the likely consequences of any decision in the long term,

    (b) the interests of the company's employees,

    (c) the need to foster the company's business relationships with suppliers, customers and others,

    (d) the impact of the company's operations on the community and the environment,

    (e) the desirability of the company maintaining a reputation for high standards of business conduct, and

    (f) the need to act fairly as between members of the company.

(2) Where or to the extent that the purposes of the company consist of or include purposes other than the benefit of its members, subsection (1) has effect as if the reference to promoting the success of the company for the benefit of its members were to achieving those purposes.

(3) The duty imposed by this section has effect subject to any enactment or rule of law requiring directors, in certain circumstances, to consider or act in the interests of creditors of the company.

However, section 172 is itself the subject of many debates. Many scholars argue that this section requires directors to have regard to the interests of employees, creditors, consumers and the community ((a)–(f) above), making it

---

[20] Ibid., p. 963.
[21] *Greenhalgh v. Arderne Cinemas Ltd.* [1951] Ch. 286 cited by Plowman J in *Parke* n19 above p. 963.

more inclusive than the common law. Others argue that the duty firmly guides directors toward seeking shareholder value and to consider other stakeholders only if to do so enhances shareholder value. Others argue that the duty is enforceable only by shareholders and that having 'regard' does not designate any substantive behaviour from directors. The latter concern is addressed somewhat by the Companies (Miscellaneous Reporting) Regulations 2018, which require companies to include in their strategic report[22] a statement (clearly delineated) on how directors comply with section 172 in respect of having regard to those goals and persons noted in (a) to (f).[23] Nonetheless, whether we consider section 172 more or less shareholder-orientated, both the statute and common law are concerned to underline the directors' role as creators of wealth for shareholders. The idea that issues like those identified in (a)-(f) should be treated as ends in themselves is ruled out in both case law and the review that led to the 2006 Act.

Directors' duties also guide the exercise of the powers directors possess under the articles to act on behalf of the company. Their authority must be exercised in the interests of the company, invariably interpreted as the interests of shareholders – the duty to act in good faith and for proper purposes. For example, directors were in breach of their duty when they used their powers to issue shares to create a sufficient majority to resist the election of three new directors wanted by the existing majority shareholders.[24] Using the power to issue shares to create a new majority is a strategy that directors have used to thwart unwanted takeovers. For example, when the hostile takeovers that emerged in the 1950s became more frequent in the 1960s, directors often used their powers to issue shares under the constitution to create a scheme that would block the takeover.[25] The response by the courts in such cases was to set aside allotments or issues of shares as a breach of duty because duties must not be used to manipulate control, [26] nor must their proper powers by used for an improper purpose.[27] With little care for the consequences to the enterprise, the courts were proactive in ensuring that directors could not subvert an opportunity for shareholders to sell their shares to the highest bidder.[28]

The law has developed many principles restricting directors' ability to extract wealth for themselves. Strict prohibitions on benefitting personally on a

---

[22] Required by s.414 CA 2006.

[23] This applies to all companies that are not small - specifically having two out of the three criteria on a turnover of more than £36 million, a balance sheet of more than £18 million or more than 250 employees.

[24] *Piercy v Mills & Co.* (1920) 1 Ch. 78.

[25] *Hogg v Cramphorn* (1967) Ch 254, *Howard Smith Ltd v Ampol Petroleum Ltd* (1974) 1 All ER 1126.

[26] Ibid., *Hogg v Cramphorn* ibid.

[27] Op cite *Howard Smith Ltd v Ampol Petroleum Ltd*.

[28] See Johnston, Chapter 9.

transaction with the company, albeit one that benefitted the company, were introduced in the 19th century.[29] Historically, directors were construed as akin to trustees, and the principle that directors should not allow their personal self-interest to conflict with their duty to the company remains foundational. For practical reasons, the courts allowed directors to manage conflicts of interest by being completely transparent, which is now part of the Companies Act under section 177. However, any failure to disclose when legally necessary renders the director in breach of duty, and the old equity rules apply, making directors liable to account for any personal benefits to the company:

> it is a rule of universal application, that no-one, having such duties to discharge, shall be allowed to enter into engagements in which he has, or can have, a personal interest conflicting, or which may possibly conflict, with the interests of those whom he is bound to protect[30]

Similar controls are in place for directors who use information they glean from their position for personal financial benefit. The House of Lords, ruling in *Regal (Hastings) Ltd v Gulliver*, stated that 'one occupying a position of trust must not make a profit which he can acquire only by use of his fiduciary position, or, if he does, he must account for the profit so made'.[31] Furthermore, liability of this kind 'does not depend upon breach of duty but upon the proposition that a director must not make a profit out of property acquired by reason of his relationship to the company of which he is director'.[32] Reform in the Companies Act 2006 does shift some power to directors as it allows directors to benefit personally provided that they comply with the provisions under section 175, which permits board approval. However, in practice, this apparent shift of power to the board applies to companies in which the directors are also the majority shareholders.[33]

Debate 3
The claim that shareholders are entitled to company wealth depends on political context – Ideas are important

Although I would argue that company law has consistently backed the primacy of shareholders and their extraction of wealth from companies, the same cannot be said for legal scholarship and public policy. Unlike company law, legal scholarship has enjoyed extensive periods when it considered shareholder

---

[29] *Aberdeen Railway Company v Blaikie Brothers* (1854) 1 Macq 461.
[30] Ibid.
[31] *Regal (Hastings) Ltd v Gulliver*. [1942] 1 All ER 378 at p. 395.
[32] Ibid.
[33] *Kleanthous v Paphitus* [2011] EWHC 2287.

primacy outdated and unjustifiable. Public policy embodied a similar view for much of the 20th century.

In the period leading up to the Wall Street crash, scholars assessing corporate America voiced concerns about the dominance of large corporations and their ability to suppress competition (Louis Brandeis) and privilege profits for shareholders over the production of socially useful commodities (Thorstein Veblen). Following the Wall Street crash, and the country's first flirtation with Keynesianism, new theories emerged that challenged shareholder claims to extract value, and the corporation's purpose became a more mainstream topic of discussion in both scholarship and government policy. Most famously, Adolf Berle and Gardiner Means, in *The Modern Corporation and Private Property*, showed how massive share dispersal in the largest corporations had fundamentally transformed the nature of share ownership. Responsibility, they argued, had devolved to management because dispersed shareholders were unable to exercise the rights generally attributed to private property ownership and indeed had no moral entitlement to do so. As passive outside investors who are protected by limited liability and who contribute nothing to the development of the corporation, shareholders had effectively 'surrendered the right that the corporation should be operated in their sole interest'. Accordingly, they had 'released the community from the obligation to protect them to the full extent implied in the doctrine of strict property rights'.[34] In a similar vein, Peter Drucker argued that shareholder passivity made their control rights anachronistic and that shareholder voting rights should be removed.[35] Scholars like Veblen and Berle developed a new approach referred to as institutional economics, which maintained that the emergence of the large corporations had subverted market forces. Competition, as a driver of growth and wealth creation, had been replaced by corporate organisational goals. Accordingly, as the organisational norms of corporations determined production and distribution, the modern corporation could be a force either for social progress or for oppression, depending on your perspective. For Berle and other scholars from 1930 to 1960, it was the former. The corporation was a force for social progress – potentially, at least. And, in the US, in the period following the Second World War, this rang true. The pervasiveness of large economic organisations and the weakness of shareholder demands resulted in a corporate management who saw their role as collaborative, working with government and trade unions to ensure growth, stability and fair distribution.[36]

However, by the end of the 1960s, when corporate growth and profit started to fall off, this 'golden age' drew to an end. Then, corporate power was viewed as a dark controlling force. Corporations created alienating,

---

[34] Berle and Means, *Modern Corporation*, p. 312.

[35] Peter F. Drucker, *The New Society: The Anatomy of the Industrial Order* (Windmill Press Kingswood 1951) 320.

[36] A. Crosland, *The Future of Socialism* (London: Robinson Publishing, 50th ed, 2006).

dehumanised working environments. They determined individual consumption patterns and defined what was desirable and undesirable. They persuaded people to adopt a particular sense of self, suppressing individual self-expression. The cultural reaction against this, and the bureaucratisation of the social world, was expressed in the quest for individuality and freedom in the bohemian youth culture of the 1960s and 1970s. As Harvey notes, this quest for individual self-expression – liberty from the bonds of bureaucracy and corporatisation – was exploitable by neoliberals able to pose as champions of freedom and individualism against the forces of bureaucratic oppression.[37] Corporations, neoliberal theorists and politicians all claimed they could provide that freedom and self-expression if they removed stifling welfare provisions, resisted oppressive collective union action and promoted individual shareholder entitlement. Similarly, neoliberal theorists sought to reject the notion of corporate authority and hierarchy and to re-establish the primacy of the market peopled by contracting, property-owning individuals. This naturally elevated shareholders as possessors of claims to the profit created by corporations while providing justification for corporations per se.

The most famous of these scholars included Ronald Coase, whose early work in the 1930s represented a sort of halfway house between managerial and neoliberal theory.[38] Coase's theory retained the 'firm' (which would normally be controlled by a corporation) as a distinct organisation with its own internal resource allocation dynamic, much like the managerialists. However, unlike the managerialists, he did not think that large organisations subverted market forces but that they emerged because of the market and specifically the costs associated with transacting in the market. Coase's central thesis here was that hierarchical firms emerge when they are more economically efficient than discrete market transactions undertaken by small entrepreneurs since these firms remove or reduce the costs of transacting in the market. In Coase's theory, large firms could supersede market forces, so that whilst price mechanisms directed resource allocation outside the firm, within the firm 'market transactions are eliminated'[39] and replaced by 'the entrepreneurial co-ordinator, who directs production'.[40]

Coase's theory was resuscitated by emerging neoliberal theorists in the late 1960s, feted and substantially redeveloped. Its closest adherent is Oliver Williamson, who made a number of refinements to Coase's market and the operation of organisations. Williamson noted that markets were prone to inefficiencies and failure. Transaction costs arose from the imperfection and

---

[37] David Harvey, *A Brief History of Neoliberalism* (Oxford University Press 2005).

[38] Ronald Coase, 'The Nature of the Firm' (1937) reproduced in *The Nature of the Firm, Origins, Evolution, and Development* (Oxford University Press 1993).

[39] Ibid., 24.

[40] Ibid.

knowledge deficiencies of the individuals involved, their 'bounded rationality'.[41] The market ideal was never the reality and therefore organisations were bound to emerge to reduce the ensuing transaction costs. Unlike Coase, Williamson did not differentiate so sharply between organisations and markets. He viewed organisations themselves as exchanges between individuals, subject to transaction costs. Williamson represents the 'new institutional economics' perspective which retains the concept of an organisation whilst conceiving it as the chosen environment of, and for, contracting parties.

Other economists revised Coase's theory much more comprehensively. In their seminal 1972 article, economists Alchian and Demsetz denied the existence of Coase's hierarchical firm, which supersedes the market.[42] Instead, they claimed that firms were a form of internalised market. Firms they were teams, coalescing around a particular sector or expertise, and concerned with profit-maximising. The firm existed but as a 'team productive process' in which the team nominated a monitor, the manager, to ensure that shirking was minimised and success was rewarded.[43] In this reciprocal arrangement, shareholders held the manager to account because, as the ultimate beneficiaries of efficient team activity, they found it was in their interest to do so. The proper functioning of the team was in everyone's interest, and monitoring ensured optimum commitment from 'resource owners'.[44]

Jensen and Meckling further developed the idea of the firm as a form of the market with no distinct organisational form, which essentially extinguished Alchian and Demsetz's team production remodelling of the firm. They argued that the firm exists only as a legal fiction, an administrative convenience, which describes a nexus of contracting individuals.[45] In fact, the firm *was* the market, peopled by contracting individuals in another guise, so that 'it makes little or no sense to try to distinguish those things that are "inside" the firm (or any other organisation) from those things that are outside of it'.[46] There was no hierarchy or group monitors.

Jensen and Meckling's approach explicitly justified shareholder entitlement. They didn't refute Berle and others' contention regarding the ownership claims of shareholders – an argument too compelling in both law and practice to defeat head on. Instead, they set out a new justification. They contended that shareholders as one group of contracting individuals had exchanged capital for

---

[41] Oliver Williamson and Sydney Winter, *The Nature of the Firm: Origins, Evolution and Development* (Oxford University Press 1993) 131.

[42] AA Alchian and H Demsetz, 'Production, Information Costs, and Economic Organisation' (1972) 62 Am. Econ. Rev 777.

[43] Ibid., 778.

[44] Ibid., 777.

[45] M Jensen and W Meckling, 'Theory of the Firm: Managerial Behaviour, Agency Costs and Ownership Structure' (1976) 3 Journal of Financial Economics 305.

[46] Ibid.

the possibility of variable return, and management were accordingly 'contractually' obligated to pursue those returns for shareholders. However, in contrast to other contracting individuals in the nexus who had negotiated a price for their inputs, shareholder contracts were not complete. There was no guarantee they would receive any returns. They were the residual risk bearers. For this reason, other measures were in place to bolster shareholders' position, thus providing the rationale for directors' fiduciary duties that supported shareholders' interests (Box 7.3).

Box 7.3 Prioritising Returns to Capital Implies Reducing Returns to Labour

Evidence clearly shows that labour is in a weaker position vis-à-vis capital today than it was for much of the post-war period when it claimed around 75 per cent of the gross national product in most developed countries. A 2015 Organisation for Economic Co-operation and Development study showed that from 1990 to 2009 the labour compensation share of national income fell from 66.1 per cent to 61.7 per cent. It estimates that on average labour share fell 0.3 per cent each year from 1980 to the late 2000s.[47]

Another outcome of the nexus of contracts conceptualisation of the company and the corporate governance reforms it inspired is to free companies from social obligations or purpose. As the company does not exist as an entity, it is incapable of possessing a moral position. This also negatively impacts on labour.

The flaw identified by contractarians in the manager/shareholder 'contract' has underpinned much of the thinking in corporate governance policies, codes, and in the law. The concern is that the managers/directors will find their duties as an agent for the shareholder (principal), come into conflict with their own self-interest, and they will be inclined toward the latter. For contractarians, redressing the imbalances between duty and self-interest entails costs in monitoring the agent, and costs to incentivise the agent to act in the interests of the principal – agency costs (see Attenborough, Chapter 8). From a policy perspective, monitoring and incentivising the agent to act in the interest of the principal has entailed specific corporate governance strategies. The hard end of monitoring is delivered by the so-called market for corporate control (Box 7.4), through which the companies of poorly performing directors will be targeted for a hostile takeover and the management removed. This is discussed in detail by Johnston (Chapter 9). The soft end is delivered through performance-related pay, discussed next.

---

[47] https://www.oecd.org/g20/topics/employment-and-social-policy/The-Labour-Share-in-G20-Economies.pdf

Box 7.4 The Market for Corporate Control

The emergence of hostile takeovers was understood by Henry Manne to present an opportunity for shareholders to assert their dissatisfaction with managers who were delivering insufficient shareholder value. He called it the market for corporate control. The share price mechanism indicated management performance: strong share prices indicated good management, and low share prices were an indication of under-performance. Shareholders could make bids for low-priced shares in other companies in such numbers as would allow them to take control of the company and dispense with the managers who didn't enhance shareholder value. This approach allowed Manne to show shareholders as active owners and the market as functioning and efficient. Manne's market in corporate control justified shareholder entitlement and ongoing hostile takeover activity, notwithstanding that this was largely pursued by private equity firms (and not company shareholders) who funded leveraged buyouts through junk bonds (see *Barbarians at the Gate* for a ripping account of the buyout of Nabisco). And, although their role was to extract years of accumulated value while creating massive transaction costs in the process, the claim to efficiencies from shareholder activism in the market remained.

Debate 4

Addressing the 'agency problem' relies on shareholder value and shareholder governance – both are regressive

Incentivising directors to pursue shareholder interests has largely involved aligning executive performance (defined as the enhancement of shareholder value) with personal reward, thereby aligning executive and shareholder interests. The mechanism for achieving this alignment was to remunerate executives with share-based rewards, and from the 1980s, rewarding executives in this way was ubiquitous in large companies. Shareholders were happy and executives were happy. The public, however, were less happy, particularly when the executives of newly denationalised industries became quickly and undiplomatically wealthy. Executives were dubbed fat cats for exploiting their position to skim wealth, motivated by unapologetic greed. In contrast, shareholder enrichment was barely acknowledged.

And there's the rub. If agency costs are real, performance-related pay creates a steady structure by which directors are incentivised to deliver shareholder value in the course of business. It is a more stable mechanism than the destabilising threat or actuality of a hostile takeover. However, if directors successfully deliver that which contractarians believe is the entitlement of shareholders, it will necessarily result in high director remuneration. High executive remuneration, therefore, arises not because executives are intrinsically greedy (although individually they may be) but because shareholders want high returns and these claims are not challenged. Policymakers believe in shareholder value and create governance norms that promote the alignment of management reward with shareholder value. A coalition has emerged in which executives and shareholders share corporate wealth at the expense of employees and other stakeholders (Box 7.5).

Box 7.5 Statistics on Rising Director Remuneration

In 2000, a FTSE 100 Chief Executive earned 47 times more than a full-time employee, by 2014 they earned 120 times more, and by 2017 145 times more.[48]

Average FTSE 100 CEO was paid £5.66 million in 2017, an increase from £4.58 million in 2016.[49]

The average remuneration of the top 350 CEOs in the US was $18.9 million. These CEOs earned 312 times more than the typical worker in their company.

Historical Shift

1965, typical CEO earned just 20 times that of the typical worker.

1989 typical CEO earned 58.2 times that of the typical worker.

1995 typical CEO earned 112.3 58.2 times that of the typical worker.

2000 - typical CEO earned 343.5 times that of the typical worker 343.5.

In the US, from 1978 to 2017, executive compensation increased an average of 1070 per cent. The typical worker's pay increased just 11.2 per cent in the same period.[50]

Regulatory and governance responses to high executive remuneration have, if anything, exacerbated the problem. They rely on transparency and reporting, in large part to improve shareholder monitoring. They rest upon motivating and empowering shareholders, the group least motivated to reduce shareholder value, which is the basis of executive remuneration.

Following the Cadbury Report (1992), which set out a regime for good corporate governance in quoted companies, the Greenbury Committee (1995) was charged with providing a solution to the embarrassment that was rising executive pay in the newly privatised industries, which had been publicly owned. Executive pay had been rising in the private sector throughout the 1980s without causing much concern. Greenbury assessed in detail the benefits of aligning director and shareholder interests through share-based remuneration packages and recommended a more formalised approach to performance-related pay. This approach was endorsed in subsequent Codes. The Codes thereon have recommended that all listed companies should have a remuneration committee, peopled by non-executive directors, to award

---

[48] Thomson Reuters New Release, 'FTSE 100 Directors' Total Earnings Jump by 21% in a Year' (http://www.incomesdata.co.uk/wp-content/uploads/2014/10/IDS-FTSE-100-directors-pay-20141.pdf).

[49] CIPD and High Pay Centre, *Executive Pay: Review of FTSE 100 Executive Pay*, August 2018.

[50] L. Mishel and J. Schieder, 'CEO Compensation surged in 2017', Economic Policy Institute, 16 August 2018, Table 1, https://www.epi.org/publication/ceo-compensation-surged-in-2017 (last visited 6th January 2020).

remuneration packages according to formal, transparent rules and terms of reference on the policy for creating these packages.

However, as this approach endorsed and formalised performance-related pay, rather than nip it in the bud, executive pay continued its rapid upward trajectory throughout the 1990s. Unwilling to renounce performance-related pay as the culprit, the government merely introduced more hard law reform to reporting on pay and to empowering shareholders. The Directors' Remuneration Report Regulations 2002 included provisions requiring all companies other than the smallest to include in their annual accounts details of directors' remuneration and other benefits. They also provided for an annual vote to shareholders on remuneration pay. The vote, though advisory only, has often resulted in voluntary resignations by executives when shareholders exhibited their discontent with a remuneration policy (AstraZeneca and Trinity Mirror in 2012). The annual advisory vote on the remuneration report (which has become ever more detailed[51]) was later incorporated in the Companies Act 2006 (section 439). In addition, section 439A introduced a binding shareholder vote on the remuneration policy every three years.[52] If voted down, the company cannot remunerate its directors and any payment made without an agreed policy is void.

Recent reforms have opted for more disclosure to assist investors further to monitor remuneration. By requiring companies to report on executive pay levels and their relationship to employee wage levels, it is also hoped that directors will moderate their demands. In December 2018, an Investment Association Public Register was established by the Investment Association (the trade body representing investment managers) to record shareholder opposition to remuneration of 20 per cent or more. The Companies (Miscellaneous Reporting) Regulations 2018 require UK-listed companies with more than 250 employees to reveal the ratio of executive pay to that of the typical employee in that business and to provide a narrative explaining the ratio in the context of the workforce in general.[53] All companies of a significant size, including very large private companies, must include a statement in their directors' report setting out which corporate governance code it has adopted and their compliance with the code, which must necessarily include a policy on remuneration. The reforms (part of Teresa May's new Industrial Policy) were prompted by overwhelming public disgust at the level of directors' pay at a time when most workers had experienced wage freezes, or cuts, and indirect losses through austerity welfare cuts. It is unclear how giving more detail on these inequalities will address the problem when shareholders are the only group with the rights or influence to do anything to redress the problem and they so clearly benefit from inequalities (Box 7.2).

Like the UK, level executive pay at the EU level is being dealt with by enhancing shareholder powers. Amendments to the EU Shareholder Rights

---

[51] Latest iteration, Large and Medium-sized Companies and Groups (Accounts and Reports) (Amendment) Regulations 2013/1981.

[52] Introduced by the Enterprise and Regulatory Reform Act 2013.

[53] These were presented to parliament on Monday 11 June 2018 and apply to company reporting on financial years starting on or after January 2019.

Directive are designed to increase shareholder rights, to engage institutional shareholders in corporate governance and to introduce shareholder 'say on (executive) pay'.[54] All of these provisions are designed to retain the old alignment of performance to pay and to make pay schemes based on this premise work better. This is particularly interesting given that the Business, Energy and Industrial Strategy (BEIS) Select Committee on corporate governance, which looked into the problem of executive remuneration (among other issues), concluded that share-based incentive schemes should be replaced by wages and bonuses based on broader corporate responsibilities.[55]

Today, as everyone is aware, directors' remuneration has not become more rationalised, nuanced, moderate or fair. Instead, it has massively increased. One glance at the statistics in Box 7.4 (above) makes that abundantly clear. However, there is a generalised unwillingness to shift from performance-related pay (the EU's cap on bankers' pay being the rare exception), which I argue here is rooted in a fundamental commitment to shareholder entitlement, enhanced by increasing shareholders' legal power to determine and monitor remuneration.

CONCLUSION

This chapter has aimed to draw out some fundamental themes and debates that students will find in their company law course in which students are frequently presented with a long list of shareholders' legal rights without the tools to challenge whether it is wise for shareholders to hold these rights. If, as the chapter claims, shareholders escaped the charge of exploitation because they became rentiers, why do they continue to hold control rights in the company? This chapter examines some of the key historical developments that shed light on this. The chapter also looks at theories around shareholder entitlement to show how these rights are not 'natural' or common sense but are particular ideological positions that can be challenged. Finally, the chapter looks at how excessive director remuneration is one of the outcomes of pursuing shareholder entitlement. It concludes that this controversy is inextricably bound to supposedly non-controversial shareholder value. Of course, the problem of shareholder entitlement goes further than director remuneration. It has impacted employee pay and conditions, examined in detail by Villiers and Russell in Chapter 3. As a recent study noted, high executive pay and shareholder returns have directly eaten into wages. 'As a mathematical matter, had there not been the redistribution upward – to the top 5 per cent, but which is mostly about the top 1 per cent – the wages of the bottom 90 per cent could have grown twice as fast as it actually did'.[56] Shareholder claims have also reduced investment in production as company capital is used to fund share buybacks rather than invest in

---

[54] EU Shareholder Rights Directive 2017/828 amending Directive 2007/36/EC.
[55] The Business, Energy and Industrial Strategy (BEIS) Select Committee report on corporate governance, published on 5 April 2017.
[56] https://www.theguardian.com/business/2018/aug/16/ceo-versus-worker-wage-american-companies-pay-gap-study-2018.

productivity. From 2017 to 2018, UK companies repurchased £15 billion of their own shares.[57] American companies bought back $797.9 billion of their own shares in 2018. Returning monies to shareholders has also led to huge corporate debt. The International Monetary Fund recently reported that by the end of 2018, in the US, non-financial corporate debt to gross domestic product was 73 per cent, close to levels seen just prior to the global financial crisis.[58] Indeed, corporate debt is likely to be the site of the next financial crisis. The pursuit of shareholder entitlements has huge social costs. This chapter queries our acceptance of it.

FURTHER READING

Rob Bryer, 'The Mercantile Laws Commission of 1854 and the Political Economy of Limited Liability' (1997) 1 *Economic History Review* 37.

S. Deakin, 'The Corporation as Commons: Rethinking Property Rights, Governance and Sustainability in the Business Enterprise' (2012) 37 *Queen's Law Journal* 339–81.

S. Deakin, Jonas Malmberg and Prabirjit Sarkar, 'How Do Labour Laws Affect Unemployment and the Labour Share of National Income – The Experience of Six OECD Countries, 1970–2010' (2014) 153 *International Labour Review* 1.

D. Harvey, *The Enigma of Capital and the Crises of Capitalism* (Profile Books, 2011).

B. C. Hunt, 'The Joint Stock Company In England 1830–1944' (1935) 43 *The Journal of Political Economy* 331.

A. Johnston, 'The Shrinking Scope of CSR in UK Corporate Law' (2017) 74 *Washington and Lee Law Review* 1001.

T. Veblen, *Business Enterprise* (New York: Charles Scribners, 1904).

Charlotte Villiers, 'Executive Pay: A Socially-Oriented Distributive Justice Framework' (2016) 37(5) *Company Lawyer* 139–54.

---

[57] https://www.telegraph.co.uk/investing/shares/share-buybacks-soar-can-spell-bad-news/.
[58] IMF Global Financial Stability Report April 2019.

CHAPTER 8

Debating Theories of the Company and Separate Corporate Personality

*Daniel Attenborough**

INTRODUCTION

The corporate form of business organisation is today a fundamental feature of modern life and modern law. In large part, its ubiquity is due to the principle of separate corporate personality, which is of central importance to company law and entails the complete separation of the company and its members. Indeed, this single idea provides a unique and powerful force for viewing the company as a juridical entity, or 'thing', which is capable of suing, and being sued, in its own name, entering into contracts, incurring debt, and owning property. However, the company's independent legal existence has long generated difficulties for the law and how we think about that law. For over a century, philosophers, political scientists, economists, and, above all, jurists and judges have fervently debated how best to understand the essential nature of the company. The distinct theories advanced not only provide doctrinal explanations, in point of law, of what the company *is* but also seek to determine questions, of a normative nature, about how the company *should* be understood. This fascinating and intellectually rich discourse tends to focus, as a historical matter, on philosophical and metaphysical questions that invoke what is commonly regarded as the 'fiction/artificial entity theory' and the 'real entity theory' or, more recently, on the economic 'contractarian/nexus of contracts theory'. However, different theories are not readily comparable as they frequently deal with different aspects of corporate personality. Consequently, their influence upon company law has been to generate misunderstanding and conflict.

This chapter thus sets out to introduce the theories of corporate legal personality and, at appropriate intervals, to situate some of the emergent questions or controversies within subject-wide debates. It sketches the importance of

* The author is especially grateful to the editors for their helpful insights and advice about this chapter. The usual disclaimers apply.

context to our understanding of this issue and how each of the concepts has seemed stronger at different times in British and American legal history. Most obviously, the ultimate purpose of our inquiry is to show the real-life significance of different theories of the company. More specifically, the lens through which we conceptualise companies is important because it helps frame problems and provides answers to the way in which perceived problems are – or ought properly to be – addressed. In this way, the theories can be presented in both positive (i.e., describing what essentially *is* the company) and normative (i.e., describing what *ought* to be the way of thinking about companies that leads to the most efficient doctrinal and policy objectives) terms. This chapter presents some of the most widely theorised and debated ideas about the nature of companies.

Debate 1

Is the company a public or private entity?

One of the points of contention between contributors to this debate, which is often a dispute splintered along ideological lines, has been about whether the company is a public or private institution. Our understanding of this issue is crucial because it determines the rights, protections and remedies to which companies are entitled and how the rest of law and regulation is to be applied to them. On the one hand, we might usefully characterise the company as a 'private' initiative, which has been allowed to develop as nothing more than a set of freely negotiated contracts between asocial, self-interested economic agents and where the role of the state is limited to the enforcement of those private bargains. On the other hand, the company can be viewed as a 'public' institution, which has been profoundly influenced by public policy choices expressed through the political system, the workings of the legal system, and the social relations within which companies are embedded. These two distinct and conflicting positions will be set out in more detail below (after Box 8.1).

Box 8.1 HSBC plc: Public or Private?

If we take the example of the British banking group, HSBC plc., we might choose to regard this corporate form as merely a vehicle for bringing together people with business ideas, people with financial wherewithal, expert managers, and employees with specific skills, etc., to use and invest the company's resources in the ideas and projects that have the highest positive expected value. On this view, we elect to emphasise the 'privateness' of the company, where overt government involvement seems distinctly secondary to the creative impulse of the amalgamation of entrepreneurs who are responsible for the venture. In the alternative, we could say that there is something about the essence of HSBC, and of its place within society, other than just the contingent fact of its having been the subject of social and political systems, which conjure up an image of an impersonal decision-making entity akin to a unified person. This account contemplates the 'publicness' of the company.

a. The 'Public' Conception of the Company

The 'fiction' or 'artificial entity' theory maintains that the company is a public creation, a 'concession' from state authority, and its juristic personality exists only as a metaphor, established in the eye of the law, to grant it the legal capacity to act. In other words, the company is a legal fiction. Writing in 1840, the German jurist and historian Friedrich Carl von Savigny set out the theory in his treatise on Roman law, and it was around this formative text that mid-19th-century common law discourse pivoted.[1] The earliest scholarship on the nature of the company emphasised that companies were created by formal acts of a sovereign, which granted to a group of individuals the right and privilege to act together as a legal person for the purposes of transferring property rights, entering into contracts, suing and being sued in court, and so forth. This early conception was quickly superseded, according to Morton Horwitz, an American legal historian, because of the rapid socioeconomic transformations that occurred during the last few decades of the 19th century in the US.[2] In particular, the corporate form encompassed key sectors such as railroads, utilities, banking and manufacturing, and they became increasingly national, transcending state boundaries and thereby state control. According to Horwitz, the idea that companies had in some sense taken on a life of their own, free from state control, effectively undermined the credibility of the fiction theory's depiction of the company as a creature of the positive law. As a consequence of this failure to provide a complete account of the 'modern' company, legal scholars and philosophers switched from looking at the company as an artificial creature of law controlled by the state to seeing it as an aggregation of natural individuals engaged in a common purpose (namely a particular business activity) and therefore a real, not fictional, entity.

Although there are a number of variants of this 'real entity' theory, one commonality is that a company is not a fiction but is a 'pre-legal' or 'extra-legal' being distinct from, and more than just the sum of, its constituent human components (e.g., the company's shareholders, employees, creditors and suppliers). In this sense, Arthur Machen Jr, in an article published in 1911, opined that a company 'is an entity – not imaginary or fictitious, but real, not artificial but natural'.[3] So understood, the company has a 'natural' personality in the same sense that a human does. Once the company is detached from the distinct claims of its constituent actors, it can be regarded as a system or network that is directed towards a coherent and stable greater corporate 'good'. The

---

[1] F. C. von Savigny, *System des heutigen Römischen Rechts, vol 2* (Veit, 1840).

[2] M. J. Horwitz, 'Santa Clara Revisited: The Development of Corporate Theory' (1985) 88 *West Virginia Law Review* 173, 209–10.

[3] A. Machen, Jr., 'Corporate Personality' (1911) 24(4) *Harvard Law Review* 253, 253. For similar remarks, see, for example, R. Harris, 'The Transplantation of the Legal Discourse on Corporate Personality Theories: From German Codification to British Political Pluralism and American Big business' (2006) 63(4) *Washington & Lee Law Review* 1421, 1473, describing the company as enjoying 'social and economic' existence.

respective efforts of British legal historian Frederic Maitland and US administrative law scholar Ernst Freund imported the real entity idea into Anglo-American legal writing in the late-19th century.[4] It was invoked in the US primarily in an effort to explain and rationalise a controversial and enduring US precedent, decided in 1886, where the Supreme Court recognised companies as 'people' and thus capable of acquiring the most fundamental legal rights normally reserved for natural persons.[5] In what must have seemed like a natural step, some real entity theorists hinted that if the company is to be regarded as an entity with its *own* claims, much like those of a natural person, then the state has no greater authority to impose its moral position on corporate persons than it does on human persons.

Notwithstanding, even if one accepts the nature of the company as a real 'organism', its existence still requires a legal framework. For example, UK company law sets forth, often on a mandatory basis, the processes and constraints for the formation and continuing governance of companies during their life cycle. What is more, even in those fields where companies are the main legal actors, whose behaviour we want to manage and contain, there is a variety of substantive and procedural law that is not customarily regarded as being part of company law. Prime examples include criminal sanctions, publicly enforceable civil penalties, private civil remedies, taxation, etc., all of which bear the imprint of the various historical contexts and social and political systems in which the company was fashioned. From this perspective, unless the context indicates otherwise, the state, under the fiction theory, artificially *creates* or, for real entity theorists, subsequently *recognises* corporate personhood, to which the formal law is then applied (or not applied if the state so chooses for some policy reason). Regardless of whether it takes the form of the fictitious or real character of the corporate entity, a company is thus undeniably dependent, either explicitly or implicitly, upon readily identifiable state interventionist techniques.

For proponents of the respective theories, the normative justification for the state to retain varying degrees of jurisdiction over corporate activity originates from a well-worn concern that organisations, other than a democratically elected government, will become more powerful than the state and that this will undermine accountability to the public. To that end, the conferral of privileges of incorporation is not merely for the private benefit of economic actors but also

---

[4] Two important examples of Maitland's work are O. von Gierke, *Political Theories of the Middle Age* (F. W. Maitland, trans. CUP, 1900); F. Pollock and F. W. Maitland, *The History of English Law Before the Time of Edward I* (CUP, 1895). For an example of Freund's work, see E. Freund, *The Legal Nature of Corporations* (Chicago University Press, 1897). The source of their efforts can be traced back to O. von Gierke, *Die Genossenschaftstheorie Und Die Deutsche Rechtsprechung* (Weidmann, 1887).

[5] *Santa Clara County v Southern Pacific Railroad* 118 U.S. 394 (1886).

for the greater public 'good' in the form of legal-institutional responsibilities. But there is, nevertheless, an important distinction between the way each theory determines rights and liabilities of the corporate entity. To explain, because the fiction theory depicts the company as a creature of the state, existing only in the contemplation of the law, it should possess only those privileges and properties that the antecedent power of the state confers on it. Put differently, the theory implies that companies have no inherent rights in their relationship with the state. For the real entity theory, the natural personality of the company arises out of its material existence and so is recognised but not created by the law. Hence, it characterises companies as persons in law to whom the law both can and should address its commands. However, because companies acquire fundamentally the same rights and liabilities as human beings, the state should have no more authority to impose its will on corporate persons than it does on human persons.

In any event, John Dewey did much to terminate the debate about the real or fictitious nature of corporate personality. He argued that the entire discussion was preoccupied with a mass of abstract and non-legal concepts, in which the competing theories were essentially indeterminate and each was capable of being deployed to support conflicting ends that are politically or otherwise determined. Instead of this, he argued, the important questions about whether to treat something as a legal person or to give it certain rights and duties should be answered not by reference to some *a priori* theory but by thinking in pragmatic terms of the consequences of doing so.[6]

b. The 'Private' Conception of the Company

However, the normative questions that underlay this controversy, namely the extent to which it is legitimate for the law to direct and regulate the company, re-emerged in more recent decades. The context for this was a form of economic analysis known as 'contractarian' or 'nexus of contracts' theory. This theory first emerged in the US and, inevitably (albeit to a slightly lesser extent), spread to Britain. Perhaps the leading exponents of the contractarian view today are Frank Easterbrook and Daniel Fischel, to whose work I now turn.[7] Contractarian theory claims that the company's existence results from nothing more than a set of freely negotiated contracts, either express or implied, and that these bargains consist of many different kinds of inputs and outputs that

---

[6] J. Dewey, 'The Historic Background of Corporate Legal Personality' (1926) 35 *Yale Law Journal* 655.

[7] Frank Easterbrook and Daniel Fischel published a series of articles that developed and applied the contractarian theory. Their work culminated in a major corporate law book entitled *The Economic Structure of Corporate Law* (Harvard University Press, 1991). See also, A. Alchian and H. Demsetz, 'Production, Information Costs and Economic Organizations' (1972) 62 *American Economic Review* 777; M. Jensen and W. Meckling, 'Managerial Behaviour, agency costs and ownership structure' (1976) 3 *Journal of Financial Economics* 305; E. Fama, 'Agency Problems and the Theory of the Firm' (1980) 88 *Journal of Political Economy* 228.

are exchanged between asocial, self-interested economic agents. They do not, however, use the term 'contract' in its conventional legal sense. Instead, it has its own metaphorical meaning, the premise being that relations among individuals, which are 'adaptable' or 'worked out', become default 'hypothetical' contracts to which both parties otherwise would have agreed in an express contract. In some sense, there is at first glance an appealing simplicity to this analysis, which resonates with the essential logic of neoliberalism. It depicts the company as a community of individuals efficiently generating endogenous rules and processes, against which the state's role in shaping the company seems distinctly secondary. The company is, of course, more or less free to act from legal instruction. It can set the prices, quantities and qualities of its outputs, organise its labour processes, choose among available technologies, determine internal corporate governance arrangements, and distribute surplus profits. These 'conventional ' contracts add vigour to the contractarian argument that all elements of the company are contractual arrangements of some stripe.

Contractarian theorists argue that making contracts is a private matter and that this is both manifest and incontrovertible within the doctrinal fabric of contemporary company law. Contractarianism is thereby located in a powerful tradition of individualist philosophy, which rejects any public function of companies and any right to regulate companies in the public interest. To exponents of contractarian theory, it is of more practical importance that all rights reside in, and all duties are incumbent upon, the constituent human components of the company. This private understanding of the company resonates with economic notions of allocative efficiency and a philosophy of liberal individualism, which endorses the principle that there is a presumption against any political action that denies or restricts anyone's freedom in any way.[8] However, this assumption of equal, abstract self-maximising individuals does not reflect the variation of ability, opportunity and need among people in the real world. To apply the 'ideal' rules out state intervention to redress existing inequalities (such as fairer wages, safer working conditions, increased consumer standards) and enables the already rich and powerful (namely directors, senior managers and shareholders) to distribute surplus profits between themselves.

In what must have seemed like a natural step, this approach also implies that company law, being the body of rules that govern these complex webs of contracts, is almost always little more than a passive adjunct to the socially optimal contracting process that creates a company. Public regulation, as set down by the state or the courts, is viewed as counterproductive on the grounds that it distorts these freely agreed arrangements and is therefore inefficient. Rather than rely on exogenously given rules, economic analysis tends to idealise the self-regulatory capabilities of the market to produce and enforce endogenous 'rules of the game' for corporate activity. The substantive content of company

---

[8] For discussion of this in the tax context, see Sadiq and McCredie, Chapter 10.

law is to be determined through this process of negotiation and agreement. The presence of irrefutably mandatory legal rules is explained away on the basis that they are 'standard-form terms' that would otherwise emerge through bargaining between self-interested actors, were the costs of making adequate provision for all possible contingencies sufficiently low. A few mandatory rules aside, the rest of company law is little more than 'off-the-rack' contract terms, intended to reduce transaction costs, that can be adopted, or not, depending on whether they meet the needs of those concerned.

What is more, contractarian theory is not content to make the descriptive claim that companies consist of nothing more than contracts and that company law simply reduces the costs of putting those contracts in place. It also makes the normative claim that this is how it should continue to be. As Marc Moore has remarked, 'the underlying tendency of contractarian scholarship [is] to assert the purported superiority of private and decentralised methods of ordering intra-firm governance affairs at the micro (i.e., individual firm) level'.[9] And again, Moore goes on to suggest that the main accomplishment of the theory has been the pervasive normalising of

'the continuing relevance and legitimacy of [company] law's privity: that is to say, the traditional treatment of corporate law as an essentially *pre*-political and market-instrumental facet of private law, rather than a publicly infused dimension of regulatory law concerned with the objectives and substantive outcomes of corporate organisations within the wider fabric of economy and society'.[10]

Since company law is reduced to a set of essentially private and transaction cost-reducing default rules that serve the contractually communicated interests of its collective participants, it follows that mandatory law and governance that overrides individual bargains should be the exception. Furthermore, the deployment of macroeconomic or politically determined public regulatory techniques, which stipulate what are, and should be, the legitimate and collective preferences of the private market of individual contracting actors, must discharge the burden-of-proof and demonstrate why coercive legal rules should trump presumptively efficient private arrangements.

Debate 2
Are companies capable of social or ethical responsibilities?

Turning to the precise goals and responsibilities of companies in society, the sources and contours of this legal debate stretch from at least the 1930s to the present day. Two dominant accounts exist. On one view, 'shareholder primacy' (or 'shareholder value') typically positions the collective interests of

---

[9] M. Moore, *Corporate Governance in the Shadow of the State* (Hart, 2013) 62.
[10] Ibid., 67–8.

shareholders at the centre of the company law and governance process and assigns priority to shareholders' interests relative to all other corporate stakeholders (e.g., the company's employees and workers, creditors, suppliers, consumers and the environment). Within this framework of legal and regulatory purpose, once the 'private' characterisation of the company is accepted, it is tempting to conclude that the interests of non-shareholder constituencies can – and should – be more effectively protected through specific regulation or wealth redistribution through taxation which would apply to all businesses, whatever their legal form. On an alternative view, described customarily as 'stakeholder theory', companies are 'public' and have responsibilities to constituencies other than shareholders. At one level, it has been proposed that it is in the interests of shareholders to take account of social or public expectations and preferences. This view, which can be seen in the 'enlightened shareholder value' approach under section 172 of the Companies Act 2006, regards the development of long-term relations, trust and commitment as part of the successful development of companies. However, there is also a broader notion that companies should not simply be run in the interests of shareholders; they have responsibilities to other stakeholders, which may on occasion conflict with their objective of wealth maximisation for shareholders. Against this backdrop, the important point for our purposes is that theories of the company are of considerable theoretical and practical importance in the shareholder–stakeholder controversy and discussion of corporate social responsibility. Depending upon which theory of corporate personhood is adopted, companies can be said to be incapable or capable of pursuing social or ethical interests.

a. Companies Are Not Capable of Social or Ethical Responsibilities

Since contractarian logic denies that companies are 'persons' in any meaningful sense, it follows that a company is incapable of having social or public obligations. Within this framework of inevitable insularity, the theory focuses on private relations between corporate actors and, once these relations are identified, it is tempting to see shareholders as the most deserving of beneficial legal-governance status. From a contractarian perspective, non-shareholder constituencies are theoretically able to bargain in advance, or renegotiate along the way, for more 'complete' rights and obligations in respect to their investments, whether in terms of an employee's fixed wage or a creditor's interest rate. In contrast, a shareholder is unable to bargain *ex ante* for a specified return from her investment in corporate equity. On this basis, a shareholder is generally viewed as an 'incomplete' contractor in the company. Coming last in terms of the priority of their claim, bearing the risk that there will be no surplus, and the incentive to monitor directors to encourage maximum corporate performance, means that shareholders have a collective interest in insisting on additional legal protection and/or governance rights within the company. Similarly, the various other essentially autonomous and rationally self-interested stakeholders are implicitly prepared to concede structural protection and governance rights to shareholders because they recognise the existence of harmony between shareholder wealth and the long-term benefits for the company. In respect to any negative social or environmental 'externalities' arising out of this pursuit of shareholder value, there is no institutional capacity for having social or moral obligations since the company does not exist in any meaningful sense. On the contrary, any public regulatory intervention, which secures additional entitlements for non-shareholder groups, is regarded as socially detrimental to the functioning of the market. Any 'corrections' should be made through specific regulation (e.g., employment law, tort law and environmental law) rather than by reforming the fabric of company law itself (Box 8.2).

Box 8.2 Corporate Social Responsibility

Corporate social responsibility (CSR) aims to ensure that companies conduct their business operations in a way that produces positive social and environmental effects. There have been increased demands from customers, employees, and government bodies for companies to be more accountable for reaching, and maintaining, acceptable standards in their business practice. Despite controversy about whether CSR should be a legal norm, ethical norm, or something else, in contractarian circles there is simply no room for debate. Once it is accepted that the company is nothing more than a set of relationships among the natural persons involved in, say, the ice-cream label Ben & Jerry's, its long-standing grassroots initiatives make no sense. Since the company does not exist, as a distinct entity, there is no capacity for philanthropic obligations. Of course, proponents of contractarian theory would argue that, even if Ben & Jerry's directors were focused on maximising profits, in order to do that they will have to treat their stakeholders well. This is often called the 'business case' for social responsibility, in which stakeholders are valued merely instrumentally. Yet it is only sometimes the case that kindness will pay – there are too many cases where, unfortunately, maximising profits requires rather poor treatment of stakeholders.

However, contractarian analysis is not without its internal contradictions and methodological 'blind spots' when it comes to the true nature of corporate activity. First, the theory fails to recognise that the company's limited institutional obligation outside of contract merely 'shifts the nature of the corporate person to the responsibilities of natural persons *toward each other* [emphasis added]'.[11] This emphasis on human beings to consider the impact of their decisions on the public interest is distorted because of the theory's conceptualisation of individual rationality. Indeed, the notion of individual rationality as a higher virtue displaces individual actors from their immediate legal, historical,

---

[11] D. Millon, 'The Ambiguous Significance of Corporate Personhood' (2001) 2(1) *Stanford Agora* 39, 54.

social or political context and into a narrower, reductive sphere of economic market-oriented behaviour. However, the denial of the company's duties outside of what its shareholders have expressly agreed to in contract and presumption of rational economic behaviour is theoretically and empirically questionable. It is simply unhelpful to assert that the company has no social or moral responsibilities unless the shareholders expressly authorise directors to sacrifice profits in order to pursue socially responsible outcomes. This is principally because, in a legal sense, it is meaningless to talk about contractual rights and obligations when mere contractual imagery, rather than express contract, is involved.[12] This leads directly to the second critique, that human beings are rational economic actors. Numerous insights from sociology, anthropology, philosophy and other disciplines show that, as in corporate activity, human behaviour is undeniably and significantly *more* than the episodic interaction of atomistic and asocial individuals pursuing entirely self-originated plans for material advantage.[13] Rather, individual behaviour within the company occurs in a collective action setting and is frequently animated through a pattern of coordination, co-operation and mutual respect. Accordingly, it is perhaps possible to suggest that social relations are far more likely to cause individuals to pursue interests other than those related to the efficiency of a particular course of action, and social relations themselves can determine the relative efficiency of the various courses of action.

b. Companies Are Capable of Social or Ethical Responsibilities

The conventional way of thinking about the company as a legal fiction assumed it capable of having only a very limited set of rights and duties, either expressly or incidental to its very existence, such as the ability to transfer property rights or enter into contracts. Put differently, the nature of artificial legal persons, which represented only a small part of a human's personality, did not allow for recognition of moral or ethical rights and duties. Notwithstanding, when the personality of a company is fictitious, a concession from the state, it becomes the subject of whatever rights and liabilities might emerge from the public policy choices expressed through the political system, the workings of the legal system, and the social relations within which companies are embedded. Now there is one respect in which, when the law conceptualises the company as a public institution because of its influence or effect on society, it implies that companies are capable of having much richer responsibilities to a wider group

---

[12] See, for example, J. N. Gordon, 'The Mandatory Structure of Corporate Law' (1989) 89 *Columbia Law Review* 1549, 1549. For an illuminating, if somewhat acerbic, exchange on this subject, see the articles of Melvin Eisenberg and Fred McChesney in a symposium issue of the *Columbia Law Review*: (1990) 90(5) *Columbia Law Review* 1321–39.

[13] See, for example, R. N. Bellah, R. Madsen, W. M. Sullivan, A. Swidler, and S. M. Tipton, *The Good Society* (Vintage, 1992) 290; M. Granovetter, 'Economic Action and Social Structure: The Problem of Embeddedness' (1985) 91 *American Journal of Sociology* 481, 488–9.

of stakeholders than just the shareholders. In addition to the apparent useful-ness of the artificial entity metaphor, CSR thinking has benefitted from the view of the company as a real entity. According to this premise, if the state recognises the organic social reality of a company, it is not a historical accident or contin-gency, but for the very practical and sufficient purpose of conferring legal rights and imposing legal obligations. This much is expressed through E. Merrick Dodd, Jr's classic account of corporate citizenship. Dodd, challenging Adolf Berle's views on the proper legal beneficiary of managerial duties, submitted that, because the company is real and different from the individual shareholders who stand behind it, the company could pursue moral and ethical interests that are different from those of its shareholders.[14] Specific expectations follow legal requirements for companies to observe non-corporate legal regulations, whether legislative or judge-made, such as environmental and employment rubrics. A broader definition would include the suggestion that the company maintains considerable potential to advance moral or ethical expectations, extending beyond the particular profit-making goals of capital providers and corporate managers (Box 8.3).

Box 8.3 Patagonia, Inc.

In early 2019, US outdoor clothing company Patagonia Inc. announced its plan to donate $10 million, the full refund from a federal tax cut it called 'irresponsible', to support those fighting for environmental causes threatened by the tax cut itself. The necessary solutions involve, amongst other things, renewable energy, sustain-able small-scale agriculture that supports working families, and the protection of public lands and waters. The company already has an established strategy of main-taining responsible supply chains, benefitting lower-level workers, and focusing on climate change and conservation initiatives. These are voluntary initiatives that could certainly result in lower corporate profits and therefore a lower rate of return for shareholders. However, in the absence of such philanthropic corporate action, fiction/artificial entity theory would legitimate state regulation of Patagonia's business activity, as a creature of the state, to require it to pursue almost any socially responsible ends. Although it is slightly harder to single out for special regulatory attention a real entity, there is a basis for arguing that the company's conduct is capable of regulation if the same legal efforts can be applied to natural persons.

Yet reified corporate personhood has posed some difficulties. Although scholars widely accept the use of the real conception of the company, they

---

[14] E. M. Dodd Jr, 'For Whom are Corporate Managers Trustees?' (1932) 45 *Harvard Law Review* 1145, 1146, 1160. See also A. A. Berle, 'Corporate Powers as Powers in Trust' (1931) 44 Harvard Law Review 1049; A. A. Berle, 'For Whom Managers are Trustees: A Note' (1932) 45 *Harvard Law Review* 1365. For a general background, see J. L. Weiner, 'The Berle-Dodd Dialogue on the Concept of the Corporation' (1964) 64(8) *Columbia Law Review* 1458.

debate its implications for law and regulatory policy. First and foremost, critics of the entity conception of the company would argue that while the definition of a legal subject is a proper and practically significant inquiry, the search for an inhering essence elides the more concrete issue of identifying the specific legal relations that proceed from being juristic entities. To be sure, the insistence both that the company is a real person, distinct from its individual members, and that the company, as a person, is not *quite* real does not altogether establish significant and operative guidance about the rights or relations that the various regulatory institutions must recognise and protect. This indeterminacy is most conspicuous and acute, as mentioned above, in respect to the political and legal implications of recognising, in the US context, certain inherent and inviolable constitutional rights for companies. This approach has generated far-ranging and ongoing controversy about the regulatory structures internal and external to corporate governance, as well as raising definite concerns about the apparently anti-democratic rights of large and powerful companies to retain religious liberty, privacy, freedom of speech, and so forth. Second, in determining what may be in the company's interests, the courts have been faced with the problem of applying to a juristic person a legal understanding developed for application to natural persons. The recognition of the company's separate identity established it as the beneficiary of directors' general duties, but only natural persons have the sort of interests that could satisfy the functional requirements of the fiduciary obligation. These are political rather than legal considerations, which, however, have a significant effect on law. Third, and finally, in respect to questions of attribution to companies of the acts and states of minds of individuals, if any general rule can be laid down in current English law, it is that contextualism, rather than anthropomorphic inquiry into corporate personality, is central to providing answers. Although such an approach may assist the courts' understanding of when and how criminal or tortious liability might be imposed upon companies, the fact of the matter is that there are a number of practical difficulties in seeking to justify a company's liability for criminal wrongs and, to a lesser extent, tort wrongs.[15]

Debate 3

Can a single theory explain or predict patterns of company law?

We have already seen that the various theories of the company have much to say about the public/private dichotomy and the goals and responsibilities of companies. It is thus important to provide a brief and panoramic examination of UK and, where relevant, US corporate law and governance in order to ascertain which of these concepts properly explains or predicts the law. Given space

---

[15] See, for example, *Okpabi & ors v Royal Dutch Shell plc & anr* [2017] EWHC 89; *Chandler v Cape plc* [2012] EWCA Civ 525; *Meridian Global Funds Management Asia Ltd. v Securities Commission* (2005) 3 All ER 918.

constraints, the following examples provide merely a flavour of the influence of theory in this practical and real-world sense.

a. The Fiction Theory in Law

There is considerable historical evidence of the influence of the fiction theory of the company in common law. In the landmark decision of *The Case of Sutton's Hospital*,[16] decided in 1612, Lord Coke, in a now familiar exposition, observed that 'the [company] itself is only *in abstracto*, and rests only in the intendment and consideration of the law; for a corporation aggregate of many is invisible, immortal, and rests only in the intendment and consideration of the law'. Simply stated, Coke's words seemed to accept, tacitly, that there is such a thing as corporate personality apart from the human beings comprising it, albeit existing only as a figment of legal imagination. What is more, the fiction theory is generally regarded to have influenced corporate theory in the US 'from the Founding to the mid-19th century'.[17] The classic decision of *Trustees of Dartmouth College v Woodward*,[18] decided more than two centuries after *Sutton's Hospital*, highlights the influence of fiction theory. US Supreme Court Chief Justice Marshall characterised the company as an 'artificial being, invisible, intangible, and existing only in the contemplation of law'. Marshall stated that, as companies derive their existence by concession from the state, these entities possess only those properties that are conferred by special legislative grant, which usually limited them to purposes of a public nature. Notwithstanding, it should be noted that authority for the fiction theory, at least in the UK, could be viewed as an accepted narrative of law and society during the Early Modern period of Europe because corporate bodies embodied the power of the state and were engaged in quasi-state activities. However, as we saw earlier, this changed because of rapid changes in the industrial landscape during the 19th century.

b. Real Entity Theory in Law

The entity concept has undoubtedly developed from the early days of the modern company law era. From the middle of the 19th century onwards, real entity theory has gained a considerable ascendance amongst courts and policymakers in the UK and the US, who began to rely increasingly on the ideas it embodied in order to advance different doctrinal and normative positions. In the UK context, this paradigm shift can be traced back to a small, but functional, distinction made in

---

[16] (1612) 10 Co Rep 23a, 77 ER 960. On the significance of this decision, see W. S. Houldsworth, 'English Corporation Law in the 16th and 17th Centuries' (1922) 31(4) *Yale Law Journal* 382, 382–3.

[17] D. A. H. Miller, 'Guns Inc.: Citizens United, McDonald, and the Future of Corporate Constitutional Rights' (2011) 86 *New York University Law Review* 887, 916.

[18] 17 US (1 Wheat.) 518 at 636 (1819).

the Companies Act 1862 when compared with its 1856 antecedent.[19] The earlier statute stipulated in section 3 that 'Seven or more persons... may... form *themselves into* an incorporated company [emphasis added]'. This suggested that the newly formed company, while an entity, was made up of its shareholder-incorporators. However, the later version of this provision omitted the words 'themselves into', which meant the substitution of a collective group of members for a separate legal personality. Subsequently, this change became significant, inspiring various rules that are now regarded as fundamental to company law and governance; prime examples include directors' duties,[20] the proper plaintiff rule,[21] the *ultra vires* doctrine,[22] and the rules relating to capital maintenance[23] (see Talbot, Chapter 7). In the classic case of *Salomon v Salomon Co Ltd.*,[24] Lord Halsbury LC stated that 'once the company is formed it must be treated like any other independent person with its rights and liabilities appropriate to itself, and that the motives of those who took part in the promotion of the company are absolutely irrelevant in discussing what those rights and liabilities are'. Although His Lordship was careful to state that the company is an artificial creation of the law, *Salomon* may at the same time have allowed for an apparent partial acceptance of real entity theory. In particular, Lord Halsbury refers to the company many times in his judgment as 'real', not artificial, once legally incorporated.

Aside from the common law, recognition of the entity conception of the company is apparent in policy. Most recently, the Company Law Review Steering Group, responsible for the legislative reform project that culminated in the Companies Act 2006, talked about the business relationships that companies have as important intangible assets of *the company*.[25] It said that directors' general duties at common law are often regarded as leading to directors having 'an undue focus on the short term and the narrow interests of members at the expense of what is in a broader and a longer term sense the best interests of *the enterprise* [emphasis added]'.[26] In the modern world, despite the best efforts of policymakers, the collective influence of shareholders over the

---

[19] This argument follows closely the approach taken in P. Ireland, I. Griggs-Small, and D. Kelly, 'The Conceptual Foundations of Modern Company Law' (1987) 14 *Journal of Law and Society* 149, 150.

[20] The common law explicitly stated that the general duties were owed to the company itself. See, for example, *Peskin v Anderson* [2000] EWCA Civ 326; *Percival v Wright* [1902] 2 Ch 421. This position is now codified in CA 2006, s 170.

[21] *Foss v Harbottle* (1843) 67 ER 189. See now, CA 2006, ss 260–4.

[22] *Ashbury Railway Carriage & Iron Co. v Riche* (1875) L.R. 7 HL 653. See now, CA 2006, s 171.

[23] *Trevor v Whitworth* (1887) 12 App. Cas. 409. See now, CA 2006, Parts 18 and 20, which implement various parts of the European Second Council Directive 77/91/EEC.

[24] [1897] AC 22, 30.

[25] Company Law Review, *Modern Company Law for a Competitive Economy: Strategic Framework* (London, DTI, 1999) para 5.1.17.

[26] Ibid.

management of companies has diminished, and shareholders in UK companies are dispersed across the globe. Similarly, creditors and employees are seldom actively involved in the company's business. Hence, the notion of a free-standing entity arguably fits very well into this context.

A similar story occurred in many states in the US, where the real entity theory achieved prominence in the courts during the nineteenth and twentieth centuries. Analysis of Supreme Court decisions demonstrates that in recent years the real entity theory is firmly, though not universally, established. The law has developed from a line of constitutional law cases originating from the 1886 decision in *Santa Clara Co v Southern Pacific Railroad*,[27] where Justice Waite stated that '[t]he court does not wish to hear argument on the question whether the provision in the Fourteenth Amendment to the Constitution, which forbids a State to deny any person… the equal protection of the laws, applies to… [companies]. We are all of the opinion that it does'. These remarks have come to stand in American jurisprudence for the protections of due process and equal protection. By holding that companies have certain rights, the Supreme Court has applied the protections of the Constitution to companies in the same way, if not with the same content, as it does to natural persons. However, perhaps because the Supreme Court rarely considers what a company is, the real entity theory ebbed and flowed in subsequent decisions. In seeking to reconcile conflicting lines of its own precedent, the Supreme Court in *Citizens United v Federal Election Commission*[28] struck down more than 100 years of precedent in recognising the rights of free speech of US companies. Although the majority opinion did not explicitly state that companies are real persons, the theory retains a serious role in explaining the reasoning of this landmark decision. In particular, the opinion stated that 'no sufficient government interest justifies limits on the political speech of non-profit or for-profit corporations'. Besides the particular visibility in the constitutional law arena, the real entity theory's ascendance has made its mark on US corporate law in a number of ways. Historically, the real entity theory helped support the trend to grant corporate entities limited liability, served as the ultimate object of directors' plenary powers, and strengthened the so-called 'business judgment rule' that applies in most states in the US.[29]

---

[27] 118 US 394 (1886). For some examples of subsequent decisions that affirm this decision, see, for example, *First National Bank v Bellotti*, 435 US 765 (1978); *Pacific Gas and Electric Co. v Public Utilities Commission*, 475 US 1 (1986); *Copperweld Corp. v Independence Tube Corp.*, 467 US 752 (1984). Conversely, in other cases decided during that period, the fictional nature of the company prevailed. See *United States v White*, 322 US 694, 698 (1944); *Wilson v United States*, 221 US 361, 383–4 (1911); *Hale v Henkel*, 201 US 43, 74 (1906).

[28] 558 US 310 (2010), 365. On this point, see generally Miller, above n 15, 893; J. Macleod Hemmingway, 'Thoughts on the Corporation as a Person for Purposes of Corporate Criminal Liability' (2011) 41 *Stetson Law Review* 137, 138.

[29] R. S. Avi-Yonah, 'Citizens United and the Corporate Form' (2010) *Wisconsin Law Review* 999, 1018–19.

c. Contractarian Theory in Law

The contractarian theory offers a more plausible explanation or prediction of the US corporate law rather than UK company law and governance. In brief, the first unique doctrinal characteristic of much of US corporate law, which is consistent with the general de-regulatory and market-facilitative ideology of the contractarian analysis, is the essentially default nature of many legal rules that serve the preferences of its collective participants. This transaction cost-saving component of US corporate law enables individual commercial actors (i.e., the directors and shareholders) to adopt, or reject, a default rule that is unsuitable to a company's particular business context. This tradition of adaptability and opting out of US corporate law is implied through the country's unique system of inter-jurisdictional competition. That is, while federal law creates minimum standards for trade in company shares and governance rights, all 50 states have their own state-level systems of corporate law. This enables the directors and shareholders, in a fundamental and legally unconstrained way, to choose the 'optimal' state of incorporation or where it might reincorporate later on. No doubt, one of US corporate law's enduring issues has been the extent to which a process of competition between the states produces a 'race to the bottom' in the generation of laws (i.e., increasing permissiveness rather than careful elucidation of minimum standards of directorial behaviour and enforcement). The second characteristic of US corporate law, which is central to contractarian theory, is the protection of the internal governance affairs of the company from external regulatory intervention. Directors and shareholders are in a position to determine the general strategy and policy of the company at the intra-corporate level, largely uninhibited by judicial scrutiny or state regulation. This deference to internal contractual autonomy is also established at the fundamental level of US corporate governance in the jurisprudential foundations of the board of directors itself, whose essential existence and plenary powers would appear historically to predate extraneous regulatory initiative.[30] This is one of the many reasons why it is more ideological than descriptive. It conceptualises arrangements, developed in a more entrepreneurial form of capitalism, which have long since been surpassed by large corporations. It explains the present using concepts appropriate to the past.

In contrast, significant dimensions to the UK legal-institutional framework are set out, to a greater extent than in most states in the US, on a mandatory and irreversible basis in the Companies Act 2006. Most obviously, this includes, but is not limited to, directors' duties, shareholder voting rights, and capital maintenance. However, the contractarian analysis does provide some explanatory value when it comes to the presence of flexible and reversible

---

[30] For a fundamentally more detailed and complete account of the practical manifestation of the contractarian paradigm within US corporate law and governance, see Moore, above n 8, 99–135; B. R. Cheffins, *Company Law: Theory, Structure, and Operation* (OUP, 1997), esp. Chapters 7, 8 and 10.

internal governance rules. Most notably, the model articles of association contain default governance rules that shareholders are free to adopt or alter. They set out a constitutional structure and divide corporate power between the board and the general meeting of shareholders.[31] Typically the power of management is vested in the board of directors (who are generally permitted to delegate to managers below board level), and although companies invariably follow the default rules, this is formally a matter of private ordering under each company's articles rather than being embedded in substantive law (as it is in, say, Delaware).[32] The articles, according to section 33(1) of the Act, are binding on the shareholders in their dealings with each other and on dealings between shareholders and the company. On this basis, the de-centralised and generally consensual rule-making processes of the articles implicitly 'acknowledge contract as *the* animating force within company law'.[33] The rationality of inter-personal association legitimates the collective entitlement of shareholders to retain and exercise formal sovereign prerogative over the directors and management. Furthermore, although the US business judgment rule and statutory *ex ante* exculpatory provisions for directors are not formally part of the UK's doctrinal legal fabric, the English courts customary deferral to the exercise of executive discretion and what shareholders have actually agreed in the corporate constitution[34] implicitly affirms the contractual conception of the company.[35]

CONCLUSION

Undoubtedly, the dialogue over the 'essence' of corporate personhood has provided a crucial intellectual tradition for company law and governance. It places the constitutive legal doctrines and legal decisions of the discipline within a broader theoretical framework that gives meaning and coherence to them. It will be recalled that the main theories range from characterising the company as a legal fiction or as a real entity or, more recently, as a nexus of contracts. Simply stated, the point of these descriptive explanations of when

---

[31] See, for example, Companies (Model Articles) Regulations 2008 (SI 2008/3229), arts. 3 and 4.

[32] See Talbot, Chapter 7 for a historical explanation of these aspects of English company law.

[33] H. McVea, 'Section 994 of the Companies Act 2006 and the Primacy of Contract' (2012) 75(6) *Modern Law Review* 1123 at 1123. For a representative authority, see *Fulham Football Club (1987) Ltd v Richards & Anor* [2011] EWCA Civ 855. On 22 February 2012, the Supreme Court refused permission to appeal the CA's decision.

[34] This judicial deference pre-dates registered companies as can be seen in *Carlen v Drury* (1812) 1 Ves & B 154, 158, per Lord Eldon. See also, *Re Smith & Fawcett Ltd* ([1942] Ch. 304; affirmed more recently in *Edge v Pensions Ombudsman* [2000] Ch. 602, CA, 627E–630G; *Equitable Life Assurance Society v Hyman* [2002] 1 AC 408, HL, [17]–[21].

[35] For a greater breadth and depth of analysis of this part of the chapter, see Moore, above n 21, 136–76.

and why companies come into existence, and how company law may affect these processes, is to provide a particular normative agenda, setting and justifying regulatory or facilitative goals that may influence policymakers. Yet these prescriptions for company law and governance remain intensely debated because each of these attempts to explain the nature of the company has failed to universally convince. Now there is one respect in which, because of the apparently unresolvable tensions and controversies in this debate, ascertaining the precise nature of the company is no closer to resolution today than it ever has been. But in a fundamentally more reasonable and nuanced respect, it is pertinent to note that '[m]ost theories simply describe matters a little, or even a lot, differently from the next one'[36] to the extent that each of the respective conceptualisations has 'some validity and contributes to a better understanding of the full dimensions of a "remarkably fluctuating reality"'.[37] So understood, it is perhaps more plausible or readily arguable that the company is in a real-world sense 'simultaneously a legal fiction, a contractual network, and a 'real' organisation'.[38]

FURTHER READING

P. I. Blumberg, 'The Corporate Personality in American Law: A Summary Review' (1990) 38 *American Journal of Comparative Law* 49.

W. W. Bratton, 'The New Economic Theory of the Firm: Critical Perspectives from History' (1989) 41 *Stanford Law Review* 1471.

G. F. Canfield, 'Scope and Limits of the Corporate Entity Theory' (1917) 17 *Columbia Law Review* 128.

J. Dewey, 'The Historic Background of Corporate Legal Personality' (1926) 35 *Yale Law Journal* 655.

F. Easterbrook and D. Fischel, 'The Corporate Contract' (1989) 89 *Columbia Law Review* 1416.

R. Harris, 'The Transplantation of the Legal Discourse on Corporate Personality Theories: From German Codification to British Political Pluralism and American Big Business' (2006) 63(4) *Washington & Lee Law Review* 1421.

M. J. Horwitz, 'Santa Clara Revisited: The Development of Corporate Theory' (1985) 88 *West Virginia Law Review* 173.

A. Machen, Jr., 'Corporate Personality' (1911) 24(4) *Harvard Law Review* 253.

M. Moore, *Corporate Governance in the Shadow of the State* (Hart, 2013) Chapters 4–5.

M. Radin, 'The Endless Problem of Corporate Personality' (1932) 32 *Columbia Law Review* 643.

---

[36] D. Wishart, 'A Reconfiguration of Company and/or Corporate Law Theory' (2010) 10(1) *Journal of Corporate Law Studies* 151, 160.

[37] G. Teubner, 'Enterprise Corporatims: New Industrial Policy and the 'Essence' of the Legal Person' (1988) 36 *American Journal of Comparative Law* 130, 130–3.

[38] P. I. Blumberg, 'The Corporate Personality in American Law: A Summary Review' (1990) 38 *American Journal of Comparative Law* 4, 50–1.

CHAPTER 9

Hostile Takeovers: Corporate Governance Solution or Social Cost?

Andrew Johnston

Introduction

The hostile takeover is perhaps the most important and controversial – and certainly the most spectacular – feature of the UK corporate governance landscape. This chapter begins with the conventional description of takeovers, which insists that they are simply transfers of shares from dispersed shareholders to a new majority shareholder. It then looks at how changes to law and soft law turned transfers of shares into transfers of corporate control, which in turn came to be viewed as a solution to the 'agency' problem of corporate governance. Managerial discretion was truncated as directors focused on keeping the shareholders happy and the share price high in order to head off the threat of takeover. It then explores some of the critical debate about takeovers, focusing on the arguments that they create social costs, encourage short-termism and allow the breach of implicit contracts between employees and companies. It concludes with some thoughts on the prospects for reform.

Takeovers Are Simply Transfers of Shares

A takeover occurs where one company (referred to here as the 'bidder' company) successfully acquires enough of the shares of another company (referred to here as the 'target' company) to allow it, as the dominant, majority or 100 per cent shareholder, to take control of the target's general meeting. Like any shareholder who controls the general meeting, the bidder can then replace the board of directors and then the senior management of the target below board level. Following the takeover, the bidder may merge the business of the target company into one of its own subsidiaries or it may preserve the target as a separate company within its own group structure. A bidder company will normally prefer to acquire all of the shares in the target company because this allows it to run the target company in its own interests without having to consider the position of minority shareholders. In addition, takeover regulation, in the UK at least, is not favourable to partial offers, and they are rare.

The bidder company launches its takeover bid by making a public 'tender offer' to purchase all the shares in the target company from its dispersed share-holders. The law gives a bidder who acquires 90 per cent of the shares in a target a legal right to 'squeeze out' (i.e., compulsorily acquire the shares of) the remaining minority shareholders. Therefore, tender offers are normally condi-tional upon 90 per cent of the target shareholders accepting the tender offer, although the bidder often reserves a power to lower this threshold to 50 per cent. The bidder company may offer to pay cash for the shares it wants to acquire, it may offer shares in itself, or it may offer a combination of the two. Clearly, the bidder company must offer consideration for the shares which is sufficiently attractive to persuade 90 per cent of the shareholders to accept the offer. Where the target is a listed company, the bidder normally offers a pre-mium above the three-month average market price of 10 to 40 per cent. Target shareholders who are considering accepting shares in the bidder have a more difficult decision to make as they have to form a view of whether the bidder's plans for the combined business post-takeover are satisfactory.

Takeovers may be 'friendly' or 'hostile'. In a friendly takeover, the bidder company approaches the target directors and asks them to recommend the offer to their shareholders. This normally implies that a friendly takeover will not result in the removal of the target's directors and senior management team. It also allows the bidder to gain access to better information about the target company's finances and other aspects of their operations. Where the target directors refuse to co-operate or where the bidder company anticipates that they will do this, they may launch a 'hostile' bid, bypassing the target directors and making a public tender offer directly to the target's shareholders. In that situation, it is likely that at least some directors and senior managers will be removed, and the absence of co-operation means that the bidder company will only have access to publicly available information about the target. In the case of listed public companies, this will be quite far-reaching; in the case of public companies which are not listed, there will be considerably less.

Takeover bidders may be companies in the same industry (and so in the largest takeovers, competition law may come into play), and there may be an industrial logic behind the takeover (acquisition of assets such as intellectual property or other technologies[1]), cost-cutting through synergies such as uni-fied distribution networks, common administration, and so on). Alternatively, bidders may be financial entities such as private equity firms and other invest-ment vehicles, in which case the logic is likely to be economic and financial (cost-cutting through reducing production costs, balance sheet restructuring). Private equity firms very often collaborate with senior managers of the target

---

[1] See Harrison, Chapter 4.

company, in which case the takeover may be termed a 'management buyout'; the private equity firm provides the finance (much of it borrowed) and uses a shareholders' agreement to set strict performance conditions for the senior managers (who will remain minority shareholders) for incentive purposes. Where the bidder company uses borrowed money in addition to its own equity capital to finance the bid (something that is very common where the takeover has a financial motivation), the takeover is referred to as 'leveraged'.

A bidder will normally establish a 'foothold' in the target company before launching the bid but this will remain below 30 per cent because a bidder who crosses the 30 per cent threshold in the UK is required to launch a bid for all the shares in the company. It may also remain below 10 per cent because where the bidder has acquired 10 per cent or more of the target's shares before launching the bid, the minimum price payable for the remaining shares will be set at the highest level paid during the previous 12 months or during the bid itself. In addition, there are rules requiring disclosure of significant acquisitions of shares, which may alert shareholders (and other investors) to the possibility of a tender offer, potentially triggering price rises. This serves to emphasise the importance of secrecy and speed for the bidder as well as the possibility of insider trading (the possibility of a takeover is very price-sensitive information).

Takeovers Involve More Than Simply Share Transfers

A. Transfers of Corporate Control Became Possible Because of Historic Regulatory and Policy Choices

The historical development of company law and takeover regulation shows that takeovers involve more than just share transfers. A series of intentional and unintentional regulatory and policy choices had the effect of making control of companies contestable, paving the way for the takeover to emerge. The rules ensured that bidders who acquired a majority of the shares would be able to take control of the general meeting and board of the company and that target companies could do very little to prevent this. As we will see in this section, early company law and practice made companies virtually immune from hostile takeover. Legislation opened them up to hostile takeover, whilst case law and self-regulation introduced by financial interests made it progressively harder for companies to defend themselves against unwelcome takeovers.

In the late 19th century and early decades of the 20th century, amalgamations between previously separate companies were carried out by an agreed merger between two or more companies, either through a share exchange or through the formation of a holding company. Key decisions were taken by the directors, and there was little involvement from the shareholders. Mergers normally occurred between companies in the same or related lines of business and were often anticompetitive (there was little meaningful control of monopoly until after World War II), and companies aimed to form cartels in areas such as textiles, tobacco and cement.[2] Following the merger, the previously separate companies were often still managed by the same people under the umbrella of a parent company. After the First World War, there was a growing emphasis on 'rationalisation', driven by unfavourable comparisons with Germany and the US, which had developed more big business, leading to reforms in the Companies Act 1929 intended to facilitate economies of scale. In particular, that Act gave the acquirer of 90 per cent of a company's shares the power to make a compulsory purchase of the remaining 10 per cent of shares and this 'squeeze out' provision turned out to be crucial to the later emergence of the hostile takeover. It is worth noting the emergence of theories of 'scientific management' around the same time, something that was promoted by government, and an emergent view that 'conscious and purposeful organization' was superior to unconstrained market competition.[3] Around this time, there was a broad consensus that the role of newly professionalised corporate management was to balance the competing interests at stake in the company.[4] There remained concerns about directors (who were often constitutionally entrenched and significant shareholders) either retaining their seats on the board of the merged company or being paid to relinquish their position (expropriating some of the value of the business that would otherwise have been paid to shareholders). However, policymakers were also beginning to express concern about the implications of the growing dispersal of shareholders, and the Companies Act 1948 marked the beginning of an effort to put shareholders back in control of companies.

The early 1950s witnessed the emergence of the hostile takeover in the UK, as bidders bypassed the board of directors, whom they intended to remove once they acquired control of the company, and approached the shareholders of the target directly. Until this point, both quoted and unquoted companies had been largely self-financed, relying on retained earnings,[5] and directors were able to rely on hidden reserves, paying out only sufficient earnings to keep shareholders content. Property was often undervalued on balance sheets.

The emergence of the hostile takeover and its establishment as a practice was driven by the coincidence of a number of legal and institutional changes. The Companies Act 1948 abolished hidden reserves and modernised accounting, giving bidders more reliable information and allowing them to target companies that were underperforming or had undervalued assets. Equally importantly but less discussed, that Act introduced a power for shareholders to remove the directors by ordinary resolution (simple majority) rather than the 75 per cent stated in most companies' constitutions, which strongly entrenched

---

[2] L Hannah, *The Rise of the Corporate Economy* (Methuen, London, 2nd ed, 1976), pp. 21–2 and 42.

[3] Hannah 1976 at 31–2.

[4] See, for example, LCB Gower, 'Corporate Control: The Battle for the Berkeley' (1955) 68 *Harvard Law Review* 1176.

[5] Hannah 1976 at 62.

many incumbent directors (who were significant minority shareholders).[6] This made the control of many companies contestable overnight, and bidder and incumbents raced to gain the support of the majority of the shareholders and, with it, control of the company. Once these changes ensured that takeovers operated to transfer control of companies, the 'squeeze out' rules introduced in 1929 came into play, allowing a bidder who acquired 90 per cent of the shares to make a compulsory acquisition of the remainder, eliminating potentially irritating minority shareholders. Institutionally, the 1950s witnessed the gradual replacement of individual shareholders by institutional investors, who were less likely to follow management's advice and were more focused on short-term financial returns, whilst bidders gained easier access to debt finance as the City of London changed its views on hostile takeovers.

As the hostile takeover developed, incumbent directors did not remain passive in the face of the threat. Far from it. They began to undertake many of the actions that bidders favoured, such as increasing dividends to shareholders and selling off assets and then leasing them back. This marked an important transformation in managerial practice, away from balancing the competing claims of different groups towards a focus on creating value for the shareholders and keeping the share price sufficiently high to keep the shareholders happy (and head off the threat of hostile takeover). The social norm of shareholder primacy was thus quietly born during the early days of the hostile takeover era. More problematically from the perspective of those who favoured this new mechanism, however, directors began to use the broad discretion given to them by company law to take actions that made takeovers considerably less likely to succeed. These 'defensive measures' included issuing increasing numbers of non-voting shares, issuing shares to friendly parties and setting up structures, like employee share trusts, which appeared not to be a breach of directors' duties because they were aimed at what the directors considered in good faith to be 'the interests of the company'. A Board of Trade report on defensive measures taken by the directors of Savoy Hotel Ltd anticipated the development of the common law approach by the courts in *Hogg v Cramphorn Ltd*[7]: the directors would be acting for an improper purpose if they took action for the purpose of retaining control or preventing the majority from exercising its rights. *Howard Smith Ltd v Ampol Petroleum Ltd*[8] subsequently confirmed that an issue of shares 'purely for the purpose of destroying an existing majority, or creating a new majority which did not previously exist' would be unlawful. Although the courts accepted in both cases that the directors were acting honestly, this line of case law made it harder for directors to take defensive measures. Yet it was not exactly encouraging of hostile takeovers either since

---

[6] For further discussion of this, see A Johnston, B Segrestin and A Hatchuel, 'From Balanced Enterprise to Hostile Takeover: How the Law Forgot about Management' (2019) 39(1) *Legal Studies* 75.

[7] [1967] Ch 254.

[8] [1974] AC 821.

they are normally time-critical. The legality of defensive measures was assessed by the courts on an *ex post* basis on the basis of (contested) evidence about the primary purpose for which directors acted. When the directors created an employee shareholding trust, were they acting to incentivise the employees (lawful) or to prevent an unwelcome takeover (unlawful)? When the directors issued new shares, were they acting to raise capital (lawful) or to prevent a takeover (unlawful)?

Early takeovers were also characterised by numerous procedural abuses that put pressure on shareholders to accept the tender offer. Financial institutions in the City of London gradually developed a system of soft law regulation of take-overs in the form of the 1959 *Notes on Amalgamations of British Businesses*, which were revised in 1963. The City was able to use its self-regulatory capacity (essentially a power to deny access to markets to those who flouted its rules) to impose its preferred norms on the conduct of takeovers. However, the *Notes* did not address defensive measures explicitly, confining themselves to stating that takeovers should not be 'artificially impeded' and that there should be 'no interference with the free market in shares and securities of companies'. These early efforts at self-regulation by the City 'made almost no difference to the conduct of takeovers in Britain'.[9] Dissatisfaction with the regulation of take-overs during the boom in the second half of the 1960s prompted the Bank of England to set up a working party that led to the development of the City Code on Takeovers and Mergers, administered by a Takeover Panel consisting of appointees from City institutions. Unlike the common law and the earlier *Notes*, the City Code imposed a strict prohibition on the directors taking any action that might result in an actual or potential takeover bid being frustrated. This provision effectively superseded the courts' jurisdiction over takeovers, closing off any possibility of directors taking defensive measures against the bid. It has remained a mainstay of takeover regulation ever since (the current iteration is Rule 21 of the Takeover Code) and has formed a blueprint for takeover regula-tion in many other jurisdictions (the main exception being Delaware in the US, whose approach is closer to the pre–City Code common law approach).

B. Takeovers Solve a Corporate Governance Issue:
The 'Agency' Problem

From Adam Smith[10] to Milton Friedman,[11] economists have claimed that the separation of 'ownership' and control reduces the capacity or incentives of shareholders to supervise directors and so allows corporate managers to be

---

[9] R Roberts, 'Regulatory Reponses to the Rise of the Market for Corporate Control in Britain in the 1950s' (1992) 34(1) *Business History* 183.

[10] A Smith, *The Wealth of Nations*, Book V, Chapter I, Part III.

[11] R Van Horn, 'Reinventing Monopoly and the Role of Corporations: The Roots of Chicago Law and Economics' in P Mirowski and D Plehwe (eds), *The Road from Mont Pelerin: The Making of the Neoliberal Thought Collective* (2009, Harvard University Press) at 215.

inefficient, incompetent or self-serving. In this context, efficiency has long been understood narrowly to mean serving the interests of shareholders or, in its more extreme formulation, maximising shareholder value.

The use of the term 'ownership' to describe the shareholders' claims on the company is controversial because it is not legally correct yet closes off wider arguments about whose interests the company and its management should serve. It is true that Berle and Means described the shareholders' interest as 'ownership' in their seminal 1932 work, but they also recognised that the nature of property had changed in the modern corporation. This led them to conclude that company directors should not simply serve the interests of the shareholders; it seemed more likely that they would 'develop into a purely neutral technocracy, balancing a variety of claims by various groups in the community',[12] a conclusion that was entirely in line with the dominant managerialist ethos at the time. Nowadays, company law academics are virtually unanimous that shareholders do not own the company[13]; instead, they own their shares, which give them a bundle of rights in relation to the company which fall far short of what lawyers normally refer to as 'ownership rights'.[14] For example, shareholders have a right to a dividend only if the directors declare one and, unless the company is in liquidation, have no claim on the company's assets. Nevertheless, Berle and Means' shorthand of 'ownership' has, along with the residual appeal of the logic of partnership, which for historical reasons influenced the internal allocation of powers within the company, influenced policymakers. The result has been a series of reforms intended to increase the powers of shareholders in relation to directors in an attempt to reunite 'ownership' and control. For example, during its 1942–45 review of company law, the Cohen Committee reverted to simple assumptions about shareholders as owners and those on whom the first loss falls. In its final report, it recommended allowing the shareholders to remove the directors by simple majority as a 'means of making it easier for shareholders to exercise a more effective general control over the management of *their* companies'. The justification for introducing this unusual mandatory rule into company law was the 'illusory nature of the control theoretically exercised by shareholders over directors' which 'has been accentuated by the dispersion of capital'.[15] This logic continues to the present day: although recent initiatives to empower institutional shareholders may be justified on the basis of 'sustainability' or 'long-termism', the policy aim has always been to ensure that companies serve shareholder interests. Whilst we will see in what follows that economists no

---

[12] A Berle and G Means, *The Modern Corporation and Private Property* (1991 edition, Transaction Publishers) at 312–13.

[13] See, for example, L Stout et al, *The Modern Corporation Statement on Corporate Law* (2016) available at https://papers.ssrn.com/sol3/papers.cfm?abstract_id=2848833.

[14] See J Kay and A Silberston, 'Corporate Governance' (1995) 153 *National Institute Economic Review* 84.

[15] *Report of the Committee on Company Law Amendment* (Cm 6659, 1945), Para 5, emphasis added, and Para 7.

longer demand shareholder primacy on the grounds of ownership, as recently as 2016, a UK Government Green Paper on *Corporate Governance Reform* repeatedly referred to shareholders as owners, implicitly ruling out any fundamental rethinking of corporate governance.[16]

Since at least 1980, economists, led by Eugene Fama,[17] have abandoned the notion of shareholders as owners and have tended to analyse the relationship between shareholders and directors as an economic 'agency' relationship; the directors are cast as agents and the shareholders as principals. The shareholders depend on their agents for their returns but are vulnerable to 'agency costs' where the directors serve their own interests or the interests of other groups rather than those of shareholders.[18] By reframing the old 'ownership' debate in economic terms and claiming that shareholder value is the sole reliable indicator of economic efficiency, agency theory has exercised a huge influence on corporate governance debates over the last 40 years and provided a powerful retrospective justification of takeovers and the UK system of takeover regulation.

Henry Manne, a key neoliberal thinker, is generally – but erroneously – credited with discovering the market for corporate control, where 'the control of corporations [which] may constitute a valuable asset' can be traded, with a number of advantages, including 'more efficient management of corporations, the protection afforded non-controlling corporate investors, increased mobility of capital, and generally a more efficient allocation of resources'. The takeover mechanism 'provides some assurance of competitive efficiency among corporate managers and thereby affords strong protection to the interests of vast numbers of small, non-controlling shareholders'.[19] Although Manne might have coined the term 'market for corporate control', the substance of his argument had been around for some time in the UK, where hostile takeovers emerged much earlier than they did in the US. Various commentators had spoken approvingly of the hostile takeover since its first emergence.[20] The City of London and the Bank of England had come around to the desirability of hostile takeovers by the late 1950s,[21] and in 1962, the Jenkins Committee, which was reviewing company law, endorsed takeovers as a 'convenient method of amalgamation'. A minority of that Committee, led by Gower, the UK's leading academic company lawyer,

---

[16] Department for Business, Energy and Industrial Strategy, *Corporate Governance Reform*, Green Paper, November 2016.

[17] E Fama, 'Agency Problems and the Theory of the Firm' (1980) 88 *Journal of Political Economy* 288–307.

[18] See Attenborough, Chapter 8.

[19] HG Manne, 'Mergers and the Market for Corporate Control' (1965) 73 *Journal of Political Economy* 110.

[20] See, for example, *The Economist*, 23 January 1954, p. 254, describing the bidder as 'performing an economic service to the community'; G Bull & A Vice, *Bid for Power* (London, Elek, 3rd ed, 1961) at 25–6, noting that 'takeover bidders, with their short-term outlook' will tend to make 'the most efficient use of a company's assets'.

[21] Roberts at 187 and 191.

added the further gloss that takeovers were a spur to managerial efficiency.[22] By 1963, economists such as Marris were beginning to formalise the theory that takeovers produce efficiency-enhancing effects.[23]

In the conventional approach, takeovers are viewed as contributing to efficiency in two ways. First, like consensual mergers, they allow the creation of synergies, as existing businesses can be streamlined to take advantage of costs savings. Second, they reduce agency costs because inefficient, incompetent or self-serving management is replaced by new managers, who will prioritise the interests of the (new) shareholders in an attempt to recover the premium paid for control and more. The agency cost explanation of takeovers relies on the efficient markets hypothesis, which, in different formulations, claims that all publicly or privately known information is reflected in the company's share price. The share price reflects market participants' view of the present discounted value of the future income streams generated by the company's assets under current management.[24] The bidder offers a premium to that market price reflecting the improvements they will make once the takeover has been consummated, and that premium demonstrates that the assets are moving into the hands of corporate controllers who value them more highly (producing allocative efficiency).

Takeovers certainly 'constrain managers to work in the shareholders' interest',[25] but it is the threat, rather than the execution, of a takeover which puts pressure on managers. The UK's regulatory regime works very well in this regard, making it practically impossible for directors to do anything that might lessen the threat of takeover. As we saw above, the advent of the hostile takeover swiftly transformed management's approach towards a shorter-term, financialised approach, in which shareholder interests were prioritised. The broad discretion given to directors and management in company law is truncated by the hostile takeover, and the effect is even stronger where takeovers are leveraged because free cash flow is further cut by the legal obligation to service debt.[26] The hostile takeover, along with executive pay practices and boards dominated by non-executives in line with the UK Corporate Governance Code, continues to play a key role in ensuring that companies are run along shareholder primacy lines. The conventional view is that UK takeover regulation is a paragon to be followed by other jurisdictions.

[22] *Report of the Company Law Committee* (Cmnd 1749, June 1962), para 265 and Note of Dissent, Para 9 (by Gower and two others): 'Efficient directors who have treated their shareholders fairly and frankly should have little to fear from a raider'.

[23] See R. Marris, 'A Model of the "Managerial" Enterprise' (1963) 77(2) *Quarterly Journal of Economics* 185 at 190.

[24] See Cullen, Chapter 12.

[25] R Romano, 'A Guide to Takeovers: Theory, Evidence, and Regulation' (1992) 9 *Yale Journal on Regulation* 119 at 129.

[26] MC Jensen, 'The Agency Costs of Free Cash Flow' (1986) 76 *American Economic Review* 323–9.

Not all of the conventional approach to takeovers is positive. A whole swathe of academic research recognises that bidder shareholders often suffer losses in the form of falls in the share price when the company in which they hold shares completes (or even announces) a takeover. This form of agency cost has been explained on the basis that bidder directors are affected by over-confidence (or 'hubris') and so overpay for their acquisitions.[27] Alternatively, it may be that directors of bidder companies are 'empire building' as a means of self-aggrandisement and as a defence against takeovers since larger companies are less likely to become targets.[28] Takeover regulation focuses on the protection of target shareholders and is silent on the position of bidder shareholders. They receive some protection from board structure (non-executives should, in theory, limit the ability of executive directors to launch unwise takeovers) and from the incentives provided to executives (which reward them for increasing the share price). In addition, the Listing Rules provide (and have done since 1975) a degree of protection for bidder shareholders, requiring general meeting approval of transactions that exceed 25 per cent of the total value of the company under one of four tests.[29] Bidder company directors will have to discuss the proposed acquisition with powerful institutional investors and proxy advisory services within a very short time frame after the bid is made public, and the takeover offer will be made conditional on the relevant resolutions being passed. Recent research suggests that shareholders tend to give approval under the Listing Rules, that listed companies tend to pay lower takeover premia for listed targets, and that shareholders do not refuse to approve takeovers.[30] This bidder shareholder protection is stronger than that which exists in the US and Germany. However, beyond the Listing Rules, bidder shareholders have little protection.

In contrast to this concern with target (and, to a lesser extent, bidder) shareholders, the conventional approach to takeovers offers no recognition that anything is at stake for the company's employees, who are assumed to be protected by their contracts, or the rest of society, which is assumed to be protected by legislation across various fields.[31] Although, as we will see below, the Takeover Code contains a number of provisions ensuring publication of information about employment post-takeover, this is squarely aimed at informing shareholders who are deciding whether to tender their shares, particularly

---

[27] R Roll, 'The Hubris Hypothesis of Corporate Takeovers' (1986) 59 *Journal of Business* 197–216.

[28] R Marris, *The Economic Theory of 'Managerial' Capitalism* (London: Palgrave Macmillan, 1964).

[29] See LR 10.5.1R.

[30] M Becht, A Polo and S Rossi, 'Does Mandatory Shareholder Voting Prevent Bad Acquisitions?' (2016) 29 *Review of Financial Studies* 3035.

[31] See, for example, the Winter Report produced for the European Commission (*Report of the High Level Group of Company Law Experts on Issues Related to Takeover Bids*, 10 January 2002) at 21.

where the offer is of shares in the bidder rather than cash. Nor does the conventional approach pay much attention to the high costs to both bidder and target of using a range of professional advisers, such as investment banks, accountants and lawyers, which may amount to more than 1 per cent of the cost of the acquisition.

TAKEOVERS CREATE SOCIAL COSTS, ENCOURAGE SHORT-TERMISM AND ALLOW THE BREACH OF IMPLICIT CONTRACTS

Although the conventional approach has dominated policy debates, recent controversial takeovers of well-known companies in the UK have focused more attention on the critical approach to takeovers. The starting point is that the focus of management has shifted from the interests of the company or enterprise to the interests of the shareholders. Company law did nothing to prevent this, whereas takeover regulation positively encouraged it. What was lost in this reorientation of management? The critical account emphasises that takeovers drive short-termism and so undermine the productive enterprise which is under the control of the legal entity and give rise to significant social costs.

The debate about short-termism in UK corporate governance is long-standing,[32] and concerns about the impact of takeovers – and asset stripping in particular – on the long-term future of businesses date back to the 1950s.[33] By the end of that decade, under growing threat of removal, incumbent company directors were stripping assets from their companies in the same way as takeover bidders with the aim of increasing returns to shareholders. The debate about short-termism never went away, rearing its head periodically each time a controversial takeover came to public attention. Most recently, in his 2012 Review, leading economist John Kay characterised executive behaviour as 'hyperactive', being focused on 'financial engineering or mergers and acquisitions at the expense of developing the fundamental operational capabilities of the business'.[34] The imperative to increase returns to shareholders undermined the practice of 'retain and reinvest', which allowed companies to finance most of their growth from retained earnings. Nor have companies issued new shares to raise capital since this would reduce return on equity and, with it, the share price. Instead, companies rely more heavily on borrowing, leveraging their balance sheet and becoming more fragile as they must necessarily service their debts or face insolvency. Although there was a period of de-leveraging following the global financial crisis as banks were unwilling to lend, global

---

[32] Concerns about the lack of a close relationship between finance and industry date back to at least the Macmillan Committee of 1929: see B Feigh, 'Short-Termism on Trial: An Empirical Approach', LSE Working Papers in Economic History No 19/94 at 5–6.

[33] H Callaghan, *Contestants, Profiteers, and the Political Dynamics of Marketization: How Shareholders gained Control Rights in Britain, Germany, and France* (OUP, 2018) at 49–50.

[34] BIS, *Kay Review of UK Equity Markets and Long-Terms Decision Making* (July 2012) at 10.

non-financial corporate debt is now higher than it was in 2007.[35] Increased distributions to shareholders in the form of dividends and share buybacks (which have been permitted out of profits since the 1980s), coupled with increased reliance on debt finance, require companies to cut costs. It is here that social costs enter the picture.

The danger of cost-cutting affecting the future of the business is perhaps most obvious and pronounced in relation to research and development (R&D), where the UK's expenditure (which is largely driven by companies) is far lower, as a percentage of gross domestic product, than that of its main competitors and emerging economies. The threat of hostile takeover (coupled with the increasingly short tenure and short-term incentives of executives) creates pressure for immediate returns to shareholders. R&D, which will pay off only in the long-term, and the returns to which are uncertain are obvious targets for cuts. Although cutting R&D will boost short-term returns for shareholders, it clearly undermines the future prospects, and even survival, of companies and reduces the innovative and competitive capacity of the economy as a whole. This is becoming an increasingly sensitive political issue but is currently addressed on an ad hoc basis: during the recent takeover of engineering firm GKN by Melrose, the Business Secretary announced that Melrose had made binding commitments to maintain GKN's current level of investment in R&D for five years and to remain a UK business.[36]

Less visible, but arguably even more important, is the impact of cost-cutting on employment, wages and training.[37] Although this is often framed as a 'social' issue, critical economists have demonstrated that it also has an economic dimension where it relates to investments in firm-specific human capital (FSHC). The argument, explored most fully in the work of Margaret Blair,[38] is that it is economically desirable for employees to specialise their skills to the specific needs of their employer because it enhances the firm's competencies and competitive advantage and, in turn, its long-term profitability. However, if those employees lose their jobs and are re-employed elsewhere, they will no longer earn a return to that part of their skill set (or 'human capital') which is firm-specific. The risk of this occurring – made salient by the waves of takeovers and downsizing – makes employees reluctant to specialise, leading to lower productivity and trust throughout the economy.

This argument has made little impact on the conventional approach, which largely ignores it or claims that employees do not make these investments. At most, agency theorists claim that employees are – or ought to be – fully

---

[35] G Tett, 'The corporate debt problem refuses to recede', *Financial Times*, 8th February 2018.

[36] See letter from Chief Executive of Melrose to Business Secretary of 27 March 2018.

[37] Pendleton summarises that the 'evidence mainly supports' the argument that hostile takeovers have more adverse impacts on employment than agreed takeovers: see A Pendleton, 'The Employment Effects of Takeovers' in J Cremers and S Vitols (eds), *Takeovers with or without worker voice: workers' rights under the EU Takeover Bids Directive* (ETUI, 2016).

[38] See, for example, M Blair, *Ownership and Control* (Brookings Institute, 1995).

protected by their employment contracts. If they fear losing their jobs in the event of a change of control, the argument goes, they ought to bargain and pay for protection. This overlooks the steering effect of company law, which by default gives only shareholders voting rights and so imposes transaction costs on employees (or anyone else) who want to depart from the default governance structure. More importantly, it ignores the problems facing employees if they attempt to use contract to protect investments in FSHC. Indeed, it can be argued that employees and shareholders face similar barriers to making legally binding contracts with companies about how their interests will be protected and advanced in an uncertain future. Mainstream economists use shareholders' contracting problems to justify giving them the rights to appoint and remove directors that form the foundation of the market for corporate control.[39] Yet, when it comes to employees, they assume that they will be able to anticipate the extent of their investments and how they should be rewarded far into the future. Hence, employee expectations have to be protected by more informal mechanisms, such as 'implicit' contracts between employees and managers, in which the employer agrees to reward the employee over time in line with increases in their productivity. This shows up in the form of wages rising with seniority, and above market levels, as employees progress up a career ladder within the organisation. Managers honour the informal undertakings they have made to employees because they want to maintain relations of trust and a reputation for doing the right thing. However, these 'implicit contracts' are vulnerable in the event of a hostile takeover. The new controller can replace the managers who made commitments to the employees, breach the implicit contract and expropriate the contractually unprotected surplus wages. As Shleifer and Summers put it, 'ousting the managers is a prerequisite to realizing the gains from the breach... Not surprisingly, then, takeovers that transfer wealth from stakeholders to shareholders must be hostile'.[40]

The imperative to cut costs following a takeover can also pose a threat to company pension funds. As the pension fund is an unsecured creditor of the company, it is potentially vulnerable to decisions made by the new controller, such as sales of assets and changes to capital structure, which may give new creditors priority over the pension scheme. The Pensions Regulator (TPR) has a statutory duty to protect pension scheme members' benefits, and a takeover is one situation in which corporate governance practices might impact on them. TPR has a power to require a new corporate controller to make a contribution where it considers the takeover an event that materially weakens the employer covenant that underwrites the scheme.[41] There has been criticism of TPR's failure to act when Philip Green sold his shareholding in BHS for £1 to

[39] See further S Deakin and G Slinger, 'Hostile Takeovers, Corporate Law, and the Theory of the Firm' (1997) 24 *Journal of Law and Society* 124.
[40] A Shleifer and L Summers, Breach of Trust in Hostile Takeovers' in AJ Auerbach (ed), *Corporate Takeovers: Causes and Consequences* (University of Chicago Press, 1988) at 41.
[41] s38 Pensions Act 2004.

a former bankrupt with no retail experience. At the time of the sale, the BHS pension fund was in significant deficit (c. £350 million) and Green had declined to remedy the deficit throughout the period of his control. Aside from its criticism of Green, a Parliamentary report termed TPR 'reactive' and 'slow moving': even though it was 'materially detrimental to the pension schemes', the sale of BHS did not require approval of TPR as it was sold as a 'going concern', and TPR did not launch an anti-avoidance investigation until after the sale.[42] In its 2017 election manifesto, the Conservative Party accepted that regulators' powers were inadequate and committed 'to give pension schemes and the Pensions Regulator the right to scrutinise, clear with conditions or in extreme cases stop mergers, takeovers or large financial commitments that threaten the solvency of the scheme'.[43] However, this commitment, which was demanded by TPR,[44] was dropped on the grounds that it might 'stifle legitimate business activity'.[45] Under strong public pressure, Green agreed to make a voluntary payment to the pension fund. Beyond the specific case of BHS, however, it is clear that pension funds are highly vulnerable in the event of takeovers and financial engineering and that public pressure cannot always be relied upon. The Takeover Code does require a bidder to disclose 'its intentions with regard to employer contributions into the offeree company's pension scheme(s) (including with regard to current arrangements for the funding of any scheme deficit)'.[46] However, as we will see next, these commitments merely need to be made honestly and can be reneged upon where there is a 'material change of circumstances'. Serious reform is required here.

Employees Receive some Protection from the Takeover Code

It is true that, since 1974, the Takeover Code has included a rule requiring a bidder to state its intentions with regard to 'the future business of the offeree company', to continued employment and conditions of employment, and to 'its strategic plans for the offeree company', including 'repercussions for employment'.[47] When introducing the rule, the Takeover Panel made clear that the aim is to assist the shareholders in deciding whether to tender their shares: the 'likely effect of any such intentions on the future livelihood of the offeree company's employees may be a significant factor for shareholders in deciding

---

[42] House of Commons Works and Pensions and Business, Innovation and Skills Committees, *BHS*, Report HC 54, 25 July 2016, paras 43 and 49.
[43] Conservative Party Manifesto 2017 at 17.
[44] J. Cumbo, 'Pensions regulator wants veto on mergers and takeovers after BHS', *Financial Times*, 12 August 2016.
[45] J. Cumbo, 'UK ditches plan to give pensions regulator powers on takeovers', *Financial Times*, 19 March 2018.
[46] Takeover Code Rule 24.2(a)(iv).
[47] Takeover Code, Rule 24.2(a).

whether or not to accept an offer'. The aim is to ensure that shareholders know whether there is a 'fundamental business rationale' for the bid. In practice, this requirement is satisfied by 'boiler plate' clauses. Beyond this, the target board is also required to give its opinion on 'the effects of implementation of the offer on all the company's interests, including specifically, employment'[48] and, since 2006, has been required to append opinions from the employee representatives and pension scheme trustees where these are received in good time (within very tight time frames).[49]

Although this disclosure regime imparts a mild stakeholder flavour to the Takeover Code, these disclosures offer little in terms of protection for the target's employees. Since Rule 21 (which prohibits defensive measures) sidelines management as a means of protecting employees, the latter are wholly dependent on the shareholders as regards the outcome of the takeover. Yet it seems rather unlikely that the consequences of a takeover bid for either employment or the target's pension scheme will influence many shareholders.[50] Most shareholders will focus exclusively on the adequacy of the premium being paid for their shares in light of their expectations for the company. Statements by the bidder about their future plans will be relevant to target shareholders accepting shares in exchange for their shares, so retaining an interest in the company after the takeover. However, their concern is likely to be limited to evaluating the credibility of the bidder's business plan. The precise details about repercussions for employment are unlikely to sway any but the most socially responsible shareholders (and, even then, there is a lack of clarity in practice as to how far pension funds are legally permitted take account of 'social' considerations when making investment decisions).

The 2010 takeover of Cadbury by Kraft highlighted the weakness of these provisions. During the course of its bid, Kraft stated more than once that 'we believe we would be in a position to continue to operate' a factory that Cadbury had already planned to shut down. After the takeover was completed, Kraft discovered that it would not be viable to reverse the planned closure. In considering whether Kraft had violated Rule 19.1 of the Takeover Code, which requires statements to be made 'with the highest standards of care and accuracy', the Takeover Panel noted that Kraft 'chose to make the statement as one of belief' because it did not have detailed knowledge of Cadbury's plans for the facility. The Panel ruled that the Code requires not only a genuine and honest belief but also 'a reasonable basis for so holding that belief (an objective test)'. Given the prominence of the statements and the importance attached to them by the employees, 'particular care was required in relation to the statements regarding the Somerdale facility'. Although Kraft held an honest and genuine

---

[48] Rule 25.2.

[49] Rule 25.9

[50] See, for example, the report prepared for the European Commission by Marccus and Partners, *The Takeover Bids Directive Assessment Report* (Brussels, 2013) at 46.

belief, it did not have a reasonable basis for that belief, given its lack of information. Accordingly, Kraft suffered the sanction of being publicly 'criticised for not meeting the standards required under Rule 19.1'.[51] It is not clear that its chocolate sales in the UK have suffered as a result of this.

In response to this takeover, the Code was amended in 2011. It now requires offerors who foresee no repercussions for employees to include a statement to that effect.[52] Such offerors are to be 'regarded as being committed to that course of action for a period of 12 months from the date on which the offer period ends... *unless there has been a material change of circumstances*'.[53] However, it seems likely that hostile bidders will continue their current practice of stating that 'their intention is to undertake a review of the offeree company's business following completion of the takeover'.[54]

WHAT WOULD REFORM LOOK LIKE AND IS IT LIKELY?

Conventional accounts claim that the hostile takeover is the result of market forces and therefore both legitimate and efficient. The market for corporate control is a simple mechanism to align managerial incentives with those of shareholders, and American agency theorists look at the UK's takeover regime with admiration. From their perspective, little change is needed (although some are not in favour of the mandatory bid rule, which deters some transfers of corporate control).

In contrast, the critical account emphasises that the market for corporate control did not emerge simply from exchanges among shareholders. Historically, the transfer of shares was not in itself sufficient to bring about a change in corporate control since shareholders had actually purchased their shares on the basis that corporate management would be fairly strongly entrenched. In this context, the market for corporate control came into existence only as a result of a contingent combination of legal, self-regulatory and institutional changes and was therefore, in considerable part, the outcome (whether deliberate or accidental) of policy choices. In other words, the 'marketisation of corporate control' is the product of 'the social and political constitution of markets' rather than something inherent in the market itself.[55]

For the critical account, takeover regulation is not merely a technical exercise; it is a politically charged decision that reflects assumptions about the purpose of companies and scope of company law as well as the interests of dominant

---

[51] See Takeover Panel, 'Kraft Food Inc Offer for Cadbury Plc' (Opinion 2010/14).

[52] Rule 24.2(b) of the Takeover Code.

[53] See Note 3 to Rule 19.1, emphasis added.

[54] The Takeover Panel, *Review Of Certain Aspects Of The Regulation Of Takeover Bids*, 21 July 2011, para 7.2.

[55] B van Apeldoorn and L Horn, 'The Marketisation of European Corporate Control: A Critical Political Economy Perspective' (2007) 12 *New Political Economy* 211 at 212.

actors. The 30-year debate that preceded the adoption of the European Takeover Directive clearly illustrates the controversy to which takeover regulation gives rise when it is examined in a political forum. Such were the disagreements between Member States that the Directive could be adopted only by making its most controversial provisions (including the prohibition on defensive measures) optional, accommodating Member States that wanted to make takeovers more difficult in order to protect a range of different interests. A number of EU Member States took advantage of this flexibility to permit directors to take some defensive measures. For example, in Germany, hostile takeovers remain rare though not unknown. In part, this is because the German codetermination law requires companies above a certain size to give their employees the right to appoint representatives to sit alongside shareholder representatives on the supervisory board, which monitors the management board that runs the company.[56] Codetermination potentially acts as a 'poison pill' because the supervisory board is permitted (within limits) to authorise defensive measures, including share issues and disposal of key assets. It also provides support for employee investments in FSHC, as employee representatives are able 'to protect employee interests and reduce the capacity of hostile raiders to engage in *ex post* redistribution of wealth following takeovers through collective dismissals'.[57]

No such political debate ever took place in the UK, where takeovers remain largely regulated according to the blueprint drawn up by financial institutions in the City of London in 1968. The UK's active market for corporate control has become a mainstay of its corporate governance system, and politicians view it as a key driver of foreign 'investment' (purchases of existing claims on existing companies) in the UK economy. Hence, there is little political appetite at present for serious reforms to takeover regulation despite a number of recent controversial successful (Cadbury, GKN) and unsuccessful (Pfizer's bid for AstraZeneca) hostile takeovers, which pose a threat to high-quality employment and innovation in the UK.

Conventional thinking about how takeovers are to be regulated tends to start from the perspective that managers should be passive in the face of a takeover and that shareholders – as the only group affected by the takeover – should decide on the outcome. Once we recognise that the interests of other groups may be affected by takeovers – and cannot protect their interests by means of explicit contract – then we have to consider how these economic externalities (adverse effects on third parties) should be addressed. One common response is that, in practice, companies are constrained to act in a socially responsible manner. Yet it seems unlikely that social pressure alone will be sufficient to steer takeover bidders towards minimising social costs: as a report produced for the European Commission concluded, many takeovers are characterised by a

---

[56] For an overview, see A Conchon, 'Workers' Voice in Corporate Governance: A European Perspective' (ETUI, 2015).

[57] M Höpner and G Jackson, 'Revisiting the Mannesmann takeover: how markets for corporate control emerge' (2006) *European Management Review* 142 at 145.

'community control gap', in which those controlling the bidder are far removed from the social consequences of their decisions.[58] In the absence of constraining social norms, the law often intervenes where private actions produce adverse effects on third parties who are unable to protect themselves. Takeover regulation does not do this, so there is an argument that it should be reformed to address this problem.

Reform proposals can be broadly grouped into three categories.

The first is governmental intervention in takeovers. The Business Secretary has the power to intervene in a takeover where it raises public interest concerns in relation to national security, including public security, freedom of expression and financial stability.[59] These areas can be changed by the secretary of state using delegated legislation, so it would be relatively easy to permit intervention on the basis of a wider range of concerns. Indeed, in its 2017 manifesto, the Conservative Party pledged to allow government to 'require a bid to be paused to allow greater scrutiny' of takeovers 'driven by aggressive asset-stripping or tax avoidance'.[60] This pledge appears to have been quietly dropped. In any event, this type of intervention would be ad hoc and highly politicised, making it unpredictable for bidders, targets, shareholders and stakeholders.

The second group of reform proposals aims to regulate takeovers differently. One proposal is to give directors more discretion to defend against hostile takeovers. However, simply repealing Article 21 of the Takeover Code – though permissible under the EU Takeover Directive – would be unlikely to result in greater protection for stakeholders for two main reasons. The first reason is that board and executive decision-making is powerfully shaped by the broader corporate governance system: they have internalised the social norm of shareholder primacy and view themselves as agents of the shareholders rather than as owing duties to the company or acting to balance competing interests. Under the influence of the UK Corporate Governance Code, boards now consist largely of non-executive directors without long-term investments in FSHC. The Code also encourages companies to align executive pay with 'long-term shareholder interests',[61] which in practice means rewards for increasing the share price over a specified time frame. If a takeover is launched during that time frame and the share price increases, the executives will benefit directly. This makes it highly unlikely that they would use new powers to defend against a takeover. Hence, any attempt to rely on management to protect stakeholder interests in the takeover context would require both changes to soft law and a far-reaching reconsideration of the role of management and the purpose of the company. The second reason is that English law would simply revert to the common law position, according to which managerial decisions are reviewed

---

[58] Marccus and Partners report at 34.
[59] ss42 and 58 Enterprise Act 2002.
[60] Conservative Party Manifesto 2017 at 17.
[61] See Financial Reporting Council, *UK Corporate Governance Code*, July 2018, Provision 36.

against the proper purposes duty. A disgruntled shareholder seeking to challenge defensive measures might also rely on section 172 of the Companies Act 2006 to argue that directors defending a takeover with a view to protecting stakeholders are in breach of their duty to 'promote the success of the company for the benefit of its shareholders as a whole'. So, reform to company law would also be necessary. Perhaps inspiration could be drawn from the numerous US states that introduced constituency statutes during the 1980s, explicitly permitting directors to take account of the effect of a takeover on stakeholder groups such as employees.[62]

The third type of proposal is to give employees more powerful rights in the takeover context. Above, we saw that, at present, employees have largely ineffective rights to information and consultation. If employees were given rights to appoint board-level representatives, this (if combined with changes to takeover regulation) would increase the potential for their interests to be taken into account. A promise by the (then) incoming Prime Minister, Theresa May, to mandate employee and consumer representation at the board level has been watered down to a 'comply or explain' obligation in the 2018 edition of the UK Corporate Governance Code, requiring companies to appoint a director from the workforce, set up a formal workforce advisory panel, or designate a non-executive director to engage with the workforce.[63] Leaving aside doubts about whether this weak measure allows meaningful employee participation, it is certainly inadequate to offer any meaningful input from employees on takeovers.

CONCLUSION

Critical approaches to takeovers have been gaining ground in recent years, arguing that takeovers redistribute wealth from stakeholders to shareholders and encourage managerial short-termism. These arguments are not reflected in the current system of takeover regulation, which was designed by, and serves, financial interests. Although wholesale reform of takeover regulation does not look likely at present, the UK's shareholder primacy system of corporate governance, which is underpinned by the threat of hostile takeover, continues to generate scandals (Carillion's collapse in 2018 was the most recent). These scandals have led to the most far-reaching debate about corporate governance in recent decades. For example, a Parliamentary report expressed cautious support for employee representation on boards as a means to greater diversity of thinking and concerns about the incentives provided to company directors.[64]

---

[62] For discussion, see, for example, E Orts, 'Beyond Shareholders: Interpreting Corporate Constituency Statutes' (1992) *61 Geo. Wash. L. Rev* 14.

[63] See *UK Corporate Governance Code*, 2018, Provision 5.

[64] House of Commons, Business, Energy and Industrial Strategy Committee, *Corporate Governance*, Third Report of Session 2016–17, 30 March 2017 at 39 and 57.

Reform of takeover regulation has not been central to those debates so far but may become so if the coming years witness yet more asset-stripping takeovers. At the very least, TPR should be given increased powers, and wider stakeholder representation is desirable, both on the Takeover Panel, which is dominated by financial interests, and on company boards. Most fundamentally, the influence of takeovers on directors and managers must be reduced. This would certainly require reform of takeover regulation but would also require a wider reappraisal of the social purpose of companies, followed by legal and cultural changes to ensure that that purpose is achieved.

FURTHER READING

B. van Apeldoorn and L. Horn, 'The Marketisation of European Corporate Control: A Critical Political Economy Perspective' (2007) 12 *New Political Economy* 211.

M. Blair, *Ownership and Control: Rethinking Corporate Governance for the Twenty-First Century* (Brookings Institute, 1995).

S. Deakin and G. Slinger, 'Hostile Takeovers, Corporate Law, and the Theory of the Firm' (1997) 24 *Journal of Law and Society* 124.

L. Hannah, *The Rise of the Corporate Economy*, 2nd ed (Methuen, 1976).

A. Johnston, 'Takeover Regulation: Historical and Theoretical Perspectives on the City Code' (2007) 66 (2) *Cambridge Law Journal* 422.

A. Johnston, B. Segrestin, and A. Hatchuel, 'From Balanced Enterprise to Hostile Takeover: How the Law Forgot about Management' (2019) 39 (1) *Legal Studies* 75–97.

J. Kay and A. Silberston, 'Corporate Governance' (1995) 153 *National Institute Economic Review* 84.

D. Kershaw, 'The Illusion of Importance: Reconsidering the UK's Takeover Defence Prohibition' (2007) 56 *International & Comparative Law Quarterly* 267.

CHAPTER 10

The Taxonomy of Taxation

Kerrie Sadiq and Bronwyn McCredie

INTRODUCTION

Tax law is inherently political. At the very least, it introduces an underlying tension in politics but is more often at the forefront of political debate. Tax is at the centre of political ideological conflict, and elections are won or lost based on tax policy. Political parties often define themselves by their position on tax with a spectrum of views ranging from a pro-business, free market economy platform to a pro-worker, egalitarian platform. 'Taxation without representation is tyranny', generally quoted as 'no tax without representation', eloquently captures the political nature of tax. More recently, reform of the tax system has been influenced by the global financial crisis and fiscal conservatism. The international tax system in particular has undergone significant reform in an attempt to address base erosion and profit shifting by multinational entities. This reform has seen jurisdictions around the world reforming their domestic tax regimes to more closely align with 21st-century corporate practices and ensure effective and efficient taxation of global corporate groups and networks.

The political tax debate, and hence the design of any tax system, has at its heart the issue of 'fairness'. Few would doubt that tax in some form is needed to ensure societal order, as taxes fund core government services such as defence, the courts and policing. However, many argue that this alone is insufficient and that taxes should also be used for additional purposes. Consequently, tax takes on its secondary role of redistribution, supporting macroeconomic stability (e.g., tax credits for low-income taxpayers), internalising negative externalities (taxes on carbon emissions), and steering behaviour (taxes on alcohol and tobacco). This chapter outlines and discusses the following four debates, which should be considered by anyone with an interest in tax: (1) Why do governments tax? (2) How do we justify a society's choice of redistributive model and market interference through the taxation system? (3) How do we design a tax system based on society's choices? (4) What could a modern corporate tax system look like?

Debate 1

Why do governments tax?

A basic definition of tax, derived from the Latin *taxare*, which means 'to assess', is that it is a compulsory exaction of money by the state, levied on the income or property of individuals or organisations in order to fund various public expenditures. Over time, different words and phrases have been attached to tax. 'Duty' is sometimes used, as is 'levy', thereby employing political rhetoric to suggest an obligation to pay without the negative connotations that tax often elicits. However, tax is simply a label placed on certain mandatory payments to government which can be distinguished from payments in exchange for rights, such as royalties paid for the right to extract natural resources, and from penalties imposed for certain breaches of law, such as speeding fines.

States impose direct or indirect taxes (or both) to pay for agreed national needs and government functions. Whereas some states impose high levels of income tax, others impose very little. This is the same for consumption taxes and taxes on capital gains. Corporate taxes also vary significantly across states; some states charging a tax on both corporate income and dividends paid to shareholders, whereas others provide dividend credits to reflect corporate tax paid and so avoid double taxation.

Although tax itself is defined as a compulsory exaction of money, taxes in modern society are used by governments for three distinct purposes: to raise revenue for necessary government functions, to redistribute wealth, and as a regulatory tool that can steer behaviour and contribute to macroeconomic stability.[1] Each of these purposes requires state and societal decisions on how much government intervention is appropriate.

Where a state determines that it wishes to fund certain activities, questions also centre on the type of intervention adopted. States can provide public and merit goods free of charge. Public goods are those that can be consumed by all without depletion (e.g., street lighting), whereas merit goods are provided on the basis of need. For example, in the UK, merit goods such as school education and health care are provided without cost to users. Alternatively, certain goods and services may be subsidised (e.g., dental care in the UK). However, the state may decide not to use tax at all here and rely on regulation to put responsibility on the individual. For example, the state may require citizens to purchase certain goods such as health insurance or motor vehicle insurance in order to avoid the need for the state to fund those activities.

The most important function of tax is its role in income-raising, and the effectiveness of the tax system in raising that revenue is essential to the running of government. No doubt, taxes are the most prevalent source of government revenue, but borrowings, foreign aid and earnings are alternatives. The

---

[1] Avi-Yonah, Reuven, 'The Three Goals of Taxation' (2006) 60(1) *Tax Law Review*, 1.

prevalent view is that taxes fund the state which, in turn, provides goods and services to its citizens.[2] Funding the state involves raising sufficient revenue for effective government and this entails a political decision as to how the state should raise funds (primarily taxation or borrowing) as well as about which 'essential' services a state wishes to provide to their citizens and, in turn, which goods and services are demanded by its citizens.

The second function of tax, which is clearly linked to its revenue-raising function, is to redistribute wealth (i.e., the transfer of income and wealth from certain individuals to others to ensure all citizens attain a minimum standard of living). Taxes are often the predominant way in which wealth is redistributed in society, although charity and other methods also contribute. The tax transfer system serves the dual purpose of both redistribution and social spending on programs designed to overcome poverty and inequality. Progressive taxes on income are generally viewed as the obvious way to achieve a redistribution. However, there is an argument that current tax regimes are failing to adequately address growing inequality because capital is accumulating faster than income. This conclusion is evidenced in Piketty's *Capital in the Twenty-First Century*,[3] a work that has inspired a number of policy proposals recently, including by US Democratic Party presidential candidate Elizabeth Warren.[4] One driver of this is automation, which causes gains to accrue to capital at the expense of labour, and is discussed below in Debate 4. Economists assess and quantify such equality, pre- and post-tax, by using the Gini coefficient.

The Gini Coefficient

The Gini coefficient, also known as the Gini index when expressed as a percentage, measures the statistical dispersion of income or wealth of a nation's residents. It is a broad measure of inequality which ranges from zero (perfect equality) to one (perfect inequality). Over the last three decades, the distribution of wealth in Organisation for Economic Co-operation and Development (OECD) countries indicates a trend of rising inequality. Findings indicate that currently the richest 10 per cent of the OECD population earns 9.5 times more than the poorest 10 per cent.[5] Furthermore, the Gini coefficient has increased in OECD countries on average by three points from 0.29 in 1980 to 0.32 in 2012.

---

[2] For an alternative view, in which taxation follows spending and is a means by which the government controls the amount of money circulating in the economy, see Johnston, Cullen and Pugh, Chapter 11.

[3] See Piketty, T., (2014), *Capital in the Twenty-First Century*, The Belknap Press of Harvard University Press, Cambridge, MA.

[4] The Warren proposal recommends an annual tax on wealth in America. See https://theintercept.com/2019/01/24/elizabeth-warren-proposes-annual-wealth-tax-on-ultra-millionaires/.

[5] According to Benioff (2017), the top 1 per cent of the world owns more than 50 per cent of the world's wealth, while the bottom 50 per cent of the world owns less than 1 per cent of the world's wealth, and that gap is widening as the fourth industrial revolution progresses.

The third function of tax is to operate as a regulatory mechanism to steer behaviour and promote economic stability. This raises the fundamental political economic question of how much the state should interfere in the economy. One response to this question focuses on perceived or predicted market failures. Tax policy should not interfere with market-determined allocations unless there is a reason to do so. So taxes may be used to correct externalities; 'Pigovian' style taxes may be imposed on alcohol and tobacco in order to bring the private cost of drinking or smoking closer to the social cost of providing public health care. Taxes can also be used to encourage or promote certain activities. It can be difficult to set these taxes at a level that accurately prices the social cost or encourages the activity in question. From a macroeconomic perspective, fiscal policy (i.e., public taxation and spending) needs to be designed and operated so as to achieve society's goals, which are often defined in terms of a trade-off between employment, inflation and growth. Tax cuts are often used as a means to stimulate the economy; the targeting of those tax cuts is one of the most controversial decisions made in a modern polity.

In meeting these functions and achieving the three distinct purposes of tax, governments must adapt the tax system in light of social and technological changes such as globalisation and automation (discussed in Debate 4). For example, states are currently grappling with challenges around how to tax emerging digital technologies such as e-commerce, crypto-currencies, and blockchain transactions. The issue is whether such transactions and activities can be taxed by adaptations of existing tax regimes or whether an entirely new form of digital tax is required. Reforming the taxation of the digital economy is a key action underlying the OECD's Base Erosion and Profit Shifting (BEPS) project.

Reforming the Taxation of the Digital Economy

The aim of Action 1 of the OECDs BEPS project was to identify the main challenges that the digital economy poses for the application of existing international tax rules and to develop detailed options to address these difficulties, taking a holistic approach and considering both direct and indirect taxation.

In November 2017 in the UK, the Government published a position paper 'Corporate tax and the digital economy', which was updated and reissued on 13 March 2018, following a period of consultation. The UK has a fast-growing digital tech-sector that employs more than 1.5 million people and, in 2016, accounted for £6.8 billion of investment, which was 50 per cent higher than that of any other European country. The position paper clearly articulates the current misalignment between where digital businesses are taxed and where they create value. It also recognises that this threatens to undermine the fairness, sustainability and public acceptability of the corporate tax system. The UK government has stated that it hopes to find a multilateral solution to this challenge and that the OECD provides a roadmap for a coherent, proportionate and sustainable long-term solution.

Similarly, demographic trends, particularly the ageing of populations, are placing significant strain on fiscal systems. As people are living longer and having fewer children, the fastest-growing segment of the population is the over-65s. In the UK, the Office for Budget Responsibility, in its annual fiscal sustainability report, has forecasted that the ageing of the population is likely to put significant pressure on government spending in the future.[6]

Finally, governments should keep their taxation systems under review, responding to research that identifies unintended consequences or failures of the existing regime. For example, feminist legal theory has shown that the tax system often has negative effects on work, family, women and children. For women, there may be impacts in relation to filing joint tax returns with their spouse, such as the loss of certain benefits like tax offsets and deductions. These offsets and deductions are often meant to assist the secondary or low-income earner, most often a woman, yet the benefits can be lost under joint filing. Studies on the extent to which tax impacts differentially on same-sex couples have also been carried out. In the UK, for example, taxpayers who are married or in a civil partnership cannot file joint tax returns, but part of the tax-free personal allowance may be transferred between spouses.

Debate 2

How do we justify a particular tax system?

Once we recognise that governments tax for particular purposes, the next question is how a particular tax system is justified. Fiscal policy entails imposing taxes and providing transfers, which in turn influence social and economic outcomes. Hence, these public policy choices raise questions of morality and justice. At the core of economic justice is the notion that everyone should pay tax on their income for the common good. Supreme Court Justice Oliver Wendell Holmes, Jr., claimed 'Taxes are the price we pay for a civilized society',[7] which in turn leads to questions concerning the nature of a civilised society.[8] Individually, tax appears as a loss of money, but it rests on decisions that are taken collectively. Society acting through the political process must decide not only how much it must collect for the efficient running of government (however defined) but also what a morally acceptable redistribution of wealth looks like. This is ultimately a 'who should pay', 'how much should they pay', and 'what should they pay for' dilemma within a group contest.

Distributive justice offers a framework in which to evaluate these various considerations. It is concerned with the distribution of not only wealth but also income, status and power in society. Depending on the underlying philosophical approach adopted, the distribution of economic resources can be justified by reference to merit, effort, equality, need and/or social contributions. In this debate,

---

[6] Office for Budget Responsibility, *Fiscal sustainability report*, July 2018 (https://cdn.obr.uk/FSR-July-2018-1.pdf).

[7] *Compañía General de Tabacos de Filipinas v. Collector of Internal Revenue* 275 US 87, 48 S. Ct. 100, 72 L. Ed. 177.

[8] Leviner, Sagit, 'The Normative Underpinnings of Taxation' (2012) 13 *Nevada Law Journal*, 95.

three important normative philosophies on distributive justice are considered and contrasted; the aim is to highlight how each can be used as a critical tool in the development and analysis of a tax regime. The theories discussed are utilitarianism, libertarianism, and John Rawls's theory of justice as fairness. These theories have been selected on the basis that they offer an insight into classic distributive justice theories. However, this does not suggest that other theories are not relevant; Ronald Dworkin's theory of equality of resources and its implications for redistributive taxation, for example, could also form part of any discourse.[9]

Utilitarianism

Utilitarianism is one of the most influential approaches to modern normative justice. Jeremy Bentham[10] and John Stuart Mill,[11] the most well-known scholars in this field, concerned themselves with legal and social reform. Bentham focused on human welfare or 'utility'. For Bentham, the utility of a policy could be calculated. The calculation – the *felicific calculus* – was that which produced the greatest pleasure for the greatest number, after deducting the 'pain' for some, which would inevitably accompany any policy. Bentham assumed that wealth contributed to individual happiness whereas poverty caused pain. Therefore, a redistribution of resources was necessary to maximise total social well-being (given that no one person is worth more than another). The level of taxation was broadly calculable: how much should be taken from some people's wealth in order to alleviate extreme poverty? Whilst it might be assumed that the adoption of a Benthamite redistribution policy would ultimately lead to an equal distribution of economic resources and, with it, maximum happiness, this is not the case: Bentham believed that once poverty was alleviated, the pleasure derived from wealth diminished. Equality, therefore, might not necessarily result in the greatest happiness.

In terms of designing a public policy model, utilitarians do not prescribe specific types of tax rules. Utilitarians consider such issues as the ideal type of ownership, the way of organising production and distribution, authority arrangements within the production process, material incentives, and the nature and extent of welfare provisions.[12] Two propositions stand out as exemplifying the modern

---

[9] See, for example, Duff, David G., Tax Policy and the Virtuous Sovereign: Dworkinian Equality and Redistributive Taxation (2017). Philosophical Foundations of Tax Law, Monica Bhandari, ed. (Oxford: Oxford University Press, 2017), 167–89. Available at SSRN: https://ssrn.com/abstract=2808197 or https://doi.org/10.2139/ssrn.2808197.

[10] Bentham, Jeremy, 1789 [PML]. *An Introduction to the Principles of Morals and Legislation*, Oxford: Clarendon Press, 1907.

[11] Mill, John Stuart, 1843. *A System of Logic*, London: John W. Parker. 1859; Mill, John Stuart, *On Liberty*, London: Longman, Roberts & Green., 1861 [U]; Mill, John Stuart, *Utilitarianism*, Roger Crisp (ed.), Oxford: Oxford University Press, 1998.

[12] Shaw, William H and Vincent, E Barry, *Moral Issues in Business*, 12th ed (2013), Wadsworth Cengage Learning, p. 111.

utilitarian approach to distributive justice: greater worker participation and greater equality of income. Beyond this, utilitarianism as popularised by Bentham has been modified and expanded in many ways in modern times. For example, Karl Popper discusses the concept of negative utilitarianism, which requires the least amount of suffering for the greatest number of people and does not consider maximising pleasure. A distinction has been drawn between 'act' utilitarianism and 'rule' utilitarianism. 'Act' utilitarians aim to achieve the greatest net utility, whereas 'rule' utilitarians adopt a process of following moral rules which are justified on the basis of a code that creates more utility than another rule. From a tax perspective, an 'act' utilitarian might conclude that the act of imposing income taxes on a wealthy individual in order to redistribute income to those less fortunate will achieve the greatest net happiness. A 'rule' utilitarian, on the other hand, would look beyond a particular action to consider what the general rule should be: in this case, that wealthier individuals should pay tax to ensure a wealth transfer system to those less fortunate.

Utilitarians generally favour greater equality of income on the basis that it increases happiness or, at least, that inequality in wealth leads to numerous social problems such as lower life expectancy, economic insecurity and infant mortality. Building on Bentham, utilitarians rely on the economic concept of the declining marginal utility of money (income and wealth), a concept popularised by Alfred Marshall in the late 19th century.[13] The idea is that individuals derive less enjoyment, welfare or happiness from each successive dollar they earn. Money is first used to buy essential goods and services, and preferred needs (non-essential and luxury goods and services) are purchased according to remaining funds and based on individual satisfaction. This certainly supports an egalitarian approach to economic distribution of wealth, and taxes can contribute to this by ensuring greater equality in after-tax income. It is also consistent with the payment of taxes representing an individual loss of utility but a social welfare gain (as part of the aggregated utility measure and objective of maximising total utility). Progressive taxes on income are the obvious way to achieve a redistribution.

However, although utilitarianism supports a progressive rate of tax, it leaves many questions open. It does not quantify the decreasing value of money, nor does it factor in the incentive effects that higher rates of tax have on productivity and innovation. Utilitarians leave to economists the question of how to ensure that the individual utility lost through payment of taxes is less than the utility gained from spending or redistributing the tax revenue.[14] Economists have attempted to determine the optimal tax rate (with a balancing of interests), and Arthur Laffer's 'Laffer curve' is perhaps the most well known of these. Although the Laffer curve has been widely discredited, it does

---

[13] 'The additional benefit a person derives from a given increase of his stock of a thing diminishes with every increase in the stock that he already has' – Alfred Marshall, *Principles of Economics* (1890).

[14] Leviner, Sagit, 'The Normative Underpinnings of Taxation' (2012) 13 *Nevada Law Journal*, 95.

demonstrate the relative cost of income taxes on workers and the rationale for not increasing taxes beyond the point at which individuals will elect not to undertake further work. It also demonstrates the tension between taxation helping to achieve wealth redistribution and high rates of tax reducing incentives to work and invest.

The Laffer Curve

The Laffer curve attempts to show the relationship between taxes and the amount of tax collected by government. It suggests that as tax rates increase, tax collected will also increase until it reaches an optimal level at which point an increase in tax rates decreased tax collected because there is no incentive to work or produce. Once taxes hit 100 per cent, governments would collect no tax because all revenue is lost. The Laffer curve has been criticised for its simplicity (single tax rate), failings in fundamental assumptions (less tax equals more jobs) and failure to factor in different taxes and rates.

Utilitarianism is not without its flaws, and two stand out in particular in the context of economic distribution. First, by focusing on the aggregate maximum utility of society, it creates a danger that the utility of individuals will be lost in pursuit of the wider social good. That is, the happiness of the group may come at the expense of the individual. An extreme example would be taxing a wealthy individual at a rate of 99 per cent on all capital and income to distribute that revenue to 100 poverty-stricken individuals. Clearly, the wider social group is much better off but at the expense of the wealthy individual, who may have experienced a great deal of hardship to place themselves in a position of wealth. Second, by using money as a proxy for utility, certain fundamental requirements of individuals, such as food and shelter, may be inadequately valued. Modern developments in the field of welfare economics attempt to address these issues by providing a guide for achieving optimal distribution of income by mapping satisfaction of individual preferences against collective choices. Since wealth (money, property and goods) and welfare are different constructs, an approach that takes both into account is surely desirable. Although a comprehensive discussion of the works of Amartya Sen is outside the scope of this chapter, his work on welfare economics, social choice theory, and economic and social justice delve into the problems associated with using money as the sole indicator of utility and, therefore, economic justice. Sen's concept of the 'conversion handicap' encapsulates the problem. Sen explains that, for a handicapped person, not only is it more difficult to raise an income, but the cost of living is also higher.[15] Sen has argued that, from a tax perspective, the state must play a role in the redistribution of income through a progressive taxation system.[16]

---

[15] A Sen, *Development as Freedom* (OUP, 2001).
[16] https://taxjustice.blogspot.com/2010/03/amartya-sen-power-and-capability.html.

Libertarianism

Libertarianism (which is a modern incarnation of classical liberalism) is a philosophy of individual political and economic liberty and confines the role of the state to protecting individual rights such as the right to property.[17] Justice is equated with personal liberty and requires that each person should be able to order their life how they choose without undue interference from others. This entails duties not to interfere with the way of life and choices of others and not to coerce others so as to prevent them from living according to their own choice. Consequently, basic rights co-exist with basic obligations. Whereas utilitarians accept that, in order to achieve maximum social well-being, a degree of interference with personal choices may be justifiable, libertarians believe that personal liberty is paramount and that even government does not have the right to interfere with individual choices. Hence, the role of government is greatly circumscribed, being confined to law enforcement and protection of citizens, a kind of night watchman role that does not interfere with individual choices. Libertarians oppose the levying of taxes on individuals to support less privileged people on the basis that forcing people to support activities is a violation of personal liberty because they have not consented to this. In terms of the funding of public services, this translates into a preference for 'user pays' over 'universal access' systems.

John Locke's theory of justice provides the foundations of libertarianism, and the rights to private ownership of property are central to its application to tax policy. Locke's theory of private property begins with his well-known assertion that all 'men' have property in their own person, an inalienable right, which requires the state to protect: 'life, liberty and estate'. Property in self may be sold by the owner as labour – this is key to the market economy. For Locke, property in self also provides the justification for liberty from feudal obligations or slavery. It is from this progressive position that Locke constructs his (much contested) theory of private property. For Locke, all things that derive from nature are communally owned by all men. Only property in one's own person is private property. However, once a person expends his property in self upon a thing from nature, he makes it his property. It is a thing that is fixed with the person's property in self. Individuals become entitled to own and use property as they choose because they have applied their labour to natural resources. In terms of tax, interference with that natural right to hold property cannot be justified, subject to two provisos. First, accumulation of private property must not result in wastage. For example, leaving private property vacant would not be acceptable. Second, accumulation is permissible only where there is enough left for others. Otherwise, the right to labour and to own property must be protected by society and this can be financed through a tax system that shares the costs of policing and courts across the individuals who make up society.

---

[17] Vallentyne, Peter and van der Vossen, Bas, 'Libertarianism', *The Stanford Encyclopedia of Philosophy* (Fall 2014 edition), Edward N. Zalta (ed.), URL = <https://plato.stanford.edu/archives/fall2014/entries/libertarianism/>.

More recently, Robert Nozick's entitlement theory, described in his book *Anarchy, State, and Utopia*,[18] offers a libertarian interpretation of Locke's theory of justice. Like Locke, Nozick adopts the view that entitlement to ownership of property is paramount. However, he also emphasises the right to dispose of property. Nozick's notion of economic justice is based on the notion that if individuals are entitled to justly acquired property, they should also be entitled to dispose of that property however they choose. Freedom of disposal implies freedom to spend on anything, and to give away property, provided that this does not infringe anyone else's rights. Like Locke, Nozick suggests that the state's powers are limited to protecting these rights through enforcement and defence against such things as theft and fraud. In summary, Nozick's entitlement theory holds that distributive justice primarily consists of three principles: one, the principle of justice in acquisition; two, the principle of justice in transfer; three, the principle of rectification for violations of one and two.

In terms of justifying taxation, Nozick argues that taxation of wages or profits is the equivalent to seizing the results of someone's labour or directing a person to carry on certain activities (a violation of principle one). He does not view equality as a guiding principle in justice but rather believes in the right to dispose of property freely and without interference via the market or otherwise (principle two). As such, the only legitimate taxes would be those that raise the revenue needed to maintain institutions such as police and courts needed to protect private rights and the operation of the market (principle three).

Libertarians present a marked contrast with utilitarians. Where utilitarians focus on aggregate social well-being and are willing to restrict personal liberty and interfere with personal choices in order to achieve this, libertarians believe that taxing the wealthy to support the poor violates the liberty of individuals as they are forced to part with their property against their will.

Rawls's Theory of Justice

Arguably, the most influential theory of economic justice of recent times is John Rawls's *A Theory of Justice*.[19] In his work, he focuses on fairness (as opposed to happiness within utilitarianism or rights in libertarianism). Rather than start from an individualistic view of justice, Rawls treats society as a co-operative venture. As such, Rawls adopts a form of social contract theory to determine what society should look like. Social contract theory is the notion that an individual's moral and political obligations are bound in a contract between all members of society and according to an agreement as to the society in which they want to live. Under a social contract, individuals have consented to surrender some of their rights to the state in return for protection of their remaining rights. Locke, discussed above, was one of the earlier philosophers

---

[18] Nozick, R., 1974, *Anarchy, State, and Utopia*.

[19] John Rawls, *A Theory of Justice*, Cambridge, MA, 1971.

to use the notion of the social contract in his work. However, he adopted a very narrow view of what individuals needed to give up under the social contract, arguing that the only right that is surrendered for there to be a civil society is the right to punish people for violating rights (i.e., vigilantism). Rawls, on the other hand, goes much further.

Rawls asks what principles individuals would choose to govern their society if they were in the 'original position'. The 'original position' is an artificial construct in which it is imagined that people come together for the purpose of deciding the rules for their society and in particular the rules for determining economic distribution. Rawls asks what principles people would choose as the principles of justice if – hypothetically – they were deciding from behind a 'veil of ignorance'. This veil removes self-interest bias by imagining that the people making the decision as to what is just do not know their characteristics, skills, wealth endowment or social position. Thus, the phrase 'original position' is used as choices/decisions are made without any bias. Once the principles of justice are agreed upon and revealed, they form the basis of the social contract.

Rawls argues that, once the various options and possibilities are considered, two basic principles of justice emerge from the original position to govern society. The first is that 'each person is to have an equal right to the most extensive basic liberty compatible with a similar liberty for others',[20] limited only by the idea that the liberty of one member should not impinge on the liberty of another member. This principle takes priority over the second and guarantees both equal liberty and as much liberty as possible. The second basic principle is that 'social and economic inequalities are to be arranged so that they are both: (a) to the greatest benefit of the least advantaged, consistent with the just savings principle, and (b) attached to offices and positions open to all under conditions of fair equality of opportunity'.[21] The 'just savings principle' provides that the current generation should provide sufficient material capital to maintain just institutions over time, thereby providing for future generations.

The 'difference principle', which provides that inequalities are justified if they advantage the least well off, is salient in the tax context. Many tax systems provide tax concessions to low-income earners, single parents, mature age workers, and retired individuals, to name a few. These concessions are discussed in more detail below. They are known as 'tax expenditures', and they fall within Rawls's difference principle on the basis that a particular group of taxpayers or a particular activity is subsidised in order to benefit the least advantaged.

Rawls's theory of justice is viewed as an alternative to the utilitarian approach to economic redistribution on the basis that the latter may result in an unfair distribution of benefits and burdens as pleasure and pain are treated as

---

[20] John Rawls, *A Theory of Justice*, Cambridge, MA, 1971, p. 60.
[21] John Rawls, *A Theory of Justice*, Cambridge, MA, 1971, p. 302.

interchangeable and traded off against each other in order to maximise total societal well-being. Rawls argues that the rights secured by justice cannot be bargained away or subject to utility aggregation. His 'difference principle' modifies utilitarianism to achieve this by excluding the possibility of justification of inequalities 'on the ground that the disadvantages of those in one position are outweighed by the greater advantages of those in another'.[22]

Rawls also rejects the modern libertarian approach of Nozick on the basis that transactions between individuals do not represent the starting point of system design. Rather, the 'basic structure is to secure just background conditions against which the actions of the individuals and associations take place'.[23] Rather than, as might be expected, support a progressive income tax, Rawls is a proponent of a consumption tax on the basis that it taxes what is taken out of the pool rather than what is added to it.[24] Rawls stated that 'income taxation might be avoided altogether and a proportional expenditure tax adopted instead, that is, a tax on consumption at a constant marginal rate. People would be taxed according to how much they use of the goods and services produced and not according to how much they contribute'.[25] For example, wealthier individuals will consume more goods and services as they have more discretionary funds, so where a comprehensive consumption tax is applied to goods and services, wealthier individuals will pay a higher amount of tax than the less wealthy on the basis of greater consumption.

Once a society has determined the basic principles that underlie its notion of justice, it must design and put in place a tax system that will raise and distribute revenue, and perform such other functions as are required, so as to further that notion of justice. This will involve consideration of issues such as the extent to which education should be publicly funded, how health care should be funded and provided, the extent to which the state or the private sector provides infrastructure, and so on. This leads us to Debate 3: How do we design the elements of a tax system?

Debate 3

How do we design the elements of a tax system?

Any tax regime can be thought of as containing two distinct sets of provisions: technical tax provisions and tax expenditures. Technical tax provisions are designed principally for the purpose of raising revenue, whereas tax expenditures are designed to encourage certain activities or provide transfers to particular

---

[22] John Rawls, *A Theory of Justice*, Cambridge, MA, 1971, pp. 64–5.

[23] John Rawls, *Political Liberalism,* New York: Colombia University Press (1993), p. 226.

[24] Leviner, Sagit, 'The Normative Underpinnings of Taxation' (2012) 13 *Nevada Law Journal*, 95, 129. For an analysis of the application of Rawls to tax policy see: Linda Sugin, Theories of Distributive Justice and Limitations on Taxation: What Rawls Demands from Tax Systems, 72 *Fordham L. Rev.* 1991 (2004).

[25] John Rawls, *Justice as Fairness: A Restatement*, 2005, 161.

taxpayers. Tax regimes are designed with underlying principles in mind and then are adjusted in order to achieve specific aims. In practice, therefore, tax systems always embody social and economic policy judgments. These judgments have nothing to do with revenue-raising and, in fact, quite often reduce the amount of revenue collected through the tax system.

Components of a Tax System

Any discussion around the allocation of liabilities to pay tax focuses on two distinct – and often conflicting – principles: 'benefits received' and 'ability to pay'. The 'benefits received' principle suggests that, according to the goods and services they consume, citizens should either pay tax to governments or make purchases directly from governments. Taxes that apply to specific goods such as fuel or alcohol as well as tolls or permits to use roads fall into this category. In contrast, the 'ability to pay' principle implies that the tax burden should be assigned on the basis of income and wealth, so that those who have more are required to pay more in taxes. Whether a state adopts 'benefits received' or 'ability to pay', a process is still required to determine how that will be implemented. A functional and effective tax relies on five essential elements.[26]

First, there needs to be a base upon which to impose the tax, which can consist of an amount (income/cash flow), transaction (consumption), or property/asset (capital or wealth).

Second, there must be a filing unit, or unit of taxation, which is responsible for paying the tax. Common tax units are individuals, families, corporates and trusts. The most controversial question around the tax unit is whether the relevant unit for income tax purposes should be the individual or the family. In the latter, family members' incomes are aggregated and tax imposed on the total. This apparently simple choice is actually highly complex and involves a trade-off between treating individuals with equal incomes equally and treating families with equal incomes equally. It also gives rise to definitional difficulties, such as the meanings of 'equal' and 'family'.

Third, a tax rate must be set. The expression 'tax rate' often refers to the legislated tax rate. However, 'tax rate' can refer to the marginal rate or effective rate of tax. These are technical tax terms but it is important that they are understood in any tax debate. The marginal tax rate refers to the rate of tax that applies to each additional pound or dollar earned by a taxpayer. Marginal rates are particularly important where a progressive income tax is imposed on individuals. The marginal rate identifies the tax payable on additional income earned by a taxpayer and does not affect the tax paid on income already earned. As such, it may have a significant influence on the incentives to engage in additional economic activity as demonstrated in the above discussion on the Laffer

---

[26] See Brooks, N., 'The Logic, Policy and Politics of Tax Law', p. 19.

curve. That is, the higher the tax rate on additional income, the less likely a taxpayer will take on additional work. The effective rate of tax refers to tax actually paid as a percentage of total income and differs from the statutory (legislated) rate of tax because it takes into account any progressivity in the rates scale as well as things like exemptions, deductions and credits which are embedded in the tax system.

Fourth, there needs to be a tax period for the levying and collection of the tax. Fifth, administrative arrangements must be in place to collect the tax.

Types of Taxes

It is necessary to consider the types of taxes that will be introduced. Generally, taxes can be divided into direct and indirect taxes. A direct tax, for example, income tax, is normally levied directly on individuals and corporations so that the burden cannot be shifted by the taxpayer to someone else. On the other hand, an indirect tax, such as a sales tax, is levied on goods and services where the burden can be shifted to another person or entity. This is because an indirect tax such as value-added tax (VAT), whilst collected by a seller of goods and services, is normally embedded in the retail price, shifting the burden to the ultimate consumer.

Taxes can also be proportional, progressive or regressive, depending on their effect on the distribution of wealth. A proportional tax, such as an income tax, imposes the same relative burden on all taxpayers, whereas a progressive tax imposes a larger-than-proportional increase in tax burden relative to income, so that higher earners pay relatively more. A regressive tax, such as VAT, imposes a less-than-proportional increase in tax burden compared with income, so that higher earners pay relatively less than lower earners. Administrative considerations also drive the decision to impose one type of tax over another. For example, it is relatively simple to impose an import tax on goods and also is more politically palatable. Furthermore, it is relatively simple to collect income taxes from employees through an employer collection system. Real property taxes are another example of a tax that is relatively easy to administer because it is easy to ascertain the location and value of real property. Intellectual property, on the other hand, is much harder to value and can be located in a jurisdiction of owner choice.

Common examples of direct taxes are income taxes, expenditure taxes, death taxes and payroll taxes. Commonly cited benefits of direct taxes include price stability as they don't tend to have inflationary tendencies and, when progressive, are considered by some to be highly equitable. Disadvantages include the complexity of the system itself, the effect on disposable income, the disincentives to further activity created by a progressive scale, the narrowness of the base and an inability to shift the incidence.

Common examples of indirect taxes include sales tax, VAT, goods and services tax (GST) and import duties. These taxes are levied on the production or consumption (or both) of goods and services or on transactions involving imports/exports. Countries such as the UK, consistent with the recommendations of the Meade Report, which advocated for a tax on an individual's total consumption (measured by calculating the difference between receipts and payments during the tax year), are placing increasing reliance on consumption taxes rather than income taxes. Customs duties, excises, stamp duties and luxury taxes such as those on motor vehicles also fall within this category. The reason for this shift from direct to indirect taxation, as explained in the Meade Report, was to improve incentives to earn and to invest income.[27] Other commonly cited benefits of indirect taxes are that they are easy to collect, provide a wide base and, because they are included in the price of goods and services, shift the incidence of tax to the ultimate consumer. Disadvantages include their regressive nature, especially when there is a wide base so that low-income earners are taxed for the goods and services consumed, and their inflationary tendencies, which have the potential to disturb prices.

Tax Expenditures

Tax provisions which form part of a government's policy of supporting particular taxpayers or activities and which have little to do with revenue-raising are known as 'tax expenditures'. Tax expenditures are an important part of fiscal policy and essentially represent a reduction in the burden imposed on a taxpayer rather than a direct expenditure by the government on the same taxpayer or subsidy to a particular product or service. However, the net effect is the same as if the government spent the money on the taxpayer (taxpayer net income or wealth is higher and government revenue is lower). Tax expenditures play an important steering function in society and can be very controversial from a distributional (and hence political) perspective.

As a starting point, a benchmark is determined to see what the state would collect if 'everything' were taxed. The benchmark, which is a normative tax construct, requires a standard tax treatment that applies to similar taxpayers or types of activities. Any benchmark generally includes the tax base, tax rate, tax unit, and tax period: that is, the amount to be taxed, the percentage of the tax, the taxpayer, and the timeframe for taxing. The benchmark for consumption taxes is normally the supply of all goods and services in the particular taxing jurisdiction. As deviations from the benchmark, tax deductions typically involve exemptions, deductions, offsets, concessional rates, and deferrals of tax liabilities. That is, they reduce a taxpayer's tax liability.

The most common, and most costly, tax expenditures tend to be those related to individual taxpayers. Concessions around capital gains and retirement savings often result in billions of dollars or pounds being forgone in

[27] Chick, M. 2018 "Incentives, inequality and taxation: The Meade Committee Report on the Structure and Reform of Direct Taxation (1978)", *Business History*, DOI: 10.1080/00076791.2018.1456531.

annual tax collections. For example, most capital gains tax systems provide an exemption for any gains on a taxpayer's main residence. Concessionary rates are also often present for some classes of assets which are intended to encourage investment in certain capital assets such as small businesses. Income from retirement savings is also often taxed at a lower rate compared with regular income in order to encourage long-term savings and independence in retirement.

However, businesses also benefit from numerous tax expenditures. Small businesses receive concessions in the form of extra deductions from income or corporate tax intended to encourage spending or investment (or both) in certain activities. For example, immediate write-offs are permitted for assets that are normally capitalised and amortised (i.e., depreciated or written off over a length of time). So an item normally classified as an asset for tax purposes is instead treated as an expense, changing the tax treatment and reducing the taxpayer's taxable income. Another common example is increased deductions or offsets for investment in research and development, which results in a lower assessable income so that less tax is payable. Tax expenditures are also found in the rules of domestic regimes which apply to international transactions. For example, it is common to exempt foreign branch profits from income tax on the basis that they are taxed in the foreign jurisdiction, and reduced withholding taxes (an amount levied on payments of certain income earned in one jurisdiction and paid to a resident of another jurisdiction) apply to taxpayers in a tax treaty partner jurisdiction. Other tax expenditures are simply a matter of administrative ease such as threshold exemptions on integrity rules. For example, in many countries, VAT or GST is not charged on low value importations as the administrative burdens are simply too high.

Tax expenditures in the form of concessions often apply to certain industries on the basis of a government policy to support certain economic sectors. These commonly include primary producers, the film industry, tourism and philanthropy. For example, primary producers (farmers) may be offered the option to defer paying their taxes if certain criteria are met, and producers of films who invest in a jurisdiction may be given extra deductions as an incentive to locate in a certain place. Legislation often allows taxpayers to deduct donations to registered charities from their assessable income, even though there is no link or connection between the expense and the earning of income.

Negative tax expenditures are also possible. In Debate 1, we saw that it is possible to use taxes to steer behaviour. Negative tax expenditures can be used to implement Pigovian taxes to address negative externalities. Negative tax expenditures result in revenue-raising beyond the comprehensive tax base and contribute to the fiscal purse. The most obvious of these are additional or pecuniary taxes on polluting activities or pollution, as well as on tobacco and fuel, all of which are intended to steer behaviour in what is considered a socially desirable direction. Double corporate taxation is also claimed to be a negative tax expenditure. That is, a corporate tax is imposed on the entity and then an individual income tax is imposed on the shareholders when they are paid a dividend, meaning the same amount is taxed twice. Furthermore, the non-deductibility of certain expenses such as entertainment expenses, fines, and penalties is an obvious category of expenses that are denied for social policy purposes.

Debate 4
What could a modern corporate tax system look like?

In addition to raising revenue, redistributing, and steering in an efficient and effective manner, a modern corporate tax system should be flexible and able to respond to rapidly changing circumstances such as those discussed in Debate 1: digital technologies (e-commerce, digital currencies, and blockchain transactions) and demographic trends (an ageing population and subordinated groups of taxpayers, including women, minorities and same-sex couples). In this final debate, we consider the changes in approach that are required in the face of how transformative change, in the form of globalisation and automation are affecting current tax regimes. We follow the approach advocated in the Mirrlees Review of seeking to put in place a long-term, considered, and systematic tax policy.

The Mirrlees Review was commissioned in 2011 by the Institute for Fiscal Studies to identify the characteristics of a good tax system for any open developed economy in the 21st century, to assess the extent to which the UK tax system conforms to these ideals, and to recommend how it might realistically be reformed. The review concluded that the current system is 'inefficient, overly complex and frequently unfair'[28] and made a number of recommendations designed to increase output and welfare. These include a progressive income tax with a transparent and coherent rate structure, a largely uniform VAT, a consistent price on carbon emissions, a standard income tax schedule applied to income from all sources and a single rate of corporation tax.[29] With the ultimate goal of establishing an 'economic ideal' rather than facilitating a popular political process, the conclusions reached in the Mirrlees Review put forward a case for radical tax reform. A similar approach is arguably required to address globalisation and automation.

GLOBALISATION

While trade and technology facilitate the growth of global, mobile businesses, tax authorities remain constrained by national borders. This gives rise to opportunities and loopholes through which multinational corporate groups

---

[28] See https://www.ifs.org.uk/publications/5674.
[29] Mirrlees, J., Adam, S., Besley, T., Blundell, R., Bond, S., Chote, R., Gammie, M., Johnson, P., Myles, G., and Poterba, J., 'The Mirrlees Review: Conclusions and Recommendations for Reform' (2016) 32 *Fiscal Studies* 331–59.

can aggressively manage their tax practices, shifting assets and using debt to move profits between jurisdictions so as to reduce their tax burden. Although the legal practice of tax avoidance had been well known for decades, the global financial crisis of 2008 brought it into sharper focus. The collapse of financial markets was followed by fiscally conservative policies of austerity, ostensibly intended to stimulate economic growth, as well as expansive monetary policy, which made it easier for large corporations to borrow.[30] As the offshore assets of the largest companies ballooned, there were growing concerns from civil society that the largest corporate groups were not paying their fair share of tax.[31] Perhaps most strikingly, the Panama Papers leak sent shockwaves across the globe and prompted the call for a unified and strategic global response.[32]

According to Owens,[33] governments can respond to the challenge of globalisation in one of three ways: (1) they can withdraw behind national borders and take an isolationist or unilateral approach to global tax issues, (2) they can seek harmonisation of the international tax system via a global tax code and a global tax authority, or (3) they can respond by strengthening their co-operation with other jurisdictions through measures such as transparent systems and an open exchange of information across borders. Tasked by the G20 to provide guidance on increasing international tax co-operation and transparency to tackle tax evasion practices, the Organisation for Economic Co-operation and Development (OECD) adopted the third response in 2008. This led to proposals for radical tax reform via a global action plan on the Base Erosion and Profit Shifting (BEPS) Project.

The OECD's BEPS Project provides 15 action items designed to equip governments with both domestic and international instruments to tackle the problems of base erosion and profit shifting, two symptoms of aggressive tax avoidance. Of these 15 action items, four are referred to as minimum standards requiring urgent action because of the potential for negative spillovers if jurisdictions take no action. Specifically, the minimum standards are designed to harmonise the national approaches in order to stop multinational corporations from reducing their taxes through highly aggressive tax planning strategies and secretive arrangements. These strategies exploit differences in national tax regimes and find gaps that allow income to be tax-free or minimally taxed.

As jurisdictions have incorporated the action items into their domestic tax policies and as monitoring and review has increased, there has been significant reform of the international tax system. National actions have, however, been inconsistent

---

[30] For more discussion of this, see Johnston, Cullen and Pugh, Chapter 11.

[31] ActionAid (2011) "Tax responsibility: The Business Case for Making Tax a Corporate Responsibility Issue", *ActionAid*, <https://www.actionaid.org.uk/sites/default/files/doc_lib/tax_responsibility.pdf>.

[32] https://www.icij.org/investigations/panama-papers/.

[33] Owens, J. 2002 "Taxation in a global environment", *OECD Observer*, <http://oecdobserver.org/news/archivestory.php/aid/650/Taxation_in_a_global_environment.html>.

and implementation is patchy,[34] and there are marked differences between capital importing and capital exporting jurisdictions and between developed and developing jurisdictions. In part, this has been driven by differing social and economic goals, but critics have also highlighted the lack of involvement of developing jurisdictions in the initial design of the BEPS program, as well as a lack of sophistication in the tax regimes of many of those jurisdictions.[35] Whatever the reasons, the OECD, if it is serious about addressing the impact of globalisation on tax, has much work to do to facilitate the coherent adoption of the BEPS program.

Automation

The so-called fourth industrial revolution has seen advances in technology, communication and connectivity dramatically improve the efficiency of business and organisations through automation. These advances, however, bring with them drawbacks in the form of negative externalities such as labour displacement and rising inequality. Current estimates of these externalities suggest that between 30 and 50 per cent of human, wage-related activities, totalling almost $15 trillion globally, could be lost due to automation by 2035 if technical progress, costs, and social and regulatory acceptance align.[36] If these estimates are realised, the losses will perpetuate the 21st-century trend of rising inequality as income and wealth stratification grows, giving rise to a number of social issues, ranging from greater health and social problems to managing conflict and disparities in consumption, particularly in education. As such, radical tax reform is required.

The solution to the possible impact of automation proposed by most commentators is that, if and when jobs are replaced by automation, those affected will have to be supported and sustained by payments from the government (e.g., via a universal basic income). However, for these payments to be possible, governments must put in place fiscally sustainable tax systems, something that is challenging because the fiscal purse is eroded as there are fewer workers to tax.[37] In 2017, Bill Gates, co-founder of Microsoft, asserted that such a system should be sustained by taxing automation.[38] This bold, unconventional or

---

[34] Sadiq, K., Sawyer, A., and McCredie, B. 2019 "Tax Design and Administration in a Post-BEPS Era: A Study of Key Reform Measures in 18 Jurisdictions", Fiscal Publications, Birmingham UK.

[35] Sadiq, K., Sawyer, A., and McCredie, B. 2019 "Jurisdictional responses to base erosion and profit shifting: a study of 19 key domestic tax systems", 16(3) *eJournal of Tax Research* 737.

[36] McKinsey Global Institute (2017), "A Future that Works: Automation, Employment, and Productivity", McKinsey & Company, <https://www.mckinsey.com/~/media/McKinsey/Featured%20Insights/Digital%20Disruption/Harnessing%20automation%20for%20a%20future%20that%20works/MGI-A-future-that-works_Full-report.ashx>; PWC (2017), "UK Economic Outlook" Price Waterhouse Coopers <https://www.pwc.co.uk/economic-services/ukeo/pwc-uk-economic-outlook-full-report-march-2017-v2.pdf>.

[37] For a contrary view, see Johnston, Cullen and Pugh, Chapter 11.

[38] Bill Gates, cited in Delaney, K. (2017) "The Robot That Takes Your Job Should Pay Taxes Says Bill Gates", *Quartz*, <https://qz.com/911968/bill-gates-the-robot-that-takes-your-job-should-pay-taxes/>.

radical notion suggests a shift from taxing income to taxing capital, consistent with the conclusions of Piketty.[39]

Piketty tracks the growth of capital (essentially income-producing wealth) above income over the last century and forecasts further significant increases, coupled with an unequal distribution, of capital, due to wage inequality, low economic growth, and high returns on capital. Piketty asserts that inequality is propagated by automation and suggests a worldwide tax on capital as the solution, an audacious goal given the largely uncoordinated and unilateral response to the BEPS program.[40] This would include a progressive annual tax on capital (15 per cent) and inherited wealth (80 per cent) along with an automatic exchange of banking data regarding information on assets held in foreign jurisdictions and the use of inflation to redistribute wealth downwards.

Other possible ways of shifting from taxing income to taxing capital include a Pigovian tax on capital, a tax on economic rents, and an appreciation tax. A Pigovian tax on capital is a tax on investment in automation to force businesses to internalise the costs of worker displacement. This tax would be set at a level to offset the social cost of the externality that automation presents, namely the costs to re-educate and support displaced workers. This calculation will be extremely difficult and will require close, continual monitoring and evaluation to balance the competing concerns of equity and impediments to innovation. A tax on economic rents is a tax on surplus or excess profits due to automation (i.e., a tax on those earnings over and above the average market return). Such a tax is similar to the Australian Petroleum Resource Rent Tax (PRRT), which has been in operation since 1987. The PRRT provides a fiscal regime that encourages investment in the exploration and production of petroleum while ensuring a fair and adequate return to the Australian community via a tax on profits generated. A tax on automation is expected to deliver the same results, to encourage innovation and automation, whilst securing an adequate return to cover additional costs on society. Finally, an appreciation tax is a tax on capital appreciation (as opposed to depreciation). This proposed tax is particularly relevant given the unique nature of the fourth industrial revolution, where growth and returns on capital investment could be exponential because of the self-learning capabilities of artificial intelligence.[41] At present, capital gains tax is payable when capital items are sold and gains are made. An appreciation tax would accrue and be payable annually.

Each of these solutions, whilst unconventional, is not entirely outside the realms of possibility. Piecemeal approaches taken by governments globally toward a fairer tax system indicate a nascent shift in the current tax regime from

---

[39] Piketty, T., (2014), *Capital in the Twenty-First Century*, The Belknap Press of Harvard University Press, Cambridge, MA.

[40] For further information, see Sadiq, K, Sawyer, A and McCredie B, 2018, "Jurisdictional responses to base erosion and profit shifting: a study of 19 key domestic tax systems", *eJournal of Tax Research*, vol. 16, no. 3, pp. 737–61.

[41] See International Bar Association (2017) "Artificial Intelligence and Robotics and Their Impact on the Workplace", last viewed 14 February 2018, <https://www.ibanet.org/Document/Default.aspx?DocumentUid=c06aa1a3-d355-4866-beda-9a3a8779ba6e>.

taxing labour to a broader tax on capital. For example, there are commitments to reverse cuts to the capital gains tax and a 5 per cent increase (freeze) in income tax for the top 5 per cent (bottom 95 per cent) in the UK; wealth taxes in France, Norway, Spain and Argentina; and proposed legislation in Australia to eliminate refunds for franking (dividend) credits and negative gearing (allowing offsets of interest charges incurred to hold assets against other income) as well as a 50 per cent increase in the capital gains tax liability when newly purchased assets are sold. Although these developments are largely uncoordinated and unilateral, it is hoped that a coherent multilateral approach is taken in the future to build on these baby steps and bring about systemic change.

CONCLUSION

Tax in the modern world is more than just a means of raising revenue for necessary government functions; it is a political process tasked with redistributing wealth and steering certain behaviours to achieve fiscal and macroeconomic stability. As such, taxation is typically developed in a piecemeal fashion; governments avoid tough and unpopular policies, opting instead for transiently popular or politically palatable ones. This approach has resulted in improvised and incoherent tax systems that require constant independent and intense scrutiny to ensure that they remain fit for purpose.

The purpose of this chapter is to complement important studies such as the Meade Report and Mirrlees Review by offering a preliminary taxonomy of taxation that highlights the fundamental components of an economically ideal tax system. Debate 1 explores why governments tax and how developmental changes such as digitisation and demographic trends affect these functions. Debate 2 discusses how a particular tax system can be justified using normative philosophies of distributive justice, including utilitarianism, libertarianism, and Rawls's theory of justice. Debate 3 outlines the five elements of a tax system and how they should be designed. These elements are (1) a base upon which to impose the tax, (2) a filing unit or unit of taxation which is responsible for paying the tax, (3) a tax rate, (4) a tax period for the levying and collection of the tax, and (5) administrative arrangements to collect the tax. In addition, types of taxes (direct and indirect) and tax provisions or expenditures are defined and evaluated. Finally, Debate 4 details what a modern corporate tax system could look like when responding to transformational changes such as globalisation and automation.

Taken together, these debates provide the foundation for an economically ideal tax system. For this to endure, however, as indicated in the Mirrlees Review,[42] governments need to be honest with their electorates and to be willing to listen, understand and explain; to put long-term strategy ahead of short-term tactics; and, above all, to be bold.

---

[42] See Mirrlees et al., 2011 at 359.

FURTHER READING

M. Burton and K. Sadiq, *Tax Expenditure Management: A Critical Assessment*, Cambridge Tax Law Series (Cambridge University Press, 2012), particularly Chapter (Introduction) and Chapter 5 (The Politics of the Tax Expenditure Concept).

T. Dagan, *International Tax Policy: Between Cooperation and Competition*, Cambridge Tax Law Series (Cambridge University Press, 2017), particularly Chapter 1 (Dilemmas of Tax Policy in a Globalised Economy) Chapter 2 (Global Planners and Strategic Players) and Chapter 3 (International Tax and Global Justice).

C. Evans, J. Hasseldine, A. Lymer, R. Ricketts, and C. Sandford, *Comparative Taxation: Why Tax Systems Differ* (Fiscal Publications; Birmingham, 2017).

P. Harris, *Corporate Tax Law: Structure, Policy and Practice*, Cambridge Tax Law Series (Cambridge University Press, 2013), particularly Chapter 1–3 (Taxation of Corporate Income when Derived, Taxation of Corporate Income when Distributed, and Taxation of Corporate Income).

J. Mirrlees, S. Adam, T. Besley, R. Blundell, S. Bond, R. Chote, M. Gammie, P. Johnson, G. Myles, and J. Poterba, *Tax By Design* (IFS, 2011), particularly Chapter 2 (The Economic Approach to Tax Design), Chapter 4 (Reforming the Taxation of Earnings in the UK), Chapter 14 (Reforming the Taxation of Savings), and Chapter 20 (Conclusions and Recommendations for Reform).

B. Obermayer and F. Obermayer, *The Panama Papers* (Revised ed., Oneworld, 2017).

T. Piketty, *Capital in the Twenty-First Century* (The Belknap Press of Harvard University Press; Cambridge, 2014).

K. Sadiq, A. Sawyer and B. McCredie, *Tax Design and Administration in a Post-BEPS Era: A Study of Key Reform Measures in 18 Jurisdictions* (Fiscal Publications; Birmingham, 2019).

N. Shaxson, *Treasure Islands: Tax Havens and the Men who Stole the World* (Palgrave, 2011).

CHAPTER 11

The Law and Regulation of Banks and Money

Andrew Johnston, Jay Cullen and Trevor Pugh[*]

INTRODUCTION

The global financial crisis (GFC) moved banks and money to the centre of the public's attention. The aim of this chapter is to move beyond the conventional account offered to law students and to show that banks and money give rise to a number of fundamental questions about how we order our society and distribute wealth. Whereas conventional economic accounts pay little attention to money, other, more heterodox accounts show that both central banks and private banks can create money out of nothing. The state relies on interest rates set by the central bank as well as banking regulation to prevent private money creation from resulting in economic and financial instability, but these tools are necessarily imperfect. The chapter then looks at the response of the state to the financial crisis, contrasting the politically driven arguments in favour of fiscal austerity with the more relaxed approach to monetary policy, which has further entrenched income and wealth inequality. We conclude with a call for more scrutiny of private banks and politicians.

THE FUNCTION OF BANKS

The Conventional Approach in Law

Most books about banking law focus on the relationship between banker and customer, being content to tell the student the surprising and counterintuitive news that, in law, the customer is the creditor of the bank. The effect of this is that the deposit in the customer's account is not 'their' money in the sense that it remains their property; it is instead merely a contractual claim on the bank

---

[*] We are grateful to Rohan Grey for helpful comments on a draft of this chapter; all errors remain our own.

and one that is threatened if the bank becomes insolvent and cannot pay its debts. There then follows a detailed exposition of the law relating to cheques, payments, and so on.

From a critical perspective, these traditional explanations depoliticise the role of banks in the economy because they fail to consider what money is and where it comes from. Under these accounts, the existence of money is taken for granted, and lawyers apparently feel no pressure to explain where it came from.[1] It simply facilitates transactions, and banks assist with this function by intermediating between savers and borrowers; they borrow money from savers for the short term and lend it to borrowers for the long term. The only issue arising is whether those who have borrowed from banks will pay it back with interest, making the bank profitable, or whether they will default, either reducing profitability or endangering the solvency of the bank, bringing the state into the picture through deposit guarantees and possibly bailouts, raising the question of regulation.

Getting Deeper into Banking Regulation

More interesting accounts of banking explain that states guarantee banks' liabilities to their depositors, both explicitly in the form of deposit guarantee schemes offered to retail depositors who hand over their savings to banks and implicitly to larger depositors such as corporations and financial institutions.[2] The deposit guarantee scheme was, until the financial crisis, poorly understood and it remains fragmented. For example, bizarrely, in the UK before the financial crisis, only the first £2,000 of deposits per customer was guaranteed, and 90 per cent of the rest was guaranteed up to a limit of £35,000. Any deposit balance over £35,000 was uninsured. Now, deposits are guaranteed 100 per cent, up to a limit of £85,000. These guarantees are essential for two reasons which are normally lacking from the conventional account of banking normally offered to law students.

The first is to preserve confidence in the banking system; without them, depositors would rush to withdraw 'their' money at the first hint of a problem with the bank, thereby converting that hint into a self-fulfilling prophesy of the bank's failure. This is often referred to as a 'bank run' and is what we saw in 2007 in the UK with the 'run' on Northern Rock. Conventional accounts of banking explain the rush to withdraw money on the basis that banks practise 'fractional reserve banking', which means that they retain only a small fraction of the money that has been deposited with them and lend the rest out to

---

[1] A notable exception is C. Proctor, *Mann on the Legal Aspect of Money* (7th ed, OUP, 2012), Chapter 1.

[2] The EU requires the Member States to establish deposit guarantee schemes covering deposits up to €100,000 per depositor: see Directive 2014/49/EU of the European Parliament and of the Council of 16 April 2014 on deposit guarantee schemes OJ L 173/149, 12.6.2014). In the UK, this function is performed by the Financial Services Compensation Scheme.

borrowers. Borrowers in general then deposit these funds in another bank, a process that is repeated a number of times. This results in a so-called 'money multiplier' effect, whereby repeated relending of deposited funds by banks generates ever greater volumes of money, which can be used to purchase assets and fund investment. The money multiplier implies that the money supply increases as banks lend. In fact, by far the largest form of 'money' in the modern economy is in the form of bank deposits (or 'bank money'). Bank lending thus has implications for inflation and price levels. It also implies that not all depositors can withdraw their money at once since only a small 'fraction' of the deposited funds is retained by the bank as cash (bank reserves) to support loans. Since depositors know this, they will rush to the bank to withdraw their money at the first hint of trouble. An explicit, but limited, guarantee from the state is supposed to reassure depositors that their money is safe and to head off runs on banks from the very beginning. However, when a crisis hits, these *ex ante* limited guarantees are often converted *ex post* into blanket guarantees. The Irish government, for example, issued a two-year guarantee without limit of the liabilities of Irish-controlled banks (including deposits), whereas the UK government first extended its deposit guarantee and then made it unlimited as the financial crisis spread. These pragmatic extensions are justified on the grounds that their aim is to reassure depositors, deter runs and banks and, ultimately, head off systemic risk (discussed next), but they can also be criticised for giving rise to moral hazard (effectively relieving savers of any obligation to check the solvency of banks).

Second, banks are also highly interdependent: as we explain below, they tend to lend lots of money to each other, so the failure of one bank can cause other banks to fail through no fault of their own. Hence, a run on Bank A can cause the otherwise entirely healthy Bank B to fail, either if Bank A defaults on its debts to Bank B or if Bank B's depositors withdraw from Bank B on the basis that the run on Bank A has made them start to worry about the solvency of Bank B. The central bank has the power to step in and guarantee *liquidity* to banks at times of market stress, which allows banks to swap non-cash assets (e.g., government bonds) they hold for central bank money (reserves or 'base money'). One way in which it exercises its power is through the 'lender of last resort' (LOLR) facility, which, in the UK, is in general administered by the Prudential Regulation Authority, which is part of the Bank of England. This account concludes by explaining that, since they guarantee their liabilities and offer them access to liquidity, states impose regulation on banks with the aim of reducing the risk of these unfortunate events happening.

A DIFFERENT VIEW OF MONEY

Modern Monetary Theory (MMT) builds on the work of a number of well-known and not so well-known economists, including Keynes, Minsky, Godley, Innes, Knapp and Lerner. Although some of its normative prescriptions are controversial (and are discussed in the final section of this chapter), the foundation of MMT is a painstaking description of the actual operation of the monetary system and it is for this reason that we focus on it in this chapter. MMT explains that banks and money are more deeply intertwined than the conventional account suggests. Although the state plays a role by creating base money, it is banks that play the dominant role in creating most of the money we use on a daily basis, determining how much of it there is in the economy and allocating it to borrowers.[3] However, the 'fractional reserve banking' explanation of the banking system is inaccurate because banks do not need existing savings to create money. As a Bank of England paper put it, rather than intermediate between savers and borrowers, 'in the real world, the key function of banks is the provision of financing, or the creation of new monetary purchasing power through loans, for a single agent that is both borrower and depositor. The bank therefore creates its own funding, deposits, in the act of lending, in a transaction that involves no intermediation whatsoever'.[4]

'Base money' is created by the state electronically out of nothing. This new money is then used by the state to purchase goods and services from its citizens. The state endows this base money with value by decreeing that it must be used by citizens to pay their taxes and fines. In other words, base money is an IOU of the state, which can be used by citizens to discharge their tax debts to the state (as Wray put it, it is a 'basic law of credit' that 'you must take back your own IOU when it is presented to you in payment'[5]). This part of MMT draws on the 'chartalist' theory of money, which sees money as having value because the state declares this (hence it is referred to as 'fiat' currency), and it is backed by law, [6] as opposed to, say, a commodity, which derives value from some other function it may play in the economy, as well as on Innes's view that 'credit and credit alone is money'.[7] We return to taxation in the final part of this chapter.

Base money primarily takes the form of reserves held by private banks in their account at the central bank, but it also includes coins and notes, although these constitute less than 15 per cent of base money.[8] Hence, when the state spends (e.g., paying a teacher or nurse for their work), it simply adds reserves equal to their pay to the central bank account of the private bank where the

---

[3] For a helpful introduction to MMT, see R Rojer, 'The World According to Modern Monetary Theory', The New Inquiry, 11 April 2014 (https://thenewinquiry.com/the-world-according-to-modern-monetary-theory/). A more detailed treatment is in LR Wray, *Modern Money Theory* (Palgrave, 2nd ed, 2015).

[4] Z Jakab and M Kumhof, 'Banks are not intermediaries of loanable funds – and why this matters', Bank of England Working Paper No 761, 26 October 2018.

[5] Wray, *Modern Money Theory* (2nd ed) at 138.

[6] GF Knapp, *The State Theory of Money* (Macmillan, 1924) at 1.

[7] AM Innes, 'What is Money?' in LR Wray (ed), *Theories of Money: The Contributions of A Mitchell Innes* (Elgar 2004) at 31.

[8] As of September 2018, there were £75 billion of notes in circulation compared with £488 billion of commercial bank reserves at the central bank (www.bankofengland.co.uk).

teacher or nurse has an account, and the private bank then creates a deposit in the teacher or nurse's current account (a liability of the private bank to pay the teacher or nurse). No physical money is ever printed and this entire accounting operation takes place electronically (the metaphor of 'keystroking money into existence' is often used here to denote this very mundane process). The state's debt to the private bank is reflected in the bank's reserve holdings (effectively IOUs of the state), and the private bank owes money to the teacher or nurse as represented by the deposit. This is effectively an IOU from the bank to its customer, as the conventional legal account of banking confirms, but it is 'bank money' not 'base money'.

The teacher or nurse can then do three things with their 'bank money' deposit. First, they can withdraw it from the private bank in the form of cash and spend it (banks promise to allow customers to convert their 'bank money' deposits into 'base money' cash on demand). Where a depositor makes a withdrawal, the private bank reduces the size of their deposit balance and hands over cash to the depositor. To do so, it must draw down its reserves from the central bank. If the private bank needs more cash to meet the demands of its depositors, it can obtain it from the central bank in exchange for reserves. Second, they can buy goods from someone with an account at the same private bank, paying for them by writing a cheque or, more realistically, electronically transferring the money to the seller. If they do that, the private bank reduces the balance in their account and increases the amount in the seller's account. At no point does any 'physical' money change hands. Third, they can buy goods from someone with an account at a different private bank. If they do that, their bank reduces the amount in their deposit account, transfers some its reserves with the central bank to the seller's private bank, and the seller's private bank increases the amount of the deposit in the seller's account. The second and third of these activities are pure accounting activities. In either case, the seller will accept a bank deposit as payment for goods because 'bank deposits are any modern economy's dominant medium of exchange'.[9]

Here is where it gets interesting. If the teacher or nurse decides (or is persuaded) that they need to borrow money to satisfy their needs, their private bank can, of course, oblige. As soon as the teacher or nurse gives a legally binding promise to repay the prospective loan with interest, the private bank simply increases the amount in their account by the amount of the loan. Just like the central bank, the private bank 'keystrokes' the money lent into existence, increasing the amount of the IOU to its customer, although this time it is offset by an IOU from the borrowing customer to the bank. The borrowing customer can then use this 'bank money' in the same way as the existing deposit that reflects the salary paid by the government.

Hence, the creation of 'bank money' *reverses the conventional account of banking*, rather than banks requiring deposits before they can lend, bank loans

---

[9] Jakab and Kumhof.

actually create deposits. This is not some quack theory; this account has been endorsed by the Bank of England.[10] The amount of the loan from the bank to the teacher or nurse is created out of thin air in just the same way as the state created money from nothing at the beginning of this story. However, its creation was not dependent on prior bank deposits.

What Is the Function of Bank Reserves?

The conventional fractional reserve banking account claims that the central bank can limit the extent to which private banks increase the supply of money in the economy by changing reserve requirements. By requiring private banks to hold more reserves in their account at the central bank relative to total deposits issued, reserves which therefore cannot be lent out, the central bank can control the expansion of loans and deposits, and therefore money, in the economy. So, if the central bank believes that too much credit is being created, it can force banks to hold more reserves, reducing their capacity to multiply these reserves up into more deposits.

This account has been persuasively rebutted by both MMT theorists and central bank economists, who highlight the limited role of reserves in the monetary system. There is a hierarchy or pyramid of money. Individuals and companies use 'bank money' in the form of bank deposits to settle most of their liabilities to each other and to private banks. Alternatively, they can convert their 'bank money' deposit into cash (which is 'base money') and use that to settle their liabilities. Banks use 'base money' in the form of reserves held at the central bank to settle liabilities between themselves, moving them from one account to another.[11] Reserves never leave the accounts held by private banks at the central bank except when they are converted into currency to meet customer demands for cash (e.g., cashing cheques or withdrawing cash from an ATM). In this situation, the central bank will supply cash to the private bank in exchange for reserves (which are cancelled). If the private bank does not have sufficient reserves to meet the demand for cash, it will have to borrow them, normally from other banks. Interbank lending of reserves occurs on a short-term basis, either on an unsecured basis in the interbank lending market or on a collateralised basis in the 'repo' market. A repo is a 'repurchase agreement': that is, the sale of an asset, say a bond, with an agreement that the seller will repurchase after a specified time period for a specified price. The seller (here, a bank which needs reserves) wants to borrow, whilst the buyer (here, a bank with surplus reserves) wants to lend. This interbank lending is the cause of the interdependence of banks discussed above. In a financial crisis, banks will become wary of lending to each other, and so banks that are short of reserves

---

[10] M McLeay, A Radia and R Thomas, 'Money creation in the modern economy', (2014) *Bank of England Quarterly Bulletin* (Q1) at 1.
[11] Wray (2012) at 86.

will have to approach the central bank in its role of 'lender of last resort'. It is only where the private bank can no longer borrow money from other private banks or from the central bank that it will fail and will default on its promise to convert deposit liabilities (bank money) into cash (base money). In that situation, as we discussed above, the government guarantees a portion of those deposits. Only banks benefit from this privilege, and it illustrates the key influence that banks have over the supply of the everyday monetary instruments that most people use in the economy.

So How Does the Central Bank Control the Supply of Money to the Economy?

Since banks do not lend out reserves, central banks find it very difficult to control lending through reserve requirements (which is why MMT says that banks are not 'reserve-constrained'). Instead, central banks control private bank money creation indirectly. The central bank has the power to set interest rates, and it uses this power to set the price of base money at a level that it considers appropriate to hit its inflation (or other) targets set by the legislature. Since most lending is interbank, the central bank's task is to ensure that the price of borrowing reserves in the interbank market is as close as possible to the base rate, and they do this by adding and removing reserves from the system through 'open market operations'. If the market rate for reserves is too low, the central bank will drain reserves from the system by selling bonds, reducing the supply of reserves and so forcing the market rate up. Conversely, if the market rate is too high, it will inject reserves into the system by buying bonds. By controlling the base rate in this way, the central bank indirectly influences the willingness of borrowers and banks to create money.

Why Is the Financial System Unstable?

Whilst financial instability has been around for as long as we have had a banking system, conventional accounts of banks and money cannot adequately explain financial instability other than by reference to exogenous shocks such as natural disasters or political or technological changes.[12] Conventional economists only recently (and after a devastating bank-driven financial crisis) began to acknowledge collectively the contribution of banks to financial instability. One explanation for their prior failure is their belief in the 'fractional reserve banking' account, discussed above. Another is their failure to pay any attention to where money comes from, treating it as a neutral veil that facilitates transactions but does not otherwise influence the economy. This omission stemmed from the desire of neoclassical economists to develop an 'equilibrium' model of the economy, one where supply and demand are balanced in the absence of

---

[12] See, for example, M Wolf, *The Shifts and the Shocks* (Penguin, 2014), preface.

outside disruptions. However, in order to make mathematical modelling possible, it had to make a number of 'heroic assumptions',[13] including ruling out 'the existence of money, time, uncertainty, and expensive capital assets',[14] that limit its utility for real-world policymakers.

An alternative account explains that financial instability is endogenous to the banking system; that is, it is produced by the very way in which banks and other financial institutions operate. The reason for this is that, unlike 'base money' which is created by the state going into debt to its people and then destroyed by taxation, every pound or dollar of 'bank money' created by private banks is backed by a private debt that must be repaid. Since around one sixth of the money in our economy is base money and the remainder bank money, the retail money supply is backed by a lot of private debt. Indeed, before the launch of quantitative easing (QE) in 2009 (discussed below), bank money represented as much as 97 per cent of the money supply.[15] This means that if banks lend too much money or lend unwisely, borrowers may not be able to repay, calling into question the solvency of banks. When bank balance sheets are impaired, they are unlikely to be expanding the credit supply in the economy and ultimately this will result in a reduction in demand across the economy. This was recognised long ago by the heterodox economist Hyman Minsky, who noted that this was a common feature across a range of financial institutions that engaged in 'money-creating' behaviour.[16]

Why Are Banks So Unstable?

The fragility of banks, and bank-like financial institutions more broadly, results from their use of leverage. This means that they use debt (borrowing) as well as equity (their own funds) to finance their assets. Almost all corporations operate with some degree of leverage, as do individuals. An individual may put down a deposit of 20 per cent of their own money (equity) to buy a house (an asset) and borrow the remaining 80 per cent from a building society. Similarly, a large company such as Royal Dutch Shell, for example, has total assets of around $410 billion, funded by shareholder equity of around $201 billion and debts and other liabilities of around $209 billion.[17] Banks operate with leverage levels that far exceed those of other private actors, so that their assets (the loans

---

[13] Minsky, Stabilizing an Unstable Economy, 1986 (2008) at 50.

[14] KJ Arrow and G Debreu, 'Existence of an equilibrium for a competitive economy' (1954) 22 Econometrica 265 at 270.

[15] McLeay et al (2014) at 2.

[16] For further discussion of Minsky, see Cullen, Chapter 12.

[17] Royal Dutch Shell 1st Quarter 2018 results, https://www.shell.com/investors/financial-reporting/quarterly-results/quarterly-results-2018/q1-2018/_jcr_content/par/toptasks_1119141760.stream/1524681330328/3d5a0a10d9a7b36a82ee8e412b791a15ac0a51afca298ec032539a3591c73b93/q1-2018-qra-document.pdf.

they have made) may be financed 3 per cent by equity and 97 per cent by debt. In terms of a leverage ratio (i.e., total assets divided by equity), Royal Dutch Shell is 2:1, the individual in our example is 5:1 and the bank is around 33:1. This use of leverage by banks is inherent in the system of bank money creation. When bank customers promise to repay, banks gain an asset, but they also incur a liability when they credit their customers' accounts in response to that promise. These assets and liabilities come into being at the same time (when they are keystroked into existence) and disappear together when the customer repays (and the balance sheet entries are deleted). For the duration of the loan, the bank bears the risk of default.

Although the quality of the loans is important, the key issue from a stability perspective is the amount of debt on the balance sheet: the more leverage, the more fragile the bank. If lots of depositors demand to convert their deposits into cash, the bank might face a crisis of liquidity and need to access LOLR facilities at the central bank. More dramatically, if the bank's borrowers default on their repayment obligations in significant number, the solvency of the bank may be called into question. This is because any defaults must be absorbed by equity capital (which is a small sum compared with the amount of loans that the bank has made), and once this is used up, the bank will have insufficient assets to meet its liabilities to its depositors, making it insolvent.

Can Banking Regulation Help Protect the Public Against the Financial Instability Caused by Banks?

Given that there is no physical upper limit on the amount banks can lend (provided that people are prepared to hold their IOUs in the form of bank deposits), regulation is clearly required to prevent bank lending from generating financial instability. The Basel Accords, which are issued by the Basel Committee on Banking Supervision and are essentially soft law, coordinate national banking regimes. In general terms, they attempt to make the financial system more stable by requiring banks to hold more equity capital to support their loans (and so reduce leverage) as well as by regulating the amount of equity held against different kinds of loans. So, for example, loans secured against residential property are given a lower risk-weighting, and so require (or 'use up') less equity capital, than unsecured loans or loans to businesses.[18]

The Basel Accords are based on a correct understanding of the process by which banks create money but, like all regulation, are imperfect. Following the financial crisis, it was recognised that the Basel Accords were not preventing banks from using far too much leverage and so there was too much risk in the financial system. Once losses began to emerge at some banks, the interbank

---

[18] Jay Cullen, 'Securitisation. Ring-Fencing and Housing Bubbles: Financial Stability Implications of UK and EU Bank Reforms' (2018) 4 *Journal of Financial Regulation* 73.

lending system seized up and many banks simultaneously suffered solvency and liquidity problems.

It became clear that regulators had been focusing on the solvency of individual banks at the expense of considering the implications of bank lending for the financial system as a whole. To use an analogy, regulators tended to focus on the likelihood of an individual tree falling over rather than on the potential for a forest fire. New macroprudential regulations (such as the countercyclical buffer) were introduced by Basel III, giving bank regulators considerable power to require private banks to build up additional equity capital where they consider that lending is expanding too quickly. Regulators can take this decision on the basis of factors such as credit/gross domestic product (credit/GDP) ratios and asset price inflation, the latter commonly being a leading indicator of financial problems.

Furthermore, banks had been circumventing the limits on lending imposed by banking regulation by securitising (packaging up and selling off) many of the poor-quality loans they had made. Before the crisis, securitisation was praised for allowing investors to diversify according to their risk preferences and for distributing risk more widely beyond banks. However, securitisation actually contributed to the financial crisis as banks and other financial institutions often remained highly exposed to the risks from securitised loans. The complexity of the securities made them effectively impossible to value, spreading uncertainty and losses around the financial system but without reducing overall risk. As a result, legislators have enacted greater restrictions on securitisations (see box), and there are moves to put in place a simpler system.

Securitisation

With banking regulation limiting lending by reference to equity, banks use off-balance sheet entities to increase their lending capacity. One of these processes is known as securitisation. By removing assets from bank balance sheets, the risks and returns of those assets are transferred to the pool of outside investors who hold claims on the entity. This allows the banks in question to make new loans. For example, if a bank makes a 25-year mortgage loan to a borrower, it consumes balance sheet space, and banking regulation limits the ability of the bank to originate new loans. If, however, the bank can find a way to remove that loan from its balance sheet, it can lend more (which is what bankers want to do as it generally increases profits, return on equity and bonuses).

To achieve this, the bank sells the receivables (i.e., the repayments due) from its assets (loans) to an outside 'special purpose vehicle' (SPV). The SPV then issues debt securities (normally bonds) to investors: it uses the sale proceeds from the debt issuance to fund its purchase of the receivables from the bank. The cash flows from borrowers are then used to service the repayments due under the debt securities.

The law – in particular principles of property law, contract law, company law and insolvency law – is crucial to the securitisation process. For example, the SPV's securities are often constituted under a trust deed, and the investors in the securities hold a beneficial interest that is held by a trustee appointed by settlor (normally the bank that set up the SPV). SPVs are also 'insolvency-remote', so that if the original asset-originator (the bank) becomes insolvent, it will not affect the interests of the purchasers of the SPV's securities.

Finally, banks, as public companies, were significantly influenced by the corporate governance system, and banking regulation did not take account of the pressures (and incentives) for bankers to generate shareholder value in the short term at the expense of undermining the long-term health of the institution. Bankers were generally expected to be concerned about the riskiness of their bank's balance sheets and ultimately their bank's solvency.[19] However, the neoliberal approach to corporate governance insists that, in order to encourage them to 'create shareholder value' by raising the share price, executives should be rewarded with pay packages that are tens or even hundreds of times higher than those given to their companies' ordinary employees. Like their counterparts in other public companies, senior managers and executives at banks are rewarded with salaries and various forms of bonuses that incentivise them to increase return on equity, which in turn raises their bank's share price. Bankers are able to do this very effectively in the short term by increasing leverage (i.e., funding the bank's assets with debt rather than equity). In essence, this means lending more money, so that assets and debt liabilities increase, leaving equity constant. Where regulation prevents this, they can raise return on equity by relying more heavily on securitisations. The EU has introduced a – controversial, for some – cap on bankers' bonuses, which is supposed to remove some of the incentives for excessive risk-taking, [20] as is the introduction of a binding 'say on pay' for shareholders in the UK and the EU, even though shareholders pushed executives before the GFC to take more risks.

THE PROBLEM OF ASSET PRICE BUBBLES

Aside from the financial stability concerns to which bank money creation gives rise, bank lending decisions, which determine how quickly the supply of money to the economy increases and decreases, can create asset bubbles, especially in

---

[19] Jakub and Kumhof refer (at 5) to bankers' 'own assessment of the implications of new lending for their profitability and solvency' as 'the most important limit, especially during the boom periods of financial cycles when all banks simultaneously decide to lend more'.

[20] A Johnston, 'Preventing the Next Financial Crisis? Regulating Bankers' Pay in Europe' (2014) 41 *Journal of Law and Society* 6–27.

post-industrial economies. This has already been seen twice in the UK housing market in the last 15 years, where, as in other advanced economies, loans against property dominate bank lending.[21] If newly created money is spent primarily on purchasing already-existing assets, such as houses or company shares, which are in limited supply, rather than investing in the development of new productive capacity, its only effect will be to drive up the price of those assets. This effect is amplified when investors use bank credit to speculate on such assets (e.g., investors in buy-to-let housing). That in turn will allow the holders of assets to pledge those assets as security for further borrowing and further money creation, making bank solvency heavily dependent on the price of the assets that they have accepted as collateral and creating a political imperative to keep asset prices increasing. In the mainstream view that prevailed until the financial crisis, ever-rising asset prices were viewed as virtuous, making us all (or at least those who own assets) richer, particularly given that inflation was confined to asset prices (policymakers regularly referred to this period as 'the great moderation'). Indeed, while a bubble is expanding, there will be no shortage of willing borrowers to maintain or increase the amount of money circulating in the economy (although the quality of the loans will decrease as those borrowers act in the expectation of further asset price increases).

However, when a bubble inevitably bursts the process of borrowing and asset price inflation goes into reverse, there is a danger that a self-sustaining loop of de-leveraging (paying down debt) and asset price deflation will emerge. The reason for this is that, the more asset prices fall, the more borrowers are likely to default, forcing banks into fire sales of collateral, which produce further price falls and so on. As asset prices fall, banks find that they no longer have sufficient security for the loans that they made and so their solvency can be called into question.

As we saw during the financial crisis, governments honoured (and even extended) their deposit guarantees and bailed out banks – and other critically important financial institutions – with public funds. Central banks played their part too, engaging in LOLR operations and slashing interest rates to historically low levels. Lower interest rates effectively put a floor under property prices, protecting banks against insolvency and benefitting asset owners but transferring wealth from savers to debtors. Following that, central banks engaged in QE, an unconventional monetary policy, which flooded the economy with liquidity (a course of action which is discussed in more detail below) and was (at least in part) intended to increase asset prices. All of these actions were taken as a response to excessive bank lending during the period leading up to the financial crisis, and the central bank, as Minsky puts it, used its 'ultimate weapon for validating a debt structure'.[22] However, this also creates moral

---

[21] A Turner, 'High tide for house prices is engulfing our economy', *Financial Times*, 25 July 2014.

[22] H Minsky, *Stabilizing an Unstable Economy*, 62.

hazard, a situation in which a risk-taker can enjoy the benefits that result from risk-taking whilst knowing that another party will bear any losses that result. The financial crisis showed bankers that, even if their risk-taking results in losses that make their banks insolvent, the government will not allow this to happen.[23] Moreover, as Minsky pointed out, interventions in the heat of crisis make it imperative to then introduce regulation that will constrain or prohibit the practices that led to the crisis. Failure to do so would mean that 'another situation requiring intervention will occur'.[24] Although there have been regulatory tweaks since 2008, the main policy solution chosen was not far-reaching regulation but rather to stimulate new borrowing to reflate a bubble originally inflated by too much borrowing. This was done in order to prevent asset prices from falling, in part to keep the banks solvent and in part in the hope that renewed asset price inflation would lead to increased demand on the part of asset owners.

Although these policy responses to the collapse of the global property bubble may have prevented an immediate and far deeper crisis in the financial system, this has come at the price of contributing to a wider political and economic crisis.

First, putting a floor under asset prices has led to a further concentration of wealth in the hands of those who own assets. With wages stagnating for long periods in the UK since 2008,[25] those who depend on work-generated income no longer earn enough to purchase property and are forced to rent. The result is rampant wealth inequality; the top 10 per cent own 45 per cent of the wealth, with an average of £1.2 million, whereas the top 1 per cent have an average of £3.2 million.[26] There is also lesser but still significant income inequality; the top 10 per cent earn 31 per cent of the income.[27] Even within the top 10 per cent, incomes are massively skewed towards the top. The average income of the top 10 per cent is £107,937, whereas that of the top 1 per cent is £253,927 and that of the top 0.1 per cent is £919,882.[28] Although there were clearly many drivers, there is some suggestion that growing inequality contributed to the outcome of the referendum on Brexit as wealth inequality correlated with the vote to leave.[29]

---

[23] See Adam Tooze, *Crashed* (Allen Lane, 2018), especially Chapter 7.

[24] Ibid. at 59.

[25] See Villiers and Russell, Chapter 3.

[26] ONS, Wealth in Great Britain, Wave 5: 2014 to 2016, https://www.ons.gov.uk/peoplepopulationandcommunity/personalandhouseholdfinances/incomeandwealth/bulletins/wealthingreatbritainwave5/2014to2016.

[27] G Hervey and M Scott, 'Inequality and Brexit', 24 December 2017, https://www.politico.eu/article/brexit-economy-inequality/.

[28] https://www.equalitytrust.org.uk/scale-economic-inequality-uk.

[29] Ibid and http://blogs.lse.ac.uk/politicsandpolicy/brexit-inequality-and-the-demographic-divide/.

Second, those who are sanguine about constant asset price inflation ignore the rising private debt that necessarily accompanies the creation of private bank money that drives asset prices higher. The growth of private debt not only causes problems for individual indebted citizens but also has far-reaching implications for the future trajectory of the economy. If a private citizen spends bank money on consumption in the current period, it is clear that they will consume less in future periods as debt plus interest has to be paid back to the bank. If a private citizen spends bank money on an asset – such as a house – in the current period, they have to service the debt they took on to purchase the asset in future periods. As they pay the interest and principal falling due under the loan, the effect is to divert money away from circulation in the economy towards the bank. Moreover, as the principal is paid down, the amount of money in circulation falls as the bank's liabilities reduce in parallel with its assets, and unless there is new borrowing or the state creates new money, there is a danger of deflation in the price of goods and services and of the economy shrinking. Monetary policy and the injection of liquidity into the economy were used to offset this dynamic by supporting asset prices. In contrast, there were strong political pressures to cut government spending (fiscal policy), which brings us to the debate about austerity and the role of fiscal policy in offsetting recessions.

How Should the State Respond to Economic Downturns?

The role of private banks in creating money goes largely under the radar of public debate, and few concerns are expressed about central banks playing a greater role in addressing economic downturns through unconventional monetary policies such as QE. However, much more critical attention is paid to the possibility (and alleged dangers) of the state creating (or borrowing) money to stimulate the economy or to protect the economically vulnerable.

From Keynesianism to Austerity

Until the 1980s, the conventional approach, widely attributed to John Maynard Keynes,[30] was that the government should spend on public works to stabilise the economy in the event of a shortfall in effective demand. The 'Keynesian consensus' gradually developed into an expectation that governments should ensure continuity of demand, and, with it, employment, by means of counter-cyclical fiscal policies. This entailed running deficits, borrowing and spending money into the economy during downturns (when the private sector was

---

[30] See, for example, JM Keynes, 'How to Avoid a Slump' in D Moggridge (ed), *The Collected Writings of John Maynard Keynes*, Vol 21 (Cambridge University Press, 1982); E Perez Caldenty, 'Chicago, Keynes and Fiscal Policy' (2003) 62 *Investigación Económica* 15, especially at 29–30.

saving or paying down debt), and withdrawing it through taxation, paying off debt and running budget surpluses during expansions.

However, this type of response to a recession is now much more difficult because of the ideology – shared by neoliberal political parties and newspapers alike – of fiscal austerity, which limits the state's capacity to spend in order to offset recessions and depressions and to offset the growing inequality discussed in the previous section. Austerity has been highlighted as one of the drivers of the rise of populism and the outcome of the Brexit referendum.[31]

Although few objected when the UK government increased its debt in order to bail out the banks or to a short round of fiscal stimulus in the immediate aftermath of the GFC, there have been attempts to put in place legally binding rules restricting deficit spending, both in the UK and around the world. In the UK in 2015, then-Chancellor of the Exchequer George Osborne introduced a Fiscal Spending Charter under the Budget Responsibility and National Audit Act 2011, requiring the government to run a budget surplus – which means it would be spending less than it collects in taxes – in 'normal economic times' (when the economy is growing by 1 per cent or more). Similar ideologies led the US government to cut spending drastically. In 2013, the US Congress approved cuts of $1.2 trillion in the federal budget over a 10-year period, following the passage of the Budget Control Act 2011 and the American Taxpayer Relief Act 2012. Similarly, the EU's 1999 Stability and Growth Pact, which requires Member States to limit their deficits to 3 per cent of GDP, was ignored in the aftermath of the financial crisis when bank bailouts were required, but fiscal austerity was re-entrenched with the 2012 Treaty on Stability, Coordination and Governance, which requires signatories to create binding budgetary rules to prevent deficits where national debt exceeds 60 per cent of GDP.

Austerity is justified by the idea, popularised by neoliberal governments since the Thatcher administration,[32] that states face a similar solvency constraint to households and firms. Hence, states must live 'within their means' and avoid sustained budget deficits or issuing high levels of public debt. This provides intuitively logical support for fiscal austerity in the face of persistent deficits. Having run up massive debts (in large part from bailing out insolvent banks) and with a decline in its tax take because of the depressed economy, ideologues of all stripes insist that the state must also de-leverage by slashing fiscal spending. Although bringing a household or firm's budget into surplus is normally a good thing, this is less clear in the case of a state. Supporters of austerity claim that, in addition to undermining the budgetary soundness of the government, state spending risks 'crowding out', or reducing the

---

[31] T. Fetzer, 'Did Austerity Cause Brexit?', University of Warwick Centre for Competitive Advantage in the Global Economy Working Paper No 381, June 2018 (https://warwick.ac.uk/fac/soc/economics/research/centres/cage/manage/publications/381-2018_fetzer.pdf).

[32] See, for example, Margaret Thatcher, Speech to Conservative Party Conference, 14 October 1983, equating the government budget with those of households and businesses.

confidence of, the private sector.[33] This may be true when the economy is strong, but withdrawal by the state of its demand during a downturn (when private actors are de-leveraging or saving, and there is spare capacity) is likely to lead to a deeper recession (and with it lower business confidence). Another argument for austerity is the need for a country to become more competitive internationally in order to attract foreign investment (i.e., external sources of funding and money). Keeping wages and prices down allows this to happen, although foreign exchange movements could offset the benefits. In the case of a currency union such as the Eurozone or a pegged currency, this policy may well succeed, but if many countries are attempting it at the same time, it will not.[34] The demand for austerity in the Eurozone post-crisis can be seen as driven by creditor countries and banks seeking to protect their loans and to prevent debtor countries from profligacy, such as engaging in high levels of domestic investment (at the expense of seeking additional international invest-ment), although it is far from clear that this is successful.[35]

Is Fiscal Austerity Really Necessary?

Most economists continue to follow Keynes and deny that fiscal austerity is necessary.[36] Although there is a broad spectrum of post-Keynesian thinking, MMT takes perhaps the most radical approach and we will focus on it here. It argues that states that are sovereign currency issuers do not have to tax in order to spend; instead, they have to spend in order to tax (because without prior spending, there would be no 'base money' to collect), and they have to tax in order to create demand for their sovereign currency.[37] As Randall Wray pithily

---

[33] For a helpful summary of these arguments, see N Fraccaroli and R Skidelsky, *Austerity vs Stimulus* (Palgrave, 2017) at xviii–xix.

[34] See Mark Blyth, *Austerity: The history of a dangerous idea* (Oxford, 2013).

[35] See Ashoka Mody, *Euro Tragedy* (Oxford, 2018).

[36] See, for example, S Wren-Lewis, 'A general theory of austerity', *University of Oxford BSG Working Paper Series 2016/14*, May 2016 (https://www.bsg.ox.ac.uk/sites/default/files/2018-05/BSG-WP-2016-014.pdf).

[37] There is a long-standing controversy in economics about the source of value: from Locke to Marx, many economic theorists have viewed labour as the true source of value and this is the approach taken by Villiers and Russell (Chapter 3) and Talbot (Chapter 7). Hence, most accounts of the economy, including modern neoclassical economics, have no space for money, viewing it as a trivial way of simplifying complex barter transactions and not impacting on the way in which assets are valued. In contrast, monetary theories formed a separate line of inquiry running from Quesnay through Keynes to Minsky, who emphasised that money has powerful implications for the stability and performance of economies. In this approach, money is not merely a nominal overlay of the economy; it is produced through a complex system of credit which confers legal rights over economic resources. It was only following the financial crisis that interest was revived in this strand of economic research. For early recognition of this divide, see JR Commons, *Institutional Economics* (1934, reprinted as University of Wisconsin Press, 1959) at 51–2.

puts it, 'The government does not "need" the public's money in order to spend; rather the public needs the governments money in order to pay taxes'.[38] When the public pay their taxes to the government, they do this through their banks and using their bank deposits. The taxpayer writes a cheque to the government, the private bank debits their deposit, and the central bank debits reserves from the private bank's account at the central bank and credits the Treasury's account.

According to MMT theorists, the state's task is to ensure that the economy has the right amount of money circulating in it, and it does this by spending and taxing (in that order), although it can, of course, also use taxation to achieve other policy goals, such as redistribution of wealth, discouraging negative externalities and encouraging positive ones, and allocating the costs of public services to particular individuals.[39] This means that government deficits do not matter as ends in themselves. Unlike households, governments can create money out of nothing. This does not mean, however, that governments face no spending limits since government spending can lead to inflation. If the state prints lots of money to spend (e.g., on improving public services), the effect of this will be to increase the supply of base money and therefore the total supply of money. As creation of new money increases spending faster than the underlying real economy can produce new goods and services, the purchasing power of money is likely to fall. The reason for this is that people in the UK, for example, have to hold only pounds in order to purchase the output of the UK economy and pay taxes to the UK state. If there are more pounds than are necessary for these two purposes, there will be inflation in the sense that there is more money chasing the same supply of assets and consumption goods. (Likewise, if there is insufficient money, there will be deflation.)

Drawing on functional finance, MMT argues that the state should conduct fiscal policy so as to achieve full employment and price stability. Excess money should be withdrawn through the economy through taxation, and the state should spend (or cut taxes) where unemployment is too high. Critics of MMT argue that it is very difficult to set tax rates at the correct level to achieve this, and they explain that budgetary constraints are a political choice imposed in the name of 'sound money'.[40] Advocates of MMT respond that taxation should be adjusted on an ongoing basis, that inflation is caused not only by excess demand but also potentially by the pricing power of big companies (which requires regulation), and that excess demand can – and should – be addressed by changes to financial regulations to reduce bank lending and speculation.[41]

---

[38] LR Wray, Understanding Modern Money (Elgar, 1998) at 18.

[39] LR Wray, *Modern Money Theory* (2nd ed, 2015), 143. See further Sadiq and McCredie, Chapter 10.

[40] G Ingham, *The Nature of Money* (Blackwell/Polity, 2004) at 143–4.

[41] S Fulwiler, R Grey and N Tankus, 'An MMT response on what causes inflation', FT Alphaville, 1 March 2019, https://ftalphaville.ft.com/2019/03/01/1551434402000/An-MMT-response-on-what-causes-inflation/.

Beyond this, they claim, the state should anchor the currency and ensure full employment by offering a 'jobs guarantee', effectively acting as 'employer of last resort' where the private sector is not hiring. Such a jobs guarantee would be offered to anyone willing and able to work and would be the main tool used under MMT to control inflation. This debate goes beyond the scope of this short chapter, but its very existence demonstrates that there is considerably more space for fiscal policy than advocates of austerity admit.

If Fiscal Policy Is Ruled Out, What Can Still Be Done by the State When There Is an Economic Downturn?

In contrast to the heated debate over fiscal policy, the monetary policy actions of central banks around the world in the aftermath of the GFC have given rise to less controversy. Central banks, which are institutionally separate from governments for ideological reasons and are responsible for controlling inflation and ensuring financial stability, cut interest rates to historically low levels following the GFC. When this did not encourage the private sector – which was de-leveraging – to borrow more money, thereby increasing investment and effective demand, the major central banks pursued extraordinary monetary policies known as 'quantitative easing'. This policy appears to have first been suggested by Milton Friedman as a means to stimulating the real economy through increasing asset prices.[42] It involves the central bank creating enormous quantities of reserves (base money) out of nothing, which then are used to purchase government bonds from private actors (government bonds are essentially debt contracts giving their holders claims against the government). QE is essentially an asset swap whereby the central bank withdraws interest-bearing assets (bonds) from the economy and replaces them with lower interest-bearing assets (reserves).[43] The policy has encouraged individuals and companies to seek out higher returns by buying riskier assets. Those who used to hold government bonds now find themselves holding bank deposits, which carry only a very low rate of interest. In order to increase their returns, they can use those bank deposits to buy equities, real property and other riskier financial assets. Others can borrow money from banks at very low interest rates and use that borrowed money to buy stocks, other financial products and property.

One effect of QE has been to drive stock markets to unprecedented heights and reflate property bubbles around the world, but for the typical worker, real earnings are now *lower* in the UK than they were before the crisis.[44] The Bank

---

[42] M. Friedman and A. Schwartz, 'Money and Business Cycles' in A. Schwartz (ed), *Money in Historical Perspective* (1987, University of Chicago Press) at 65 originally published at (1963) 45 *The Review of Economics and Statistics* 32–64.

[43] See M Joyce, M Tong and R Woods, 'The United Kingdom's quantitative easing policy: design, operation and Impact' (2011) *Bank of England Quarterly Bulletin* (Q3) at 200.

[44] Institute for Fiscal Studies, '10 years on – have we recovered from the financial crisis?' 12 September 2018.

of England, which introduced this policy in the UK, recognises that it has resulted in an unprecedented redistribution of wealth towards the richest in society.[45] In particular, it has reduced the income of those who rely on interest and it has made defined benefit pension schemes appear unviable whilst making borrowers better off by lowering the rate at which they can borrow. Besides putting a floor under asset prices and encouraging investment by reducing long-term interest rates, central banks expected QE to improve the performance of the real economy by encouraging the asset-rich to spend some of their gains. Certainly, luxury goods manufacturers have been experiencing unprecedented demand, but the principal effect appears to have been further asset price inflation.

In the final analysis, fiscal spending by governments arguably would have been a more effective – and equitable – way of lifting the economy out of recession but was ruled out by the ideology of fiscal austerity. Indeed, even central bankers – not renowned for their political speeches – have hinted that fiscal austerity is harming growth and that 'monetary policy cannot do it all'.[46] Yet central banks have been forced into these extraordinary policies by politicians who claim that fiscal austerity is necessary. There is a pressing need for more honest debate about the role of the state in the economy. The simple, but misleading, analogy between the public finances and household finances should be abandoned. As Alan Greenspan, former chairman of the Federal Reserve, put it:

> ... government cannot become insolvent with respect to obligations in its own currency. A fiat money system, like the ones we have today, can produce such claims without limit.[47]

CONCLUSION

This chapter has sought to show that the law relating to banks and money has far-reaching implications for financial and economic stability and for the distribution of wealth in society. Both the state and private banks can, in principle, create money at will and without any limit. However, private banks, constrained

---

[45] See 'The distributional effects of asset purchases' Bank of England Quarterly Bulletin (Q3) 2012 at 254.

[46] Before the House of Lords Economic Affairs Committee on 25 October 2016, Governor of the Bank of England, Mark Carney stated that 'monetary policy cannot do it all' and had been 'overburdened in terms of providing support to the economy'. (https://parliamentlive.tv/Event/Index/aee168f2-616e-429b-85ef-27e164c399c2). In his 2016 Report to the Treasury Committee, Carney simply noted that 'Trade and fiscal policy continued to drag on growth' (see https://www.bankofengland.co.uk/-/media/boe/files/about/people/mark-carney/mark-carney-annual-report-2016).

[47] Federal Reserve Board, Remarks by Chairman Alan Greenspan at the Catholic University, Leuven, 14 January 1997 (https://www.federalreserve.gov/boarddocs/speeches/1997/19970114.htm).

only by relatively flexible banking regulation, currently have far greater latitude to create money than the state, which faces politically motivated and ultimately self-imposed budget constraints. The financial crisis showed that the creation of money by banks and other financial institutions can have the same stimulatory – and possibly inflationary – effect as creation of money by the state, although it tends to create inflation primarily in asset prices rather than consumption goods. The resultant wealth effect for the 'asset-rich' may be one reason why there is so little public debate about the role of bank money creation. Another is that the debt which is its inevitable counterpart exercises a strong disciplinary effect on the borrowers who make up the majority of the population.

Although these ideas are becoming more widely known, banking law remains, for the most part, an anodyne subject that steers well clear of these important questions. MMT holds out the prospect of governing money in an entirely different way and, at the time of writing (April 2019), had become highly topical (and, of course, controversial). Its potential to contribute to a Green New Deal was being canvassed by, among others, Alexandria Ocasio-Cortez. Although the issues raised in this chapter are technical, they are no more technical than many of the other topics addressed on an undergraduate law programme. We hope that this chapter will encourage law students to play a greater role in holding banks and politicians to account and pressing for the abandonment of socially and economically damaging austerity policies. What is needed now is fiscal policy that benefits everyone in society, rather than monetary policy that benefits only the few who own large quantities of assets.

FURTHER READING

M. Blyth, *Austerity: The History of a Dangerous Idea* (Oxford University Press, 2013).

G. Ingham, *The Nature of Money* (Blackwell/Polity, 2004).

P. Mehrling, 'The Inherent Hierarchy of Money' in L. Taylor, A. Rezai and T. Michl (eds), *Social Fairness and Economics: Economic Essays in the Spirit of Duncan Foley* (Routledge, 2012).

H. Minsky, *Stabilizing an Unstable Economy* (McGraw-Hill, 1986).

A. Mody, *Euro Tragedy* (Oxford, 2018).

L. R. Wray, *Modern Money Theory*, 2nd ed (Palgrave, 2015).

S. Wren-Lewis, *The Lies We Were Told: Politics, Economics, Austerity and Brexit* (Bristol University Press, 2018).

CHAPTER 12

Financial Regulation and Market (In)Efficiency

Jay Cullen

INTRODUCTION

In 2014, a Harvard law student wrote in an essay that the 'most repeated word in my first year curriculum was not justice, or liberty, or order. It was efficiency'.[1] This rather troubling observation reflects the way in which much modern legal scholarship approaches questions of law and financial regulation. Over the past few decades, lawyers have ceded much of the intellectual ground for legal and regulatory analysis to economists, and the line between law and financial regulation is becoming increasingly blurred. Because the principles of such laws are derived from 'mainstream' economic analysis, legal systems, particularly in the Anglo-American spheres, increasingly reflect what is taught in mainstream economics classrooms about the behaviour of financial markets.

In this chapter, I will argue that basing financial regulation on the predominant principles of mainstream economics is deeply flawed. Such principles are, in many cases, no more than superstitions: convenient myths that, though somewhat useful for academic exercise, fail to reflect reality. The emergence of this mythical framework can be traced in part to the evolution of economics scholarship over the past 50 years, during which economists have attempted to emulate the physical sciences with equivalent mathematical formalism and methodologies. Mirowski argues that this 'physics envy'[2] has led to the production of elegant, internally logical and highly complex models that, based upon certain assumptions about human behaviour and the removal of institutional structures, are supposed to generate predictions with universal application, independent of institutions and sociological context.

---

[1] Ted Hamilton, Why Law School's Love Affair with Economics Is Terrible for the American Legal System, Salon 26 July 2014, http://www.salon.com/2014/07/26/whylaw_school-sloveaffair with economicsneedsto-stop/.

[2] Philip Mirowski, *More Heat than Light: Economics as Social Physics, Physics as Nature's Economics* (Cambridge University Press, 1989).

Indeed, the fundamental aim of scientists in the study of physical or natural systems is the pursuit of 'truth': objective facts or discoveries that function (for now) in both theory and practice. In this way, 'hard science' operates in a normative vacuum: scientists describe how things are and how they come to be and falsify alternative theories or hypotheses through a constant process of experimentation and improvement, relying on empirical data to support their hypotheses. Yet, despite the claims of many economists, studying economies and markets in this way is not possible; the central truth about economics as a discipline is that it is *not* a hard science. Although economists may point to similarities in language and methodology between academic economics and physical science, the study of economics – unlike, say, that of physics – cannot be divorced from its legal, political and sociological contexts. To take a crude example, markets do not exist in vacuums: they exist only because of the law. Such markets – particularly those in the modern world – cannot function without significant legal interventions. Markets are not 'things' that appear spontaneously in the absence of rules, customs and laws; they are designed and crafted. As noted by Campbell in the context of neoliberal law and economics:

> Most of [the] belief [in free markets] has been furnished by economists, but it is the professional deformation of most economists that they are so fixated on what they believe is spontaneous order that, when they deign to give the fundamental issues of social theory any thought, they will tend to believe this stuff! Lawyers who are concerned with the law as the main institution necessary for the market to work, and who should appreciate the evidence of how hard it is to get it to work that is in front of their eyes, should not fall for this so easily.[3]

One of the most persistent myths informing financial regulation – the so-called 'efficiency of markets' – is the focus of this chapter. Related theories inform financial market law and regulation, both at the micro (individual firm and consumer) and macro (entire economy) levels. Because markets are presumed to be efficient and self-correcting, the character of much financial regulation until the global financial crisis (GFC) was overtly light-touch. However, although grand models do an excellent job of explaining how financial markets approach so-called 'equilibrium' (or 'balance') in theory, in practice financial markets experience crises of one sort or another on a regular basis. This is amply demonstrated in the empirical record; over the past 30 years and more, the global economy has been rocked by frequent boom and bust episodes as well as countless other regional crises. According to efficient markets theory, such crises should not happen. Indeed, efficient market advocates often contend that such crises happen *only* because of external interference, especially by government.

---

[3] D Campbell, 'The End of Posnerian Law and Economics' (2010) 73 *Modern Law Review*, 305, 312.

The inability of these dominant theories adequately to explain financial crises, as well as their inconsistency with the empirical record, matters because these theories drive policy recommendations and regulation intended to prevent future crises. Happily, there are alternatives to the mainstream approach, which reflect reality to a greater degree, in part because they do offer theories of crisis and, indeed, recognise the impact of law and other forces in shaping market behaviours.

The essential take-away from this chapter is that financial markets – far from being stable in the absence of external interference – tend towards instability in the absence of targeted law and regulation. The potential for such instability is not benign; the recession of 2008–13 was the deepest in the UK since the Second World War, and the GFC cost the UK economy as much as £7.4 trillion in lost output.[4] Many savers and other stakeholders suffered immense damage from the GFC; ironically, it was partly market *in*efficiency that facilitated rent-seeking (i.e., using one's resources or position to extract existing wealth rather than create new wealth) on the part of insiders and led to unprecedented financial and economic losses. Yet, despite the failures evident in financial markets over the last decade or more, regulators continue to insist that any reforms to financial regulation must be 'grounded in a commitment to free market principles'.[5] This is why a new paradigm is required.

The Relationship Between Law and Financial Regulation: The Mainstream Approach

We start with a discussion of the relationship between law and financial regulation, and of how the influence of mainstream economics on financial regulation gradually increased, in particular over the second half of the 20th century. The overarching principle underlying the mainstream approach is the notion that free markets are the best solution for generating economic growth and wealth creation. This necessitates the vast bulk of economic activity being controlled by private individuals and enterprises rather than the state, which is imagined to be inferior to the market in terms of efficient resource allocation. The tradition underpinning this movement can be traced to Adam Smith, whose work has been selectively seized upon by free market economists to suggest that, where individuals follow their own self-interest, this will produce optimal welfare outcomes for all. His famous 'invisible hand' metaphor suggests that markets adjust to new circumstances automatically and produce efficient outcomes in the form of increased wealth for

---

[4] Andrew G Haldane, 'The $100 billion question' Comments at the Institute of Regulation & Risk, Hong Kong, 30 March 2010.

[5] G-20, The Declaration of the Washington Summit on Financial Markets and the World Economy, 15 November 2008, Washington, DC, http://www.un.org/ga/president/63/commission/declarationG20.pdf.

individuals and, therefore, society as a whole.[6] The implication of this 'self-correcting' mechanism is, of course, that government or state 'interference' in markets will simply distort what would otherwise be an efficient outcome.

As politics mirrored mainstream economics, so too did financial regulation. From the 1970s, the post-war dominant Keynesian economics consensus – under which governments were trusted to stabilise economies – was gradually dismantled and replaced with a much more 'efficiency-focused' approach to the management of economy. This was the genesis of 'modern finance theory', the generic term used to describe a collective set of theories that dominate the study of financial markets. The most significant of these are arguably the efficient market hypothesis (EMH) and the rational investor model (RIM).

The central claim of the EMH is 'the simple statement that security prices fully reflect all available information'[7]: prices should react quickly to news regarding a security and the implications of this news should be incorporated rapidly and correctly (i.e., prices should not 'over- or under-react'). Prices should also not move away from fair value unless the news relates to the fundamentals of the security. The EMH therefore excludes the potential for money to be made from 'stale' information; profit cannot be made from trading on past news, as all historical information on a security will have already been incorporated into its price.

The RIM holds that investors are rational in their choices; that is, investors' financial decisions are based upon all available information and they do not make systematic mistakes (they possess so-called 'unbounded rationality'). At a more technical level, this means that investors use all available information to generate a correct expectation of the distribution of future cash flows derived from each and every security, appropriately discounted for risk. The RIM endows market actors with very specific attributes:

> Individuals are fully informed about all their decision alternatives, the probabilities of their outcomes, and their consequences, and there are no cognitive limitations in the perception or processing of this information. Individuals base their decisions on cost-benefit calculations and choose the alternative that generates the highest expected utility.[8]

Consistent with Smith's invisible hand, 'utility' in this context means 'selfish egoism', and human actors are assumed to strive simply toward the maximisation of financial gain, and social institutions and structures have no influence

---

[6] Adam Smith, *An Inquiry into the Nature and Causes of the Wealth of Nations* (Edwin Cannon, ed., Univ. of Chicago Press 1976) (1776), 477–8.

[7] Eugene F. Fama, 'Efficient Capital Markets: II' (1991) 46 Journal of Finance 1575.

[8] Rafael Wittek, 'Rational Choice Theory' in *Theory in Social and Cultural Anthropology: An Encyclopedia* (R. Jon McGee and Richard L. Warms (eds): Sage 2013), pp. 688–9.

on their behaviour. In such models, even acts of altruism are regarded either as (i) a 'signaling' device by the perpetrator of the apparent altruistic act to increase the likelihood of future reward or (ii) a selfish act designed simply to make the perpetrator feel good about herself.

The implications of rational choice theory for economic and financial market performance are profound: 'the [RIM] is built on the assumption that investors, through some miraculous but unspecified process, gain perfect knowledge of the future'.[9] If this prediction about economic agents holds, across the economy:

> [w]ages and prices will adjust instantaneously to new conditions, because these conditions will have been anticipated and will already be incorporated in the prices which people charge and expect to pay for their services. No departure from real long-term values is possible even in the short run.[10]

The importance of the EMH and the RIM to the study of financial markets is therefore the 'prediction that, even though all information is not immediately and costlessly available to all participants, the market will act *as if* it were'.[11] A further implication is that *only* a completely unanticipated exogenous shock (e.g., a terrorist attack or a natural disaster) will move market prices to any great degree.

The EMH is well supported in some contexts; for example, it is well established that the vast majority of investors fail to 'beat the market' on a regular basis since price movements are random in general and therefore unpredictable. This dictates that, all things being equal, investors will over time receive higher returns through taking passive positions in the entire stock index rather than attempting to pick individual stocks for investment. This benign prediction of the EMH is perfectly sound. Of course, markets also usually provide the 'best guess' available regarding the future profitability of companies and returns on shares and such indicators are very useful for certain risk management purposes. In particular, it is clear that financial markets exhibit considerable relative efficiency; that is, the relative prices of individual securities are in most circumstances very accurate.[12] On the other hand, as the remainder of this chapter will outline, this says nothing about financial market prices as a whole (Box 12.1).

---

[9] James R. Crotty, 'The Realism of Assumptions Does Matter: Why Keynes-Minsky Theory Must Replace Efficient Market Theory as the Guide to Financial Regulation Policy' (2011) Political Economy Research Institute, University of Massachusetts at Amherst Working Paper No. 255.

[10] Robert Skidelsky, *Keynes: The Return of the Master* (Penguin 2009) 32.

[11] Ronald J. Gilson & Reinier H. Kraakman, 'The Mechanisms of Market Efficiency' (1984) 70 Virginia Law Review 549, 552.

[12] Andrew W. Lo, 'Efficient Markets Hypothesis' in L. Blume and S. Durlauf, *The New Palgrave Dictionary of Economics* (2nd Ed. New York: Palgrave Macmillan, 2008).

Box 12.1 Financial Market Modelling

The assumptions made under so-called neo-classical economics provide principles that may be used to inform the design of models, at both the macro and micro levels. The economists who design such models argue that the assumptions they make about the economy are needed for 'tractability'; that is, they allow the designers to construct workable models. Otherwise, economic models would be too complex and too unwieldy. Recognising the difficulty with such simplifying assumptions, Milton Friedman went as far as to suggest that the assumptions made in economics don't actually matter, only whether or not the predictions made by the theory are true.

In spite of this, it is useful to take a look at some of the simplifying assumptions used in one of the foremost models used in financial markets: the Modigliani-Miller theorem.[13] This model is widely used in financial markets, and its basic argument is that the proportion of debt to equity in a firm should not affect its value. In other words, two firms with identical prospects will have the same value no matter how much debt they carry. The (clearly unrealistic) assumptions required to make the model work mathematically are the following:

- There are no taxes: there is no tax benefit to debt over equity.
- Transaction cost for buying and selling securities is zero: there is unlimited liquidity.
- No-one defaults: no-one ever fails to meet their financial obligations or breaches a contract.
- There is perfect information: all agents have perfect information about financial instruments.
- Investors are rational: all agents know with certainty the statistical distributions of future cash flows.
- Capital markets are perfect: the cost of borrowing for companies and investors is identical.
- There are no costs to listing on a stock exchange: there are no broker fees, no investment banking fees, and so on.
- There are no financial institutions.

How Efficient Market Theory Informs Financial Regulation

The principles of efficient market theory laid out above are used to support the view that deregulation of financial market activities is a critical requirement for their efficient operation and, therefore, for greater economic welfare. Regulatory approaches to managing risk in markets are heavily informed by modern finance theory. In particular, in the context of law and regulation, modern finance theory assumes that efficient markets offer a complete range of

---

[13] F. Modigliani and M. Miller, 'The Cost of Capital, Corporation Finance and the Theory of Investment' (1958) 48 American Economic Review 261–97.

financial contracts which will allow market actors to precisely satisfy their preferences for risk and return; markets are sufficiently rational as to justify a strong presumption in favour of market deregulation; and even where regulators suspect irrational behaviour is occurring, they will never know with certainty whether to intervene and should refrain from doing so.[14]

Significantly, these principles are incorporated in the models used by financial institutions to manage risk and to make investment decisions. In fact, the EMH (and its offshoots) even informs regulatory assumptions about the amount of debt with which companies and financial institutions can safely operate. The creation of mountains of debt and the associated fragility of the contracts that have arisen over the past 40 years or so is due partly to the use of such models: the most significant mainstream models of financial markets assume that debt levels – or leverage – will not produce dangers since rational investors always choose an optimal debt position and always charge the correct risk premium based upon the relevant debt structure (and so eliminate the possibility that companies will use 'excessive' leverage). MacKenzie claims, for example, that the introduction of option pricing models in the 1970s led the US Federal Reserve (one of the main financial regulators of the US) to change its regulations and substantially loosen the use of credit by parties in options markets.[15]

This form of analysis was championed from the 1970s onwards under the doctrine of the 'self-correcting nature of markets', leading axiomatically to their deregulation. In the financial services market in the UK, this began in 1986 with so-called 'Big Bang'[16] implemented under the Financial Services Act 1986. By 1997, under New Labour's economic policies, many existing financial supervision structures were dismantled and placed under the umbrella of the newly established Financial Services Authority (FSA).[17] Tellingly, the FSA trumpeted its 'light-touch' regulation; Gordon Brown, as Chancellor of the Exchequer, for example, just one year before the GFC, had congratulated himself on 'resisting pressure' to toughen up regulation of banking activities.[18]

Deregulation was even more explicit in the US. Legal academics and judges between the 1970s and 1990s seized upon the aforementioned economic

---

[14] Financial Services Authority, *The Turner Review: A regulatory response to the global banking crisis* (March 2009) 40.

[15] Donald MacKenzie, *An Engine, Not a Camera: How Financial Models Shape Markets* (MIT Press: 2008) p. 166.

[16] Big Bang ended fixed commissions on fees for share transactions on the London Stock Exchange as well as removing the distinction between 'jobbers' and 'brokers'.

[17] Established in 1997 and given extensive powers by the Financial Services and Markets Act 2000 (Ch. 8).

[18] Speech by the Chancellor of the Exchequer, the Rt Hon Gordon Brown MP at the Mansion House, London, 20 June 2007.

analyses to argue that most laws and regulations governing financial markets were unnecessary: freedom of contract and well-delineated property rights combined with rational choice would suffice to ensure allocation of resources to the user which values them most highly, increasing aggregate social welfare. Based on such analyses, the underlying prescription for financial market regulation has been to promote increased information flows to market actors, allowing them to 'crunch' the relevant information and effortlessly and accurately price financial assets (as only supremely rational investors can). These assumptions support deregulation: the deconstruction of financial market law and regulation to remove obstacles to free contracting and the removal of the state from 'private market' affairs. By the late 20th century, in the US, the Glass–Steagall Act was repealed (removing the restriction on banks having both commercial and investment banking operations), and in 2000, the Commodities and Futures Modernization Act was introduced, exempting many financial derivatives and swaps from regulation. Further significant loosening of bank regulation followed in the mid-2000s.

THE EMH AND THE RIM ARE FLAWED

This part of the chapter will discuss alternative theories of investor behaviour and market operation – theories that, it will be argued, are much more consistent with the empirical record than those associated with efficient markets and rational investors. For starters, as alluded to above, mainstream economic approaches to law and regulation have no room for 'bubbles' (long-term deviations of securities prices from intrinsic value). Asset bubbles are impossible in the presence of full information because market prices always convey the fundamental value of assets. In fact, mainstream economics has no need to explain crises because it assumes that rational bankers, investors, and other market participants will not assume risks that cause their firms or investments to collapse.

However, history refutes such claims: asset bubbles do arise and they arise frequently.[19] In 1990, for example, Japanese stocks accounted for over half of the global equity index before collapsing by almost 60 per cent in a year. Ten years later, tech stocks represented over 45 per cent of the US stock exchange before the dot.com bubble burst. By 2018, despite the presence of tech giants such as Amazon, Google and Facebook, the tech portion of the US stock exchange had returned to represent only 26 per cent of US stock indices, indicating how extreme

---

[19]A non-exhaustive list of bubbles includes Tulip mania (Holland) (1634–37); the South Sea Company (Great Britain) (1720); the Panic of 1837 (1834–37); the Panic of 1857; the US farm bubble and crisis (1914–18, crash 1919–20); the Roaring Twenties stock-market bubble which presaged the Wall Street Crash (US) (1921–29); the Japanese asset price bubble (Japan) (1986–91); the dot-com bubble (US)(1995–2000); the US housing bubble (US) (2002–06); and the Cryptocurrency bubble (2016–18).

the valuations of the early 21st century were. As documented in the chart below, the price of one Bitcoin increased from about $1000 at the beginning of 2016 to over $19,000 by the end of 2017, yet its price at the time of writing (March 2019) was about $3500. If these are not 'bubble episodes', what are they? More importantly, how can we explain the occurrence of such extreme price rises and crashes in so-called sophisticated (and, moreover, rational) markets? (Boxes 12.2 and 12.3).

Box 12.2 What Is an Asset Bubble?

Generally, bubbles may be defined as instances when current market prices for a class of assets, such as stocks or real estate, diverge from the fundamental value of those assets. An asset's fundamental value is, in turn, defined as the present discounted value of all future cash flows (i.e., income) from that asset. The characteristics of such bubbles are described by Kindelberger as 'mass hysteria [which leads to] an occasional deviation from rational behaviour'.[20] The stages of bubbles have been categorised in the following way:

(i) Displacement: the emergence of a new technology or investment class (e.g., the internet)

(ii) Boom: slow price rises eventually give way to greater momentum, spurred by media coverage and increased speculation, often in spite of a lack of information and uncertainty surrounding the new technology or innovation.

(iii) Euphoria: investors are captured by speculative fever, a wider range of investors join the stampede, and 'the greater fool' theory emerges everywhere, reducing investors' risk aversion. (The 'greater fool' theory holds that it is possible to make money by buying assets, whether or not they are overvalued, by selling them for a profit at a later date. There is thus an implicit assumption that there will always be someone – i.e., a greater fool – who is willing to pay a higher price.)

(iv) Profit-taking: many sophisticated investors spot the emergence of the bubble during the euphoric stages and consider selling out of a market, although it is difficult to spot the peak of the bubble, and many will remain invested, attempting to eke out any profit left before the bubble collapses.

(v) Panic: as realisation of the bubble dawns across markets, investors panic, rushing to sell the overpriced assets and flee to safe havens. However, the glut of these assets on the market depresses their price and sends a signal to remaining investors that the assets in question were likely highly overpriced. This amplifies negative price movements and the bubble pops.[21]

---

[20] Charles P. Kindleberger and Robert Z. Aliber, *Manias, Panics and Crashes: A History of Financial Crises* (6th ed, Palgrave Macmillan 2011) 26–7.
[21] Gary Giroux, Business Scandals, Corruption, and Reform: An Encyclopedia (Greenwood: 2013) 381.

At the same time, it should be remembered that, in general, mainstream financial economists refuse to acknowledge the existence of bubbles. Fama, for example, commented in 2010 (after the GFC) that 'I don't even know what a bubble means. These words have become popular. I don't think they have any meaning ... I want people to use the term in a consistent way. For example, I didn't renew my subscription to *The Economist* because they use the world bubble three times on every page. Any time prices went up and down – I guess that is what they call a bubble. People have become entirely sloppy'.[22]

Box 12.3 Bitcoin

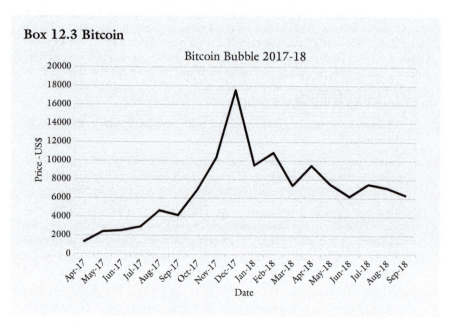

In fact, a separate tradition within economics – led by John Maynard Keynes and Hyman Minsky – has repeatedly emphasised the possibility and significance of instability in financial markets. This instability arises thanks to a simple truism: rather than being a system populated by a collection of hyper-rational supercomputing investors with perfect information, financial markets are characterised by *uncertainty*, which causes frequent boom and bust episodes. Uncertainty arises because there is insufficient information concerning the probability of particular events, either because they are too irregular (i.e., outside the bounds of prediction) or because they occur too infrequently (and so may not appear in the

---

[22] See John Cassidy, 'Rational Irrationality – An Interview with Eugene Fama' *The New Yorker* (New York, 13 January 2010).

empirical record). It is these factors that build inefficiencies into the market structure since the decisions of business people making decisions today may turn out to be the 'wrong' decision in the future (i.e., they take on too much or too little risk). Far from market outcomes and risks being calculable given a full information set, under conditions of uncertainty, the likelihood of future events is actually indefinite and incalculable. Such an analysis provides explanatory power for the bubbles, panics and crashes witnessed with increasing frequency in financial markets.

Therefore, a more realistic view is that investors ought to be classed as 'boundedly rational' agents who make frequent cognitive errors. Bounded rationality has influenced a number of fields, including relational contract law and corporate governance.[23] However, it has made no real inroads into mainstream financial economics. Heterodox economists, in contrast to those in the mainstream, argue that it is abundantly clear that investors should not be characterised as unboundedly rational. For example, it is clear from research that humans possess 'limited computational skills and seriously flawed memories'.[24] Such investors also operate with incomplete knowledge and understanding of how particular factors will interact and determine future performance, a point noted by Crotty:

> The economic outcomes we observe over time are generated by a system of ever-changing agents, agent preferences, expectations, risk-aversion, innovations, and economic, political, and social institutions. Thus, the mechanisms that generate future outcomes cannot possibly be known in the present... The best agents can do is base their decisions on fallible expectations of some kind. These fallible expectations guide agent choice today and thereby influence the future trajectory of the economy.[25]

In such analyses, the value of assets is always *ex ante* unknowable, and expectations about the future are incomplete, fragmented, and subject to intractable uncertainty. In the words of Keynes, this leads to the recognition that '[in] a world ruled by uncertainty, with an uncertain future linked to an actual present, a final position of equilibrium, such as one deals with in static economics, does not properly exist'.[26]

Incomplete knowledge may also arise from the complexity and opacity of the financial network, something ignored by the EMH and RIM but acknowledged by Minsky as a potential source of instability. Financial claims and the chains of transactions between institutions are often highly complex, as are

---

[23] See Morgan, Chapter 1, Attenborough, Chapter 7 and Johnston, Chapter 9.

[24] Christine Jolls, Cass R. Sunstein & Richard Thaler, 'A Behavioral Approach to Law and Economics' (1998) 50 Stanford Law Review 1471, 1477.

[25] James R Crotty, The Realism of Assumptions Does Matter: Why Keynes-Minsky Theory Must Replace Efficient Market Theory as the Guide to Financial Regulation Policy (2011) Political Economy Research Institute, University of Massachusetts at Amherst Working Paper No. 255, March. p. 18.

[26] John M. Keynes, *The Collected Writings of John Maynard Keynes, Volume 29: The General Theory and After: A Supplement* (Macmillan 1979).

some of the financial instruments used to generate them. It is not always clear, to either market participants or regulators, where losses will eventually fall in the event that default occurs. For example, there is convincing evidence that, during the GFC, many senior managers of financial institutions were unaware of the risks their institutions were taking, and many of the investments that eventually became toxic were regarded as safe for risk management purposes.[27] On this view, it is not just that the market *cannot* be efficient, it is that instability and inefficiency in financial markets arise as a result of *endogenous* (i.e., internal to the system) processes, so that booms and busts are inherent aspects of the system rather than, as the conventional approach claims, the result of some unanticipated external (exogenous) shock.

MINSKY'S FINANCIAL INSTABILITY HYPOTHESIS

The uncertainty referred to above is crucial to the operation of Minsky's financial instability hypothesis (FIH), the theory he is most closely associated with (Box 12.4).

Box 12.4 The Financial Instability Hypothesis

Minsky regarded human behaviour as having a fundamental effect on both the structure and performance of the financial system, thereby refuting the orthodox view that the economy is predisposed to a static equilibrium. In many ways, Minsky was a forerunner of modern behavioural economics, which views human behaviour as inherently procyclical, leading to herding and feedback processes that may generate boom and bust cycles.[28] Minsky realised that a theory which understands that the quantity of money in an economy is elastic, and that economic agents use that elasticity to finance positions in assets, has to recognise that there is a danger that agents will overpay for assets, creating the possibility of financial instability as that process of overpayment is reversed in the form of forced asset sales. This danger is recognised in Minsky's pithy phrase, 'stability creates instability', as economic agents become complacent about the prospects of reductions in asset prices and overcommit in terms of finance.

Since the GFC – which is often referred to as a 'Minsky moment' – his work has been rediscovered and it has important implications for regulating money and the banking system. The FIH provides an explanation for how increasing

---

[27] For example, many of the so-called 'toxic mortgage assets' were highly rated by both credit rating agencies and internal financial analysts. See Johnston, Cullen and Pugh, Chapter 11 for a discussion of securitisation.

[28] George A. Akerlof & Robert J. Shiller, *Animal Spirits: How Human Psychology Drives the Economy, and Why It Matters for Global Capitalism* (Princeton University Press, 2008).

bank lending during financial booms can eventually cause a financial crisis if the loans made during such periods do not pay off in the sense of being validated by the future evolution of the economy and the trajectory of prices. In modern economies, debt is often used to finance assets, and it is banks in general which create this debt. Minsky's FIH therefore places banks at the centre of the analysis: investment decisions are only validated over time when it becomes clear that they do (or do not) generate the cash flows needed to service the cost of the capital used to acquire the assets in question. Whether or not particular investments will be validated in this way cannot be known when it is made; it emerges only later on.

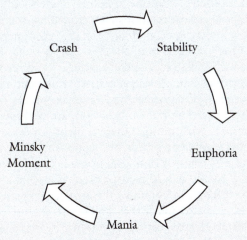

The FIH explains in two propositions how financialised economies are prone to crisis and market pricing cannot be efficient. First, the FIH states that there are two forms of financing regime: one that is consistent with stability and one that subjects the economy to instability. Second, over protracted periods, even 'stability is destabilising' and stable economies will become progressively more unstable because of investor behaviour, in particular the twin traits of optimism (euphoria) and pessimism (panic).

The FIH focuses on the use of debt to finance purchases by economic actors of assets. Under the FIH, asset price increases are natural products of the expectations of investors that positive economic conditions experienced in the recent past will persist. In turn, these asset price increases form the basis for decisions to increase borrowing and make speculative investments, which will eventually fatally undermine the investment structure of the economy. In particular, following a crisis, and as the memory of it fades:

> [R]isk aversion dissipates and financing terms ease. As a modest economic expansion replaces stagnation, financial institutions and balance sheets in general become more robust. Continued success sets the groundwork for failure. Financial

robustness that is deemed excessive leads to the development of new instruments. Once again, power in the belief of creative finance emerges. Even as optimism reigns, financial robustness is eroded: the domain of financial fragility increases.[29]

Consistent with this, according to the FIH, bankers are naturally sceptical about lending money to finance the purchase of financial assets and their view of risk will be influenced both by the composition of their portfolios and by their views about future economic prospects. Minsky argued that, in the absence of certainty or perfect foresight, economic actors instead fall back upon recent experiences and memories to use as a frame of reference to guide future investment. In such conditions, investors, lenders and other market participants are predisposed to expectations-changing influences such as optimism, pessimism or overconfidence, depending upon the recent performance of their investments and wider conditions in the financial markets. Minsky's work in particular accords with investor bounded rationality and recognises that there can be no guarantee that economic agents share consistent models 'such as are needed for the existence of a rational expectations equilibrium'.[30]

Such assertions concerning human behaviour are well supported by behavioural finance research. For example, there is plenty of evidence that, in general, people are overconfident or far too optimistic, or both.[31] Individuals possess a profound bias towards optimism in predicting future events, and the levels of confidence people ascribe to their predictions and abilities are far too high. People also suffer from cognitive dissonance: they attribute too much weight to experiences that confirm their abilities to themselves whilst systematically ignoring instances that cast doubt on their own appraisal of their abilities.[32] Conversely, people have a profound propensity to underestimate the probability of adverse outcomes, often termed 'disaster myopia'.[33]

Therefore, a highly significant consequence of these influences is that where an institution or investor appears to be gaining abnormally large profits in the short term, other investors will usually attribute greater probability to those high profits continuing than is warranted by fundamentals. This may produce the result that

---

[29] Hyman P. Minsky, 'Longer Waves in Financial Relations: Financial Factors in the More Severe Depressions II' (1995) 29 Journal of Economic Issues 83, 93.

[30] Hyman P. Minsky, 'Uncertainty and the Institutional Structure of Capitalist Economies: Remarks upon Receiving the Veblen-Commons Award' (1996) 30 Journal of Economic Issues. 357, 360.

[31] Werner F.M. De Bondt & Richard H. Thaler, 'Financial decision making in markets and firms: a behavioral perspective' in Robert A. Jarrow, Vojislav Maksimovic & William T. Ziemba (eds), Handbook in Operations Research and Management Science: Finance (Elsevier 1995).

[32] Rowland Bismarck & Fernando Pasaribu, 'About Stock Bubbles' (2009) Econometric Research Institute Working Paper.

[33] Jack M. Guttentag & Richard J. Herring, Disaster Myopia in International Banking (Princeton University Essays in International Finance 1986).

'[i]n a rising stock market or any other asset market ... individuals embrace unsustainable beliefs that the price rises will continue indefinitely'.[34] Each of these factors reveals that the assumptions of the rational investor model are not only misleading but dangerous because they inform systems of regulation which take no account of the possibility that financial crises may result from the uncertainty inherent in financing decisions and the debt structure of investments.

IMPLICATIONS OF MINSKYAN FINANCIAL DYNAMICS

Underlying all of this analysis is the Minskyan rejection of the EMH and RIM. Boom and bust dynamics are propelled by investor psychology, rather than fundamentals, exercised under uncertainty. Investment decisions are influenced by the behavioural factors discussed above rather than unbounded rationality and perfect foresight. Where investors are enthusiastic about the prospects for speculative ventures, demand for credit to finance investments and, with it, the interest rates charged by banks will rise. Banks may also insist on more security from borrowers, limiting the amount of leverage that investors can use. In a growing economy with conservative financing structures in which most business ventures are succeeding, both businesses and banks come to regard the safety margins written into loan contracts as excessively risk-averse. However, if a given investment in an asset does not pay off (because the asset in question does not generate sufficient income to cover repayments), the debtor will eventually have to either sell that asset in order to make the payments due under the loan or find another income stream with which to do so. Increasing numbers of asset sales will drive down prices to levels that incorporate more realistic estimates of future income streams; however, as asset prices fall, this calls into question the ability of other asset owners to roll over the debt they are using to finance positions in equivalent assets (as bankers respond to the new, lower market prices).

At the core of this pattern is 'irreversibility': contract law insists that contracts for finance are binding and must be honoured, regardless of later changes in circumstances. This strict legal rule brings with it profound implications for financial stability. Agents in a booming and overconfident economy will carry forward asset positions acquired in the past which tie them to a need to service the debt liabilities incurred to finance those assets and to renew their borrowings where they expire. Minsky's work demonstrates that it is these financial commitments established across the economy during a boom which are the key to subsequent instability: 'the liability structures that geniuses of leverage exploited in the high-growth days become nooses for aggressive-growth firms when low growth hits'.[35]

---

[34] Emilios Avgouleas, 'The Global Financial Crisis, Behavioural Finance and Financial Regulation: In Search of a New Orthodoxy' (2009) 9 Journal of Corporate Law Studies 23, 33.

[35] Hyman P. Minsky, *Stabilizing an Unstable Economy* (2nd ed, McGraw-Hill 2008), p. 236.

This analysis reveals the perceptiveness of Minsky's claim that 'stability is destabilising'; in other words, benign economic conditions actually lay the groundwork for future crises because, during these periods, margins of safety are reduced as risk tolerance increases. From a legal perspective, any financial market contracts that were entered into during boom, or euphoric, periods cannot simply be unwound if the boom in question later turns to bust. Put simply, this means that because market actors make their contracts – or take financial positions – under considerable uncertainty about the future, it is for practical purposes impossible to design a contract at the outset which will cater for all possible futures, thanks to bounded rationality. According to the EMH and RIM, all contracts are honoured; no-one ever breaches a contract since investors possess perfect foresight and therefore can bargain at the outset and make provision for all future contingencies. Indeed, according to Goodhart, the reason that mainstream economics has no room for the concept of 'money' or banks is that the hyper-rational representative agent of the models used would never default on a contract.[36]

On the one hand, therefore, financial markets need legal validation to provide certainty and credibility. On the other, inflexibility in financial market contracts may bring down the entire financial system in the absence of implicit support from regulatory authorities.[37] However, whilst manias, panics and crashes certainly do pose dilemmas for financial regulators and politicians, this is partly because existing theories of the economy regard it as tending towards balance – in the jargon, an equilibrium-seeking system – which is pushed away from stability only by exogenous (external) forces, which are not foreseeable and therefore cannot be prevented. Andrew Lo, of MIT, has proposed 'a framework for regulatory reform that begins with the observation that financial manias and panics cannot be legislated away, and may be an unavoidable aspect of modern capitalism'.[38] Lo rightly argues that the endogenous causes of the instability of capitalism, and financial markets in particular, can be addressed by regulation, but it requires us to recognise that the debt structure of the economy – and the activities of financial institutions in particular – is important in determining financial stability.

Moreover, innovation, competition and evolution in financial markets have led to the development of increasingly complex financial products, which present regulatory challenges of their own. Such innovation was thought to lead to highly liquid financial markets which, when populated by rational and sophisticated market participants, would allocate risk to those investors

[36] Charles Goodhart, Dimitrios Tsomocos & Martin Shubik, Macro-Modelling, Default and Money (June 2013) LSE Financial Markets Group Special Paper 224.
[37] Katharina Pistor, A Legal Theory of Finance (2013) Journal of Comparative Economics, Vol. 41.
[38] See Andrew Lo, 'Regulatory reform in the wake of the financial crisis of 2007–2008' (2009) 1 Journal of Financial Economic Policy, 4, 5.

willing to bear it so that markets would need no further regulation. Because the RIM assumes that investors can completely evaluate the risks from products, however complex, regulators paid little attention to the increasingly complicated financial products that were being traded on financial markets (such as the mortgage-backed securities and other debt securities that were central to the GFC), blindly assuming that the market was pricing them correctly. There was also little thought given to how the enormous returns generated for private actors from the financial system – revealed later to be completely dependent on the guarantee of the public purse – ought to be distributed; rather, the narrow view was adopted that 'a rising tide lifts all boats' and that the whole of society would benefit from the activities of a gargantuan financial sector. Finally, the mantra of financial regulators and macroeconomists alike – with a few notable exceptions – suggested that the activities of the financial sector *in and of themselves* could not pose a risk to wider economic stability.

If we instead regard the economy as one that tends away from stability, at least two policy prescriptions flow from the analysis above. The first is that leverage matters. As noted by Avgouleas, 'Within measure, leverage can be a good thing, but uncontrollable leverage can destroy society and this is a fact that we are hiding from'.[39] On this basis, any regulatory system must ensure that losses fall – as far as is possible – on those parties that assume risk for private gain. Since allowing banks to become insolvent can pose a threat to the stability of the financial system, the choice is between bailouts, which impose the losses of private financial institutions onto the taxpaying public, and regulation.[40] Higher capital requirements (or, conversely, limiting the amount that banks are permitted to lend by reference to the value of the asset acquired) are arguably the most appropriate tools with which to ensure that bank bailouts are unnecessary. These regulatory tools force financial institutions and borrowers to operate with more of their own funds – or 'skin in the game' (share capital in the case of banks and equity in the case of borrowers) – which ought to induce a greater degree of caution as regards risk-taking. It also provides a larger reservoir of funds that can absorb losses without provoking insolvency *if and when* the aggregate predictions of the market malfunction. The possibility of such events is, of course, integral to the Keynes–Minsky paradigm but is omitted from mainstream theory.

A good deal of work in this field has been done by global regulators, in particular in relation to the banking system, following the GFC.[41] Prior to this, deregulation and financial innovation rendered the financial system so complex that estimates of risk became largely impossible. This was partly thanks to an

---

[39] E Avgouleas, From speculative to sustainable finance – can markets do good? Lecture at Murray Edwards College, Cambridge, 19 January 2017.

[40] For further discussion, see Johnston, Cullen and Pugh, Chapter 11.

[41] Some of this is discussed in Johnston, Cullen and Pugh, Chapter 11.

over-reliance on market discipline with regulators persuaded by market efficiency arguments that financial institutions ought to be able to set their own capital requirements. Unsurprisingly, such latitude resulted in lower capital levels across financial markets. In the UK, new capital regulation has been introduced pursuant to the EU's Fourth Capital Requirements Directive (CRD IV) and using the Bank of England's own rule-making powers. New capital adequacy requirements require banks to fund their assets with much more equity capital. In principle, the capital adequacy regime in the UK requires banks to have sufficient capital to act as a buffer to withstand losses or writedowns on their assets. There are also 'exposure limits' placed on banks and other financial institutions, designed to prevent them from becoming too dependent on each other for financing, thereby reducing interconnectedness. Yet these capital requirements remain inadequate: one observer has commented that the new capital requirements under CRD IV, which force banks to have at least three times more capital than previously, may sound tough, 'but only if one fails to realise that tripling almost nothing does not give one very much'.[42] Other prominent financial regulation experts have recommended that capital requirements be raised substantially. Admati and Hellwig, for example, have recommended that a bank should fund its assets with at least 25 per cent equity capital.[43]

Other reforms are also necessary. There should be a blanket removal of public guarantees for speculative financial activities. These activities take place on so-called secondary markets and dwarf the retail and corporate lending that financial markets originally emerged to facilitate. Most of what occurs on secondary markets is simply gambling (trading in commodities or currencies via derivatives, for example, is done mostly for speculative purposes) and has no public benefit or social value. Removing public support is important for three reasons: (i) in the presence of such guarantees, capital that might fund productive enterprise in the real economy is diverted towards speculative finance, distorting the economy; (ii) the use of leverage to amplify the potential gains from such speculation creates no social benefits yet creates a risk of social cost if it undermines the stability of the financial system, requiring the injection of public funds; and (iii) markets dominated by financing of speculative rather than productive activities breach the social contract according to which the state backs the financial system in exchange for its role in promoting economic growth.[44] The UK has gone to some lengths to address this by mandating the 'ring-fencing' of certain operations of large banks, in particular isolating 'core'

---

[42] Martin Wolf, 'Basel: the mouse that did not roar', *Financial Times*, 14 September 2010.
[43] Anat Admati and Martin Hellwig, *The Bankers' New Clothes: What's Wrong with Banking and what to Do about it* (Princeton University Press, 2014).
[44] Iris Chiu, Rethinking the Law and Economics of Post-Crisis Micro-prudential Regulation – The Need to Invert the Relationship of Law to Economics? *Review of Banking and Financial Law* (forthcoming, 2019).

retail deposits from 'excluded' wholesale and investment banking activities.[45] The effect is to remove any public support, including deposit guarantees, from non-ring-fenced activities. This is more prescriptive than the approach taken in either the EU or the US.

However, this is still inadequate. Any retail institution that benefits from public guarantees – either explicit through the deposit guarantee system or implicit because of their systemic importance – ought to be required to satisfy a strict public interest requirement as a condition of licensing.[46] Such a licensing requirement would recognise in law that this type of financial institution is, in effect, a public–private franchise arrangement because it has the exclusive right to dispense a vital public resource: namely bank deposits backed by the full faith and credit of the state.[47] Anything less gives a clear signal to the markets that a repeat of the cycle of damaging rent-seeking – the cardinal function of financial speculators – remains acceptable, and will be underwritten by a system that is ultimately backstopped by public funds. As Minsky put it, 'Unless the regulatory apparatus is extended to control, constrain, and perhaps even forbid the financing practices that caused the need for lender-of-last-resort activity ... another situation requiring intervention will occur'.[48] Such reforms include measures to prevent explosive growth of speculative finance. If such requirements force financial institutions to shrink, so be it. The contingent fiscal costs to citizens of insuring the liabilities of such behemoths far outweigh any putative benefits from financial speculation.

CONCLUSION

The benefits to society from free markets are significant, and in some contexts, the EMH and RIM provide useful frameworks for market analysis. On the other hand, at the systemic level, it must be acknowledged that the explanatory power of the EMH is limited. Contrary to its predictions, markets are far from stable, even in the absence of an external shock. Asset bubbles and price distortions are endogenous to the operation of financial markets, driven by investor behavioural traits and the procyclicality of investment strategies. In fact, Minsky's analysis shows that, by their very nature, financial markets are prone to instability, as economies progress from debt-fuelled periods of expansion to inevitable collapse, through increased leverage amongst market participants in the throes of mania.

Any system of financial regulation must recognise the threat posed by these dynamics to systemic stability. Some progress has been made in recent years in

---

[45] HM Treasury, 'Banking reform: a new structure for stability and growth', Cm 8545 February 2013, 2.6.
[46] R. Hockett and S. Omarova, 'Special, Vestigial or Visionary? What Bank Regulation Tells Us about the Corporation – and Vice Versa' (2016) 39 Seattle University Law Review 453.
[47] R. Hockett and S. Omarova, The Finance Franchise (2017) 102 Cornell Law Review 1143.
[48] Hyman Minsky, *Stabilizing an Unstable Economy* (McGraw-Hill, 2nd ed, 2008) p. 59.

both UK and global regulation; however, significant flaws remain, posing grave threats to the stability of the financial system and therefore to the wider economy. Lawyers and regulators must resist the narratives spun by advocates of deregulation, particularly in coming years, when memories of recent crises begin to fade and the belief in a 'new era' emerges. We must recognise that mainstream financial market theory is built upon unrealistic assumptions about human nature and so its prescriptions concerning the proper role and construction of regulatory frameworks are unreliable. We ought to embrace alternative understandings as to the nature of financial markets, which are more realistic and so provide a more appropriate basis for financial regulation.

FURTHER READING

J. Cullen, *Executive Compensation in Imperfect Financial Markets* (Elgar, 2014).

E. Gerding, *Law, Bubbles, and Financial Regulation* (2016).

C. Kindleberger and R. Aliber, *Manias, Panics, and Crashes: A History of Financial Crises*, 7th ed (Palgrave Macmillan, 2015).

H. Minsky, *Stabilizing an Unstable Economy*, 2nd ed (McGraw-Hill, 2008).

R. Shiller, *Irrational Exuberance*, 3rd ed (Princeton University Press, 2015).

INDEX OF NAMES

INDEX